THE CENTENNIAL EDITION

OF THE WORKS OF

SIDNEY LANIER

GENERAL EDITOR

CHARLES R. ANDERSON

I. POEMS
    Edited by Charles R. Anderson

II. THE SCIENCE OF ENGLISH VERSE and ESSAYS ON MUSIC
    Edited by Paull F. Baum

III. SHAKSPERE AND HIS FORERUNNERS
    Edited by Kemp Malone

IV. THE ENGLISH NOVEL and ESSAYS ON LITERATURE
    Edited by Clarence Gohdes and Kemp Malone

V. TIGER-LILIES and SOUTHERN PROSE
    Edited by Garland Greever

VI. FLORIDA and MISCELLANEOUS PROSE
    Edited by Philip Graham

VII-X. LETTERS
    Edited by Charles R. Anderson and Aubrey H. Starke

LANIER, AGE TWENTY-EIGHT, 1870

Charles D. Lanier Collection, Johns Hopkins University

CENTENNIAL EDITION
VOLUME VIII

SIDNEY LANIER

LETTERS
1869—1873

EDITED BY

CHARLES R. ANDERSON AND AUBREY H. STARKE

BALTIMORE
THE JOHNS HOPKINS PRESS
1945

CONTENTS

	PAGE
LETTERS: 1869	3
LETTERS: 1870	51
LETTERS: 1871	136
LETTERS: 1872	221
LETTERS: 1873	305

ILLUSTRATIONS

LANIER, AGE TWENTY-EIGHT, 1870	FRONTISPIECE	
PAUL HAMILTON HAYNE IN THE 1870'S	FACING	10
LETTER FROM LANIER TO HIS WIFE, MACON, GEORGIA, 1870		56
MARY DAY LANIER IN 1873		315
"BLACK-BIRDS," UNPUBLISHED MUSICAL COMPOSITION BY LANIER, 1873		335
BALTIMORE MUSIC GROUP, ETCHING BY FREDERICK DIELMAN, 1872		382

LETTERS
1869 — 1873

CHRONOLOGY

1869	Winter	Studying law, Macon, Ga. Began writing "The Jacquerie."
	Apr.–May	Business trip to New York.
	June 30	Furlow College Address, Americus, Ga.
	July 7	Admitted to the Georgia Bar.
	July–Nov.	Ill. August–September at Georgia health resorts.
	Dec.	Began law practice.
1870	Apr. 26	Confederate Memorial Address, Macon.
	May–Nov.	Ill. July at Lookout Mt., Tenn. August–September in New York, care of Dr. E. E. Marcy.
	Oct.	Returned to law practice.
1871	Winter	Ill. Renewed literary activity. Began contributions to *Southern Magazine*, Baltimore.
	Mar.	Trip to Brunswick, Ga., for health.
	June–Nov.	Ill. August–September in Marietta, Ga., for health. October–November in New York, Dr. Marcy.
	Dec.	Returned to law practice.
1872	Winter	Ill. Returned to law practice in May.
	July	Alleghany Springs, Va., for health.
	Aug.–Oct.	Marietta, Ga., for health.
	Nov.	To San Antonio, Texas, for health.
1873	Winter	In Texas, until March 1. Renewed literary and musical activity.
	Spring	In Brunswick, Ga.
	May–Sept.	In Marietta, Ga., planning to give up law for literature and music. Visited Baltimore, September 18–23, and met Asger Hamerik, Director of the Peabody Institute.
	Oct.–Nov.	In New York, seeking a musical career.
	Dec. 1	Began engagement as first flute in the Peabody Orchestra. Lived at 161 St. Paul St.

1869

To Virginia Hankins [1]

[Macon, Ga.? Feb., 1869?]

". . . A certain May arose
From out that sea that 'twixt three larger lands
Lies like a violet midst of three large leaves,
Arose from out this Violet and flew on
And stirred the sad soul of the woods of France,
And smoothed the brows of moody Auvergne hills,
And wrought warm sea-tints into maidens' eyes,
And calmed the woody air of market-towns
With faint suggestions blown from distant buds,
Until the land seemed a mere Dream of land,

[1] Previously published, *Southern Literary Messenger,* II, 9-10 (Jan., 1940).
This undated letter to Virginia Hankins is an answer to her letter of Dec. 10,
1868, and is in turn answered by her letter of Feb. 17, 1869. A reading of the
sequence seems to place Lanier's letter nearer the latter date.

Though no letters by Lanier during Jan., 1869, have been discovered, one
sidelight on his life at this time is shed by a notice in the *Banner of the South,*
I, 6 (Jan. 2, 1869), which announces Lanier as one of the performers in a series
of concerts to raise money for the "Ladies Memorial Association" of Georgia,
for a cemetery at Marietta to bury the state's Confederate dead. The first concert
was scheduled at Columbus, Ga., Jan. 4, 1869; the second at Savannah, Jan. 7;
and others at Augusta, Atlanta, and Macon. Other performers listed were Lanier's
Macon friends Mrs. J. M. Ogden and Mrs. A. O. Bacon (formerly Augusta and
Virginia Lamar), a Prof. Schmidt and Mr. Maas also of Macon, Miss Leila
Howard of Columbus, and Mrs. R. Hines of Albany.

Another glimpse is afforded in Paul H. Hayne's letter of Jan. 14, 1869,
acknowledging receipt "last night" of a lost letter from Lanier—"your kind
note, (with the accompanying poem)." This was a part of Lanier's long narrative
poem, "The Jacquerie" (I, 171), submitted to Hayne, who promised detailed
criticism after giving the poem the study it deserved. For the present he said:
"The *first* impression left upon my mind after a perusal of 'the Jacquerie,' is,
an impression of exhuberant force, & fancy. . . . I augur the *happiest* results in
reference to your *future literary career*— for, the evidences of mental richness you
have already displayed—, are *more* than eno' to justify bright anticipations!"
Lanier seems to have worked steadily during the winter of 1868-1869 on "The
Jacquerie," ll. 61-70 of which are quoted at the beginning of the present letter.

3

And in this dream-field Life sat like a dove
And coo'd across unto her dove-mate, Death,
Brooding, pathetic, by a river, lone."—

— This, from "the Jacquerie," a long historic poem I'm
writing. I know not what there is in it that is like you: but,
because there *is* something in the Spirit of it that always
breathes your name into my Soul, and because I dreamed of
you when I wrote it a few days ago, therefore, I love it, being
mine own utterance, and often say it softly to myself when
my heart is pure and holy, swearing solemnly and cheerfully
as knights swore in the old time, that these words shall be a
wonderful shrine and that my Little One shall dwell therein
for a Shrine-heart, to light and warm the shrine, and to guard
it forever by her holiness from all unholiness.

— — —

And so, in answer to your letter, know that I am well, and
fighting fates at all points for daily bread, having withal no
vantage-ground (of patrimony, or otherwise) to fight from,
and winning, by many thrusts, but small modicum of the same.
Howbeit, I have hope, founded partly on certain faint praises
which have come from divers directions, and partly in a certain
stir in my blood which mounts and boils when people talk of
great and good men, that some day will see me fighting less
and winning more and giving much. I am in the *Law*: having
abandoned my professional life through a deep conviction that,
as matters go at present, it is too narrow for elbow-room, and
too hampered by provincialism and sect, for that large view
which one would wish to take who does not forget that God
is the God of the whole world and of the Stars and of the trees
and of the worms and of all. I live here, in Macon, and will,
for some time.

Meantime how is Mrs. Wilson, and where living, and what
were the particulars of poor Price's death?[2] And how is your
father, and do plantation operations go favorably? And Dr.
Crump, and all your brothers? Tall Mark, what doeth he?
And do you take the Round Table still, and have you seen
George Eliot's Spanish Gypsy,—that strangely-marred splendid,

[2] James Price, of Macon, had married the widow Wilson, of "Mantura," in
the summer of 1866. Both were old friends of Lanier.

pure, passionate, vigorous, inartistic book? Write me specially of this last: if you say *no,* I'll send it you.

And herewith receive the yearning desire to see you, to surround you with loving act and word, to hear your voice, to wonder at your eyes, to caress your hand, to bless you a thousand times—of

S. L.

To Clifford A. Lanier

Macon, Ga
Feby 22nd 1869

My Darling Clifford:

I got your letter and was glad to learn the very clever distinction which it conveys between the Statutory and Common Law Separate Estate of the Fenn Caveat.[3]

From a discussion which took place in the office some days ago, I became 'ware of a very pretty distinction concerning Commercial paper, which may perhaps be of value to you at some time.

By an Act of Congress, passed some time ago, no assignee of a Bill of Exchange could sue in the Federal Court unless *his Assignor* could sue in that Court. If, therefore, *you* lived in New York, and I had assigned to you a Bill of Exchange, I being an Endorser, you could not sue any one of the previous Endorsers in the Federal Court whom *I* could not have sued there. Now, in the construction of this Statute, Held, that it applies only to Notes and Bills *payable to Order,* and not to Notes and Bills payable to *Bearer:* for a Bearer is not, in intendment of this Statute, an " Assignee," but gets possession of the note (or Bill) by *delivery* merely: so that *any* holder of a Bill payable to Bearer *is* " Bearer," and could sue the Maker or any one of the Endorsers or all of them, if living in a different State, in the Federal Court, without reference to the Status of the person from whom he traces title, as in the case of the holder of a note payable to order.

---

[3] Since Clifford Lanier had also begun the study of law—some time before Sidney—it was only natural for the two brothers to write each other of legal matters.

What are you doing? I've been laboriously reviewing Black-stone, by Barron Field's Analysis; and am now in the last part of the third Book, in review.

Willie seems very well indeed, and needs nothing except *you*. When are you coming over? [4]

I saw D[r] Hall in reference to y'r Bill two days after you left. His custom is to charge, at such times, *by the month*, dating from day of confinement, depending upon the trouble which the patient gives by sickness ensuing. He therefore did not make out his a/c, but promised to do so as soon as he should want the money.

Write me of y'r goings in and out and *on*.

Love to all, From

Sid.

[Macon, Ga.? Mar. 7, 1869?]

To Virginia Hankins [5]

I've just read y'r letter: – and I am convinced that the practice of setting diamonds in black is founded upon Divine authority; for it is upon the same principle that the Heavens have set *you* in a cluster of sorrows.

I wonder what they do with these same diamond-souls in Heaven? Current traditions deny that there is *any* black in the Kingdom of Light. Ho, I see how it is: – presently the diamond will burn the jet into *another* diamond: the setting will become a gem, itself: whereat Light will prosper.

Perhaps, after two or three eternities are passed, Christ will, in this way, burn Satan into a good man, and Heaven will burn Hell into a Paradise.

That's after " two or three eternities." Most people would laugh at the idea of more than one eternity. Most people think eternity is like a very long string, which is tied at *one* end to

[4] Clifford Lanier and his wife had spent Christmas in Macon, she remaining there for some weeks thereafter to await the birth of her child—possibly because of the lack of privacy at the Exchange Hotel in Montgomery. Her daughter Wilhelmina was born on Jan. 24, 1869.

[5] The last part of this letter is missing. The conjectural dating is arrived at from the opening sentence of the following letter.

Death, but which at the *other end,* – well, it hasn't any other end, they say. How absurd! The old Egyptian idea is better. Eternity is like a ring. If you want me to, write me, and I'll demonstrate to you in my next letter, by unimpeachable mathematics, that each moment of a man's life is, in very and solid and sober truth, an eternity.

If all this is very flighty, then Logic is a humbug: – and if you should reply that all this *is* very flighty and that Logic *is* a humbug, – I would not contradict you, but would only kiss your hand and ask you if it was not nearly time for Judgment-day.

Meantime, the R'd Table is the most wonderful compound of sagacity and wooden-headedness that life ever produced, and you need never look for anything in the criticisms of the R. T. upon such a book as Charles Auchester. In such cases, R. T. is not only *ultra vires* but *ultra naturam.*

Probably, the beauty and the mystery of the Sea do not go for much, with the oyster, living, as he does, right in midst of the same; albeit the Bivalve may possess much truculent sharpness in the shell thereof, and much skill in the disposition of mud. Our friend, yonder, R. T. is an Oyster, and a fine, large, good one of his kind: upon all questions which concern mud, (such as " The Tribune," " Mr Greeley," " The proposed Cabinet of Grant," " The Civil Service," " The Finances," " Greenbacks," " The Wreath of Eglantine " &c&c&c) he brings to bear a pair of shells which have an uncommonly strong *nip,* and approves himself a Bivalve of wonderful gristle and integuments: but when it comes to beauty, especially of that exquisite, evanescent, flower-breath kind which hovers and sways and floats through " Charles Auchester " like a heliotrope-odor through a June twilight, — why, then, he can only grip and snap and sputter, after whatever awkward fashion the powers of his oysterhood make possible. — The descriptions of the " Tone-Wreath," and of Mendellsohn conducting the " Messiah," in Charles Auchester are, I think, not surpassed in our language, as specimens of *quiet, serene, powerful narratives.* [6] The book is an old friend, of mine, and of Mamie's. Do you know the other book by the same Author, " Counterparts "? If not I must try and look it up for you. I had thought

---

[6] Elizabeth Sheppard's novel, *Charles Auchester,* was based on the life of Mendelssohn.

both these books out of print. I made great efforts, some time ago, to find a copy of Ch. Auchester, but failed everywhere. Is yours a new edition? I shall be glad to hear that it is, since I think the Author a very wonderful person in some respects, and would be rejoiced to see her emerge into more general fame.

I'm replying to y'r letter immediately, and so cannot say that I have *sent* " the Spanish [Gypsy."]

x   x   x   x   x   x   x

To VIRGINIA HANKINS [7]

Macon, Ga.
March 9th 1869.

I forgot, Dear Little One, in my letter of a day or two ago, to tell you to send me, by all means, the poems of your " friend," of wh. you spoke in y'r last. I shall take the greatest pleasure in giving my honest opinions about them. Who is the *" Friend,"* you demure Creature, you! Is it *you?* I would not be less severe in my critisism, on that account: because I love you too well to be insincere with you, and I love mine Art too well to be false to it. No, no, I will not mince, even to save you pain: for I should inflict such pain in the surgeon's way, and I know *you* would never flinch. Do write me quickly, and long.

Your

S.

To MILTON H. NORTHRUP [8]

Macon, Ga
March 15th 1869.

My Dear Milton:

I have been y'r debtor for some months, for y'r very kind and interesting – not to say, *tantalizing* – letter,

---

[7] Previously published, *Southern Literary Messenger*, II, 6-7 (Jan., 1940).
[8] Previously published, *Lippincott's*, LXXV, 312-313 (Mar., 1905); excerpt reprinted, Mims, pp. 100-101.

written from Naples: and – aside from the fact that, in *epis-tolary* debts, I rarely pay more than Twenty-five cents in the Dollar: – I should have answered y'r letter long ago, but have waited to receive some intimation from you that you had returned to this Home of the Brave &c.

Y'r " promotion," My Dear Boy, gives me sincere pleasure. You'll be Duke of Albany, yet, I hope. I fancy y'r position, as Agent of the Associated Press, must be one which would entitle you to a vast deal of consideration from those whom, by a twirl of y'r pen, you can present in a very ridiculous or very sublime light, in all the morning-papers, as happens to strike y'r lordly humor. If you're like our Georgia man who has been doing the Georgia Legislature by Telegraph, you can wield more power by a " heading " than a Frenchman did with an epigram in the days of the Revolution. Use your lightning fairly. My Fine Ariel: do your spiriting gently, and let not harm come to the patriots that sacrifice even their souls in making the Laws of the Country.

With a most monstrous yawn and gulp I swallowed my envy, when I heard of y'r projected tour to the great old Lands, and genuinely rejoiced in the pleasure wh. I knew must be in store for you. As for *my* sweet old dreams of studying in Germany,[9] *eheu!* here is come a wife, and By'r Lady! a boy, a most rare-lung'd, imperious, world-grasping, blue-eyed, kingly Mannikin; and the same must have his tiring-woman or nurse, mark you, and his laces and embroideries and small carriage, being now half a year old: so that, what with mine ancient Money-Cor-morants, the Butcher & the Baker & the Tailor, my substance is like to be so pecked up that I must stick fast in Georgia, unless litigation, and my reputation, should take a simultaneous start and both grow outrageously. For, you must know, These Southern Colleges are all so poor that they hold out absolutely no inducement in the way of support to a Professor: and so last January I suddenly came to the conclusion that I wanted to make some money for my wife and my baby, and incontinently betook me to studying Law: wherein I am now well advanced,

---

[9] In his letter of Oct. 30, 1868, from Naples, Northrup had given an account of his European travels with a reference to " Heidelberg where I spent two glorious days . . . & where I did not forget that *you* would have been, had not war darkened our land."

and, D. V. will be admitted to the Bar in May next. My advantages are good: since my Father & Uncle (Firm of Lanier & Anderson) are among the oldest lawyers in the City and have a large practice, into which I shall be quickly inducted.

I have not however ceased my devotion to letters, wh. I love better than all things in my heart of hearts: and have now in the hands of the Lit. Bureau in N. Y. a vol. of Essays, I'm (or rather have been) busy too on a long poem, yclept " the Jacquerie," on which I had bestowed more real *work* than on any of the frothy things which I have hitherto sent out; tho' this is now necessarily suspended until the summer shall give me a little rest from the office business with wh. I have to support myself while I am studying law.

I shall be delighted, Dear, to see you in Macon, and can promise you a view of a beautiful City, some pleasant rides amid green leaves, some good music, and a hearty welcome.

By the way, have you ever happened to meet my friend Salem Dutcher, now on " the N. Y. World?" He writes mostly over " S. D." Should you ever meet him and mention my name, I do not doubt he will be glad to know you, and I am sure *you* will not regret it: for if you can but once manage to break his shell, you'll find him a very wonderful creature, strangely fashioned as to his heart, and a very genius as to his lightning-like play in conversation. He talks infinitely better than he writes.

And so, having drawn all this upon y'rself, believe, My Dear Milton, that I am always

Your Friend

Sidney Lanier.

To Paul H. Hayne [10]

Macon, Ga
March 15th 1869.

My Dear Mr Hayne –

Y'r forbearing goodness entirely bankrupts me: but my outstanding obligations to you lie upon me

[10] Previously published, *Critic,* VIII [o. s.], 77 (Feb. 13, 1886); reprinted in *Letters,* pp. 221-223. This is the earliest letter from Lanier to Hayne that has survived. (See facing illustration, a tinted photograph by Pelot & Coles, Augusta, Ga. See also VII, 394, note 47.)

PAUL HAMILTON HAYNE IN THE 1870'S

Courtesy of Duke University Library

so sweetly and so unlike all other debts, that I do not desire to
take the benefit of the Act relieving Insolvents, and I refuse to
be discharged. Of course I w'd not have dared to write to any
ordinary correspondent what I wrote you: for I sh'd very surely
have been told that I was a lackadaisical fool who needed work
and physic. These wonderful hells into which we descend, at
such times– – – who will picture them to one who has not dwelt
in them? It is idle to discuss colors with a blind man. As for
me, however, the good God has seen fit to arm me, very
singularly, against the dark hosts of temptations that dwell in
these places. The longing for stimulants, which I feel in
common, I suppose, with all men of like nature, always defeats
itself in my particular case, by awakening a certain *Pride* of
Pain, a certain *self-gratulation* of *Sorrow,* (how foolish this
sounds), which enables me to defy the whole damnable troop
with a power which seems thoroughly anomalous, in view of
the fact that, ordinarily, I do not think my *will* is very strong,
because my *sympathies,* which *are* strong, easily override it.
Indeed, it is not a bad thing, that I get plunged into these awful
depths: for, O My Friend, they teach me lessons which are
beyond the reach of reason, beyond the Utmost of Thought,
beyond Time, beyond *mySelf.* Have you ever felt, in those good
moments when the formulae of life sink out of memory and
the Soul comes to look at things with a sort of Before-World
simplicity,—have you felt, at such times, that you had *two
selves,* of which one stood as it were in the continual background, calm, sedate as eternity, looking with a half-amused
smile upon the slips and errors and crimes and contortions and
struggls of your *other* self in its feverish life, as if this calm
inner Self were confident that, after all the struggles and fevers,
the *struggling* and *feverish self* will come out pure and whole
and calm and strong? What do we mean when we say one is
" *master* of him*self*," " one is conscious of himself," " one
examines himself " &c?

   In these, and a thousand similar expressions of common life,
are indicated some wonderful metaphysic facts (I hate the word
psychology), which, when the metaphysicians come to find the
true source of their science, will be quickly revealed.

   At any rate, these present Spring-breezes are blowing on my
soul as on a young green leaf, and I wave and sway and rise

and fall, in the midst of the Heavens, with a wonderful love and happiness upbearing me. Ah, the exquisite, intense Calms, which are yet full of a strange quickening and stir of birth! — I have a boy, whose eyes are blue as your Aethra's.[11] Every day when my work is done I take him in my strong arms and lift him up and pore in his face. The intense repose, penetrated somehow with a thrilling mystery of *potential* activity, which dwells in his large open eye, teaches me new things. I say to myself, where are the strong arms in which I, too, might lay me, and repose, and yet be full of the fire of life? And always, through the twilight, come answers from the other world; Master, Master, Master; there is one, one Christ: in His Arms we rest.

Truly your friend,

Sidney Lanier [12]

To Mary Day Lanier [13]

[Macon, Ga. March 24, 1869]

Dear Maydie:

Mrs. Fulton and Miss Munnerlyn have been on the search for you for some time this morning. They wish you to come in – you and Sissa – immediately – to hear Mr. Poppen play, at *Emerson's*. He is at their service for the afternoon. Miss Munnerlyn insists on my flute. Please bring it: and bring *Macbeth* and the *Fürstenau* piece (that you and I used to play) and the Niobe (I believe that's the name of it: the

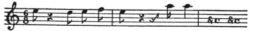

So: come in the carriage, you and Sissa, immediately: bring flute & music.

Hastily

Sid.

Office. Wed. 24/69.

---

[11] A character in a poem of the same name, by Hayne.

[12] The conclusion of this letter (" Truly your friend,/ Sidney Lanier ") does not now appear in the MS, but is given in *Letters*, p. 223.

[13] This is one of a number of surviving notes sent by Lanier from the office of

To Mary Day Lanier

[Macon, Ga. March 27, 1869]

My Darling:

Campbell & Emmell want to play some trios today.[14] Please bring down my Flute, on the Bureau, when you come this afternoon.

Don't forget.

I send Ten Dollars by Henry, & have p'd y'r other bills.

Lovingly & Hastily

Sid.

Office.
Mar 27/69.

To Virginia Hankins [15]

[Macon, Ga., Apr., 1869?]

My Friend, what have I done? What do you mean by " retort," by *my* " comfortable doctrines "? This is wonderful. How idle, how flighty, how ineffably foolish must have been my poor letter!

Listen.

If one should ask me, " in whom do you believe? " I should reply; in my Master, Christ, who is also God. If my questioner should ask " how do you know? " — I should reply, *I know.* " But *how?* " Still, I would only reply, *I know.*

Lanier & Anderson to his wife, at home. Some of them are undated, and few are important; but several, as here, suggest the half-heartedness with which Lanier had embraced the study of the law.

[14] Campbell and Emmell were two of the Georgia friends with whom Lanier serenaded his way through the Civil War. Music written for their three flutes is reproduced in part in facsimile in Starke, opp. p. 44 (MS formerly owned by Miss Louise Weed Campbell, now by her nephew John Voorhees, Morristown, N. J.).

[15] The last part of this letter is missing. The conjectural dating is arrived at from the fact that this is an answer to Virginia Hankins's letter of Mar. 23, 1869, and is in turn answered by hers of Apr. 13. A reading of the sequence seems to place Lanier's letter nearer the latter date. The quotation in the fifth paragraph is from E. B. Browning's " A Vision of Poets."

And this, my dear G., is all that I know, – this Master, whose Words are all divine, but ah! whose Words are not all intelligible to us, but are oftentimes, as they were formerly, and as He often intended them to be, " hard sayings " (You remember, somewhere, one said to Him, " Master, this is an hard saying ") : this Master, I say, is all I know, and beyond this ————————

And so much for " doctrine ": your quotation is so precisely my " doctrine," and so altogether sweet, that, as if it were a violet, I toss it back to you, for there is still, and will *always* be, clear dew upon it:

> " I *know*, is all the mourner saith,
> Knowledge by suffering entereth,
> And life is perfected by Death."

And so you are wonderfully mistaken, Miss Wisdom, when *you* " believe that the agony we endure for the *sin of another* is more intense " than the *wretch*edness of which Tiger-Lilies speaks, *i. e,* wh. comes from one's own transgression. Agony endured *for the act of another* is permeated by two blessednesses which, if they *are* overshadowed, yet still are *there* and temper the sharp sting, or, if they do *not* temper it, they so ennoble it that one would rather endure this suffering than be happy: these two are, Innocence and Unselfishness. No anguish, which is *un*selfish, can possibly be of that deadly, down-dragging sort, which one endures for one's *own* sin: Ah me, this is the sharpest sting in it all, that one is wasting one's sorrow on one's miserable *self.* How ignoble, how mean, how base, how utterly beyond all endurance, is this sentiment, when it comes crushing down upon the *already too-heavy* weight of sin's regret! To suffer, and to have no better thing to suffer *for,* than one's *self*! — This, undoubtedly, is the suffering in the Place of Woe: this is the Anguish of Him who rules there; – the anguish of *selfishness.* Tiger-Lilies is right; confess it. ——— ——— ————

As for " liking " you more, or less, for *any* cause, – I could not do so: I cannot " like " you either more or less than now.

I would not think any less of an artist who hid his dreams to keep from bartering them; – but no artist could very well do

this. Believe this, dear Friend; no artist ever publishes his best
or sweetest thought; it must ever remain his Pain, that his Best
is unutterable, *unthink*able, and only *feel*-able. —

As to the Artist's publishing *himself*; this, it must be confessed, is a very ambiguous expression; for the Artist sym-
pathizes with all things, and draws all things into himself, and
incorporates them with himself and himself with them, in such
a way that whatever he puts forth may, in one sense, be called
him*self*. – I have not time now, but I will write you again about
this. — ─────────

And about Mrs Browning, and the Sonnets, and the painful
discoveries that y'r ideas have been anticipated (oh, how
familiar this last, to *all* poets!), I'll write some other time –
I'm writing now, *mostly,* to beg another letter from you quickly.

" Mrs Lanier " thinks y'r letters are the most wonderful
letters in the world, – and frequently declares, (– put your hand
over your heart –) declares that you are the only woman in
the world who is worthy of *me* ! ! ! — — —

— I had been so accustomed to think of Seraphael as
Mendellsohn, that I had entirely forgotten he was ever *called*
Seraphael in Ch. Auchester. All the characters in

x   x   x   x   x   x   x

To Clifford A. Lanier

Macon, Ga
April 13th 1869.

My Darling Clifford:

I sit here in solitary glory, Father being at Circuit
Court in Savannah, and Uncle Clifford in Americus – How
I should beam upon you, if you might sit here, all this exquisite
Spring afternoon, and talk *law-suits* with me!

I have finished the course, that is, Blackstone, Adam's Equity,
and the Code, which are all that Uncle C. thinks will be
required at my examination. I have however made considerable
progress in Chitty's pleading, – wh. is tough but very fascinating to me – and in Powell's Evidence. I think I'm pretty
well fortified on all the primary matters of the Law: but, Shade
of Cicero, what a vista do these open, of toil, of thought, of
careful analysis, of rigorous logic, to [be] spent on the minuter

points which the actual practice develops in infinite varities! [16]

I expect to leave Macon next Monday, for New York, on business, and may be absent for three or four weeks. Maydie will go down the Country on a visit to Lilla Hazelhurst. Poor May is very thin and pale; Charlie has nearly absorbed her; and I hope the country air and change of food will be beneficial to her.

The Superintendent of the Literary Bureau has been quite ill for three months past, as I learn from a letter written to me by his wife. He is now recovering and I hope will be able to give my Essays some attention.

Willie writes that Auntie is in New Orleans. Do give her my love and a hundred kisses when she returns.

As also y'r two sweet Willies, whom I love as mine own,

As also

Your Self

To Mary Day Lanier [17]

New York, April 28, 1869.

x   x   x   x   x   x   x

I've just come from the "Tempest," at the Grand Opera House, corner Twenty-third Street and Eighth Avenue, newly

---

[16] The law books mentioned by Lanier were: Sir Wm. Blackstone's *Commentaries on the Laws and Constitution of England,* John Adams's *Doctrine of Equity, The Code of Georgia,* Joseph Chitty's *Precedents in Pleading,* and Edmund Powell's *The Principles and Practice of the Law of Evidence.*

The business that took Lanier to New York (see next paragraph) was an attempt to interest Northern capital in some Georgia property belonging to his father-in-law, Charles Day, on which iron ore had been discovered. Lanier left Macon on Apr. 20, with Harry Day, and wrote to his wife that evening from Atlanta (a brief note, here omitted), before leaving for an inspection of the property near Wills Valley in north Georgia. Mary Day Lanier (with her baby, nurse, and father) left Macon for Savannah on Apr. 23, and after a short stay went on to Waynesville to visit her friend Lilla Hazelhurst (see her letters of Apr. 24 and 30).

[17] Previously published—with two omissions and with the beginning and end missing—in *Scribner's,* XXV, 622-623 (May, 1899); reprinted in *Letters,* p. 67. This fragment is reproduced from the latter source, as the MS has not been found.

On Apr. 27 Lanier had written his wife from Harrisburg, Pa., but that letter is here omitted, because Lanier's letter of Apr. 29 to his father-in-law, which

built; and my heart has been so full . . . that although they're about to shut off lights, I must scratch you a line to carry my last thought to you before I sleep. In one interlude between the scenes we had a violin solo, Adagio, with soft accompaniment by orchestra. As the fair, tender notes came, they opened . . . like flower-buds expanding into flowers under the sweet rain of the accompaniment: kind Heaven! My head fell on the seat in front, I was utterly weighed down with great loves and great ideas and divine in-flowings and devout out-flowings, and as each note grew and budded and opened, and became a bud again and died into a fresh birth in the next bud-note, *I* also lived these flower-tone lives, and grew and expanded and folded back and died and was born again, and partook of the unfathomable mysteries of flowers and tones.

x   x   x   x   x   x   x

To Charles Day

New York
April 29th/69.

My Dear Father:

I arrived here yesterday, very much fatigued by nearly eight days of steady travelling. The Fifth Avenue Hotel was so crowded that I was unable to get a room: and so I came down to the St. Nicholas, where I am very comfortably located.

I devoted yesterday to resting, and to endeavoring to scrub off the black cuticle of Coal-smoke and dust which covered me very thickly. This morning is raining heavily, and admits of nothing but letter-writing.

I stopped twelve hours in Harrisburg. Mr [Joe] McClellan, who had heard that I was coming, met me, and was extremely kind. After conducting me over his Rolling-Mills, – which cost seven hundred thousand Dollars, and of which he has sole charge – we had a long talk about the Empire Co. I gave him a short description of the property. He was astonished at its

follows, gives a more circumstantial account of the progress of his business. In fact, of the twenty-odd letters to his wife written during the rest of his month's stay in New York, only eight are included in this edition—the others being mere love-messages or being duplicated in his other correspondence here printed.

combination of facilities, and pronounced the ore, of which I showed him specimens, first class. He assured me repeatedly that he had not the slightest doubt of my success in starting the Company, and that we would be able to make iron at little more than half the cost of its production in Pennsylvania. While not disposed to be so enthusiastic as *he* is, I am now convinced, from facts which I ascertained from McC., that with proper energy the Company *can* be started and can succeed. McC's estimate of our expense in starting a blast-furnace are very much below the ideas we had formed: and I do not doubt his ideas are correct, judging from what I saw, myself, in the blast-furnace near his Rolling-Mills. An Engine, capable of furnishing sufficient blast for two furnaces could be bought for ten thousand Dollars and laid down at Trenton for, probably, about two thousand more. McC. offered to go with me to Pittsburg, where he would give me such introductions as would enable us to purchase our Engine on three, or perhaps, six months time. He thought that, the engine once procured, the rest of the works could be completed for, at most, fifteen thousand Dollars: so that, considering twenty thousand necessary to clear off encumbrances, he thought that fifty thousand ought to set us free and start us well at work. He however agreed with me that it would be better to attempt to raise a hundred thousand: so that, in any event, we might not be crippled at the outset. McC. displays a strong anxiety to go to Wills Valley [Ga.], and a very lively interest in our enterprise. He is coming to N. Y. in a week, to see how I am succeeding.

I've written Father (*t'other* one) today, and so send no messages except to my dear Cubbie, for whom I've been yearning all the way. Will write again in a day or two.

Your Son

Sidney.[18]

[18] On May 3 R. S. Lanier wrote to Clifford: "Had a letter from Sid this morning in N. York. Had arrived safe after eight days hard travelling – which includes two or three on horseback among the mines in Dade Co. Ga. He says he was very dusty & very tired on arrival & slept long after. He had not entered upon the business which carried him there, & so he had nothing very special to write." (This letter of Lanier's has not been found.)

As his correspondence with his father shows, Lanier's trip to New York was partly in the interests of the firm of Lanier and Anderson. In a letter of Apr. 29, R. S. Lanier sent Lanier the name of a firm of bankers and brokers in New York,

To Mary Day Lanier

St. Nicholas Hotel [New York].
May 1st 1869.

My Darling Wife, You will see I am still at the St. N. I devoted yesterday to a hunt for lodgings and after some trouble found a very pleasant room at 45 East Tenth St. The room was, however, to be papered newly, and so I could not move in immediately. Today, being May 1st, we have the torrents of rain which traditionally and proverbially belong to moving-day, and so I don't know whether I'll get in before Monday.

Last night Salem and I went to hear " La Belle Helène," at Fifth Avenue Theatre. The costumes were very magnificent: the burlesque on ancient Greek customs was very funny: the calves of the *Cantatrice*, Mlle. Tastée, were immense, ditto the Chorus: all the women had *rouge* in the centres of their cheeks, powder upon all other portions, deep pencil-marks on their eye-brows, and a streak of black-paint drawn from the corner of each eye, supposed to impart a pensive and passionate expression: The gestures, the music, the songs, were all infinitely lascivious and suggestive: and yet, as there is no filth out of which *some* flower will not grow, I managed to sprout a wee violet of a dream out of all the indecency, and I kneeled before the sweet soul of My Maydie which came hovering down to me through all the lights and the flippancies and the bawd-music. Dear Spirit, my heart is pained, I am sick that music is fallen into such hands and gone to serve such passions. I try, with great struggles, to lift myself to some high place above the rushing-by of the times, from which I may look down with clear eyes and see, not *one,* but *all* of the ages, so that I may fit them together and may observe the symmetry of time and may not be dismayed by all this which seems a broken and disjointed and utterly ugly segment of life.

— If thou wert but in my yearning arms, my work were easier

on which he asked his son to call; and in his letter of Apr. 24 he spoke of making " interest with the merchants in New York & Boston, in respect to the firm of L & A. of which you are soon to be a partner – so enlarging its business."

In a brief note to his friend Northrup on Apr. 29—here omitted—Lanier urged a meeting in New York, which apparently never took place.

and my soul lighter: and yet on thy love, as Apollo on some warm up-bearing rosy cloud, I lie and float freely and rest.

Charles Lanier [19] handed me, yesterday, letters from both my fathers, from Harry, and from *you.* I was full of rejoicing to hear some true-love talk, and I dwelt on the words that spoke of my fine Man – chen.

Ah, for the blue eyes, and the sweet hands, and the smiles that shimmer, as sheens of the moon over water: and ah, for the gray serious lights in the countenance of my Mutter chen, My Wife !

Dost stay with Lily? Tell her I envy *both* of you.

Sidney.

To Robert S. Lanier

45 East 10th St. [New York]
May 4th/69

My Dear Father:

I have at length, after a good deal of trouble, secured my lodgings, as above, and moved in. We have had torrents of rain and continuous bitter-cold weather ever since I came, and this has seriously interfered with my activity: but I have managed, at any rate, to get through with the numerous preliminaries to my business. I found Mr J. F. D. Lanier and his Son Charles very cordial indeed, and the former seemed very agreeably impressed with such of his kinsmen as he met while in the South.[20]

I breakfasted with Mr J. F. D. Lanier this morning, and I am to meet him at the banking-house tomorrow to open my business with him, after which I dine at his house. I called on Mr Day's friend, Judge Herring,[21] yesterday, and am to dine with him

---

[19] Charles Lanier was the son of J. F. D. Lanier. He became a good friend of Sidney Lanier, and after his death presented copies in bronze of Keyser's bust of Lanier to the Johns Hopkins University and to the Macon Public library.

[20] J. F. D. Lanier, apparently on his way home from a visit to Florida with his wife and daughter Kate, had written Lanier on Feb. 4, 1869, of his regret that he could not travel *via* Macon, but that he had " a most agreeable visit " with Sterling Lanier and Mrs. Jane Lanier Watt, in Montgomery.

[21] Lanier had sent a copy of *Tiger-Lilies* to this family friend of the Days (see Judge Elbert Herring's letter to Lanier, Jan. 27, 1868), but had possibly not met him before May 3, 1869. Judge Herring (1777-1876) was made the subject of a newspaper article in the New York *Herald* of Apr. 6, 1875, in which he was called " the world's oldest lawyer." See Lanier's letter of Apr. 12, 1875, to his wife, and note.

at three O'clock today. It is now after two, and as it is a long
ride to Judge H's house, I have but little time to write. I was
delighted to get your *two* letters, and shall try not to disappoint
any of the hopes wh. you express. The paint business shall be
attended to.[22] The weather has so far been too inclement to
make any business calls down town. Today shows signs of
fairer skies: we have had a little warm sunlight: and I hope to
be able to work to advantage. I am to meet a real-estate man
this afternoon, with whom I have some prospect of striking a
bargain in relation to the wild lands in Clinth C'y. My visit to
McClellan in Harrisburg, Pa. wonderfully encouraged me, as
to the value of the iron property: and I feel very sure that the
time is not far distant when the great iron-manf'ing interests
of the United States will transfer themselves to Georgia &
Tennessee & Alabama.

I cannot tell you of my inexpressible longing for home and
my dear ones. This is a fearful place: and these foolish people
continually make my heart sick.

I send a thousand kisses to my Darling Sissa: and all love
to you.

Sidney.

Address me at
45 East 10th St.
N. Y.

To Virginia Hankins [23]

address as
45 East 10th Street.
New York City.
May 4th 1869

I sit here, My One Friend, late at night, in my lonely lodging,
above the monstrous turmoil of Broadway, while the endless

[22] In his letter of Apr. 29 R. S. Lanier had asked his son to get information
about paint for the house where the Laniers lived in Vineville, Macon (see
note 56, 1868).
[23] Previously published, *Southern Literary Messenger,* II, 7 (Jan., 1940). In
a letter to his wife of the same date, Lanier wrote: " I saw *one* woman look love
into a man's eye some nights ago, and this all the love I have seen in New York.
God pity the place and send me quickly to where I can find a heart." Lanier
never became reconciled to what he felt was the inhumanity of New York City.

mass of men and women rolls on beneath: and a torn-throated fire-bell blares out its alarum with a marvellous brazen gurgle: and a great gray-stone church stands gazing over against me, with naught to do, it would seem, but to keep lifting its steeple whose spire cuts far up against the sky: and the stars are wholly still about the matter:—save that when I see a star, I seem to hear thy name whispered, and so I cannot forbear to scratch thee this line, to know if thou are still struggling with over-much clouds, or still shining like these other stars, here, shining, in a clear cold Heaven, down upon seas of sin that are too muddy to mirror thee.

And I write further to say that I am here on business and will be here a matter of two or three weeks longer, and that I would be greatly builded up in my belief that honor is not gone out from among men and women like a candle in a wind-gust—a hard belief to cherish in this most ingeniously perverted and most exquisitely distorted of all civilizations which one finds in the New Yorker *at night*—I say I might still keep my arms about this most sweet faith of mine, if thou would'st write some of thy wonderful wisdom, which thou singest as the birds whistle, to

Thy Friend

Sidney Lanier.

To Mary Day Lanier

45 East 10th St. N. Y.
May 6th 1869.

So, My Wife, I come to lie down at thy feet and grasp the hem of thy garment, as I do daily lie and grasp, being alas, alas, unable to reach to thy lissome hands, or thy most sweet lips, or thine heavenly eyes, or aught of the comeliness which hath penetrated through all my soul and which on earth and in Heaven is called *mine*.

All yesterday and today have I been stoutly hewing and whacking, in the way of business, against the most fearful odds of unfavoring fortune that ever dismayed a soul: with what success I will not speak to thee since I am but beginning the preliminary skirmishing, and the main fight is to come. I am

calm about it, and I believe that by much thinking on thee and
on My Master I am very high above being cast down by a
defeat which is so probable.

Yesterday Mr [J. F. D.] Lanier gave me a very fine dinner
at Delmonico's, where I met many of his relatives, and was
cordially received by them. We had most delicious wines:
Chablis, Sherry, and Champagne; we had thirteen courses, of
all manner of delicacies: we sat, drank, and ate three hours:
and down beneath my constant stream of talk, – for I had two
ladies to entertain –, far down, thou was sitting in my heart,
and I drank wine – O rare, flaming wine – with thee, My too-
Beloved, exquisite-sweet Sweetheart.
I have called today on thy friends: Miss Carville, who was not
in: and Mr Higgins, whose family, being out of town today,
I meet tomorrow.[24] I wrote thee I had dined with Judge
H[erring].
Thy letter announcing the arrival of the teeth is come. My
beloved Boy! I do with all my soul yearn for thee and him.

I am
            Thine

To Mary Day Lanier

                              45 East 10th St. [New York]
                              May 9 /69

Dear Faithful Heart, I went this afternoon, late, to call on
Judge Herring, whom I had not seen since I dined there on
Wednesday last. I found that he had been quite unwell, and
had not left his apartment since I had been last there. He had
left instructions for me to come to his room, immediately: so
I went upstairs, and we sat together a long time, in the twilight.
I led him to speak of the olden days, and was vastly entertained
with his reminiscences of some of the great and dignified

[24] Julia Carville was a friend to whom Harry Day had appealed in Nov., 1867,
and who had taken care of the engraving of the wedding invitations at Tiffany's
for the marriage of Mary Day and Sidney Lanier (see H. C. Day to Lanier,
Nov. 27, 1867).

Foster Higgins was Mary Day Lanier's first cousin, the son of her mother's
eldest sister, and formerly a resident of Savannah, Ga.

statesmen who adorned our now-unhappy land, in the days when the ideal of Manhood was founded upon largeness of soul rather than of purse.

I left him at eight, to call on Mr Higgins' family: but they were all out, and so I trudged home: – aye, *home*: for, since thou art not actually within my arms, that spot, – even the wee table whereon I write to thee, – is most like home to me, since there I have most of thee.

I dined today with Charles Lanier and his sweet little wife. Miss Fanny Dunn, a granddaughter of Mr J. F. D. Lanier's was also there. We had a delicious salad (among other things) and good Champagne: no drop of which passed my lips without a wish for my dear Wife, and a great yearning for the day when I may lavish upon her all the delicate comforts which I see scattered about here in such profusion.

O My God, My God, I think Thou knowest I would not murmur at any hard crust which thou gavest me: but as for my wife, – Ah, this is too bitter, – it is too bitter. Good Master – Thy Will be done.

————My Darling, there's a most sweet blue vein runs round thine eye, and I have often seen the blood in it beating and throbbing with the tumultuous joy of passing so near to thy lips; so is my heart, now, vibrating, as if thy very body were near to me: – but I cannot reach to thee, I cannot reach to thy cheek, which I see, soft and fair, just before me: oh, Wife, Good Night.

To Robert S. Lanier

45 East 10th St. N. Y.
May 10th/69.

My Dear Father:

I've been down on Wall St. all day, and have come back to my third floor lodging, to rest a little. I find that the stone pavements tire me out: and I unforunately fail to find out that I *am* tired, until I am brought up standing by a feeling of *dead* fatigue such as I never experienced from walking, anywhere else. It is almost impossible to "go slow" on Wall: even if the crowd didn't hurry one on, the intense spirit of hurry which displays itself on every side is irresistibily catching, and one finds himself going at a killing pace before he is aware.

I find that my iron undertaking here is a desperately heavy job. A Wall-Street man said to me today: " The effect of the war was to bring every sort of mining enterprise into great activity: everybody invested in iron: and *I don't know a man in Wall St. who has not been bit, on iron,* to the tune of all-the-way from ten thousand to hundreds of thousands." The Chattanooga and Wills Valley iron properties, and all their relations to commerce and the markets, seem to be well-known on every side: and all whom I have seen appear to put entire faith in the *solid* character of the iron properties there, but fear the want of a market: and this apprehension seems so supported by the simultaneous offering of the Hewitt Rolling Mills, and the Cherokee Blast Furnace, for sale, that up-hill work presents itself to me. Nevertheless, this is what I expected, when I came: and I am working away, in various directions, to raise money by a mortgage on the property.

I have been diligently visiting our clients, and am pleasantly received by them. There are two houses of " Biningers " in N. Y. (the house, you remember, which owes us costs for cases against *Whipple* (?) I think). I have visited both of them and both deny ever having received any letter from the firm of L & A. or ever having sent out any such cases as those referred to. I stirred up their whole establishments: called up various clerks &c: but could get no farther satisfaction.

Charles Lanier has here a book containing the addresses of all the *Banks* in New York, Boston, Philadelphia &c. I propose, if you think it would not be undignified, to enclose one of our cards in an envelope, and send this by mail to each one of these Banks: also to all the Western Banks. This seems to be customary with Lawyers here: & I can see nothing improper in it. What does Uncle C. think?

I had a charming dinner with Charles Lanier yesterday, & his sweet little wife. He is very kind and cordial. I am to meet a family-party of Lanier, at the house of Mrs Stone, tonight, in ninth St. Mrs S. is a married daughter of Mr [J. F. D.] Lanier. I dine with Mr Foster Higgins tomorrow: and with Judge Herring again on Wednesday.

Tomorrow, I am to meet Mr Winslow, who is the proprietor

property yet: as no favorable opportunity has offered, and Mr Day did not wish it hawked about the market. On Monday I shall call on Mr Foster, and perhaps on Mr Dabney, to see if any thing is likely to be effected in that direction. I am but just beginning to feel entirely unflurried in the crowd, and to go about business, deliberately.

I'm dreadfully homesick, and long indescribably for all the dear faces at home. If I should see no further chance at the end of next week, shall probably return about that time.

Meantime, until I write again, my love rests with all my loved ones.

Sidney.

To Mary Day Lanier

[New York, May 16, 1869] [27]

O My Friend,   How the stars make me shiver!   Is it not sweet that I see thy face in among the stars: – a thousand Maydie-faces, Darling, framed in ovals of stars, looking down upon me, through my windows?   How kind and loving and good thou art, so to fill the else empty star-spaces of my Heaven! And, O God, how I love thee!

—   Today I went with Foster to St. Paul's.   'Twas Whit-sunday.   I communed with them.   I knelt and received the Bread & Wine.   Hand in hand with *thee*.   My soul went and stood before our Master and our Father.   Meantime, the organ pealed apace, and I swam on the waves of it, with thee.

I dined with Foster, stayed, talked, took tea.   After tea, we had his wonderful microscope and a great collection of marvels of God's tiny-world.   I gazed at these, with thee,

– — –   O My Dear Mistress, I wish thy hand were on my head tonight.   A mortal calm is come upon me.   It is like the awful stillness that is just before a storm.   This stillness is *above* my storm: wh. is a tempest of longing, in my heart.   How tense are the lightnings, there!   It is as if they were bows, bent till both ends met at the arrow-notch.

---

[27] Dated from the sequence and the reference to Whitsunday in the second paragraph.

I feel as if somewhere in my heart blood was dropping and trickling like water in a stone cave underground. Ah, I know why this is. I thought, a moment ago, of thy weak body, thy suffering limbs, thy pallid face. I will come back to thee very soon. I can kiss thee, thou knowest! – A parlous remedy. I wish all the heat of all my life might warm thee from one chill. To die for this would very fully satisfy me. There is only one thing that I ever greatly hated, for a long time together, that is, thy suffering.

Why do these ills come to *thee*? This is the most marvellous mystery of all my life.

Perhaps it is because God will not permit us to have our perfect Heaven *yet*. But then, might He not let thee be well, and just part us sometimes, for a very short time? Would not this do, to keep us at least on Earth, and out of Heaven, until we die? But then, God is God: and man knoweth Him not. I will not question. One thing I know, I am utterly

Thine.

To Mary Day Lanier

[New York] May 17th [1869]

By this, My Dear Mistress, thou must have recd some fifteen of the petals wh. the Rose of my Love is daily shedding, in the hope that the good winds will waft them to thee. Thy letter and thine orange-wreath are come, and I know not which is sweeter, no, not I! Surely, if I knew any woman in the world who might have written this letter as thou hast written it, I w'd do reverence to the same. Thou art very sweet: I wish I were by thee. I fear to give rein to my yearnings. But, – O Most Sweet Heavens, if ye will favor me! – I shall see thee before long. I think to leave here early in next week. Thou must stay in Savannah until I meet thee there. I shall write thee more definite news in a day or two. I cannot now tell my movements exactly. Day after tomorrow I go with Mrs Winslow to her beautiful home at Poughkeepsie to stay a day. Will call on thy Mr Rider, whom she knows well.[28]

[28] In the winter of 1860-61, Mary Day had spent seven months " as a boarding pupil . . . in Poughkeepsie, N. Y., at the school of Rev. George J. Rider, of the

This morning, Mr John Cornell took me to Trinity Church and played for me one hour on the Great Organ there. – But without thee it is a divine pain to me. Some day, thou and I will listen together. Then it will be perfect happiness, this Music, this unfathomable thing.

See, how subdued I am! I dare not venture to talk to thee now.

Good My May Lilian –

Thy Lover.

To Virginia Hankins [29]

May 17th [1869]. *N. Y.*

— Except, thou tiny Genius! – that *some* nations *can* QUITE understand and appreciate the genius of other nations; – for instance, *I,* – being a most unruly and rebellious and mountain-bandit sort of a nation, – a Mexico, as it were, – and only after a series of marvellous revolutions and passionate uprisings having succeeded in getting my internal polity into some semblance of shapely government under the Good Master; – I, being such a Nation, nevertheless understand *thee* from the very highest to the very lowest of the dainty and most strange peoples that compose thee: – and I do *not* exactly understand the warnings which thy friend, – who is a good, sweet, true, intelligent friend, evidently from the letter thereof – sends to thee. " Intellectual repose "? Thou hast an eye that looks into things, and I would *never* fear that thou, My Good Brown

Episcopal Church." (Mary Day Lanier to Edwin Mims, July 31, 1905.) For the identity of John Cornell, mentioned in the next sentence, see note 26, above.

[29] With her letter of May 13, Virginia Hankins had sent a letter (not found) from an unnamed friend, who had written her thoughts on *Tiger-Lilies.* Virginia Hankins wrote: " There can be nothing more friendly & delicate than in all she says about, ' striving through philosophy and pure & lofty sentiments, to gain the heights of intellectual repose; ' – for thus gently she wishes to warn *me.* Good Friends — unless I were to stir the dust of a ' day that is dead,' I could scarcely tell *you* by what means I have reached this stage of my life-journey. However wrong I may be – I have tried to attain that wh: in my poor power seemed the best: and at all times, God has been better than all else. Individuals are like Nations, – they have their *rebellions* & revolutions and their peace-festivals. And – no Nation can quite understand and appreciate the Genius of another Nation." Lanier's letter begins with a reference to this passage.

Bird, wouldst be caught with such chaff as the intellectual repose which some foolish people have hoped for – (how strange even the *hope* for such a thing, when one thinks of it!) but wh., fortunately, they have never found.

— Just before our Fair Father Christ left us, he said " *My Peace I give unto you.*" This Peace is so different from " intellectual repose," that it is always the very finest condition for the most intense intellectual *activity.* – Is it not strange that " Tiger Lilies " (– a foolish book, Friend, of a foolish boy; Ah, how I have outgrown Tiger Lilies in these two years since then!) should produce such *diverse* impressions upon various readers? For, some time ago, a certain Clergyman of great intelligence and of devout piety, sent to me an invitation, on this wise: " that he had read Tiger Lilies; that he did not know whether I belonged to any church; but that he was sure none but a devout Christian *could* have written that book; wherefore he desired that I would come to his Church on the following Sabbath, and join him in the *Communion* "!

— So that, I fear thy friend may misunderstand both me and thee. Surely, in the wretched Goethe-doctrines of self-culture, and the like, I, for one, put no reliance, nor ever have. Not only do I disagree with them, but I contemn and utterly despise them. That which hath to do with *Self* comes of the Devil: God is *Love,* wh. is unselfish; – this is a fundamental maxim wh. the *poetry* in my heart wrought out for itself before I was able to reason, but wh. all my maturer reason authenticates and emphasizes.

Thy news of Lucy Spiers surprises me.[30] I th't she was long ago married to her old-time sweetheart, and was probably head of a numerous progeny by this time. An I could find her, I sh'd certainly call on her; but, to say, as thou dost, that she is " in New York," is no more than to say she is in the world; for here every one is lost unless one knows street and number.

Good Little One! Do I not wish I might have been there, to take off my hat, to toss back the lank hair, and to cry " Himmel," with thee, before the sparkle of the kiss of the Wave and the Day! Well, why should I not see these things once more with

---

[30] Virginia Hankins had written: " By the way, Lucie Spiers, – you remember her? – is living in New York, & supports herself as assistant editress of some newspaper, & is also writing a book – "

thee?[81] My business is nigh done, I think to leave here next Monday (wh. will be May 24th). Write me immediately where thou wilt send a horse for me: I do not know the landings, now; or, if this sh'd come too late for a letter to reach me here, send a note for me to the National Hotel, at Norfolk, to meet me there, and inform me how best I can get to thee.

I have not written thee about the poem of thy friend Aimée because I had not time. I discern some freshness of soul in this piece & therefore I like it. I will review it, some other time. Thou canst not imagine the haste with wh. this letter is written. Pray Heaven, thou mayst read it! Meantime, I am

Thy Friend.

To Mary Day Lanier

New York,
May 18   1869

My Dear Darling:

Next Monday or Tuesday I shall start South, I now think. I have received a letter from Ginna Hankins wh. is very beautiful. In one place she says: " Will the Fates ever allow us to grasp hands again?": in so sweet a way that I can hardly resist the appeal. I had determined *not* to go and see her: because I could not at all bear the thought of being away from thee one moment longer than necessary. But, now, it seems this way: I have apparently the power to throw a little ray of brightness on this dark and noble life of Ginna's: and I regard it as a sacred duty to do so. Think *how* sacred, when I, in the discharge thereof, am kept a whole long day from *thine* Arms. O My Well-Beloved and well-worshipped Mistress!

So I will go there: and then come to thee in Savannah: but, thou seest, I am by this arrangement unable to name precise days.

[81] Virginia Hankins's letter of May 13 begins: " I was at ' Shoal Bay ' on a visit for the first time since — well — since the World ended. I dressed quickly, before the house was astir, and ran through the high grass and snow-drops and lilies of the valley, down the hill to the beach. I clasped my hands — *you* would have taken your hat off, & tossed your hair back & cried ' Himmel! ' — It was over yonder, you & Cliff lay dreaming when my voice, together with the rising mist went up to greet you & the sunlight, a bright May-morning long ago."

I write thee hurriedly from Mr Lanier's Banking office. I am thy yearning

Lover.

To Mary Day Lanier

New York,   May 20   1869

My Dear Heart: I write thee very hurriedly, to beg that thou wilt stay in Savannah, until I meet thee *there*. I have just received from y'r father a letter, stating that he knew M^{rs} [William] Duncan had written you to come to her house, with assurances of plenty of room. I therefore desire that you will remain there until I shall come.

I had not expected to go to Boston, but I *may* go,[32] and so can't tell exactly what day I will leave here for home & thine arms: *any*how, by next Wednesday or Thursday, today being Friday.

I've just returned from Po'keepsie where I saw thy Mr Rider & all his school, and enjoyed myself.

Love to all.

I send this to Savannah.

Thine.

To Robert S. Lanier

45 East 10th St. [New York]
May 26th 1869

My Dear Father:

After running about all day long, getting my traps together for the joyful homeward journey, I am so utterly worn out that, – especially in consideration I shall see you soon – I will only scrawl you a line to let you know that I start home tomorrow, (Thursday) morning. I shall stop over a day at Portsmouth, Va, and will then join Mamie in Savannah, bringing home all my dear ones.

---

[32] On May 22 Lanier wrote to his wife: " I run to Boston tomorrow night, and will not leave N. Y. for thee before next Wednesday; perhaps I may be kept, by bad connections, in Virginia two days: and so I would not reach thee in Savannah before next Monday week, probably June 1st."

I long so to see you all! This is a fearsome city: I hate it. I send a hundred kisses to My Darling Sissa.

Hastily   Sid.

To Mary Day Lanier

Norfolk.   Friday, May 28th "/69.

Here came I, O Holy Soul, at six this morning: and here must I stay until six tomorrow morning, to catch the Richmond Steamer wh. will take me to Bacon's Castle:— all of wh., had I surely known it in time, w'd I think, have caused me to go through without stopping. Yet,— I found here a letter from Ginna, awaiting, me: I enclose it [33] thee: thou wilt read in it that my going to her will be a joy in her poor uneventful life: and, from another letter I've had from her, I see that she wishes to know of many high matters wh. she does not understand, and whereon I think I can enlighten her.

To make the laggard hours go faster, I have been all day calling on my old comrades of the war, many of whom live here.[34] With much hand-grasping, my arm is tired: alas, there

---

[33] The letter inclosed, dated May 22, [1869], reads:

"'If I should meet thee
    After long years,
How should I greet thee?'

——— ——— —— "With all the joy that is in me – full tenderly & tearfully & sisterly. Albeit with few words –(– my poor tongue never failing to refuse to do the bidding of my heart –).

"Your letter only came in time to give me the faint hope that this will meet you in Norfolk & let you know that the buggy will be at Jones' Wharf on Tuesday – if you do not come it will be there again Thursday.

"I think the birds told me that a friend was coming — I put roses in my hair for you *yesterday!* Does that seem too romantic for a Head of a House? We two are old enough to have shaken hands with Romance, forever.

"This will find you in Norfolk tomorrow night – and *the next night?* — Why surely the world has not stopt!

"Already my hand trembles to meet yours — and my pen will say no more, except what it can never refuse to say, that I am your Friend

Ginna Hankins."

[34] Lanier had spent considerable time at or near Norfolk, having been encamped there with the Macon Volunteers for about eight months during 1861-1862; later he was stationed at nearby Boykins Bluff from June, 1863, to Aug., 1864 (see his letters for these dates).

is but one hand in the world now that I wish to clasp: it is thine, Thou Music's-finger!

Yonder, over the way from where I write, is the self-same building in wh. I was once imprisoned during the war,[35] along with certain thieves and cut-throats, under custody of some foolish negro soldiers. I do remember me how lonely I was, there: I think I thought once of thee, while I looked through the grated windows, and drew in a mournful-beautiful scene down the flashing waters of the bay: and if then I had known that thou wouldst one day be wife to me, this Hope would have transformed the strutting Africans into passable Angels, and I would have dreamed me a boat and embarked in it and sailed to thee; from the uttermost part of the earth.

I am very sure that I *must* get rich, ere long: because I can never go anywhere again without thee. I cannot do my work when thou are not with me. I care not whether this is because I am weak:—perhaps it is because I am strong,—in my love. Thou art so enticing – sweet, Dear Lady, that I cannot ever have patience for aught that demandeth labor, unless I am where I may quickly have my arms about thee, and my lips to thine.

How this weary month, since I last saw thee, hath dragged his slow length along! I wonder how many letters thou hast had from me? Packing up, day before yesterday, I found one or two letters to thee wh. I had written and, in the multitude, forgot, I suppose, to send.

— I am three hundred miles nearer thee, than I was yesterday morn. Perhaps, on Wednesday, I will be but the length of an arm from thee. If the Marvellous Master grant me this boon, is it possible I shall ever sin again?

— I wish to feed, for days and days, on the exquisite Mysteries in thy two gray eyes. The arches of thine eyebrows, Yoland,— arches as it were of a Bridge in Heaven,—these my soul will cross and recross.

— Altogether, as thou seest, there is in me neither coherency of speech nor idea, and there is no nucleus in this chaos which

---

[35] For the known facts about Lanier's imprisonment in 1864-1865, see Appendix C, vol. X of the present edition. According to *Tiger-Lilies*, the temporary prison in which he was kept before being sent to Point Lookout, Md., was across the river from Norfolk, at Fortress Monroe.

I am, save one: it is that before many days I will put my head on thy bosom and be at

Rest.[36]

FROM SALEM DUTCHER [37]

Augusta, Ga., 1st July, 1869.

Thou wilt see I am in the old burgh. And therewith comes a beer-some recollection. Dost remember how as we sat one night in Pfaff's of the great City I was for a time silent and then dashing the beercup therof violenter on the festive board, did say By G – d I'll do it? And, furthermore, when thou saids't Do what? I told thee of my purpose to visit this town and here venture on some high enterprises? Lo! who can equal the idle man when the same is finally aroused.

Led by great purposes I came *via* Memphis, New Orleans and Montgomery hither and am now deep in certain perilous aventures whereof O! my good Sidney I wd I cd speak face to face with thee. For a day or so back I purposed coming to Macon during the exercises of the Female M. E. College there but on divers accounts have renounced the idea, and yet wd I might be there. Certain of our clergy here and one at least

---

[36] Lanier went to Bacon's Castle on Saturday, May 29, and after a visit of a day or two he proceeded by rail to Savannah, where he joined his wife on June 1 or 2 (R. S. Lanier's letter of June 4 acknowledges receipt that morning of a letter from his son, at Savannah).

No letters by Lanier written during the month of June, 1869, have survived. Presumably he returned to Macon early in the month (see his letter to Virginia Hankins, July 7 ?, below).

[37] In the Augusta, Ga., *Banner of the South,* II, 6 (June 19, 1869), appeared the following notice: "Salem Dutcher, Esq., the 'Tyrone Powers' of THE BANNER OF THE SOUTH, favored us with a visit last week. He has been in attendance at the Memphis and New Orleans Conventions. Mr. Dutcher is an able defender of the South and the Southern people, and very few writers have labored with more zeal and success in our behalf. He will remain in Augusta for a few weeks, after which he will return to New York, from whence he will send his valuable contributions to the BANNER as heretofore." Though no contributions by "Tyrone Powers" appeared after this date, there had appeared above this pseudonym in the *Banner of the South* between June 13, 1868, and May 22, 1869, a series of thirty-five literary letters from New York (one, on Feb. 27, 1869, containing a personal reminiscence of Dutcher's war experiences under Gen. Jubal Early) and a series of six longer essays on political questions.

Although Dutcher remained in Augusta for nearly two months (see his letter to Lanier on Sept. 24, 1869), he did not see Lanier on this trip South. They had met, however, a number of times in New York during the previous May.

of our fair ones, Miss Russell by name, attend. See fair Miss —
Clare [de Graffenried] will acquaint you — and give me thy
opinion thereanent.

As I came through Montgomery beheld the babe of the
whilom Miss Willie and a sweet chuff it is. I was one blush
of shame at my bachelorhood what time I tarried in the presence
of the young child and its producers.

Looking at the Americus Tri-weekly Republican of the 29th
ult. I saw thou wert on ye morrow, being yesterday, to deliver
an oration at the College.[38] As I read I thought he will say
fine things, rare things, things not to be appreciated by the
bucolic mind, wh. mind will grow addled as the rustic mouth
opens in wonderment and to the accommodation of sundry
truculent summer flies. Beautiful picture is it not! Our Sidney
discoursing and ye insect hordes almost alone reaping benefit
thereof. Tone thy fancy — people are more honest than we take
them to be but far less intelligent =

If fortune serve I may yet see thee in thine own home but
not now. And so love to thee and thine from

Salem

To Virginia Hankins

[Macon, Ga. July 7, 1869?]

Dear Far Friend. Your too-mournful letter should have been
answered immediately but for a thousand things, in the way of

---

[38] See Lanier's " Furlow College Address " (V, 247). Lanier's uncle, Clifford
Anderson, had first been invited to make this commencement oration before the
Furlow Masonic Female College of Americus, Ga.; but, being forced to decline
because he was appearing before the Supreme Court on that date, he asked his
nephew to substitute for him (see R. S. Lanier to his son, June 4, 1869). Lanier
probably spent the month of June preparing this speech and reviewing for his
bar examinations held early the next month (see note 40, below).

The Macon Telegraph and Messenger, July 3, 1869, quoted from the Americus
Republican: " The oration of Sidney Lanier, Esq., of Macon, was elegant, force-
ful, eminently suggestive and eloquent. His theme, ' The Future of the Land
we Love,' was discussed in the spirit of a broad and liberal mind. . . . There
was nothing of the politician, but all of the man of principle and integrity, of
lofty impulse and knightly chivalry, in the positions assumed and thoughts
spoken by this gifted son of Georgia. The oration was the production of a
cultivated student, glowing with the lustre and fervor of a strong and manly
imagination." (Clipping in the Charles D. Lanier Collection, Johns Hopkins
University.)

sickness, of business, of speechifying &c &c, which have kept me stirred up to my utmost energies.

I will not *write* you now: and I only scratch this off to let you know that in the midst of all cares I think of the wood-violet that is just now gone into the world of the roses.[39]

I enclose a notice of my recent speech at Americus, Georgia. You would have been glad to see the hearty applause which frequently interrupted me in the progress of the address, – sometimes so that I could scarcely proceed: – and to know that this was elicited, not by any clap-trap appeals, but by *solid* talk. I enclose a notice of the speech, taken from the Savannah Republican, wh. I doubt not, will please you. Do *return* it to me.

I underwent, this morning, my examination for admission to the Bar, and passed through it, amid many congratulations and compliments.[40]

You have not yet sent me the poem, wh. you were to arrange in rythmic order, as proof that you understood the business. Do not omit it.[41]

As for " not writing any more," – why, you *will* write more, that's all.

I will hope to hear from you very soon, and to know how

[39] Immediately after Lanier's visit to Bacon's Castle at the end of May, Virginia Hankins had gone from the tidewater to the mountains for a visit. (See Virginia Hankins to Lanier, May 28, 1869. The specific letter to which this is an answer has not been found.)
For Lanier's Americus speech mentioned in the following paragraph, see note 38, above.

[40] Lanier's petition for examination and admission to the bar of Georgia is dated July 7, 1869 (Book B, pp. 179-180, Minutes of the Superior Court, Bibb County, Ga., May Term, 1869) ; hence the conjectural dating of this letter. The certification of the petition and of Lanier as " a man of good moral character " is signed by Washington Poe and Eugenius A. Nisbet.
Lanier was ordered examined " On the Common and Statute Laws of England of force in this State " by James Jackson; "On the Law of pleading and practice " by R. F. Lyon; "On the principles of Equity " by E. A. Nisbet; and " On the revised code of this State, the Constitution of the United States and of this State, and the rules of practice in the Superior Courts " by L. N. Whittle. The order for the issuance of a license " to plead and practice law in the Superior Courts of this State " is signed by Judge C. B. Cole; the oath taken by Lanier, apparently on July 7, is not dated. He was admitted to practice in the Supreme Court of Georgia on Jan. 26, 1870. (Information through the courtesy of Mrs. Frank Jones of Lowther Hall, Clinton, Gray, Ga.)

[41] See Lanier's letter to Virginia Hankins, Nov. 30, 1869, and notes 51 and 52, below.

nearly you have succeeded in "falling in love" with any of the Professors at Lexington. To be with you, among the mountains! Would not this be an acme of life?

After leaving you, I came on to Savannah, found Wife and boy there, and spent a pleasant week among friends in that most beautiful of cities.

My wife's birthday came round some days ago: and, as is our custom I gave her a present. It was Morris' "Earthly Paradise." She has been reading some of it to me, in my sick moments. It is very *great*. It is good for *you* to read. It is simple, *toned down,* strong, unstrained, dreamy, real, sensuous, pure, and *good*. Read all the stories. You will like them better, the more you know them.

I wd. be ashamed to send you this scrawl: – if you did not *know* how entirely beyond height and depth and measurement is the friendship of

Your Friend.

To ROBERT S. LANIER

Chalybeate Springs, Ga [42]

August 18th 1869.

My Dear Father:

Sister is over at the ball-room looking on at the dancers: May is entertaining Ginnie and Gov. Bacon,[43] out in the moonlight, on our cabin-porch: and I embrace the opportunity to scrawl you a short note, using a trunk for a desk, and a crazy chair for a seat.

[42] This is the only letter written by Lanier between July 7 and Sept. 19, 1869, that has survived. The sickness mentioned in his last letter apparently proved serious enough to keep him from entering upon the active practice of law for several months. Because of his health, the summer climate of Macon was always a threat to Lanier. Hence, early in Aug., 1869, he had gone with his wife and son Charles (and his sister Gertrude and her son Edward) to the Chalybeate Springs, now better known as Warm Springs, about 60 miles west of Macon. (A letter from Salem Dutcher, Sept. 24, 1869, referring to a lost letter by Lanier, seems to indicate that Lanier did not leave Macon until after Aug. 5.)

[43] The reference is undoubtedly to Virginia Lamar and her husband Augustus O. Bacon. Though later a U. S. Senator, Bacon was never a governor; he had just been elected to the Georgia House of Representatives, however, and the title here used is apparently jocular.

We find the situation somewhat improved, by dint of one or two *rows* that I've raised with the proprietors, and what with some pleasant old watering-place acquaintances that I've found here, and the lively talk of our friend Mrs. Lockett, the time seems to go by a little more rapidly. I cannot yet tell whether the water is of benefit to me; but it seems to be improving Mamie, who is very lively and well tonight. I danced a quadrille with her last night; and indulged in a schottische and some other dances with various ladies.

Last night and tonight we looked anxiously for Grandpa and his party, but they have failed to come. I'm somewhat fearful he may not be so well: tho' we ought to have heard by letter, if anything serious had happened.

Sister wishes to go to Lookout as soon as possible, and if she were sure you would be ready to leave Macon, would join you there on Monday next. She will however wait here until she gets a letter from you, informing her when you can go with her. Some one is constantly leaving here for Macon, and I can put her in charge of some party at any time, when she is ready to leave.

Charlie and Eddie return you their very hearty thanks for the newspapers, wh. were quite acceptable. Have you subscribed for the Telegraph for me?

Mamie joins me in much love for you. We have no news of course. Hope to hear from you tomorrow.

Your Son,   Sid.

To Virginia Hankins

Newnan, Ga.[44]
Sep. 19th 1869.

A long illness, — which was so ambitious an illness that, not content with body, it must seize also upon mind and heart — has prevented me from acknowledging your last fine letter,

---

[44] Lanier had apparently left Chalybeate several weeks before, to try the springs at Newnan, Ga., a small town about 25 miles to the northwest (see Clifford Lanier to Sidney, Aug. 29, 1869).

The letter from Virginia Hankins to which this is an answer has not been found.

which gave me more *unselfish* enjoyment than I have ever before received from any of your letters. *More enjoyment*: because I read that you had made friends with the faithful Mountains, and I knew that they would remain with you and bear you up on their great bosoms, long after they had faded from your sight on the horizon: and more *unselfish* enjoyment, because I saw here a pleasure for *you,* and did not have *merely* that delight which always comes to me from the noble tones of your letters: a delight which crowns, as foam crowns a wave, the on-rush of long-enduring and faithful friendliness which sweeps over me always, like the unceasing billowing of the sea.

And how fine must have been the influx of new thoughts on your soul, which, in your loneliness there, has so long been lying fallow! If these " ideas " should not yet give themselves shape: if you find yourself, in your lonesome after-musing upon the mountains and the men and the colleges and all, unable to form anything *definite* and outlined and serviceable, – be not discouraged. After a long time the metals in the crucible cease to boil and bubble and fiercely intermingle: then they cool and presently the perfect crystals appear. This is the way that beautiful crystalline ideas result from the swift and hurried mountain-visits.

———————

I'm up here for my health: – you'll see " Newnan " at the head of my letter – a place given over to invalids, Chalybeate-water-drinking, inquiries as to whether or not " you had a bad night last night? " and such other cheerful conversation as people with chronic liver-complaints and demoralized digestions indulge in. To hear Jones talk by the hour upon the subject of heavy bread, which lies heavy upon him as anvils: and Brown discussing the question of fried meats, a thing which throws him into a paroxysm of indignation at " the people in *this* country ": and Mrs. Brown and Mrs. Jones comparing the " effects of the water " upon their separate organizations, together with much strong-minded talk about the propensity of boarding-house-keepers to be niggardly in the matter of clean towels and pillow-cases: – is, altogether, a wonderful and a fearful thing, and I do not think I shall improve, here. I go home tomorrow-week: [45] where write me.

———

[45] Lanier presumably returned to Macon at the end of September. But since

Wife and Boy are here with me: both unwell. May sends you all loving messages. She read y'r mountain-letter over and over: and spoke of it in terms of unmeasured enthusiasm.

May I hear, very soon, if you have passed the summer – well?

Always

S.

FROM PAUL H. HAYNE

" Copse Hill " [Ga.], 30th Oct, 1869.

Very pleasant, My Dear Mr. Lanier, was the sensation with which I opened, & perused your letter of Oct 18th.

I had not, you may be sure, forgotten you – (for I have a *trick* of remembering friends) – but some *hard* literary work had put me *physically, hors de combat*, & I was endeavoring to *rest.*

It really GRIEVES me to hear of your continued ill health. A man whose lungs, or *liver,* or heart, or vital organs of any description, happen to be deranged, is but *half* a man !

May the Fates in this respect change their frowns to sunniest smiles !!

As for POVERTY, accept the lean, *attenuated* hand of a Brother, and try to appropriate whatever warmth so comparatively fleshless a member may be enabled to convey !

How I wish that I could have you here by my humble hearthstone, to discuss many a topic of literary, and philosophic interest !

John [Stuart] Mill – whom you mention –, is one of those men of genius, with whom, try as I may – I find it *impossible* to Establish any genuine intellectual *rapport.* My *own* fault of course!

You are correct about " THE Spanish *Gypsy,*" and correcter (excuse Grammar!), in what you *hint* concerning " *Lisa, & the King.*" – I marvel how an *Artist,* and woman of genius like Mrs Lewes, *could* have written *such stuff.* Not only is the

---

no letters by him between Sept. 19 and Nov. 6, 1869, have survived, it is impossible to say just when he resumed his legal work. The evidence of the following reply to Lanier's lost letter of Oct. 18, 1869, to Paul H. Hayne indicates his depression at this period, as well as his continuing interest in literary matters.

STORY thin, & vapid, but look at the *versification* !! Why there
is hardly a musical Alexandrine from beginning to end!! Did
you ever behold such reckless disposition of the *Caesura,* for
example? *'Tis* jaw-breaking!!
Wm Morris I am ready to swear by. I like him a thousand
time better than *Swinburne.* – Indeed, often in reading his marvellous tales the question *involuntarily* arises, " has *Chaucer*
come back to Earth"? — Just think his " *Psyche*," & his
" *Doom* of King Acrisius " !!

A healthful, noble, picturesque poet is this Wm Morris !
How *Keats* would have loved him !! and Charles Lamb, and
Coleridge !!

To drop from *great* things to *small*, you refer to " *Krishna.*" [46]
Somehow, I hope that piece pleased you. It was composed at
least, in an out gush of feeling.

What, my *friend,* are YOU doing, at present, in *Literature* ?
For Heaven's sake don't allow " *Tiger Lilies* " to be your *first*
& your LAST *work!* Exert the genius God hath given you.
How much more have you written upon that Poem of the
Jacquerie?

The beginning is *very* fine, and the poem *ought* indubitably
to be continued.

In *Jan.* I shall have a *legend* (versified) of my own to send
you.[47] The style is *Morris'* – *tho* the *major* portion of the Tale
was written before I knew of M's existence.

Pardon so abrupt a note. Write soon, & Believe me,

Ever Faithfully yours,

Paul H. *Hayne.*

P. O. Box 635, Augusta *Geo* —

TO MARY DAY LANIER

Brunswick, Ga.
Nov. 6th 1869.

Good Wife, I could think of little else but you & Chartie last
night, and, for thinking of the same, didn't sleep for a long

---

[46] A poem by Hayne.
[47] " Daphles: an Argive Story," published in the *New Eclectic Magazine,* Mar.,
1870 (see Lanier's letter to Hayne, Mar. 5, 1870, below).

time. This morning, my fingers are so cold that I can scarcely write, and I have many thngs in the way of business [48] to look after, so that I will but send you a hundred loving kisses and finish.

It will, I believe, be impossible for me to see our Lily. The B & A. R. R. only runs about ten or twelve miles: which leaves a gap, between the end of the road and Waynesville, of about ten miles, and I can't get any conveyance to bridge this over. So fly my hopes. I'm pretty well. The weather has been quite cold since I came here, and my throat feels a little rough this morning; with which exception I'm quite vigorous.

How sorry I am that you couldnt go to the Greshams! Father assured me that he could go, not more than half an hour before I left.

I had a pleasant stroll and talk with McLellan in Savannah. Called on Mrs. Duncan, but couldnt see her: she was suffering with one of her terrible headaches. Saw Mr. Duncan, and had a pleasant chat with him.

Dear Lady Mary, If thou knewest only my infinite loneliness when I am not with thee! I have been entirely lifted over the rough talk of men, by so much companionship of thine: and I know not if any man's talk will ever again give me any pleasure. Well, next Thursday I hope to have thee in my arms: and so, till then,

Thine.

If, as is quite possible, I should not arrive on Thursday, be not alarmed at all, since there are many things that might detain me here some time longer.

S.

To Mary Day Lanier

Brunswick, Ga
Nov. 10th 1869.

My Darling Wife:

    I've just read y'r letter in reference to the Concert for the Church. If I play, it will, I fear, place me in a

[48] The nature of this business trip to Brunswick is not entirely clear. It may

very strange position, in the eyes of Mrs. Gordon: but of course *I'll play.* I have to wait here until Friday to see a man with whom I have some prospect of making an arrangement wh. will utilize the brick-clay on Father's land. It breaks my heart to stay over for two days more: but it seems like a duty, as "the man" in question is said to be a man of means, and is looking for just a place as we can give him.

I wrote you and Father and Hal on Monday, and hoped for answers today, but get none. If any important arrangements should necessitate it, I will not hesitate to stay here until Monday: for, since I am *here,* I must try and make the most of the expense so far incurred; – all of which I say, that you may not feel alarmed in the event I should fail to be home on Saturday morning.

You can say to your Father (wh. will make this letter serve for both) that Mr. (*not Baron*) Drury will remain here all winter, and wishes to get the agency for the sale of the lots now being laid off on the Day & Bloom tract. As to the desirability of this, I will report further when I come home.

And so, Wife, Wife, across the large waters, here, there come to me sweet floating *Eidola* of thee, and enter into my soul, and fill me with longing and love-sickness.

They drift in upon me, as it were white blossoms blown off the top of the sea.

Today a quiet soft rain falls, and the sea is gray and still; as thine eye is, sometimes.

Nevertheless, tomorrow the Sun will shine, and there will again be gleaming of waves, and laughing foam, and glittering lights shooting down the water, and the robust vigor of billow-sport, and wild birds rejoicing therein.

So, too, thou art the habitant of the old forests where I have been wandering, and swayest upon the long vines of the woods, and always goest with me. I saw thee, two days ago, come floating down a long straight sun-beam that shot, between

have been partly in connection with preparing an audit for the Brunswick & Albany Railroad, a job offered him by Harry Day in his letter of Sept. 16. But the following letter indicates that it was principally concerned with the extensive landholdings in Brunswick of his father-in-law, Charles Day.

many tree-trunks, right out of the Sun. What wast doing in the Sun, Little Girl? Warming me?

———

I thank thee, that thou art My Wife, and that I am thine

Husband.

———

A hundred kisses for Sissa & Eddie. Love to Father. – How I long for my Chartie!   S.

To CLIFFORD A. LANIER [49]

Macon, Ga.
Nov. 19th 1869.

My Dear Clifford:

       Your letter anent the Cotton Mill business waited for me a day or two, during my absence at Brunswick.

I have given the project very serious consideration: and with every moment of such consideration, the objections to it seem to multiply.

Out of a host of these, I select but one, which seems to be controlling.

Neither you nor I know anything whatever of the business. It is a business which requires a life-time of experience and a varied course of reading, to enable a man even to penetrate into the vestibule of it. It is full of *ins* and *outs*: and of these ins and outs you and I are *wholly ignorant*.

Upon what possible foundation, then, could we present ourselves to Capitalists, and ask them to embark in such an enterprise? The very first question wh. wd. be asked, is, " What experience have you in the Cotton Mill business? " Our necessary answer to this question wd. be the death-blow to all our solicitations for capital.

I do not regard the project as a feasible one. The capital of the South is going into lands, rather than into manufactures: and rightly, too: for we know something of farming, and we know nothing of manufacturing.

I have a far more feasible project, which I have been long incubating. It is, that in the course of a year from now, you

---

[49] Excerpt previously published, Mims, pp. 99-100.

should go with me to Brunswick as a Lawyer. If the present prospects of B'k should hold good, no finer opening will ever present itself: we know something of the Law, and are rapidly knowing more: it is a business which is far better than that of *any salaried offices* could possibly be: the extensive possesssions of Mr Day at B'k w'd. probably give us some start in the Real Estate way: and the present muddle of titles in B'k w'd. start us finely in the legal way: the climate is glorious: and the material demands of life w'd. be easily & cheaply satisfied there.

I have not written you, before, of this idea, and I do not urge it now: – for the reason that I wish to make up my mind whether you had better leave the opportunity offered you by Mr Clopton,[50] for any other, however tempting. I am not sure that it *would* be better for you to abandon the practice into which, I doubt not, Mr Clopton could speedily introduce you: I'm going to think about it: and so, at present, I urge nothing.

One thing, tho', I do urge, and am perfectly confident of: it is best that you and I make up our minds immediately to be *lawyers, nothing but lawyers, good* lawyers, and *successful* lawyers: and direct all our energies to this end. We are too far in life to change our course now: it would be greatly disadvantageous to both of us. Therefore, to the Law, Boy! It is your vocation: stick to it: it will presently reward you for your devotion.

I will write you again of the matter. Brunswick seems likely to be a City. The Albany & Bk. R. R. will be pushed on to Eufala, and connect there with the R. R. from Montgomery to Eufala. This, on the completion of the Western R. R. from Montgomery to Selma, will make a straight line through from Vicksburg, Miss. to Brunswick: a line 100 miles shorter, (so the R. R. men say) than from Vicksburg to Savannah. Brunswick will in all probability be the terminus of the Southern Pacific R. R. Many persons are now moving there: and the Mayor told me there were 1600 inhabitants some months ago.

Mr Day will shortly put some Bk. Lots on the market: and as the titles are indisputable, they will probably sell very rapidly. Many applications are already recd for these. It is

---

[50] Clifford Lanier's father-in-law, Judge David Clopton.

barely possible that I may run over to Montg'y, with a view to placing some in that market.

I long to see you: and am greatly disappointed that you couldn't come to our Fair: wh. by the way, is the most stupendous *Farce* you ever dreamed of.

Love to Auntie & Willie & all.

Sid.

To Virginia Hankins

Macon, Ga. Nov. 30th 1869.

Dearest of all my Friends;   One Death and I have been waging a mighty war for a long time, and as long as the issue was doubtful. I did not like to write you: for I could not bring myself to intrude a sorrowful suspense upon the sweet tranquillity which I knew would overspread your soul after you had created so fair a work as the little poem in the " Dispatch," which you sent me.[51]

And so, to the Poem. The versification: – under which I include the rhythm, the general movement, and the rhyme; – is almost faultless. When, as I first glanced over your poem, I perceived this, I experienced a thrill of pleasure, which was very great; – and was partly selfish, since I detected my mind running back to the fair old days when I discoursed to you of Iambic Pentameter and the like.[52] But, – me aside – always have your *short* poems as nigh faultless in these particulars as possible.   Jupiter should not nod, except at a very *long* session of the Olympian magnates.

I find but one line which I desire to criticize in these particulars. It is the fourth from the last:

" Shedding serenest glory o'er earth's gloom."

---

[51] Virginia Hankins's poem " Forget Thee! " was published in the Richmond, Va., *Dispatch*, apparently under the pseudonym of " Hilda " (see her letter to Lanier dated " November 1869 "). It survives in a typed copy (Hankins Family Collection, Johns Hopkins University).

[52] In her letter of Mar. 23 (?), 1869, Virginia Hankins had indulged in a similar reminiscence of Lanier instructing her in metrics, at the time of their first friendship in 1863-1864: " I thought you knew I was *not rhythmic*, if you remembered your dull scholar, in the oak room windows, over your trochees & iambuses! "

I have two objections to this. One is prosodial entirely. *"Earth's gloom"* is a bad iambus: for " earth's " is the short syllable and is rather too *heavy* a word for that: it is rendered additionally unwieldy by its euphonic incompatibility with the *" gl "* of *" gloom "* which immediately follows it.

My other objection is (I know not what else to call it) hyper-rhetorical, and concerns the word *" o'er."* Were I you I would never use this elided form: always the full word *over.* It is far stronger; and can always be used without trouble as to rhythm: since " o'er " is as much *two syllables* as " over," and does not make the verse smoother.

You see how highly I think of you and of your poem when I exercise this religious conscientiousness in detecting its minutest *fault.*

As to the *thought* that is in the poem: surely, it is a most eloquent protest against forgetfulness!

> " — — — — — — — — Thou liest *perdu*
>   In lily cups "

delights me.

> — — — — " The twilight is my prayer
>   To thee O, Thrice-beloved, pure and true "

is an exquisite conceit set in equisite words.

> " Its answer is the silver stars which share
>   A common radiance with thine eyes divine "

is perfect music.

I like your poem: and I rejoice in it as an earnest of what I may expect from you. I pray you, Sweet Friend, write again, write often, write many poems. I do not doubt that each separate effort, when you have gotten over the wild joy of it, will be but a step upon which you will mount and see still wilder joys in your creative power. Be, I pray you, merciless with yourself, in the matter of rejecting all weak or ignoble or common-place expressions or similes. If the expression, or the figure, have been used before, or even if there is such a likelihood; cast it behind you, where the poor half-poet people will presently come along, and grasp it, and make much of it. Think, that it is not for you.

Your words all *burn purely.* They burn; and they are pure. This is a divine fire. In the wind of the Poet's Passion it will flame like a Star in Heaven. Good Beacon, Good Beacon, to all mariners, in the night! Most rare Beacon!

And now, I am curious to see the *next* poem. Send it me. Beware of the flatterers, and work hard.

This is the parting admonition of your

Friend.[53]

To Mary Day Lanier

[Macon, Ga., Dec. 23, 1869]

My Dear Wife:

Harry is a little better this morning, but is still in bed and will stay there. Come down, when the carriage comes, and stay with him. I think he will like it.

Wrap yourself well. It is very cold.

Could you bring my book – my blank-book, with my little poems &c written in it, you know — to me? But don't distress yourself looking for it. It has the word " Journal " on the back.[54]

Hastily

Office. Dec. 23/69   S. L.

[53] At some time during late November or early December, 1869, Lanier had composed " Nirvâna " (I, 19)—not mentioned in any of his letters until 1870—and had sent a copy of it in a letter, now lost, to Paul H. Hayne, who praised it as Lanier's " *ablest* Poem," his " Psalm of Life " (see Hayne to Lanier, Dec. 11, 1869). " Nirvâna " symbolized Lanier's quest for spiritual peace at this crucial period of his life when, suffering from ill-health and torn between his desire for authorship and the hard necessity of earning a living under the blight of Reconstruction, he was trying to force himself into the groove of legal practice.

J. W. Davidson's *Living Writers of the South,* containing a sketch of Lanier as a promising young author, had just been published. And in reply to Lanier's query Hayne wrote:

" Have I seen Prof: Davidson's critical publication? No! but I am tolerably well acquainted with its *material!* What do I think of *him,* & it? – Well! *mon ami,* (for your *private ear*), I think that D—— is a *windy ass,* with just eno' of half-spurious cleverness, ill-digested information, & *Twilight taste* to deceive himself – & perhaps a ' *select few*'! (Since he's sharp on *me* in some respects, th° decidedly, & unduly eulogistic in *others,* my verdict may be deemed partial).

" *Occasionally* he writes a fair essay, (like that on poor Timrod), – but on the whole, is insufferably *crochetty,* and dogmatic to a laughable extent. As an *English scholar,* he is shallow as a – *saucer!* "

[54] The reference is to Lanier's " Ledger " (Henry W. Lanier Collection, Johns Hopkins University), in which is written much of his early prose and poetry (see specimen pages, IX, facing 72). In it appears one more poem written in 1869, " Baby Charley " (I, 191), not published during Lanier's lifetime and not mentioned in any of his letters (see Clifford Lanier to Sidney, Jan. 4, 1870).

1870

To VIRGINIA HANKINS

Macon, Ga. Jany 7th 1870

Good Friend, I wrote you, about your Poem, some weeks ago, but have no reply to my letter.[1] I trust you are not tired.

I send you a copy of an address delivered by myself to the Furlow College:[2] and hope you'll like it. When you read it, remember that, in these days, the merit of a speech of that sort lies more in what one does *not* say, than in what one does say: and that I was speaking to an *agricultural* audience, principally.

I enclose also a copy of my last poem: " Nirvâna."[3] Tell me what you think of it. Of course it is a rapt Hindu who speaks.

I await your next poem. Write to

Your Friend

Sidney Lanier

To CHARLES DAY [4]

Brunswick, Ga., *February 10th* 1870

My Dear Father:

The weather has been so unpropitious since I arrived here that any business requiring locomotion has been impossible.

[1] See Lanier's letter to Virginia Hankins, Nov. 30, 1869, above. In her reply of Jan. 2(?), 1870, which crossed in the mails with this letter, she wrote: " I must thank you for your kind words of encouragement; and though I had to coax them from you, I know they are sincere and– thank you. In that line I have done nothing worth notice. . . . I need leisure, and *that* is a rare commodity, I cannot afford. It would be better for me to spoil a poem than a breakfast, you understand."

[2] Lanier's " Furlow College Address " (V, 247) was printed in the *Catalogue of the Trustees, Faculty, Alumnae and Students of Furlow Masonic Female College, Americus, Ga. 1868-1869* (Macon, Ga., 1869), pp. 19-39 (see note 38, 1869).

[3] See note 53, 1869.

[4] Early in February, 1870, Lanier accompanied his wife and child to Brunswick

51

I shall therefore remain here until Monday next. Saturday afternoon, Mr. Couper [5] is to take me out to his rice-place, to spend Saturday night and part of Sunday.

Ayres will hand you this, and will give you information as to the land etc.

Have had no enquiries for lots yet, except from Hall, who wants fifty acres at the point where the *County road* crosses the Albany and Brunswick R. R.

The Committee of Councilmen, to whom your proposition had been referred, met me at the Hotel last night. They had not arrived at any definite conclusion, except that they insisted that the terms were too high. After talking for some time, and finding that they were not likely ever to come to any conclusion, I managed to extract from them what they thought proper terms, and got them to shape a report, which they submitted to the Council, and which was adopted. I told them that they had better do this, so that the precise difference between *their* ideas and yours might become apparent. This report will appear in the paper tomorrow, and I'll send you a copy, for fear yours may not arrive.

Your letters were duly recd. By the last, I find that Harry may not have sailed until today: and I regret very much that I shall be unable to meet him here.

May and Charlie stood the journey well. Col. Avery was very pleasant, and we managed to make the time pass very agreeably.

I have to close this in order to meet Ayres in time. I write to Father by A. also.

Aff. Your Son

Sidney

To Mary Day Lanier

Macon, Feb'y. 15th 1870

Dear Heart, hither came I on Saturday last, arriving at three O'clock on the Sunday morning, having been delayed some

and probably to Waynesville, Ga., where they remained when Lanier returned 'o Macon on Feb. 12.

[5] James Hamilton Couper, a prominent citizen of Brunswick, who was probably

hours, by our inability to pass the down-train wh. had been thrown off the track by accident. Thou wilt see that I came sooner than I intended. Seeing in the papers that the Loan associations wd. meet, I resolved to forgo the trip to Cooper's, wh. wd. have detained me until Monday. Am rejoiced that I did so: since, coming here, I find all full of work even to over-flowing, and have been fearfully driven thereby ever since my arrival.

See, by the torn envelopes of the letters enclosed, that thou hast no secrets from thine audacious loving husband ! I opened the letters, greatly desiring to see some word from Hal and Clifford. Thou wilt never know how sorry was I that thou wert absent. Here found I Tom Eason and Wife, from Charleston, Ur :le & Aunt thereof. I would thou mightst have seen this royal six-feet Thomas, and heard the huge heart of the man body itself forth in the voice and the words, in round *basso*: and the Wife, – a tall, shapely, large-eyed one, full of all sweet motions and sentences. They spoke much and lovingly of thee: how thou hadst so won the hearts of the Montgomery kinsfolk (they were just from Montgomery) who never tired of talking anent thee.[6]

And so, Most Rare Comrade, I got me to my lonely room, in the night, and sat me down by my lonely fire, and fell a-musing of thee; and frequently turned the head thereof at hearing the sweet rustle of thy dress about the sacred room where thou and I have lived: and felt the heart thereof breaking, breaking, breaking for thee: and knew great pangs by reason of the bitter onset of my grief for all the sins I have done, above all, for my great, great sin: and begged thee piteously, by all tender names, " Child," and " Rare Child," and " Slender May Lilian," and " Fair Yoland " and " Enid " and Guinevere-Purer-than-Guinevere and Most Dear Ladye and Liebe and Mignonne and Ninita and Fine Sweetheart and a thousand besides, that thy wonderful loving Soul might invent some fair veil wherewith

connected with Lanier's business mission there, as was also John B. Habersham, a commission merchant and real estate agent, on whose stationery this letter was written.

[6] T. D. and Wilhelmina Eason, Lanier's uncle and aunt, had been in Mont-gomery because of the death of Sterling Lanier (Sidney's grandfather) on Jan. 31, 1870.

to cover my woful Fault, and that thou wouldst believe yet in my strength wh. thou has *not* seen, relying upon my love which thou *hast* in some little measure beheld: and thereupon I fell upon the knees thereof and spoke with my Friend, long, anent the matter: Whereto came Answer, wh. may not be told in a word but only in a life lived for thee.[7]

And now, since with vehement throbbing my heart is like to murder itself for that it cannot throb next to thy heart, I write no more, and kiss thee afar off, commending thee, O True Wife, True Wife, to the arms of Lily on earth and of God in Heaven, wh. fire no jealousy in thine

Husband.

To Mary Day Lanier

Macon, Ga. Feby 17th /70

Heart, Heart, what a Poet thou art become!
Thine of 12th, sent to B[runswic]k, has just reached me.
It is a Song in the Night, wherein the Music and the Starlight have so exchanged their sweet natures that the light is become music and the music is become light, and each hath given all its own sweetness, and each hath gained all the other's sweetness, and neither hath lost any sweetness.

And whereas I have oftentimes surmised, in my secret broodings upon thee, that peradventure Life would sometime bear hard on thy soul and compel thee to sing with thy pen as thou singest with thy ten finger-souls, – behold, now, it is done, and thou writest me here as none of the women have ever written before, nay, thou writest as none of the very best men-poets could have written, and I am not yet done with the wild shivering, of my delight in thy most musical and starlit words.

– If my heart will only not utterly break, in that I cannot put mine arms about thy neck, and look into thy gray eyes!
I have written thee, and written thee. The " spoken words " have not been wanting and presently they will come flocking about thee.

---

[7] Lanier's " great sin " was apparently his failure to provide an adequate livelihood during his first two years of marriage.

A letter today from Hal in Savannah. One enclosed: from Janie,[8] I suppose.

Thy father is well as usual. How fares thy *son*? The note anent household matters received: and will be properly attended to.

I send a Lily-cup full of love to Lily.[9]

Thine
Husband.

To Mary Day Lanier

[Macon, Ga.] Feby. 21st 1870

Thy letter is come, (of 18th) and I am wobegone,
Ma Mie, that thou hast not yet had any of the words I have sent thee since I kissed thee last. O, how long is it since I kissed thee! Rememberest thou how Mistress Juliet crieth to young Romeo, thus:

" *Jul.*   Romeo!
 Rom.   My Sweet!
 Jul.   At what o'clock tomorrow
          Shall I send to thee?
 Rom.   At the hour of nine.
 Jul.   I will not fail; *'tis twenty years till then!*"

or thus:

" *Jul.*   Art thou gone so? My love! My lord! My friend!
         I must hear from thee *every day i' the hour,*
         For in a minute there are many days.
         O, by this count *I shall be much in years*
         Ere I again behold my Romeo." —

[8] Janie Taliaferro, the widow of John Hill Lamar, to whom Harry Day was married later on this year (Sept. 19, 1870).
[9] Lilla Hazelhurst, whom Mary Day was visiting in Waynesville.

And by this count shall I not be but a mere gray memorial of antiquity, an I do not kiss thee again soon? Last night I found thy shoe, i' the room underneath the boy's wee bed, and did caress the same with marvellous satisfaction, for thou hadst worn it.

I grieve that thou art possessed of bodily heaviness, and grieve again, and over, till in midst of love and grief I am like to yield up my spirit: – or go to thee. Set thy love a-fighting thy weariness: for, when thou art weary, *I* am thrice weary. Yet I am marvellous strong, these days. I have much strength wherewith to tend thee, when thou shalt come and be my present Heaven again.

Thy household commissions are all fulfilled, I believe, by the letter. The visits, I will make when the heavens shall cease to freeze us. Today is bitter, bitter cold. An' I did not love thee so dearly, I would be but a snow-man.

Good Sissa keepeth the room thereof like unto the bed chamber of a king, – a miracle of order – and I have no trouble to find anything, save thee, thee, thee, for whom I look vainly and ah! how lovingly!

But thou must not hurry from where thou mayst get strength, even back to

Thine   Husband.

To Mary Day Lanier [10]

[Macon, Ga.] Feby 22nd 1870

Thou askest if I have written any poetry to crown thee withal. Knowest thou, My Sweet, how the husbandman saith, " this is *fallow* ground "?
In the long winter cometh the snow, and lieth on the field, and broodeth thereon. To this succeedeth a day of sunshine, where-under the snow melteth, and straightway small rills purl among the clods, and warm vapors float, and the hard earth becometh a moist and tender mould. Whereto cometh yet more snow, which again lieth and broodeth till the sun come and melt the same: and the earth drinketh it. And so, finally, the rude clay

[10] Excerpt previously published, W. M. Baskerville, *Southern Writers: Biographical and Critical Studies* (Nashville, Tenn., 1899), I, 194.

Thou askest if I have written any poetry to crown thee withal.

Knowest thou, My Sweet, how the husbandman saith, "this is fallow ground"?

In the long winter cometh the snow, and lieth on the field, and broodeth thereon.

To this succeedeth a day of sunshine, whereunder the snow melteth, and straightway small rills purl among the ~~clods~~ clods, and warm vapors float, and the hard earth becometh a moist and tender mould.

Whereto cometh yet more snow, which again lieth and broodeth till the sun come and melt the same; and the earth drinketh it. And so, finally, the rude clay is become fine arable glebe: full of all moist kindliness to germ and to root-tendril, and ready, with large benignity, to yield then manifold rewards to him that droppeth a seed therein.

— So, I. Now, am I fallow ground. I have my snows: then knowest them. Anon cometh my sunshine: then knowest it, also. Day by day, I feel arising within me a

LETTER FROM LANIER TO HIS WIFE, MACON, GEORGIA, 1870
Manuscript in the Charles D. Lanier Collection, Johns Hopkins University

is become fine arable glebe, full of all moist kindliness to germ
and to root-tendril, and ready, with large benignity, to yield
thousandfold rewards to him that droppeth a seed therin.

——— So, I. *Now,* am I fallow ground.   I have my snows:
thou knowest *them.* Anon cometh my sunshine: thou knowest
it, also. Day by day, I feel arising within me a thousand potential growths. Day by day, from my snow and my sunshine, a
thousand vital elements rill through my soul. Day by day, the
secret deep forces gather, which will presently display themselves in bending leaf and waxy petal, and in useful fruit and
grain. This product, this leaf and petal and fruit and grain, –
why shall I expend my heart to make it? Because I will then
weave all together the petal around the grain and the leaf
tendril – bound about the fruit, into a crown, which I will put
on thy brow, Thou True-Heart.   So shall I stand, and uplift
the arm thereof, and cry, " By Thy Strength, Good Master: –
is 't not brave, and beautiful, and useful, and is't not a fine
show, there, over the marvellous brows and the true gray eyes
of This One whom I love ? " ———

Thou seest how steadily I prophecy these things. O, the time
cometh, the Time cometh.

Meantime, I would I might but kiss thee, once or twice. When
comest? ———   Yet hurry not: I will wait, so that thou but
winnest a little strength. Win it, Child, win it *quickly*; – saith

Thine

My kiss for Lily.

To Mary Day Lanier

[Macon, Ga.] Feby 25th 1870.

Thou My Heart's-Ease, Today is a day that hath been dropped
by mischance out of Paradise, and there is in all things an inter-
fusion and secret throbbing of love, whereby the sunlight is like
unto a still vast caress, and the trees stand in loving expectancy
of swift-coming leaf-enchantments, and the smoke curleth into
long wreaths like wedding-wreaths, and the sky is as a large,

sweet letter, by Hal, as also thy most sweet letter by mail of 25th are come, and yield me what is next to thee:

And, finally, I long for thee, so greatly, so greatly, O thou Rare-Heart, that I number each minute gone as a marvellous blessing, – since, being gone, it standeth not betwixt thee and

Me.

To Mary Day Lanier

[Macon, Ga.]
Feby 2 Not so:
Tis March 2nd 1870.

I write thee, Fine Wife, under difficulties. Working have I been, all day, and was buried in work when the carriage came to bring us home, not knowing the hour was come. We do not wait, thou knowest, for aught: and so I jumped in:— and we have just dined, and here sit I in Father's room, with a pen execrable beyond measure, *determined* to *write* thee my twilight kiss, since, alas and alas, I can not give it as I most love.

Tonight Father and Sissa go to hear Carlotta Patti. Prame, the violinist, and Squires the tenor, and Hermans the basso, and Ritter, the pianist, are with her. As for me, I go not. What is there for me in this Music, if thou, my Soul-of-Music, art not there?

So, I stay at home to mind the baby, Eddie.

My " Nirvâna " is out, very fairly printed and placed, in the March " New Eclectic." [14] Father & Uncle C[lifford] are greatly pleased therewith.

Thy father and Hal are well as usual.

Comest thou, truly, on next week, to me?

An thou comest not, count to find here, when thou *dost* come, a man with a vial labelled " poison " in his hand, lying on the floor of thine apartment.

A letter from Cliff to me, today, declareth that the small Child thereof hath the measles, whereby Willie goeth into a muss &c.

[14] See note 16, below.

Corolla of some giant flower, – from one petal to another – ;
that is, from thy last kiss, to thy next kiss.

Float over this time-gap, sigh thyself across this wide flower-
bell, thou Mine Ineffable Divine Music, – quickly, to

Sidney

To Mary Day Lanier

Macon, Feby 28th 1870.

Anent domestic matters: the Eight Dollars were paid, as
thou directedst, some two weeks ago: William Thomas received
Three Dollars and a half, the which he did disburse for shoes,
wherein the children do now rejoice exceedingly: Madame the
laundress hath received Six Dollars, the same being for mine
own individual lavations, and for some extra service wrought
for thee before thy departure: I have been dutifully to visit our
excellent President Bonnell, and spent some three hours therewith in much high discourse: I *wd.* have been dutifully to visit
our little Mamie [12] yesterday, had not the weather forbid,
whereupon postponed the same until next Sunday: Lucy's
folk are well and prosperous, having moved into the house
thereof, and bringing word that the Chimney of the same doth
its work admirably, yea, rarely, whereat is great triumph upon
the part of the constructor thereof: The brother of the aforesaid Lucy hath broke ground for a garden around the residence
aforesaid, and already smelleth he greens in the distance, and
the like: Hal is come back, and I sleep with the same tonight,
being aweary for great loneliness: We have made the sale wh.
I was negotiating in Brunswick,[13] whereby some three or four
thousand Dollars cometh into the exchequer of thy father: I
have been bending all day long over long columns of figures
to make out my return to the Internal Tax people: Thy most

[12] Mamie Boifeuillet, niece to Mrs. Mary Wallen, and a cripple. Mammy
Lucy, mentioned following, was a much loved family servant of the Laniers.

[13] See Lanier's letter to Charles Day, Feb. 10, 1870, above. In a letter to
Clifford Lanier, Mar. 4, 1870 (here omitted), he gave the details of the scheme
for the sale of Mr. Day's real estate in Brunswick. Of a tract totalling 5,640
acres, 500 had been subdivided into lots for immediate sale. The expected completion of a railroad from Brunswick to Vicksburg, Miss., it was hoped, would
greatly enhance the value of this property.

sweet letter, by Hal, as also thy most sweet letter by mail of 25th are come, and yield me what is next to thee:

And, finally, I long for thee, so greatly, so greatly, O thou Rare-Heart, that I number each minute gone as a marvellous blessing, – since, being gone, it standeth not betwixt thee and

Me.

To Mary Day Lanier

[Macon, Ga.]
~~Feby 2~~ Not so:
Tis March 2nd 1870.

I write thee, Fine Wife, under difficulties. Working have I been, all day, and was buried in work when the carriage came to bring us home, not knowing the hour was come. We do not wait, thou knowest, for aught: and so I jumped in:— and we have just dined, and here sit I in Father's room, with a pen execrable beyond measure, *determined* to *write* thee my twilight kiss, since, alas and alas, I can not give it as I most love.

Tonight Father and Sissa go to hear Carlotta Patti. Prame, the violinist, and Squires the tenor, and Hermans the basso, and Ritter, the pianist, are with her. As for me, I go not. What is there for me in this Music, if thou, my Soul-of-Music, art not there?

So, I stay at home to mind the baby, Eddie.

My " Nirvâna " is out, very fairly printed and placed, in the March " New Eclectic." [14] Father & Uncle C[lifford] are greatly pleased therewith.

Thy father and Hal are well as usual.

Comest thou, truly, on next week, to me?

An thou comest not, count to find here, when thou *dost* come, a man with a vial labelled " poison " in his hand, lying on the floor of thine apartment.

A letter from Cliff to me, today, declareth that the small Child thereof hath the measles, whereby Willie goeth into a muss &c.

---

[14] See note 16, below.

All this, betwixt a kiss for each paragraph, hurriedly, to thee, in the hope of whose *true* divine-real kiss liveth thine

Husband.

To Mary Day Lanier [15]

[Macon, Ga? Mar. 3, 1870?]

If the year were an orchestra, O Heart, today would be the calm-passionate, even, intense, quiet, full, ineffable *flute* therein. In this sunshine, one is penetrated with flute-tones. The passion of the struggling births of a thousand spring-germs mingles itself with the mild smile of the heavens, and with the tender agitations of the air. It is a mellow *sound,* with a shimmer of *light* trembling through it.

It is like my love, when, albeit always constant, thy kiss tremulously irradiates it.

Today is a prophecy of the New Earth: as thy Music is a prophecy of Another Life, and as thy kiss is a prophecy of Heaven.

Today floats down Time, as one petal of a Lily on the bosom of a swift stream. Silently, it tells, at once, of the gap it has left in the full Lily, and of the ocean whither it drifts, to be engulfed, to die, and to live again in other forms.

Today comes as a friend with some Serene great Joy in his eyes. He whispers his sacred exultation: and will not speak it aloud, for its holiness.

Today is to yesterday as a deep smile to a wicked laugh.

Today is reconciliation: yesterday was a quarrel.

Today is like the wing of a white dove: yesterday was like the beak of a vulture.

But if thou wert with me, O Heart, I would not know the day, whether it were calm-warm, or windy-cold: I would only know that thine eyes were gray, and thy lip was dainty, and thy soul was mine and my soul was

Thine.

[15] Previously published, *Scribner's*, XXV, 623 (May, 1899); reprinted, *Letters* (New York, 1899), pp. 67-68. Conjectural dating from the evidence of the accompanying envelope.

To Mary Day Lanier

[Macon, Ga.] March 4th 1870.

Yesterday came one Turnbull, publisher of the " New Eclectic" Magazine,[16] inquiring for one Sidney Lanier, to the Office thereof. Whereupon we foregathered, and shook hands, and presently strolled, in the fair weather, to the river, and had much high discourse. And when the afternoon was come I rode out the same in the carriage, and strolled therewith through the cemetery.

A noble, quiet, handsome, beetle-browed, slender, gray-eyed fellow, he: and was like a revelation unto me from some other world: for he cometh out of the atmosphere of letters, and of men of scholarly lives, and carrieth the air thereof with him. I greatly wished thee to see him. He was pressing in his invitation to me to write for his Magazine, and spoke to me in such cheerful and tender guise that thou woulds't have loved to hear. Did I not hear thee say that Lily's family were inquiring for a Magazine whereto they might subscribe? This " New Eclectic" grows better, monthly: it is by far the best we have had in the South.

Today bringeth rain on the earth and rain on my soul, for I have no more sweet words from thee, for which I looked eagerly this morn. Is't possible my daily letters do not reach thee? I write daily.

Mr. Clifford Anderson hath had the goodness to increase the sum-total of living humanity by one (Avoirdupois 12 lbs), being a girl.

---

[16] On Aug. 28, 1869, Turnbull & Murdoch of Baltimore, publishers of the *New Eclectic Magazine,* had written Lanier that his name had been put on their complimentary list, and invited him to submit contributions, though they explained that contributors could not be paid until the magazine was self-sustaining. Two of Lanier's poems were reprinted in it—" Life and Song " in the Oct., 1869, issue, and " The Raven Days " in the Feb., 1870, issue—and his " Nirvâna " had its first printing in the issue of Mar., 1870. During this same month Lawrence Turnbull, a young Baltimore lawyer who was editor of the *New Eclectic,* passed through Macon on a southern tour in the interests of his magazine. This letter records his first meeting with Lanier. In later years the Turnbulls were to become intimate friends of the Laniers and their great benefactors.

Patti is come and gone. Cometh now Miss McCullough, with Brignoli *et al*. Next Thursday evening, being March 10th, these latter give *Martha*: and the folowing evening *Il Trovatore*. Canst thou not come and hear this with me ?

Thy father & Hal, and mine & Sissa, well .

And this is all of news I know.

Save, O My God, that thou wilt presently come to thy

Lover.

To Virginia Hankins

Macon, March 4th 1870

What is the " one idea " that hath so possessed my Friend, and of which I learn from her last letter? Is't a Book? Is't a Poem? What Theme? What Method? Drawest from thine own life, or gazest into another's life, or prophesiest of future Life?

Write and tell me.

I enclose a trifle of mine that came out in the February number of the " Nineteenth Century," a magazine published at Charleston S. C.[17]

Dost ever see the " New Eclectic," of Baltimore? Tis by far the finest magazine we have ever had in the South. In the March number appears my " Nirvâna," fairly printed. I will procure that the publishers send thee the magazine regularly.

Thy last letter, Friend, left me longing to hear from thee again.

Let me do so. Share with me the hopes and fears that agitate thy life.

I am always thine earnest

Friend.

---

[17] " Eternity in Time " (I, 12), published in the Feb., 1870, issue of the *XIX Century,* had been composed some time before (July 20, 1867). It was revised by Lanier and republished in 1881.

To Paul H. Hayne [18]

Macon. March 5th 1870

Why did'st not give us, Good Friend, the *letter* that was writ by gracious Daphles unto that love's-rebel, Doracles? Should'st have written it, and made it

> . . . " a missive tender, sweet
> Charmed with such pathos "

that one could only dream of it as having been writ upon lily-petals, and tied under a dove's wings, and sent him, so.

This is thy one offence. What shall I say of thy virtues? — –

> " . . . . Next, for a moment, she
> Stood in a timid, strange uncertainty,
> Changing from rosy red to deathly white;
> When as a Queen sustained by true love's right,
> She spoke in mild, pure steadfastness of soul:
> ' I come, O Doracles, with no mean dole
> Of transient pity, but to show thee how
> Thy mistress would exalt the abased brow
> Of one who knows her not! ' "

That this should have been spoken by a poet, living in midst of what I always call The Age of Trade, giveth me, first, Hope, and, second, courageous Pride; both being by way of solid basis to, third, the keen pleasure wherewith I thrill by reason of the inward exquisite beauty of the words themselves. —

> " She lifts her dim eyes, hearkening, as though 'ware
> Of mystic voices calling on her name:
> Therewith her cheek, whence the quick fevered flame
> Had quite pulsed out, with one last quiver, she
> Drops on the cushioned dais passively;
> For death, more kind than love, hath brought her peace."

In the very flow of these words, I hear the uneven flutter of a gentle

[18] Previously published, *American Literature,* I, 34 (Mar., 1929). This letter is an appreciation of Hayne's poem, " Daphles: an Argive Story."

heart, breaking for tenderness. Dear Mr. Hayne, thou hast here made Death *dainty*!

On the whole, this poem can be likened unto nothing except that same rare maiden, Daphles, herself: and it is, *me judice,* the fairest child of thy genius. I hope, in my deepest heart, that thou wilt wrest from Time a-many days, yet, wherein to people the otherwise sadly-empty heaven of our poor South with these radiant creatures of a genius wh. none more heartily or reverently admires

than thy Friend

Sidney Lanier

To Mary Day Lanier

Macon, March 8th 1870.

Thy letter to thy father, dated March *4th,* came *yesterday*: and thine to me, dated March *2nd,* came *today*. I greatly regret that this last should have been so long delayed, as I fear that thou may'st have needed the medecine, therein mentioned. I have sent the medecine, today, enclosed to Armstrong,[19] at Brunswick, with instructions to him to hand to thee on thine arrival at B'k, inasmuch as he can not get it before Thursday morning, and so would not be able to send it thee earlier. It may, so, relieve some pang of Friday.

The only letter of mine thou mentionest is one written many days ago. I believe I have written thee about every day since then: hast received?

And thy letter of March 2d remindeth me of Mr. Bonnell's books, and the weather &c: whereas I wrote thee, days and days ago, that I had spent several hours on a visit to Mr. B.

---

[19] Most of the letters that Lanier wrote to his wife while she was in Waynesville were sent to her in care of J. S. Armstrong, of N. S. Finney & Co., Factors & Commission Merchants, Brunswick, Ga. Armstrong seems to have been a close friend of Lanier, perhaps one of his numerous Montgomery friends, but he is mentioned only casually and infrequently in Lanier's letters.

Of the twenty or more letters written by Lanier to his wife during this separation (see his letter of Mar. 7, 1870, here omitted), only fifteen have survived; and of these, six have been omitted from the present edition, being merely brief love-letters.

and had returned the books, and had a pleasant time &c &c.
So thou hast not received *that* letter.

Ash-Wednesday, did I dream of thee all day, and wrote thee,
and wished that thou wert here, where I might take thee to
thy sweet Church and worship with thee.

Inasmuch as thy letter of latest date declareth that thou
comest on the 11th, instead of the 15th, I will therefore not
purchase Charlie's present to Eddie, until thou canst select the
same in person.

This, therefore, is the last letter I may write thee: unless I may
send thee a little note, tomorrow, to meet thee in Brunswick.

Mrs. De Graffenried, I am told, hath a fine boy. Miss Josie
[Wingfield], saw I at Church on Sunday, but spoke not thereto,
the same having a man pendant, unknown to me.

Heart, Heart, Heart. I lie in a wild expectant dream until
then, being meantime, utterly

Thine.

To Paul H. Hayne [20]

Macon, Ga. March 21st 1870

My Dear Mr. Hayne:

I thank you very heartily for your
encouraging commendations of my little poem: [21] and for your
thoughtful kindness in sending me the duplicate copies contained in two of y'r. letters.

Much reflection convinces me that *praise* is no ignoble
stimulus, and that the artist should not despise it. Once satisfied
that the praise is genuine praise for genuine art; – surely, then,
the artist may with confident delight bathe in these glorious
seas of sympathetic appreciation, and invigorate himself for
work. " Good Heavens! " cries Mrs. Browning *ex ore* Aurora
Leigh, " I shall be almost popular! " In this exclamation, one
discovers at once a true and a false philosophy. It is true,

[20] Previously published, *Critic,* VIII [o. s.], 78 (Feb. 13, 1886) ; reprinted,
Letters (New York, 1899), pp. 224-225.

[21] Hayne's praise of " Nirvâna " occurs in several of his letters. On Mar. 12,
1870, he had written that he had taken the liberty of sending a copy of it to
the English poet, William Morris.

Martin Farquhar Tupper is, in a certain sense, " popular ": but then how about Homer and Milton and Shakespeare? Are they not popular, also?

And so, whenever my one condition-requisite, above-assigned, is fulfilled; that is, whenever I am satisfied that the praiser, being himself an artist, praises what he considers good work; I appropriate this praise with entire abandon, I enjoy it without *arrières pensées* as to whether it is my right, or as to whether I am infringing upon that outwardly-fascinating, inwardly-false German doctrine that the Self of genius is sufficient for itself.

I will write you again, in a day or two: meantime, for the enjoyment of your sympathy, which I receive without question and use without hesitation, accept the sincere gratitude of

Your Friend

Sidney Lanier

To Mary Day Lanier

[Macon, Ga., Mar. 23, 1870?] [22]

Dear Heart:

Harry is not well this morning. I have just been to see him, with Dr. Hall, who assures me that he is doing well, and is not in any immediate danger. Dr. H. insists that he shall be kept *perfectly* quiet, and therefore, you are not to see him until after 12 O'clock today. Your *father* is not allowed to see him until then.

I think it probable, however, that you had better come down, *in the carriage,* and see your father, who will of course be uneasy until then. You can spend the morning with your father in his room at the hotel.

This must be done *very* quietly: it is of great importance to make *no stir* at all, observable by outsiders. Say only to Sissa that Harry *is quite ill.*

[22] The conjectural dating of this letter is arrived at from its relation to the following letter, dated Mar. 25, 1870. During the serious illness of Harry Day, which occurred shortly after Mary Day Lanier's return from Waynesville, Lanier seems to have spent several nights, at least, watching at his bedside in the hotel where he lived in town. From his office Lanier sent notes to his wife in suburban Vineville, keeping her posted as to her brother's condition.

Come, about half-past ten, to *our office*: and I will run down to the carriage, and tell you what I cannot now write. Do this when you *first* come down, and *before* you go over to the hotel.

Your

S.

To Mary Day Lanier

[Macon, Ga. Mar. 25, 1870]

Good Morning, Fine-Heart!

Hal is steadily improving. He slept well last night, and looks very bright this morning.

But your old Wolf is a little sleepy: not having lain down until four O'clock this morning.

Have just breakfasted with your father.

Don't come down at all, today. It would be better so. I shall not let your father see Hal until noon; perhaps not then. All is well: and your coming could do no good.

I send a brush and spool of thread, left in your Father's room: also a letter from Salem.[23]

Thine.

Office. Mch 25th /70.

To Virginia Hankins

[Macon, Ga. Apr., 1870?] [24]

For two weeks, I have been standing, like a faithful squire at the side of his knight, with a friend who has been doing a stout devoir in a great hand-to-hand tussle with Death.

[23] A letter from Salem Dutcher survives, dated Mar. 22, 1870, in which he wrote apropos of Lanier's admission to the bar: "I rejoice corde cordium mihi with thy glory won of late at the feet of our Georgia Gamaliels. Was I not right to tell thee, Law was thy sphere, not literature?" Dutcher had urged Lanier to become a lawyer from the first, declaring that he had the proper qualifications—"the man, reason, and the woman, persuasion, in full measure."

[24] The conjectural dating of this letter has been arrived at from the fact that Harry Day's illness had begun about Mar. 23, 1870; and two weeks after this would put the date of this letter at approximately Apr. 6, though Lanier uses the same phrase ("two weeks") in the following letter to Paul H. Hayne, dated Apr. 13.

Watching, so, night and day, I am somewhat worn: and it is almost as if this same John Death were angered at my little assistance to my friend against him, and contemplated a petulant thrust or two at me. I only mention this to let you know why I did not, as I intended, follow up my short letter with a longer one.

Y'r letter, – wh. has come to me this morning, for all the world as if it had grown up with the sweet dew-tipped grass yonder, and floated in on the living Wind of the Spring through my window to my Soul, – has been in my hands only a few minutes, and I stop all work to make *some* poor attempt to answer it.

I set so much store by yr. friendship; I derive so pure sweetness and calm strength from it; I guard it so strenuously and so vigilantly from everything in life that is not born of dew and wind and free sky; I keep it so eye-bright: that I always dwell with keen pleasure upon any expression from you which conveys to me your recognition of value in this attachment: this – which is almost the only living thing that remains to us, out of all the dead ones that have sunk into those old years, as into old graves. It delights me inexpressibly to know that you join with me in paying tribute to that fair fortune which has kept this fire a-light. It is not dimmer, now, to me, than ever. It has outlived other lights that began with far more furious burning. I can see by it, in the dark. — One loves what one has saved from a battle, trebly.

You have discovered the wisdom of my advice " not to publish for five years." You think your thoughts are " crude; " and that you know nothing; and finally you have resolved to abandon literary hopes.

Your thoughts are, in a certain sense, " crude." We call gold crude, when it is fresh from the mine. Consider what men do with crude gold. In that shape it is uncommercial: it is not serviceable: it will not buy bread and pleasure. So, one sends it to the mint-people. What is the first thing *they* do with it? They mix with it some baser metal, and harden it so: then coin, and issue. If, instead of to the mint, (where they construct *Use*) you send it to the Jeweller, (who constructs *Beauty*): his first act is the same: he mixes the baser metal therewith, and hardens the mass; – then the filigree will keep shape.

My Friend, I have here announced to you the paradox of life, – whether it be autorial life, or any other life. To corrupt oneself, and harden oneself: AND AT THE SAME TIME TO REMAIN UNALTERABLY PURE AND TENDER; aye, By Life and Death, to be at once pure and impure, to be at once angry and loving, to be at once hard and tender: – this is what is required of him who would write for, or live in, the world.

Consider Christ: who did all this. After much reflection, after much life, you will learn how He did it.

Meantime: – the statement of this paradox explains to you why I wished you to wait five years before publishing. O Good Friend, how could I bear to see the rough world finger your virgin gold; to hear the blatant people complain that here was no alloy (which, mark you, the tradespeople *must* have, – or what becomes of trade?) and no *hard* money! This terrible torture – to have one's Best mistaken for one's Worst and so reviled, and cried out against: this, I wished to spare you, and I thought that five years more of life might bring in yr. way, perhaps, that particular training which wd. teach you the way to avoid it. That you have gold, I know. Between you and me, whether you fling it out in glittering masses to the world, or furnish forth the boys, there, with it, – is not a matter of great moment, now.[25] But boys become men, you know: and the wee sister will not always be a baby: and, then, when the tall men and the grown woman shall not, as now, require *all* your life: then, with the lavish instinct of all sweet gold-growers like you, you will scatter the bright stuff abroad.

There is, therefore, one reason why I approve of your resolution to abandon writing. That reason is – that I know you'll break it! And, for the present, it is as well that you should not print anything more than small pieces. Do not your Virginia farmers let the ground lie fallow, sometimes? The rains come thereon, the winds blow thereover, the snows fall, the sunrays pierce: – and out of them all, come to the ground such poten-

[25] Virginia Hankins's letter, to which this is an answer, is dated March, 1870. In it, replying to Lanier's query in his letter of Mar. 4, she declared that her "one idea" was not literature but the education of her brothers, to whose care she had devoted herself since her mother's death in 1865. She confessed, however, that she had begun a book—"we will dignify it with the name of ' novel ' "—but, remembering her larger task, had " decided wisely no longer to entertain literary aspirations."

cies of wheat and corn and flowers as make up the awful miracle of growth and life wh. sustains the world. You, therefore, lying fallow, should not grow impatient, or do aught hasty: — be still. Accept the liberal influences of the sunlight, and also the chaste activities of the snows. Rains and winds — tears and passions — these will quietly work strange vitalities and forces in your soul.

Bold, and silent, and patient, and large: — that is the way the broad sweet fields lie fallow. How great, how noble, how still, how pathetic, how thrilling, is the broad, upturned face of a field! Walk in yours, where we have walked, and learn the lineaments of these friendly countenances. There, you will find what I have said.

I have but begun to talk to you: and yet I must close. Notice, I pray you, that to you I do not write coherencies and essays. I only write you *suggestions.* I cannot teach you anything: but I can suggest some things to you, which I know y'r. mind will catch and follow to good issue.

I will write again, presently, as to the rest of y'r letter.

Meantime I am

Your Friend.

To Paul H. Hayne [26]

Macon, Ga. April 13th 1870

My Dear Mr. Hayne:

Watching, night and day, for two weeks past, by the bed-side of a sick friend, I have had no spiritual energy to escape out of certain gloomy ideas which always

[26] Previously published, *Critic,* VIII [o. s.], 78 (Feb 13, 1886); reprinted, *Letters* (New York, 1899), pp. 225-228.

In his reply on May 12, Hayne wrote: " Your last letter to me [was] . . . , in its spontaneous eloquence, and appreciation of nature, a *poem.* The Spring with its glories has *inspired* you. Let me prove *how,* and to *what degree* your letter impressed me. I was on the point of composing an essay on ' *The Straw-berry, & Strawberry weather.*' Well, *your* enthusiastic words stole insensibly into the dialogue of the piece, and if you see yourself thus unexpectedly in *print, don't be offended* with me, *mon ami.* . . . The *interlocutor* who is represented as uttering them in the little half dialogue, half essay, is a mere *fancy-creature.*" (Hayne's essay was published in *Appleton's Journal,* III, 661-663, June 11, 1870.)

possess me when I am in the immediate presence of physical ailment: – and I did not care to write you that sort of letter wh. one is apt to send, under such circumstances, since I gather from *yr.* letters that you have enough and to spare of these dismal down-weighings of the flesh's ponderous cancer upon suffering and thoughtful souls.

I am glad, therefore, that I waited until this divine day. If the year were an Orchestra, today would be the Flute-tone in it. A serene Hope, just on the very verge of realizing itself: a tender loneliness, – what some German calls *Waldeinsamkeit,* wood-loneliness, – the ineffable withdrawal-feeling that comes over one when he hides himself in among the trees, and knows himself shut in by their purity, as by a fragile yet impregnable wall, from the suspicions and the trade-regulations of men: and an inward thrill, in the air, or in the sunshine, one knows not which, half like the thrill of the passion of love, and half like the thrill of the passion of friendship; – these, which make up the office of the flute-voice, in those poems which the old masters wrote for the Orchestra, also prevail throughout today.

Do you like, – as I do – on such a day to go out into the sunlight and *stop thinking,* – lie fallow, like a field, and absorb those certain liberal *potentialities* which will, in after days, re-appear, duly formulated, duly grown, duly perfected, as poems? I have a curiosity to know if to you, as to me, there come such as this day: – a day exquisitely satisfying with all the fullnesses of the Spring, and filling you as full of nameless tremors as a girl on a wedding-morn; and yet, withal, a day which utterly denies you the gift of speech, which puts its finger on the lip of your inspiration, which inexorably enforces upon your soul a silence that you infinitely long to break, a day, in short, which takes absolute possession of you and says to you, in tones which command obedience, *today you must forego expression and all outcome, you must remain a fallow field, for the sun and wind to fertilize, nor shall any corn or flowers sprout into visible green and red until tomorrow,* – mandates, further, that you have learned after a little experience not only not to fight against, but to love and revere as the wise communication of the Unseen Powers. ——

Have you seen Browning's " The Ring and The Book "? I am confident that, at the birth of this man, among all the good fairies who showered him with magnificent endowments, one bad one – as in the old tale – crept in by stealth and gave him a constitutional twist i' the neck, whereby his windpipe became, and has ever since remained, a marvellous tortuous passage. Out of this glottis-labyrinth his words won't, and can't, come straight. A hitch and a sharp crook in every sentence bring you up with a shock. But what a shock it is! Did you ever see a picture of a lasso, in the act of being flung? In a thousand coils and turns, inextricably crooked and involved and whirled, yet, if you mark the noose at the end, you see that it is directly in front of the bison's head, there, and is bound to catch him! That is the way Robert Browning catches you. The first sixty or seventy pages of " The Ring and the Book " are altogether the most doleful reading, in point either of idea or of music, in the English language; and yet the monologue of Guiseppe Caponsacchi, that of Pompilia Comparini, and the two of Guido Francheschini, are unapproachable, in their kind, by any living or dead poet, *me judice*. Here Browning's jerkiness comes in with inimitable effect. You get lightning-glimpses, – and, as one naturally expects from lightning, zig-zag glimpses – into the intense night of the passion of these souls. It is entirely wonderful and without precedent. The fitful play of Guido's lust, and scorn, and hate, and cowardice, closes with a master-stroke:

" . . . Christ! Maria! God! –
Pompilia, will you let them murder me? "

Pompilia, mark you, is dead, by Guido's own hand; deliberately stabbed, because he hated her purity, wh. all along he has reviled and mocked with the Devil's own malignant ingenuity of sarcasm. —

You spoke of a project you wished to tell me. Let me hear it. Yr. plans are always of interest to me. Can I help you? I've not put pen to paper, in the literary way, in a long time. How I thirst to do so, how I long to sing a thousand various songs that oppress me, unsung, – is inexpressible. Yet, the mere work that brings bread gives me no time. I know not after all, if this is a sorrowful thing. Nobody likes my poems except two or three friends, – who are themselves poets, and can supply themselves!

Strictly upon Scriptural principle, I've written you (as you see) almost entirely about *myself*. This is doing unto you, as I would you shd. do unto me. Go, and do likewise. Write me about yourself.

Your Friend

Sidney Lanier

From Robert S. Lanier to Clifford A. Lanier

Macon Geo. April 28, 1870.

My dear son,

I mailed to your address yesterday two newspapers containing copies of Sidney's address on tuesday last out at the Cemetery.[27] Please send one copy to the family at Robertson.[28] His effort was a great success & seems to have been the general talk of the Town. He spoke it so deliberately & feelingly that the large audience heard him with profound attention & were deeply impressed. Encomiums & praises came in on every hand. The boy's success did his father's heart & all our hearts good. Dr. Wills says—& many other say the speech is a poem from beginning to end.[29] Dr. W. says he covered himself with glory. A gentleman met me to-day & said he met with Mr. Holland, the eloquent preacher (who travelled in the East last year) on the cars yesterday, who had just read the speech on the train, stated to him it was the finest effort he ever read. The preachers in Macon all speak in glowing terms of it. Dr. Bonnell,—would have kissed him, I think, had they been alone. But I forbear. Judge for yourself. You will find two errors in want of punctuation by the printer: but you will readily correct them.

We are all pretty well. Our home looks very sweet & pretty

[27] On Tuesday, Apr. 26, 1870, Lanier delivered the "Confederate Memorial Address" (V, 265) at the exercises held by the Ladies Memorial Association, Rose Hill Cemetery, Macon. The address was printed the next day in the Macon *Telegraph and Messenger*.

[28] Slip for Robinson Springs.

[29] Dr. David Wills, minister of the First Presbyterian Church in Macon, 1860-Sept., 1870. In a letter of May 12 to Lanier, Hayne praised the address similarly: "A noble poem throughout! a poem *tho not* metrically rendered. . . . In it, you managed to strike an original *key-note* from the beginning! And from beginning to end it was beautifully *maintained,* or suggestively carried off into many exquisite and pathetic *minors.*"

since the warm weather came. The garden doing pretty well, & the flowers all aglow.

Sid started to Brunswick, on business, the day after his speech. Your check rec^d. Thanks.

Kiss my dear Willie & *the* babie for me & for all of us. And give love to all the family.

Your aff. father,

R. S. Lanier.

This was intended to be written yesterday but I was too busy.

To Jane L. Watt

Macon, Ga., May 18th 1870

My Darling Auntie:

I've had a very severe illness; [30] — and I want to put my arms around your neck. I haven't said anything to anybody about it, yet: but I think of taking my little family early next week, and running over to see you for a day or two. I write, now, to find out if you'll be at home next Tuesday and the week succeeding? If you *will,* you needn't answer, as I wouldn't have time to get your letter: but if *not,* telegraph me, so that I can time my visit differently. If I get no telegram from you, I think I shall start over about next Tuesday.

Some one told me you expected to go to Charleston shortly; and I write this, fearing I might miss you.

[30] See Lanier's letter several months later to Virginia Hankins, Aug. 26, 1870, below, where he said: " shortly after delivering the Soldier's Address, I had quite a severe hemorrhage from the lungs, which completely disabled me for some time, and left a cough wh. suggested quite lively suspicions of consumption."

Lanier had apparently written to Salem Dutcher of this illness at the time of its occurrence, in a lost letter inclosing a copy of his " Confederate Memorial Address," for Dutcher's answer, dated New York, May 24, 1870, rebukes Lanier for working " so unceasingly." Apropos of Lanier's speech, which he had already read in the Augusta, Ga., *Banner of the South,* he wrote: " It shows me, and my heart leapt at that showing, thou art not so in love with ' Progress ' as thou wert. Art more Aristotelic and less Baconian. More in favor of antidoting anger and less for the supreme beauty of making shoes. It was the one defect, me judice, of thy character that thou seem'st at one time given overmuch to the Modern and regard'st not sufficiently the glory of the Old."

Dutcher's letter was forwarded on May 28 by R. S. Lanier to Montgomery, where Lanier had gone with his wife and child.

I long to see you, and the other dear ones. Love and kisses to all,

From Your

Sid.

To Virginia Hankins

Macon, Ga, May 20th /70

I send you a copy of my address before the Memorial Association. It was spoken from a stand erected among the graves of the soldiers, which were covered with a great glory of flowers. Your friendly soul would have been pleased with the reception of the speech. Congratulations and kind messages have come to me from manifold directions. I hope you'll like it, and the art of it.

Have no time to write today.

Your Friend

Sidney Lanier

To Lilla Hazelhurst

Macon, Ga.   June 15th, 1870.[31]

My dear True-Heart:

As I lie here on my sick-bed I have been greatly discomforted with the reflection that my poor mind had not even the energy to select one out of the thousand poems which are always growing and budding for you in my heart, nor the skill to frame it in fair words and send it to you, for my birthday wish. Yet, on better reflection, what matter? There is, after all's said and done, but one Poem: there is, either for

---

[31] Lanier had apparently returned to Macon in time to try a case on June 4 (see R. S. Lanier's letter, May 28, 1870, informing his son that his case had been set for this date). But he was far from being recovered from his illness. On June 9 Wilhelmina Lanier—who seems to have accompanied him on his return from Montgomery—wrote from Macon to her husband: " Sid will probably leave for Lookout [a mountain resort in Tennessee], next week– all believe a speedy change very necessary for him."

birth-day or death-day, but one true wish, and the Poem and the true wish are, Love.

If therefore on this birthday of yours I write with whatever tremulousness of weak fingers, and scrawling of unsteady pencil, that I love you, my white-throated and swaying-stemmed Lily, heartily, freshly, earnestly, and full warmly; that I set on high, above all other love or friendship that I have known, that noble devotion which you always render, with unspeakable sweetness, to her with whom God has made me one; and that besides the intrinsic delight of this rare affection, it has, as it were, an outer glory, in the strong and unfailing light it sheds on my sometimes-wavering faith in the possibilities of the human heart; that the steadfast constancy and splendid unselfishness which beam at once from your life and from your gray eyes remain always with me as distinct, unaccountable, lovable wonders, as stars which I see by day and by night, – and that my finest wish for you is that you may be always *strong in loving* — if, I say, I write this, I have written the best Love, – that is, the best Poem, and the best Wish of

Your friend

Sidney Lanier.

To Virginia Hankins [32]

[Macon, Ga.? *ante* June 20, 1870?]

My Dear Clara Benette, I wish to know, in the first place, who was the " brilliant woman," and who was the " literary critic " ?

In the second place, I wish to submit to your judgment,—

[32] Previously published, *Southern Literary Messenger*, II, 7-9 (Jan., 1940). The allusion in the salutation is to the heroine of Sheppard's *Charles Auchester.*

Virginia Hankins's letter to which this is an answer has not been found. In it, apparently, she had sent him a copy of an essay she had written two years before entitled " An Appeal to my Countrywomen" (see her letter of Mar.-Apr.?, 1870), which Lanier comments on in some detail in the present letter.

Her reply to Lanier's letter is dated June 20, 1870—hence the conjectural dating here given. It was sent to Macon but forwarded to Chattanooga (Lookout Mountain), where Lanier had gone towards the end of June with his wife and boy and his Aunt Jane, Mrs. Abram Watt (see Lanier's letter to Virginia Hankins, Aug. 26, 1870, below).

which is ordinarily a very cool judgment for a woman's, even for a man's—the following facts and considerations, which do NOT go to show that " the taste of the age is immoral," or " that the people's mind will not be strained to anything higher than Puck."

(a) Who are the writers that have claimed and secured the attention of the age? They are Dickens, Thackeray, George Eliot, Chas. Reade, Anthony Trollope, William Morris, Tennyson, Miss Rossetti, Jean Ingelow, Mr. Gladstone, Mr. Mill, the author of " Ecce Homo," [33] Longfellow, Emerson, Victor Hugo, Sainte Beuve, Auerbach, Hans Andersen, and the like. Are *their* works immoral?

Because some people will read Ouida,[34] shall we judge the taste of the age from *that* one indication, when a thousand *other* indications show us that the age—as indeed *all* ages do—will always respond to the great thoughts of genius, and will always gaze with admiration upon the pure creations of poetry? Does not the age evidently love the Eighteen good writers that I have just named in a breath? Is it exactly fair to the age, to forget its manifest, real appreciation of the true writers, and to remember only its apparent, short-lived enthusiasm for the false one?

(b) But, moreover, the age, as an age, don't read Ouida; while it *does* read Tennyson. Outside of a certain class of people who are addicted to the Young-Ladies-Boarding-School-Literature, Ouida is not read at all. People do not translate Ouida into German, and French, and Swedish, and Spanish and Russian.

(c) So that, on the whole, the critic who made this remark was probably in error, and the fact seems to be that a writer with genuine stuff in him will not only meet his reward at the hand of this age, but, upon my word, I think there never was an age in which that reward followed so quickly and so surely. Indeed, the danger is, in these days, that the reward will be *too* quick, and *too* sure, so that there is hardly *enough* of the old struggle against adversity which toughened the thews and seasoned the souls of earlier writers. For example, see how

[33] Sir John Robert Seeley.
[34] Pen-name of Marie Louise de la Ramée, a prolific Victorian novelist.

flattery and swift praise have ruined one of our noblest souls,—
I mean *Ruskin!* Some of his last works are so full of disgusting
self-conceit, that they are unreadable:—yet, ten years ago, what
a singer was he!

Again, — in support of the general proposition — do but
remember what a storm of public disapprobation beat upon
Swinburne's head! And mark how he has subsided into a lowly
magazinist, and what a changed strain he sings in!

Dear Friend, be not persuaded that the taste of the world
is immoral. It is not so. The world bites at the high and the
pure and the true, as a fish at its bait. It is *only necessary that
the writer should do one of two things:* let him either *promulge
his high, his pure, his true thought in the forms which his
particular age demands,* or, *let him create* NEW *forms, and
learn the age to appropriate and utilize and enjoy them. Either*
of these methods is open to the faithful and conscientious
writer: Either is good.

Observe then that the Successful writer must look to his
matter, and to his *form.* Each age has its particular forms,
under which it can most easily recognize the noble thought of
genius. Genius must consult these forms: or, if it think of
better forms, it must learn the age (and this is a hard task)
to use the new forms,—must familiarize their faces to the
people, so that the people be not asked to a Barmecide feast,
where there is much good substance, but not in assimilable or
edible shape.

Take the deep view of things, dear Ginna, and not the
shallow one.

Under all sin, lies Love. Heaven, which is above, is also
beneath, the earth, and envelopes it on all sides. The bad is
only superincumbent on a great Good.

Life, even modern life, is aware of its own weakness, and,
at bottom, is (as is said in another form in the essay you send
me) perfectly confident that Truth and Love are the only
foundations upon which it can build securely.

Finally I like this essay very much. It is good, vigorous
writing, and shows a fine emancipation from the *Common-place*
trains of thought on this subject.

" Nothing new under the sun " is a phrase always wrongly
applied. To *God,* there is nothing new. To you and to me,

there ARE *myriads of new things under the sun.* To each soul, the whole world is new. In our growth, each day brings a new revelation.

Poets *can* sing new thoughts. Nature is undiscovered, yet. To each genuine explorer, there will reveal themselves new treasures. Goethe said a foolish thing: " Every clever thing has already been thought of." [85] This is a mere generalization which will not bear the first thrust of a probe. Examine it and see if it will.

Very hastily!

Your Friend.

To Robert S. Lanier

Lookout Mountain,
Near Chattanooga, Tenn.
July 7th 1870

My Dear Father:

I do not doubt that Mary's letters, describing our situation &c. will have been received before now. We are very comfortably located, indeed: and I think it would be difficult to find arrangements more suitable to a parcel of invalids, seeking quiet, as we are.

The temperature is remarkably cool, and I'm wearing my thick vest to-day. I find my overcoat not uncomfortable at night. The cool, dry air, the comfortable rooms, the food — which, tho' plain, is yet so well cooked as to elicit daily compliments even from fastidious Mrs. Watt — and the noble scenery, all conspire to make us content with our resting-place. If I could but rid myself of my cough, I should soon be very stout and hearty: but this holds on very tenaciously. I have been in bed two days, hoping that by lying still and taking remedies I might relieve it. I think it somewhat better today, and am up again. I've gained some strength since coming here. Bought a couple of dozen of Ale in Chattanooga:— which has the finest effect on me.

---

[85] This quotation and that in the preceding paragraph are paraphrases of ideas found in Goethe's *Faust* (Part Two), *passim.*

Charlie is suffering with his teeth today, tho' he is very much
better than he was three days ago. May is improving. Aunt
Jane suffers with boils, of prodigious size, and with red-bugs,
acquired in her long constitutional rambles over the mountain.

We have met some pleasant people here from New Orleans.
Company very small, and constantly changing: this being no
place for *pleasure*-seekers merely.

Please stir up the "Telegraph & Messenger" people. I've
rec^d no paper yet. Mr. Day sends me his New York papers
frequently, wh. somewhat compensate.

I think we are all doing well: and hope to hear similar
accounts from you and Sissa.

Love to Uncle C. & family, from Your Son

Sidney

To Robert S. Lanier

"Lookout Mountain House"
Lookout Mountain, Tenn.
July 11th 1870

My Dear Father:

Your letter of July 4th, from Robinson Springs,
reached us night before last, and we were glad to hear that
you had taken an opportunity to escape for a little while from
the heat and dust of Macon, tho' sorry to learn of your indisposition. Mary wrote Sister a long letter immediately on our
arrival, here, which ought to have reached her before your
letter was written. I hope it came to hand, tho' I fear not, as
you mention hearing of us through *Aunt Jane's* letter only.

We have had very cool weather here, and I have been wearing
my heavy overcoat: tho' we hear, from the travellers, accounts
of very warm days in the lower countries.

My cough hangs on: and, tho' not at all painful, is annoying
from its persistency. Harry sent me up a lot of remedies suggested by Dr. Hall, and I think their effect has been on the
whole beneficial. The cough is, however, not cured, and I can
only hope to wear it off, by improving in general health. This
I am doing, to some extent. I am stronger, and have more
appetite, than when I left home.

Mary is not very well, today, but, I think, has improved in flesh since we came here.

Charlie is better: and, as soon as he gets his last teeth through, I look to see him resume his old elephantine proportions. Aunt Jane has improved in complexion: is suffering today from *Colic, which* she ate cheese for supper last night.

I made a special contract with our landlord by which we get our board for $45.00 per month: half-price for Lucy, and no charge for Charlie: wh. I think cheap enough. We are very comfortably located: barring very hard shuck-beds. Our cabin is charming: has three verandahs, & three rooms, & suits our party admirably. Fare very good.

I have not been able to make up my mind about going with Uncle William, yet. I am now too weak to stand anything like Camp life. Any exertion seems to excite my cough. Will be able to tell more about it in a week or two.[36]

The " Telegraph & Messenger " has never arrived yet. I had heard through Harry of Uncle C.'s gaining the Eufala Home [Insurance Co.] Case. Am anxious to hear from the others. Have you tried anything more before Judge Cole?

I fear you are suffering from the heat in Macon, and wish I could transmit to you a few puffs of this mountain breeze which is now blowing. All send love to you.

Regards to Uncle C. & family.

From Your Son

Sidney

To Robert S. Lanier

Lookout Mountain House
Lookout Mountain, Tenn.
July 28th 1870

My Dear Father:

I wrote you day before yesterday of the conclusion to which Uncle Clifford [37] and I had arrived in regard to the trip to Minnesota, and was gratified at receiving your

---

[36] In his letter of July 4, R. S. Lanier had urged his son to join his Uncle William Lanier, who suffered much with dyspepsia, and who was planning to try tent life at Blount Springs, Blount County, Alabama.

[37] Lanier's Uncle Clifford Anderson made a brief visit to Lookout Mountain

dispatch last night, announcing your approval. We have had three consecutive days of *dry* weather, here: during which my cough has improved: and this more than ever confirms me in the belief that the climate of Minnesota would soon set me up in health.

Mr. Day and Harry arrived yesterday, the former seeming very much debilitated by the heat and fatigue of his journey.

Harry has determined not to go on to Virginia, immediately. He found a letter here from Janie,[38] announcing that in consequence of severe illness in the family, which occupied all her time in nursing, she had been unable to get ready, and would not be so within two weeks. As Hal is much interested in arranging matters at Brunswick he will go back there from here, and will carry May and the bairn to Marietta. This fits in admirably, and I leave with very much less anxiety, having the certainty that the family will be so well cared for. They will leave here on Saturday morning, next, arriving at Marietta at 2 ½, same day.

I leave this afternoon. In response to an urgent invitation from Mr. Davis,[39] I'm going by the great Greenbriar White Sulphur Springs, which are but a few miles off my route, and where Mr D. goes to spend some days. Auntie will go with me there: she and I and Mr. Day travelling together as far as Charlottesville, Va. I shall stop a day or two at Greenbriar. Mr. Davis, who precedes us, securing comfortable rooms for us.

Mr. Given [40] will probably come by Greenbriar on his way home from New York, and take Aunt Jane back to Montgomery. She had thought of going with me to Minnesota, but hearing that the Hotel was a little short of money, concluded that she wd. not spend any more. I shall go on to N. Y. after leaving the springs, where I can get a cheap through-ticket to St– Pauls.

I have drawn on you, at five days sight,– in favor of Harry Day, who, having more money than he needed, cashed my

at the end of July to discuss plans for the recovery of Lanier's health (see R. S. Lanier's letter to Sidney, Aug. 1?, 1870).

[38] In a letter of July 19 to Lanier, Harry Day had announced his engagement to Janie Taliaferro Lamar.

[39] Jefferson Davis, formerly President of the Confederate States of America.

[40] The lessee of the Exchange Hotel, Montgomery.

draft – for $200.00. I will be glad if you will, within the next
ten days, send $100.00 to Mamie, at Marietta. I have given her
some of my funds: which with the 100 from you, will cover all
her expenses until she gets back to Macon. You will know so
well, My dear Father, with what distress and reluctance I make
these heavy drafts upon you, — that I will not speak of it. I
still hope that I may not be compelled to spend my share. It
is quite possible that a day or two of change at the White Sul.
Spgs. may so advance the little improvements of the last three
days, that I will not need to make so extensive a journey. I leave
here just in the nick of time. It is now clouding up, and
thundering: and a day of wet weather wd. undo all the three
days of dry have done.

Mr. Davis goes, about the middle of August, to England,
intending to bring back his family, – whom he had left – about
the middle of September. He urged me greatly to go with
him, and promised all sorts of pleasant things. Of course, I
couldn't think of it, – the cost being about $500 in gold – but
it was pleasant even to *have the chance* of going under such
favorable auspices! – wh. wd. have carried me into the society
of several of the greatest men in England.

Mr. Day, without my knowledge, has given me a one-third
interest in the net profits of the brick-yard at B'k, wh. he thinks
likely to bring me in at least $500 per year, and perhaps con-
siderably more. Hazard, Apthorpe & Co., of N. Y., have sent
an Agent to Europe, who is to offer two thousand acres of the
B'k property (including city lots) at $100,000: and two thou-
sand other acres at $40,000. I have thought that the war [41]
might perhaps direct investments there in this way, in consequence of the insecurity of European finances at present.

You probably misunderstood May's letter, in regard to the
number of letters rec'd by us from you: she laughed when she
saw y'r remark in that connection & thinks you didn't have your
specs on when you read her letter. We have rec'd all y'r letters,
in due course.

Write me at N. Y. care Winslow, Lanier & Co, 27 & 29
Pine St.

I was greatly gratified to learn, thro' a note sent from Uncle

---

[41] The Franco-Prussian War.

C. by Harry, of y'r success in the Liver Case.[42] This certainly completes a very brilliant round of victories.

May will add a line. Tell Uncle C. his telegram (answer from Hammond) arrived here *yesterday.* I suppose the information wouldn't be very valuable to him now.

Love to all inquiring friends. Will write you immediately on arriving at the Sp'gs.

God bless you.

Yr Son

Sidney.

To Mary Day Lanier

Greenbriar White Sul. Spgs. [W.] Va.
July 31st 1870

My Dear Heart,   If there has been any one moment, of my sleeping or waking life ,– since I left you, in which my heart was not all one agony of yearning for you, – I know it not.

Thou knowest the Undertone of the Sea, which booms forever, down beneath the infinitesimal voices of the foam. This yearning for thee is *my* undertone.

With which Invocation, I proceed to relate to thee that we have had a delicious journey, with a noble termination thereof.

Except for about fifty-miles of dust, the elements were all favorable, the air cool, the cars clean, and our company pleasant.

At Chattanooga, I had the pleasure of meeting L. Q. C. Lamar.[43] He came up from the supper table and spoke to y'r father, who immediately introduced me. He was in a great hurry, having to rush off to the Memphis train, wh. was about leaving. Grasping my hand and keeping hold thereof, he said: " I'm very glad to meet you. I know you very well, I've read y'r

---

[42] A case concerned with a patent infringement of the trade-mark of Gutin & Co.'s " Liver Regulator " (see R. S. Lanier's letter to Sidney, July 13, 1870).

[43] L. Q. C. Lamar (1825-1893), U. S. Senator from Mississippi; formerly a resident of Macon.

book, I am greatly interested in your future– ” – and, without giving me time to reply, was off.

After getting on our train at Chattanooga we met General Pope Walker, (Confed. Sec. of War) and his wife. Mrs. Walker was very beautiful, and was from Huntsville:– two lovely traits of character which attracted me. I talked with her – she came with us nearly to this place – and she was pleased, to testify her appreciation of me in certain remarks wh. she made to Auntie's private ear, wh. remarks of course were *not* told to me by Auntie, and wh. I of course shall *not* tell to thee.

From Charlottesville here is 130 miles by the Chesapeake & Ohio R. R. Such a 130 miles is not to be found elsewhere in the world. I will not try to tell thee about it, until I am ready to write the poem wh. will be born of this summer.

Finally we arrived here, parting with y'r father, (who seemed to stand the journey well, and protested he was better than when at the mountain) at Charlottesville.[44] Mr. [Jefferson] Davis came to us, and secured us very comfortable quarters. ———— The place is more beautiful than I could describe to you, and the hotel a marvel of spacious elegance. The dining-room is said to be the largest in the world. I find the fare excellent, and I wished that I could *telegraph* to you the fine mutton-chop wh. I had this morning.

I hear fine accounts of the Red Sulphur Springs (forty miles from here) in cases like mine, and think I shall go there before leaving this place. ————————

Charlie fairly snapped my heart, as I drove off from Lookout. I wanted to slip off: but he saw me, and waited, with widening eyes, until I had mounted, and the horses started: when he leaned his head on Mammy's shoulder, and cried as if *his* heart wd. break, too. Tell Mammy Lucy why I didn't say good bye to her: tho' doubtless she recognised the situation. God bless the boy, how my soul is twined about him! The haunting images of his great loving eyes fill me with strange dreams and noble anticipations and strong longing.

My fine, stately baby! He will be Prospero and Ariel in one.

I have been a little hoarse today, (for thou wilt smite me if

---

[44] Charles Day went on with his son Harry to visit Janie Lamar in Orange, Va., and then alone to New York.

I tell thee not of my cough): otherwise, the cough is about as usual. I have no more night-sweats, and slept finely last night. Here are no flies at all. I've not seen one even in the dining-room. Auntie is recovered, and is doing great detriment to the commisariat, here.

I send my love to thy two angels, Mrs. Duncan & Mrs. Wallen.[45] Tell them to ply the wings thereof vigorously in thy behalf: for thou art my all.

And so, Meine Einzige, thou and I are again apart:– and there is nothing in my life besides one thought,– to see thee again. Unto the Master of all Health, in Whose power it lies that I may see thee again quickly, I commend thee, as I lay me down here, to-night, on the strong shoulder of this mountain, where I wd. thou wert, with

Thine.[46]

To Robert S. Lanier

Greenbriar Wh. Sul. Sprgs. [W.] Va
August 2nd. 1870

My Dear Father:

We arrived here safely, after a pleasant journey, free from heat or dust, through the most beautiful country in the world.

Mr. Davis met us, and secured comfortable quarters for us. We find the crowd not nearly so large as it was last year: there being only about seven hundred people here at present. This is rather an advantage, and while we have enough for gayety, we have not enough to compel us all to scuffle for our living. The hotel, the cottages, and the grounds, are on a scale of magnitude which I had not expected. It is said that fifteen

---

[45] Mr. and Mrs. William Duncan of Savannah and Mrs. Mary Wallen of Macon seem to have gone regularly to Marietta for the summers.

[46] A wealth of letters by Lanier have survived covering his quest for health during the next two months. More than a score of them (mostly to his wife) are here omitted, only those being included which contribute to the narrative of his life.

hundred people can eat at one time in the vast dining-room.
The Hotel and most of the Cottages are of brick, and the former
is quite an imposing structure. The fare is very good, and I do
entire justice to it three times a day.

I think I am steadily improving. My cough is certainly better,
and my strength and flesh increase daily, by small but steady
additions. I hope sincerely you will have a similar account to
give of yourself. The nights have been remarkably cool since
I came here. I sleep under *two* blankets and a thick spread !
which will sound apocryphal to *you* I don't doubt, in the great
sweltering city.

Besides Mr. Davis we have met some pleasant friends, here,
and our time passes charmingly. If only my dear Wife were
with me, I could be very happy here for a month or two.

I leave for N. Y. tomorrow afternoon, stopping at Orange
C. H. one day to visit Janie. I do not know yet what route
I shall take from Washington, and so can't say what day I'll
reach N. Y. especially as I may stop one day in Washington.

I hope, however, by Saturday or Sunday, to be in the city.
Shall not go to the Red Sulphur Springs, Va. Auntie sends
love to you: wh. receive, with that of

Your Son

Sidney

To Mary Day Lanier

Greenbriar Wh. Sul. Spgs. [W.] Va
Aug. 4th 1870

They say that we are here on the mighty Southern Slope of
the great Alleghany, and that all the waters run from here into
the Gulf of Mexico.

So I am on the Southern Slope of life, and Thou are my
sweet warm Sea, and all my thoughts stream to thee. Dost not
feel the in-rushing of this great tide of love wh. flows to thee
down from this mountain?

God bend a fair sky over thee, thou tender and great Heart,
beating for me as the Sea pulsates for the Earth, receiving my
love as the sea receives the rivers, picturing the sky and holding

cloudy intercourse with heaven, – Thou, in whom all the motions of my soul find their climax and terminus.

I am just packed and ready to start Northward. Auntie, Mr. Davis and I go together as far as Gordonsville, where I turn down the road to visit Janie, the other two keeping on to Washington.

We have met some nice people here, and altogether I think my time has been profitably spent.

My cough is about as yesterday. I now cough about six times a day, pretty regularly: once after each meal, and once between. The cough is quite loose, and a large quantity of phlegm follows, each time. – I believe I improve in strength.

I long to see thy sweet handwriting: but thou wilt be busy, and must not be at trouble to write me.

Thou wilt kiss my young Ariel, and wilt cause him to kiss thee, for

Me.

To Mary Day Lanier

Orange Court House, Va.
Aug. 5th 1870

All day, through such a liquid air as must be the atmosphere of Heaven, the far mountains have palpitated, like agitated breasts. They breathed and breathed, and breathed *thee* forth: and like an exhalation thou camest across the fertile wide valleys to me. The sun was mad, with his own glory, all day, and through his awful splendors thou didst float, in thy sweet white robes, over the vast corn-fields, across the river, to me. Always floatest over to *me*, – dost not, My mountain's-thought, My breath-of-the-hills? Thou knowest no other spot to float to, but *me*, is it not so?

And oh, how thou didst fare bravely across the enchanted valley: how thou didst flash upward along the strong vertical sun-rays, how thou didst slant swiftly earthward on a sloping wind, how thou didst poise thyself, anon, in short ecstasies, how thou didst sail on the quiet air, calmly and confidently, straight into my heart!

And thou wert habited in thy sweet white wh. I love, and thine eyes were great and gray and no fuller of love than they have always been, and thine arms were outspread in an enfolding gesture, and I received thee into my soul, and we were one, My Wife.

Wh. meaneth that I am just returned from Janie's, where I drove, behind a pair af spanking grays, this morning just after breakfast, companied by a young lady from this place who was going over to see her. Janie fairly bubbled over with happiness, to see *me*. We talked, we walked arm in arm upon the hills, we found a fair spring in the woods and drank thereout, we ate a monstrous dinner, we walked again, I played the piano in the twilight, the moon rose and glorified the mountains and the trees; – and so, at nine o'clock tonight, we started back to this place, where we arrived at half past ten, after a glorious drive thro' the moonlit hills and fields. Having packed my trunk, I am ready now for N. Y. I leave here in an hour, for that place. I cannot sleep, for my longing after thee, and thy sweet eyes: and so I write thee my daily invocation of worshipful love.

Thy father prospered finely at Janie's. She told me he was in great spirits, took long walks with her, and declared himself so stimulated by the fine air, that he was better than in a long time before: – the best proof of all which is, that he staid there two days.

I found it the most suitable place I have seen for me. The air was perfect Champagne: dry and crisp and cold. I think it not at all unlikely I shall return there from N. Y. and spend a week or two. I have pretty much given up Minnesota. I hear that Mr. [C. C.] Clay has not improved: and the cold weather has commenced there. I am daily getting better, I believe; & there is surely no finer air in the world than at Janie's. Thou shouldst have seen the mountains! It was a blue such as we have never seen. I had nearly died for thee.

I will see thy father tomorrow afternoon at 4 O'clock, if God speed my train. Auntie went on with Mr. Davis this morning at 1 O'clock, to meet Mr. Given at Washington. Poor heart, she seemed greatly grieved to part with me.

And now, with my heart glowing warmly upon thee even as

the down-going sun glowed upon this Mountain this eve, I cry
adios to thee over the dark land, until the morrow, being meantime and always

Thine Husband.

I have not said that I rec^d thy letter from Janie's hands. I have
sent thee my address, I think in one of my letters from Wh.
Sul. Spgs. 'Tis always " care of Winslow, Lanier & Co. 27 &
29 Pine St. N. Y."

TO MARY DAY LANIER

New York, August 7th 1870

Dear Heart, There are here no mountains, – save of iniquity –,
no streams, – save of sin – and no fine airs, – save those of Theo.
Thomas' Orchestra, and so there is nothing out of which thou
wilt arise and come to me, save the music, wh. I will therefore
go to hear tomorrow-night. There, in the music, I well know
that I will find thee, thou sweet-toned Soul: and there I long
to be.

I find thy father doing finely. We dined together yesterday
afternoon, immediately after my arrival, and he ordered a bottle
of claret in honor of such an event. We are at Fifth Avenue
Hotel. How the good Father loves this luxury of cut-glass and
magnificence! He seems more at home here than anywhere-
else in the world.

We went to bed early after dinner. I was greatly fatigued
by travel, and my head was splitting. I put ice on it, and
relieved it enough to go to sleep. How I longed for thy tender
hand-strokes.

Salem [47] came to me before I was out of bed this morning,
bringing thy two dear letters. I tho't I had written thee to write
me care of Winslow & Lanier, 27 & 29 Pine St. 'Tis well, tho',
so: else I could not have seen thy dear words until tomorrow,
today being Sunday.

[47] Salem Dutcher had written a letter on July 24, 1870, inviting Lanier to
stay with him in New York. Lanier remained at the Fifth Avenue Hotel (on
whose stationery several of the following letters were written) until Aug. 15;
then he moved to Dutcher's house on East 49th St. for the rest of his stay in
New York.

I am dreadfully tired. The cinders, from the coal-engines on these Northern railways, affect me badly; and make me cough. I am more than ever inclined to go to back to Janie's: tho' y'r father has seen Sherman,[48] who gives a fine account of Minnesota: & he urges me to go there. I will determine by tomorrow. I am tired, now. I long for thine arms and thy hands and thine eyes, and I am thy Husband.

TO MARY DAY LANIER [49]

[New York, Aug. 8, 1870?]

And to-night, I come to thee out of what might have been Heaven, an thou, – who only canst listen to music *with* me – had'st been at my side. — 'Twas opening night of Theo. Thomas Orchestra at Central Park Garden: and I could not resist the temptation to go and bathe in the sweet amber seas of the Music of this fine Orchestra: and so I went, and tugged me through a vast crowd, and, after standing some while, found a seat: and the *baton* tapped and waved, and I plunged into the sea and lay and floated: Ah Wife, the dear flutes and oboes and horns drifted me hither and thither, and the great violins and small violins swayed me upon waves and over-flowed me with strong lavations and sprinkled glistening foam in my face: and in among the clarinetti, as among waving water-lilies with flexile stems, I pushed my easy way: and it was always as if I bore thee on my arm yet could not bend my arm about thee, nor kiss nor clasp thee, nor draw thee fully and closely on my bosom, – O Wife, O Wife, O Mistress, O All, I verily thought I could feel thy breath on my cheek and yet, if I turned, thy lips, which I saw plainly, were not available for kisses, for I knew that I only dreamed thee, and yet clung to the dream because I feel that thou, being only *dreamed,* art still sweeter and better and more to me than all others in actual presence: – And so, even lying in the Music-waters I floated and flowed with my awful sacred love for thee, – whom God now take in

[48] An unidentified cousin of Mary Day Lanier.

[49] Previously published, *Letters* (New York, 1899), p. 70, where it is misdated 1871. Conjectural dating from the sequence, the accompanying envelope, and the reference in the second sentence to Theodore Thomas's opening concert.

His tender care, – because now my soul is utterly bent and prostrate before my Shrined Sweet, My Body-of-Music, My Wife.

To Mary Day Lanier

New York, Aug. 9th 1870

Thou Dear Rose-petal about the Rose-core of my life, how bare
am I without thy soft enclosure!

Even the summer-wind, so, is cold to me, and there is no
warmth in life, nay, there is no life in life, but only death in life.

This afternoon thy father and I start for Saratoga. We will take
the five Oclock Steamer for Albany, from which place 'tis but a
short journey by rail. I stay there two days: then return to
Janie Lamar's.

I go not to Minnesota. I cannot endure the coal-dust wh.
comes from the engines. Three days of that wd. do me more
harm than cd. be compensated by any climate. Whatever can
be done by *air,* I feel confident, will be done at Janie's.

Thou shouldst have many letters from me, by this time. Thy
two dear ones per. Salem, are come.

Thy father is greatly improved. He wishes me to go to
Saratoga with him, otherwise I shd. go immediately back to
Janie's. He is very enthusiastic in regard to his trip to J.'s, and
frequently declares her one of the sweetest women in the world.
She was more *herself* than I ever saw her before: free, and
sweet, and winning. I have written Hal that I made love to
her all day, and besought her to break with him and fly with
me: – but cd. not cause her, in her blindness, to see the beauty
of so doing.

So, thou art ogling thine old Frobel,[50] eh? Ah, thou dear
Mamie Day. This carries me back into certain haunted sunshine of certain enchanted days of old glory. Dost not
remember? – But, how much sweeter is life, now, when I call
thee Wife! Thou art now not only my Sweet Heart, but also
my Sweet Wife.

[50] A former suitor of Mary Day (see her letter to Lanier, Jan. 16, 1867).

God bless thee, My Dear Wife, will I never come to thy warm lips again?

I find I have forgotten to say that my cough is about as usual, and that I am pretty well otherwise. Tell me if my dear boy is getting well again. Thou speakst of more cold, and the like. Tell me also of my fair True-Heart, My fine Essence-of-a Soul, My Thought-of-a-Violet,   My

Twin.

To Paul H. Hayne [51]

New York, Aug. 9th 1870

My Dear Mr. Hayne:

Y'r. letter, containing the poem, reached me at Lookout Mountain, Tennessee, where I had been spending some weeks.

I received it at night, about midnight. Some friends, — one of whom was Mr. Jefferson Davis—were sitting in the porch of my cottage, and I could not resist the temptation to read the poem aloud to them. So, – while my fair wife held the candle and shaded it with rounded white hand from the mountain-breeze, I read: and I feel very confident you would have been gratified with the sentiments of approval which followed, in hearty sympathy with the piece. I like it better than anything you have written: it has in it the *magnetism* wh. distinguishes genuine poetry from culture-poetry. Write me some more like this, good Friend!

I am travelling for my health. If you know what this phrase means, you know to what a melancholy state I am come. It wd. seem that the foul fiend, Consumption, hath me on the hip. Against him, I still fight: but God knows the event thereof. I had started for Minnesota: but I find the journey so disagreeable that, after resting here a day or two, I'm going back to Orange C. H. Va. where I have a friend living among the Sweet mountains, with whom I shall stay some weeks: and

---

[51] Previously published, *Critic,* VIII [o. s.], 89 (Feb. 20, 1886) ; reprinted, *Letters* (New York, 1898), pp. 228-229. Lanier refers to Hayne's letter of July 16, 1870, containing his poem, " A Summer Mood."

where, an thou hast any bowels of compassion left in thy Soul's abdomen, thou wilt write me, " care Charles Taliaferro, Esq."

I do no work at all. I am too ill. This is Apollyon's unkindest cut of all. In this he hath wounded my sword-arm. Well, well. And so, write me, dear Mr. Hayne, and believe that I always enjoy heartily your cheering words, and that I am always Your Friend

Sidney Lanier

To Mary Day Lanier

Saratoga Springs N. Y.
Aug. 11th 1870.

Yesterday, O my Heart, I was tired, and my soul was full of cinders.

Therefore I did not send to thee my worship; for worship and cinders go not well together.

Thy father and I came here by the night-boat. We entered the Highlands in a great *salvo* of moonlight. As we sat out on the forward deck, thou didst compound thyself of the water-sheen, the mist, and the mountain-influence, and didst sit by me. Nor captain nor clerk nor any but me knew that thou wert a passenger on the St. John: and I felt some qualms of conscience in smuggling thee aboard and getting thee this free ride, insomuch that, like friend Uhland, I wd. have paid passage for two: but, O God, I was too busy yearning about thee and loving thee, and ministering to thee.

And the river lay in his awful trance under thee and me, and we fared wavily on betwixt sweet mountains and many lights, and thin-voiced salutes of stars and moonshine, and jet-black shadows of hills, and shore-curves.

I thank thee for this divine Voyage. Who but Thee might be *compagnon* to me at such a time. There is no one in the world besides thee.

There is no one in the world besides thee.

Thy letter, to care of Winslow & Lanier reached me in N. Y. I had written thee why I cd. not go to Minnesota. The journey was too fearful. I go back to N. Y. this afternoon, having spent two pleasant days here with thy father. Will be there a day or so, when I think to go back to Janie's for a week or two. My cough is about as usual: not annoying, save from the persistency thereof. I will consult a medical man in N. Y.

Thy father seems to improve rapidly, and is very devoted to Ye Congress Spg. He eats amazing quantities of beef and mutton, and drinks black tea by the barrel. I know not what will become of the poor dear gentleman's stomach and bowels.

I will write thee tomorrow from N. Y. God Almighty guard thee and my bairn, for

Thine Husband

To Mary Day Lanier

Fifth Avenue Hotel, N. Y.
Aug. 12th 1870

Last night, My little Trueheart, I came down the Hudson, on my return from Saratoga, where I spent a day and a half with thy father. The full moon was up: and midst of the wild war of radiances betwixt shining moon and shining river, we rode all night. Thou and I sat on the upper deck, aft, right in the full magnificence of water and of planet, and thine arms were about my neck: wherein we had greatly the advantage of a certain couple of lovers who sat over against us on t'other side the deck, and who gazed in each other's eyes and longed and longed to throw arm about each other's necks,– but dared not by reason of many eyes of by-sitting passengers.
Thou, however, thou spirit of my Soul, thou wert there for me only, and thine arms, being not visible to others, were yet love-strong and firm-clinging to me, and thy lips warm and thine eyes gray.
O my tender Phantasy, My sweet-arm'd, warm-lipped and large-eyed Dream, My hovering White Cloud, Mine Ever-Present, My Wife,– there is no one in the world besides thee.

At thy father's request, I have been to consult Dr. Marcy.[52]

[52] Dr. E. E. Marcy, a Swedish physician of New York, to whom Lanier went

He examined my chest. He says the upper part of the left lung is obstructed, in consequence of the long bronchial trouble: that I need *treatment,* not *air*: that he *thinks* he can cure me if I will stay here for three months (!!!) so that he may see me frequently. After much deliberation, I have determined to stay *one* month,— i. e.— until about the 10th or 12th of September — to try his remedies: by which time I can better tell what to do: — all the said arrangement being subject to the approval of Father and Dr Hall. I wrote Father today, telling him Dr. Marcy's words, as above, and asking him to consult Dr. Hall as to the advisability of placing myself, for at least one month, under Dr. M's treatment.

Dr. M. is mainly right, I think. While my cough is quite loose, it has evidently ceased to be *entirely* a bronchial one, and the expectoration is quite copious. In general health, I think I am probably improving.

Salem spent an hour with me this morning. He is quite hard at work: has entirely left off drink, keeps house with his two [53] sisters, and looks greatly sobered.

Thy father improved *momentarily* at the Springs. He was full of kindness to me, would not let me pay for anything at all, showed me all the springs and places of interest, and smiled consciously at all my expressions of admiration. I think he feels a sort of proprietary interest in the place: he showed off all the points of it as if it belonged to him, and chuckled at my encomiums as if they were personal compliments to *him.*

And in the midst of all the gobbling, and guzzling of waters, and disfiguring of figures,— I never cease to long for thee and my dear bairn. Send me the picture whereof thou spokest. Address me still to care Winslow & Lanier 27 & 29 Pine St. I go tomorrow to spend a day or two with Salem.

I am always thy faithful

Husband.

for treatment and advice for the rest of his life. He had consulted Dr. Marcy before going to Saratoga with his father-in-law.

[53] Actually three (see Dutcher to Lanier, July 24, 1870).

To Mary Day Lanier [54]

N. Y. Aug. 13th "/70

Flutes and Horns and Violins,– Celestial sighs and breaths slow-drawn, penetrated with that heavenly woe wh. the deep heart knoweth when it findeth not room in the world for its two-great love, and is worn with fasting for the Beloved:– fine Purity, fiercely attacked by palpitating Fascinations, and bracing herself and struggling and fighting therewith, till what is Maidenly in a man is become all grimy and sweat-beaded, like a warrior: – dear Love, shot by some small arrow, and in pain with the wound thereof: divine lamentations: far-off blowings of great winds; flutterings of tree and flower leaves, and airs troubled with wing-beats of birds or spirits; floating hither and thither of strange incenses and odors and essences: warm floods of sunlight, cool gleams of moonlight, faint enchantments of twilight: delirious dances, noble marches, processional chants, hymns of joy and of grief: —— Ah, knowest thou that thou sat'st with me last night, in the first chair next to Theo. Thomas' Orchestra?

Knowest thou that we met Maj. Pegram, who spoke to us; and Miss Ross, who simpered when we raved of the Violon cello solo and looked a little frightened at our wild declarations as to the Violin, – I mean Miss Maggie (?) Ross, of Macon– : and Mrs. Hill, neé Wells, marching about the garden, who, encountering us, did not see thee, and so enquired after thy whereabouts and I told her thou wert in Marietta (!!): and Col. Best, who had scraped an acquaintance with the man that bloweth the French Horn, and was wild in the pursuit thereof during the interlude?

Thy letter, of eight pages, enclosing Mrs. W[allen]'s geranium is come. Thou wilt deliver to that dear woman my kiss and my thanks and my holy remembrances.

Thou wilt see from letter of yesterday to thee that all thy requests had been anticipated, save the photographic One, wh. shall be attended to. Am sorry Father has not rec'd my letters.

[54] Previously published, *Scribner's*, XXV, 623 (May, 1899); reprinted, *Letters* (New York), pp. 68-69, where it is misdated Aug. 15, 1870.

Have written him three, (I think *four*) times since leaving
Lookout. Wrote him yesterday. My poor kid, – how hardly
his fang is born! I am now grown so that I cannot bear to say
I long for thee and him.

I am thy Husband.

To Mary Day Lanier [55]

N. Y. Aug. 15th "/70

Ah, how they have belied Wagner! I heard Theo. Thomas'
Orchestra play his overture to Tannhäuser. The " Music of the
Future " is surely thy music and my music. Each harmony was
a chorus of pure aspirations. The sequences flowed along, one
after the other, as if all the great and noble deeds of time had
formed a procession and marched in review before one's *ears,*
instead of one's *eyes.* These " great and noble deeds " were
not deeds of war and statesmanship, but majestic victories of
inner struggles of a man. This unbroken march of beautiful-
bodied Triumphs irresistibly invites the soul of a man to create
other processions like it. I would I might lead a so magnificent
file of glories into Heaven!
    Wouldst not thou, too, My Wife?

Salem is going to fix me a room, at his house. I dined there
yesterday, with him and his three sisters. It is charmingly
arranged. My room is next to, and communicates with, Salem's.
I am to live there. 'Tis altogether the cleanest and nicest-
looking place in town, and is within a few steps of the cars.
Thou shouldst see the table-linen and crockery! The former is
like driven snow and the latter, speckless, invites the lip. I am
greatly pleased with the arrangement. Thou wilt address me
hereafter at No. 226. E. 49th St.
    I had a little diarrhœa yesterday, wh. made me feel some-
what badly. It is well, today. My cough is about as usual. The
weather is quite cool and pleasant: Thermometer ranged yesterday between 70 and 80. I have not heard from thy father since
leaving Saratoga.

[55] Previously published, *Scribner's,* XXV, 623 (May, 1899) ; reprinted, *Letters*
(New York, 1899), p. 68.

In thy sufferings, I yearn over thee until my heart is all melted into tears. Thy weary weeks are mine also: I count them, as thou dost. God deliver thee, O thou tender Heart, Thou, My Wife, out of pain, into some rest, – prayeth thine

Husband.

To ROBERT S. LANIER

N. Y. Aug. 19 ″/70

My Dear Father:

Y'r letter dated Aug. 16th reached me this morning.

A week ago I wrote you requesting earnestly that you would consult Dr. Hall, – who knows Dr. Marcy well –, and send me the former's opinion as to the advisability of my placing myself under the treatment of the latter, as recommended: and I announced in the same letter that I would wait here one week for y'r reply.

Yr. only answer is that you find y'rself embarrassed in giving me advice, and that while you have strong convictions on the subject, you prefer for me to follow my own judgment.

My dear Father, this is a severe and wholly unlooked-for disappointment to me.

On arriving at N. Y. from the White Sul. Spgs. at the earnest request of Mr. Day I consulted Dr. Marcy. After two interviews with the latter, in which he repeatedly and confidently declared that the condition of my lung required *treatment* and not air: after many assurances, from Charles Lanier and others, that Dr. Marcy was one of the most skillful and reliable physicians in New York: – in addition to my own conviction that the obstruction wh. had caused me so much trouble needed some active remedy: – after all this, it seemed to me that my duty, either to myself or to others, would not permit me to disregard Dr. Marcy's advice, without further light. To obtain this, I wrote you to confer with Dr. Hall &c: believing that Dr. H. wd. understand the probable condition of my disease, and that, if he should agree with Dr. M. in the course referred to, the *agreement* would form an argument wh. plain duty wd. compel me to regard as decisive.

With these views, I waited anxiously for your reply. It is

here: and contains not a word in answer to my application, or by which I can guide myself.

I do not allow myself to feel wounded, because I am perfectly confident that you could not, upon such a subject, *intend* to say anything cruel. I am only puzzled to know what it all means: *why* you could possibly be "embarrassed" in advising me: why you w'd. not see Dr. Hall; and why you refrain from giving me your "settled convictions," when I should have gladly hailed anything that could help me to see my duty in the matter, and when, if ever in my life, I sorely needed advice. I am so wholly in the dark as to the considerations (and surely they must be very powerful ones, when my life or death is the subject-matter) which restrains you from speaking freely, that I only remark further that they *must* rest on misapprehensions, wh. I should be glad to have the opportunity of removing.

Your account of your difficulties in money matters distresses me very greatly. I had hoped that the N. O. property[56] wd. be sold, and that you wd. be at least temporarily relieved from care in this respect.

My inability to work renders it difficult for me to avoid desperate thoughts; — and so I try to keep my mind off the subject.

My cough is about the same. I am comfortably settled at Salem Dutcher's, and all are full of kindness to me.

I shall stay here one month and try Dr. Marcy's remedies: at the end of which time, I shall return, and, if benefited, continue his treatment in Macon.

I send my regards to all friends.

Your Son
Sidney Lanier[57]

TO ROBERT S. LANIER

N. Y.   Aug. 22nd"/70

My Dear Father:

Y'r letter of Aug. 18th, together with two forwarded by you from Macon, reached me this morning.

[56] The reference is to the property of Gertrude Lanier Shannon, left to her by her husband.

[57] R. S. Lanier's reply of Aug. 26, clearing up the misunderstanding, is given below.

I am daily improving, under the kindness of my friends here, which seems to know no bounds. At breakfast and at dinner, each day, I find before my plate a large goblet full of pure cream, wh. I drink at Dr. Marcy's recommendation. I go, also, every day, under his instructions, to the " Lifting Cure," from which I foresee I shall derive great benefit. 'Tis a series of rooms on Broadway where a number of machines are so arranged that graduated weights can be lifted, while the body is placed in such a position as to put a gentle strain on every muscle and fibre in it. An attendant stands by to regulate the time, weights, position, &c. Dr. M. has put me upon a course of medicine, also, from which I seem already to have derived improvement. He declares that, until winter, there is not a finer climate in the world for me than this: and my experience so far bears out his assertion. For ten days we have had perfectly dry, equable weather, with a fine bracing sou'-west breeze. Yesterday I walked four miles, with less fatigue than I could have walked four hundred yards ten days ago. My room looks out upon a large pleasant court, filled with green vines, flowers and trees. Altogether, I am greatly encouraged.[58]

One of the letters you sent me was from Mrs. Clay, in Minnesota. It would seem as if some good fate had prevented me from going there: for she says that the weather had been without parallel in that country for many weeks, hot, sultry and uncomfortable, and that Mr. Clay had not been at all improved. She thinks *winter* is the time to go there.

I wrote Sister some days ago.

Love to Uncle C. and family: and to y'rself from

Yr. Son

Sidney

To Mary Day Lanier

N. Y. Aug. 24th 1870.

My Dear Heart,   I cannot judge at all (as thou askest in thy letter of Aug. 19th) whether it is better for thee to stay in

---

[58] In a letter of Aug. 20, 1870 (here omitted), Lanier had written to his wife that he weighed 134 pounds: " I am holding my own finely, this being within 8 lbs. of the greatest weight I have ever attained in my life. . . .   My cough hath been less, I think, today, and my strength more."

Marietta: but I *can* say that if thou art not able to procure
another room, then thine account of thy situation and sur-
roundings makes me quite decided that thou wert better *go to
Macon.*[59] Perhaps this wd. be (I mean, moving into another
room) more troublesome than travelling home: and so, on the
whole, as at present informed, I believe I think it wd. be best
for thee to go home. I wish, however, that thou shouldst exercise the largest discretion: I have entire confidence in thy
judgment, and I know that I shall think as thou dost, about it.
I will only urge thee to postpone going until the last verge of
prudence, so that thou mayst get as much as possible of the
Marietta air.

Harry writes me that he and Dr. Hall have been urging thee
to stay: – but, I wish *thee* to judge, – since thou knowest the
circumstances better than *they* can. I cannot well bear the
thought that thou shouldst be with *strangers* at such a time: –
in fine, I shall be glad to hear that thou hast finally determined
to go to Macon, since thou tellest me of the uncertainty of
having Mrs. Duncan with thee, upon whom I had counted.

Harry writes that Dr. Hall thought my determination to stay
and try Dr. Marcy a good one. I see Dr. M. every other day.
I report progress to him: whereupon he thinketh a moment,
then seizeth a vial of some abstruse liquid or other, poureth
out some of the same upon a small hillock of white powder,
triturateth, wrappeth up, and crieth, take a small teaspoonfull,
or a large teaspoonfull as the case may be, every two hours, or
three hours, or the like. Sometimes I have two, wh. I take
alternately every two hours. I have two-ounce vials, in which
I dissolve what he gives me, in water.

I think I improve daily. I am promoted to lifting 130 lbs.
at the " Lifting Cure." Tomorrow, will lift 140: and I look
to do my 500 before a great while.

I enclose thee a checque for $100.00, wh. Mr. Duncan will
get cashed. I send it thus early to save thee any further thought
on the matter. I hope it will bring thee through comfortably:
if not, let me know.

[59] Lanier's wife, who expected her second confinement in October, was
bothered by noises in the boarding house of Dr. Nicholes in Marietta, and by
the passing trains. Since in Macon the Sidney Laniers made their home with his
father and Gertrude Lanier Shannon, in the latter's house, Mary Day Lanier did
not feel free to go home until Gertrude returned from Robinson Springs to
open the house. (See Mary Day Lanier's letter to her husband, Aug. 19, 1870).

I yearn to see the *eidolon* of my young Ariel.

Have called on nobody, yet. Will wait a week, first, as I have to go down daily, and do not feel like going out again when I get home.

All business, thou seest: but full of romance and of love is the heart of thine

Husband.

When thou givest the checque to Mr. D. to cash, write thy name just under mine, an inch or so below.

S.

To Mary Day Lanier

N. Y. Aug. 26th 1870.

Fair Wife, Fine Wife, True-Lover, thy letter is just come, and while the song thereof singeth still in my heart, I sing back to thee that if I have been so happy, so rare-fortunate, as to work any good for thee, it is but the reflex light that, having shone from thee originally, now cometh back to thee, whence it sprang.

The great sea sendeth her sweet waters up into the clouds, whence, after many days, the same fall back again upon the dear bosom of the deep wh. is their home.

Thou, my enchanted gray sea, art mother to all the freshness and all the purity and all the life-giving clouds that float in my sky. They return themselves to thee. Thy heart, which bore them, giveth them final rest. From heaven, to heaven: this is the way of what is good.

Thou inquirest how my days go. It is wonderful, quite, *how* they go. I breakfast at 8 ½: read the paper till 10: sally forth to the Doctor's, wh. consumeth till 11: thence to the Lifting Cure, wh. bridgeth over to 12: thence back to 49th st. and brush my hair, by wh. time it is 1: then to lunch with the ladies, (Salem lunching down town) whereby I arrive at 2: then up-stairs to my room, where I lie down until 3 ½: then, my letter to thee, and to others, thro' which fair lane I come to

5: then a miscellaneous hitching up of pantaloons, adjusting of collars, brushing of hair, bathing of face &c, till 6: then dinner: then, a short talk with Salem, what time he whiffeth a villainous pipe, till 7 ½: then Salem goeth back to town, I descend to the ladies in the sitting-room, lounge, dawdle and read until 9 ½ or 10: then to bed.

So the outer life: thro' all which I dance in front of the deep background of my unending Dream of thee: wh. Dream. O My God, bring thou to Actual Touch & Sight soon, soon –

I will go see the kinsfolk thou spokest of. I have seen Judge H[erring]: he faileth greatly. I told Miss Mary thou wert well some 400,000,000 times. Will talk more when I get some more paper. Have written Janie twice, also Sissa, Cliff, & Auntie, & everybody.

Thine

To Virginia Hankins

N. Y. Aug. 26th 1870

I do not know whether I have told you that shortly after delivering the Soldiers' Address,[60] I had quite a severe hem-orrhage from the lungs, which completely disabled me for some time, and left a cough wh. suggested quite lively sus-picions of consumption. I took my little family, in the latter part of June, to Lookout Mountain, where we remained, with some friends, for a month. It was then insisted that I shd. go to Minnesota, whose climate is said to be very favorable to consumptives. I sent wife and boy to Marietta, to spend the rest of the season, and started for the North-West. On the way, I deflected from my route at Charlottesville, Va, and went over to the Greenbriar White, spending several days, with friends, – among the latter Mr. Jefferson Davis, with whom I was thrown constantly, and for whom I conceived a grand passion. I came on to New York, where I consulted a skillful physician, who declared that my left lung was hurt, that I needed *treatment* and not climate, and that if I wd. stay here three months, he

<hr width="30%" align="left" />

[60] See notes 27 and 30, above.

could cure me. After a few days at Saratoga, I came back here and placed myself under his treatment.

Me voici, therefore, a slave to this unbounded tyranny of the doctor, in Babylon.

Thou knowest, Good Friend, that I do not love this Babylon. How strange, to write to such an One as thee, from such a place at this! [61]

— However, the stars shine over Babylon as they shine over Bacon's Castle and my memory of my Friend will not be more impaired than the star-beam wh. falls on the roaring street out yonder – – — ———

When I read your exposition of the article we were discussing,[62] I find that there is no quarrel betwixt us, and that my animadversions were only against my *misunderstanding* of what you wrote, and *not* against what you wrote. I am very glad, then, that we think alike on the matter.

— But there IS something new under the sun: and when I get strong enough I will prove it to you.

Is Miss Spiers (Spires?) still in New York? If so, where? Write me her address, if you know it, that I may call on her. — See how I rely on your friendship, in believing that all these details of myself and my illness will be of interest to you! But I do not doubt it: knowing how faithfully and how wholly I am *your*

                                                    Friend.

Address me at

            " No. 226, East 49th St.
              New York City."

I'll be here for a month, at least: perhaps longer. I desire to hear what you do, how you progres in y'r. favorite project,

----

[61] In her reply of Sept. 15(?), 1870, Virginia Hankins wrote: " You do not like ' this Babylon '– William Morris, whose poetry . . . brings to one so forcibly the sense of flowers & birds & long green shadows– lives in London and is an upholsterer,– most commonplace calling! There is something so pathetic in the poetry of a great city that I wonder you do not find a charm in a residence there."

[62] Earlier in the summer Lanier had sent Virginia Hankins his criticisms of an article she had written (see note 32, above). In her reply, June 20, 1870, she had defended her positions against his attack.

and how my friend, the General,[63] – to whom I send my warm
regards – fares.

S. L.

From Robert S. Lanier

Montgomery Augt 26. [1870?]

My dear son,

I reached here last night on my way to Robertson
Springs. Your letter, with some others ford to me by your
Uncle C. came down by the train I came in. I left home last
sunday & stopped some three days at Chalybeate S. Met Davy
Clopton [64] there & also Mr Lockett & others from Macon &
Montgy, & had a pleasant time. The weather was delightful
there, but it is awful hot here. I am writing early in the day &
the sweat is oozing out from every pore. Cliffd & all are out at
the Springs. Bob Watt is in charge of the House. Cliffd will
return tomorrow. I will go over this afternoon. Will probably
return home about the 1st proxo Had a short letter from your
Uncle C. who says there is but little doing. We have done
pretty well this month.

You have taken my letter too much to heart. I was vexed
that after asking my advice & getting it you did not go to
Minnesota. I had great hopes of that trip. I differ with you
entirely as to medical treatment & staying in the foul atmosphere of N. Y. I did not think I could convince you as to this
& therefore preferred to let you do as you deemed best. I stated
to you I had strong convictions as to your proper remedy; –
They are all the more so from being the result of long continued
observation, reading &C. Your remedy is an *active out-door
life,* going to bed early & rising early, living in an open house
& never going into crowded rooms. Your affection proceeds
from an hereditary taint of the blood – being an enemy within
that never sleeps & always on the watch for aggressive attack.
Medicine can mitigate symptoms but cannot, I fear, reduce the

[63] General John Hankins, her father. In her reply of Sept. 15(?), she wrote:
" He grows each day sadder and feebler " (see note 85, below).

[64] Judge David Clopton had been R. S. Lanier's law partner in Griffin, Ga.,
in the 1840s (see Mary Callaway Jones, " Sidney Lanier: A Chronological
Record," mimeographed pamphlet, n. d.). Since 1867 the two families had been
united by the marriage of Clifford Lanier and Wilhelmina Clopton.

enemy. It is only in your own persistent courage & purpose
that I find hope for this. You ought not to stay in any one
place long. You should travel from place to place. But you
should have some business. Your mind must have legitimate
work – that is it must not grow morbid. For the next three
years you must " stoop to conquer." Take any sort of employment, be a New York book agent, a solicitor of the " World "
subscriptions, a merchant drummer – an Engineer – anything
that will give honest outdoor work. And this work, if possible,
should be in *Western Texas.* There you should take up your
abode for three years. Having got strong lungs & a well knit
frame, then come home & make the distinguished lawyer you
have already shown yourself capable of being. *Our office is
always open to you & whatever is in my purse meantime will be
lovingly shared with you.* Whatever differences of opinion
we may have, & however otherwise they may affect me, will
never abate one " jot or tittle " of the great love, regard &
sympathy I have for you, my dear, big souled, sweet boy! – [65]

—   —   —   —

In a letter I wrote you some time ago allusion was made to
an interview I had with Dr Hall, in which he spoke most
earnestly of the mode of life herein suggested. From that fact
& because I differed so widely with your other Doctor I did
not ask his further opinion & if he had given a concurring one
I should still have been obliged to say " throw physic to the
dogs," get out into the country; & spend the summer in
roam[ing] about from place to place, hunting & fishing &
amusing yourself as you can. All the habits of city life are
hurtful to health. In the country people *go to bed & rise* with
the sun & so have strong nerves.
I have been trying to think whether you ought to spend the

[65] Lanier's reply to his father's proposal has not been found. But in a letter
to his wife, Sept. 5, 1870 (here omitted), he said: " I enclose thee a letter, just
come, from Father. . . . Of course, I cd. not dream of adopting the employment of wh. he speaketh, in his love. If, in two months from now, I am unable
to *speak* professionally, I will promptly repair me to Brunswick, will get yr.
father to give me a hundred or two acres to have for mine own absolutely, will
raise me a thousand or two to keep us a year or so, will build me a cabin, dig
the soil, write a book, study my law, and please God, live a free man for a year
or two until my crisis of lung is passed,—and then, By Heaven, I will see what
Love and Oratory combined can do to furnish forth a little farm and fortune
to garnish thy sweet brows withal."

winter at Brunswick. It suits admirably in all respects but one –
I fear the moist air. Western Texas involves more expense &
is far from home: but it furnishes the ground of my best hopes.

My purpose is to spend a few days with your sister & return
home by Marietta so that I may spend a day or so with Mamie
& Charlie. Write me at Macon.

Praying that all good things may happen to you
I am your devoted father,

R. S. L.

To Mary Day Lanier

N. Y. Aug. 29th /70

O, thou Mutterchen, thou and I are like Night and Day, we
have brought forth a star!

These shadows of my boy have filled me with a delight wh.
I can not picture to thee at all. If the dead *image* of his eye
be so beautiful, how divine must be his eye! I place them
before me time after time, and gaze on them with forever
hungry regard.

How beautiful he is! How perfect is his form, how exquisite
is the *balance* of soul,— the firm equipoise of spirit—in all the
small poet's features!

—And, O me, how I yearn to feel his round arms about my
neck in the old confident pressure of his love, and to satisfy
my touch with a grasp of the sturdy legs.

I took the pictures down to thy Father [66] last night, and we
took our fill of gazing, of admiration, of love.

I like the *Ferreotype,* and thou must order liberal copies
thereof. Thou sayst there is no need, now, of a *fine* copy
thereof. Must I, then, have *any* copies taken? Write me thy
wish.

In a week, or, mayhap, ten days from now, I hope to be
prepared for a grand round of visits, and I will " take up thy
parted links " for thee, with all the pleasure that cometh to me
from pleasing thee, and from seeing them that love thee.

---

[66] Charles Day had returned to New York from Saratoga on Aug. 23, and was
staying at the Everett House (see Lanier to his wife, Aug. 23, 1870).

I postpone until this time, in order that I may fairly *settle* the regular habits, of eating, of sleeping, of exercise, of medicine, &c, wh. I have been so assiduously cultivating, and to wh. I attribute much of my improvement. Write me freely of all upon whom thou w'dst. wish me to call: I have thy mention of *some,* already.

Saturday,—a divine day—Miss Julie Dutcher,—a tall, handsome, sparkling young girl who hath conceived much friendship for me— and I sallied forth to Central Park, and spent four hours, there. 'Twas a day when all are allowed to go on the *lawns,*— an unusual privilege—; and the band played, at five. If thou, My Wife, mightest have been wi' me!

I saw thy father this morning. He is quite well. I visit him regularly at 10 A. M.

I have a letter from Sissa, dated— but I will enclose it to thee. How lovingly she writeth! Thou wilt observe she speaketh of going home in *one* week: but thou knowest how uncertain are these matters. The more I think on the subject of thy movement, the more clearly I am persuaded that *thou wert better go to Macon.* I like not the yelling trains wh. pass thine habitation: they wd. distract thee, in thy weak time. It will not do: I give my judgment as *decided in favor of Macon.* I may be away: I wd. have thee among *more* friends: I shall feel far better satisfied to have thee at home. But I hope that thou wilt delay starting until the latest prudent moment, so that thou mayst get as much of the Marietta climate as possible. Write me whether thou thinkest, *now,* of the first of October, or of an earlier time, as *thy* time of motherhood.

Dear Old Mammy, — thou seest how wrapped in thee is my heart, wh. forgetteth to send messages to any but thee.

Give her my love, and tell her that I showed the pictures round to the family, here, who pronounced her boy the most magnificent fellow in the world. Tell her all the babies fall in love with me: — riding up town with Salem today, in the car, one,— a babe of nine months old, as *die Mutter,* a poor German, told me— could not keep its poor little hands off me, but grasped my arm, and held me, and played with me a long time, much to Salem's amusement. What w'd. Mammy like me to bring her from N. Y. when I come?

Thou wilt cover my boy, lip and limb, with thy dainty kisses for me: as I wd. if I might; and as I shall when I am thy happy

Husband.

To Mary Day Lanier

N. Y. Aug. 31st ″/70

So, Dear Heart, I go, day by day, through street and house, dreaming all things into images of thee, or into relation with thee, or into opposite contrasts to thee.

I measure the world by thee, and I gauge beauty by thine eyes and cheeks and brows and lips, and I weigh life with thy sweet body in t'other scale, and I estimate motherhood by *thy* motherhood and love by *thy* love.

Truthful-tongued, amiable-lipped, faithful-eyed, womanly-brow'd, modest-cheek'd, meek-neck'd: pure in passion, clear in reason, sweet in body: cherishing One Love, and Many Charities: worshipping thy sleeping child, who, when awake, worships *thee*: eager for all beauty, hospitable to all truth, yearning after all good: sorrowing chiefly for wounds to thy love, and rejoicing chiefly in the victories of love: – so, thou movest in my day-long dream.

Art thou not mine exquisite sweet *Mémidé*, and hast thou any other affair in life than to kiss, and be kissed by, me?

Thou askest about my evenings. I do not go out at night, save, very rarely, to Theo. Thomas " Garden." This is a regular Theatre, entirely enclosed with the exception of one end which opens upon a promenade in the open air. It is quite comfortable, and is as well ventilated as any dwelling house: besides, no *crowds* ever go there.

Thy father, whom I have just left, saw Dr. Marcy in relation to Harry. Dr. M. forbids further Arsenic, and gave some remedies which y'r. father despatched to Hal by mail.

I am about as usual. Nothing further from my father since he went on to Ala. Hope to hear from him fully by tomorrow.

Thy letters are like Chopin's Music to me, delicate, and pious, and half-wild and heavenly sweet. I send thee a hundred kisses for each sweet writing-finger, that weaves so great delight for

Thy Husband.

To Mary Day Lanier [67]

N. Y. Sept. 1st 1870

" Then he took the queen in his arms, and kissed her, and said, ' Most noble Christian queen, I beseech you, as ye have ever been my special good lady, and I at all times your true and poor knight to my power, *and as I never yet failed you in right* NOR YET IN WRONG, sithence the first day that King Arthur made me knight, that ye will pray for my soul if that I be slain: for well I am assured that Sir Bors, my nephew, and all the remnant of my kin, with Sir Lovaine and Sir Urre, that they will not fail you for to rescue you from the fire: and therefore, Mine Own Ladye, recomfort yourself, whatsoever come of me, that ye go with Sir Bors, my nephew, and Sir Urre, and they will do you all the pleasure they can or may, that ye shall live like a queen upon my lands.'

' Nay, Sir Launcelot,' said the queen, ' wit thou well I will never live a day after thy days: but, and thou be slain, I will take my death as meekly, for Jesu Christs' sake, as ever did any Christian queen.'

' Well, Madam,' said Sir Launcelot, ' sith it is so that the day is come that our love must depart, wit you well that I shall sell my life as dear as I may: and a thousand fold,' said Sir Launcelot, ' I am more heavier for you than for myself '."

So, Thou Loving-Heart, discoursed Sir Launcelot and Queen Guenever, when fourteen false knights had surprised Sir L. in

---

[67] This letter records Lanier's discovery of Malory's *Morte d'Arthur*, in Dutcher's library. On Jan. 15, 1871, Dutcher sent Lanier, apparently by request, a copy of Sir Bors' farewell to Sir Lancelot, from Vol. II, Chap. CLXXVI. Ten years later Lanier prepared an edition of Malory for boys (IV, 256, 355).

Another piece of evidence of Lanier's reading in Dutcher's library survives in a letter of Sept. 2, 1870, to his wife (here omitted): " Here, at this book-case where I write, I look up and behold three certain volumes bound in green and gold, with friend Shelley's name on the cover thereof. I take one down. Ah, *thou,* I doubt not, hadst marked this pencil-mark about this passage, or ere we gave to Salem." Lanier then quoted a passage from Shelley's " Epipsychidion."

the Queen's Chamber, and were waiting at the door thereof to kill him as he came thereout, : — according to an old chronicle of the same wh. I have found in Salem's library, and wh. I wd. to Heaven thou mightst read with me, for thou alone of all women in the world wouldst get to the core of the simple-hearted old writer's beauty. His tale of the love of Sir Launcelot and Queen Guenever, is for all the world like thy lip: *pathetic, straightforward, dainty, simple, ripe-red, and* STINGING-SWEET.

This morn, in thy father's room, found I M^r McClellan and Harry Jones. Mc. is on visit to New Haven, and left at three this afternoon. Looketh well. Inquired lovingly of thee and Ariel. Thy father seemeth bright: and I *am* so.

Thou art the sweetest Love was ever loved, and I thank God I am thy

Lover.

To Mary Day Lanier

N. Y. Sep 4th 1870.

Over against mine apartment in the inner court of the square, hangeth from a certain back-window a large cage, and therein a gay-souled mocking bird at this moment distilleth his heart into a many fair song, and roundelays and amorous whistlings. He is my brother; he is from my dear Sun-land, he is in prison, he singeth some Love in the warm South, night and day he multiplieth melodies in the praise of this far-off One till his small dungeon is filled with music, he stammereth not for words, he whistleth no false note, his tune runneth like a rill unfailing, from his abounding articulate store he poureth the perfect uterance of his yearning and his life, – and doubtless he thinketh to fly Southward again, some day.

So, I, in my poor daily letter wh. is as a prisoner's song that floateth out betwixt the bars, to thee.

My Mate, my Mate, art thou not true daughter of sun and air and the woods, hast thou not the sun in thy heart, the aether in thine eyes, the forest-grace and forest-tenderness in thine arms? Weave I any song-fantasy, save with thee for the theme thereof, and hath music any soul save thou breathest therein?

Unto sun and wind and trees, – unto all that gloweth, all that floateth freely, all that groweth beautiful and more beautiful forever; that is unto all that is of like nature with thee, I commit thee till the sun shine again on my song tomorrow.

Today is the fourth day since I had word from thee: – by wh. I knew that thou art well, and wh. I wd. not mention, save that I sent thee several days ago a checque for $100.00 wh. I am solicitous to know that thou hast received.

Thy Father showed me a long letter from Hal this morning, in which the latter spoke of going to Macon, and perhaps to Virginia, in ten days from date (Aug. 28th). I think he were best to marry, and cease from troubling. Doubtless Job, that did triumph of old over many boils, got much help therein from Madame his wife. Dear old Boy, what wd. I not give to see him perfectly well and happy with his bride!

I am, – as I was been, – by wh. I mean that I was, as I am been: wh. is to say that I will have been very much as I am was: *i. e,* about the same. Likewise, thy father.

Thou art my special good Ladye, and I am thy true and poor

Knight.

To Mary Day Lanier

N. Y. Sep. 7th 1870

If thou might'st only feel the wine that is in the air today!

The beam of the sun is like a great arrow of love, wh. pierceth into the Soul, and causeth the blood to bubble and thrill with a fierce joy-of-life.

It is as if God sate in the sun and tipped the rays with warm passion and shot them into our hearts.

As I walk in this shower of the weapons of Heaven, I am strong with a sense of *thee.*

Each exquisite wound is like thy kiss. It is sharp, and warm, and intoxicating. How mad are mine arms to fold thee close to my heart!

And the sweet wind is like a sigh of thine on my cheek, and the leaves in the Park, whether my Dream compelleth me to wander, wave like thy fingers when thou playest Chopin, and the Heaven is deep as thine eye, and the water rippleth as when a sweet new thought shimmereth over thy face, and Nature, that was always my Sweetheart, now doubly endeareth herself to me in that she simulateth my one tender and awful Love, wh. is my Wife.

In the last two days I have made a fine stride towards that Lake of the Blest wh. we call Health: Today I am strong and lusty and burly, and I have lost sight of the fact that I have a lung or a stomach. I pulled up 219 pounds at the Lifting Cure this morning: and, in consequence thereof, have stood straight as a pine-tree all day. A month of such progress wd. make me such a man as thou hast never yet seen me. I have talked with Dr. M. anent my law-business. He declareth that there is *no necessity* for me to quit the law: that speaking, in itself, is not hurtful: that, if I will not stay at office-work too closely, and not speak more than an hour or so at a time, I need have no fears from that cause: that I must have exercise; and, finally, in answer to the point-blank question, that I need not think of quitting the law. He thinketh me greatly improved by my stay here: and seemeth sanguine of a complete cure.

I learned from thy father this morning that Gussie was here, and so went to see her. Found her, at 44, 23rd St. Had a sweet talk with her and Monroe. He (Monroe) thinketh to leave her here until I go home; wh. will be about the middle of October, or first November. She looketh not well. Jennie Bacon & Zillah Whittle are with them; but were out, and I saw them not.

The picture of my young Ariel is fairly cased, and standeth ever open on my bureau, to my unfailing delight. O Heart of my Heart, an thou bringest me another like this, how will I worship thee enough! I cannot be more than thy faithful, utter

Lover.

To Mary Day Lanier

N. Y. Sep. 12th 1870

Thou Strange One, that art at this moment my Wife-and-Child, both in One, – thou art journeying, I doubt not, while I write these words, and my heart is there in the car with thee, fluttering about thee and making all manner of love to thee.

It wringeth my soul hard that I am not by thee in the body, whilst thou hast so much of suffering to try thy strength and thy patience. It is only that I may be of some use to thee in the future, – that I am away, now. For indeed I have naught else that I propose to myself, and no other end of projected toil or pleasure, – save to be of some use to thee, whom I have always loved since the first divine moment when thy gray eyes met mine, and whom I will love forever.

" Thy true and poor knight, to my power, *in wrong as in right,*" quoth Sir Launcelot. This is love: it hath been my love : is, and will be.[68]

I called on Gussie this morning, and talked with her alone for a half hour. The glorious sunshine and the park trees together, thro' wh. I passed, led me to talk of the sweet early days when she and I first were friends and lovers. The old girlish light gradually sparkled forth in her blue eyes, and she became just rare-sweet; until, amid tears and smiles, I kissed her and departed.

Also called I on thy friend Miss Carville this morning. She met me with warm cordiality, and fairly mangled Charlie, – whose picture I showed her – with caresses and exclamations. Tomorrow, I go to hunt out Miss Bean: being upon the track thereof through Miss Mary Bean, the Teacher. Next day, I am to journey over to the Shermans.[69] An there be anybody else, write thou; for the mood is upon me to make the whole world fall in love with me.

I improve daily. I gain no flesh: but vast accessions of strength. The constant exercise keeps down the flesh, and hardens what I have. Today, my cough is almost entirely gone. Dr. Marcy saith my recovery is the most rapid he hath ever

---

[68] In a letter of Sept. 21 to his wife (here omitted) Lanier wrote: " What I meant by Sir Launcelot's words was: – that I have sometimes done wrong, (when thou knewest it not) hoping to give thee pleasure."

[69] In a letter of Sept. 13, 1870, to his wife (here omitted), Lanier wrote: " I called today on *Miss Mary* Bean, to learn the whereabouts of Miss Fanny Bean. She was very cordial, and was greatly astonished that it could be *me*, having heard thro' Miss Fanny that I was very ill. I am to see Miss Fanny, soon as I can get a reply from her to my note. Tomorrow I go to Brooklyn to see the Shermans &c." (The Shermans were cousins of Mary Day Lanier; for the identity of Miss Carville, see note 24, 1869.)

beheld, and seemeth in fine hope for me. Thou wilt have heard of Willie's adventures.

Thy

Husband [70]

To Mary Day Lanier

[New York] Sep. 14th 1870

Today fared I forth through sunlight and over fair water to Brooklyn, and found thy cousin Pamela [Sherman]. What a melancholy work hath sorrow wrought on the face thereof! The print of his ten fingers is merciless and deep about the eyes. – After some cordial talk, I won upon the same, and she did convey me to the bedroom thereof – start not, dear Lady – where she was working upon manifold beautiful things. There staid I an hour: and in marvellous short time *Sidney,* quo' she, and *Pamela,* and *Cousin,* quoth I. Her later pictures are marvellous. She hath greatly improved since thou sawest her work. And ah me, what wild clumps of grasses and sweet weeds, what nests of leaves green, and sere and many-colored, what convolved brilliances of radiant flowers, showed she in the small bedroom, there, to me!

Mrs. Wight [71] I saw not: the same being in the midst of moving, and immersed in carpets. Pamela saith, her pictures sell well. She fell upon wee Charles' *eidolon* and devoured the same.

But *Mein Himmel,* how the tears have ploughed down the face thereof:– wh. was what I said unto myself when I saw her first, and when I left her.

Thy telegram from Atlanta reached me last night, and gave me great relief, since, knowing that thou hadst met Hal, I knew that thou wert in good hands.[72]

---

[70] In his letter of Sept. 13 to his wife (here omitted), Lanier wrote: " Yesterday I coughed but twice, with very slight expectoration: today, but *once.* Dr. Marcy declareth he hath never seen anything in all his experience to compare with the rapidity of my recovery: and seemeth now entirely sanguine. I am quite strong and bright; and impudence curleth in my beard, which I wag the same parlously, what time I lift 235 pounds at the ' Cure.' "

[71] Sister to Pamela Sherman, sometimes referred to as Cousin Lou.

[72] Mary Day Lanier had left Marietta for Macon about Sept. 10-12.

My fine Ariel! I did not forget his birthday, and I will bring
to him my reminder of the same. This boy is like a violet, and
like a violin: he draweth one's heart into one's brain perforce,
and compelleth me to think love. Thou wilt kiss him daily, and
let him not forget to call my name.

I pray thee, dear Wife, bring me another like this: or a sister
to him, worthy of him, I care not which.

It seemeth my cough will permanently go away. I am greatly
better, in that respect. Thy father is well. I long to hear that
thou art comfortable at home. Kiss my father and Sissa for thy

Husband.

To Mary Day Lanier

[New York] Sep. 16th 1870

And so I put my head in the clamp, My Heart, and came
from out the dark-and-light this *eidolon*,[73] of wh. I enclose thee
three copies. I know not if thou wilt like the same: they say
here it is very good. One thing thou wilt smile at: the beard
was *so glossy* that it could hardly be taken: hence the peculiar
grayish appearance thereof. I think some day to brush my
hair and try again.

A dispatch from Hal to Father this morning, dated at
Augusta, saith that he left thee " cheerful "; I suppose at
Macon. I am rejoiced to know that thou art safely at home:
thou couldst never dream how my soul hath attended thy
journey.

I improve on. I have not coughed today. Dr. Marcy was all
smiles when I saw him this morning, and declareth me on the
high road to health and strength again.

Thy father is well. He hath caused Mrs. Wight to buy for
thee the most exquisite *shawl-suit*, – a new and very beautiful
style of costume for this winter – and *hat* to match, – wh. he
will bring to thee. I know not if he wd. like me to speak of it, –
so thou must not let him know I have done so. How I long to
see thee, and kiss thee, in it!

[73] Apparently a copy of the 1870 *carte de viste* photograph of Lanier by Rock-
ford, New York (reproduced in the present volume, frontispiece).

Gussie is greatly improved. I see her often. She will move to 61st St. next week, close by me.

We look for Hal and Janie next week.

I send my love to Father and Sissa. Tell them how well I am growing, and kiss both for me.

Thy Husband.

I have a dozen of the pictures. Thou canst give one to Father and Sissa, and I will send thee more.

S.

To Clifford A. Lanier

226. E. 49th St.
N. Y. Sep. 16th "/70

My Dear Brother:

Y'r. two sweet letters, one forwarded from Janie Lamar's, came together, and shone with a double radiance into my heart. If I could only *write* you a kiss! —

My prospect of life grows brighter and brighter, and my physician seems now confident of a cure. My cough has almost disappeared, and my strength is treble what it was a month ago. I breathe quite freely: eat heartily, and digest well. I hope to get back home by the middle of October.

I entirely abandoned the idea of being present at May's confinement. Clear duty seemed to demand that the successful train of habits and medicines into which I had brought myself, should not be interrupted.

'Twas a great disappointment not to see you, here. I had formed many visions of how we could walk about the great city and moralize upon the many texts which there present themselves in solid reality. But I repine not: for I look to the future years when we may be together.

Is your son like *you*, Clifford? [74] *Your* son: — I am glad you do not see the tear wh. these words bring into my eye: — it is born of the same rain-cloud that overcame me that night you were married.

Tell the *mutterchen* for me, between two kisses, that out of

[74] Clifford Anderson Lanier, Jr., was born Sept. 5, 1870.

the marriage of an Oak and a Lily, I know not what sort of tree-flower will come, but that, whatever its name be, it must needs be at once tender and strong: – wh. is the greatest thing that can be said of a man.

Please raise another $100 for me, between you and Auntie. This will finish me up. Send to address as above. I acknowledged receipt of y'r. other check in letter to Auntie some days ago.

I fill my letter with love and kisses to all whom I love. – . – If you like the enclosed [photograph], will send one for Auntie & Grandma.

Bro.   Sid.

To Mary Day Lanier

New York, Sep. 19th 1870

Thou, My Star that shinest all the brighter in sunlight, – wandering through the glorious morning by this place (H. & H.'s) [75] I could not help dashing in, to make my genuflexion before thee, and to convey to thee, with adoring whisper, afar off, my morning-worship and my eternal yearning.

Yonder, outside, the broad light spreadeth itself upon the street, and thereover pass great trucks that crush it not, and filthy wheels that foul it not, and sinful feet that stain it not, and brutish feet that recognize it not. Upon palace and trade-mart and bagniᴗ and church and kitchen, it lieth, liberal and beautiful. Through hideous smack of drunken kiss, through ascending curse, through loud bargain-sound, through yell of profit and moan of loss, it cometh, serene and always maiden pure, to the open heart. – — —

So, through all these same things, goeth my love to thee this day, and there is no iron rim in the world that maketh even a track thereon, nor no sin in the world that leaveth taint therein.

Open thy heart and thine arms, O Love, to my

Love.

[75] The letter-head reads: "Hurd and Houghton, Publishers and Booksellers/ 13 Astor Place and 136 Eighth Street."

To Mary Day Lanier

N. Y. Sep. 20th 1870

Today pulled I my coat and vest away, and Dr. Marcy did beat and tap and lay ear upon the lungs thereof.

Quickly he saith, with smiling face,

" Mr. L. yr. lungs are as *sound as a nut* "!

Hast thou not a knee and a thanksgiving for Him that dealeth this mercy? – – – – – The Great Medecine further said: that there remained only a very slight irritation of the bronchial tube; and that I might leave N. Y. for home in *two weeks* from this time.

How sayest thou, My fair Wife; – is not this a brave happiness and a rare, that I am to start for thee in fourteen days?

— I have not coughed in four days past. Today I have walked a long way, and have lifted 260 pounds at the cure. Tell this to my father and Sissa.

— I am so thirsty for a little love. I wish thee to write me one letter wh. shall have in it nothing but love: tell me therein that thou lovest me, tell it again, and over, and a thousand times over. Wilt not, – for my heart's sake?

————Why my brave boy! Have they stripped thee, denuded thee of even thy diaper, and given the audacious light bold liberties with thy small person? Have they photographed thy wee rotund belly? —O, how double is his chin! And Oh! *why* did ye conceal the enginery of his manhood with that big envious leg? [76]

By Rhadamanthus and Minos and Æaeus, what austere wisdom have we here! With horrent brow and eye of calm severe, he seemeth to call men unto judgment. Did ye persuade the child that he sat in the seat of justice, delivering sentence? And why did ye not bind his diaper round that awful brow, by way of black cap?

And now, – if the father *will* come out, – showed Dan Cupid ever a rarer play of dimple, from crown to sole, than this boy?

[76] A fragmentary undated letter to Lanier from his wife, Sept. (?), 1870, speaks of having sent him on Sept. 13 " three likenesses of our Cupid—in Cupid-guise! "

His knee rounds like the swell of a great lily-petal: and his thigh pouts, like a lip. He is simply beautiful.

This morn showed I him unto Gussie: whereupon came a fair storm of kisses and rain of sweet words down on the dear flower, – I thank thee for these rare pictures.

— — Thy father went to Boston last night, tho' not very well. We look for Hal and bride Thursday morning. They were to be married on last Monday, – yesterday, – at 11 O'clock. Thy father returneth Wednesday. I *have* written Hal: & he hath acknowledged my letter. He forgot. I will attend to the music-commission.[77]

Love and kisses to father & Sissa. Thou canst show them this letter, cans't not? I don't know what's in it.

Thy

Husband

To Robert S. Lanier

N. Y. Sep. 21st 1870

My Dear Father:

I wrote May yesterday the gratifying intelligence that the Doctor pronounces my lungs free from disease, and will discharge me in a couple of weeks. He says there remains a slight irritation of the bronchial tube: which he thinks will disappear in the time specified.

I am, indeed, in many respects, in better health than for several years past. My old distressing stomachic symptoms have disappeared in the last week, and I have enjoyed a feeling of ease and lightness in that region which has been unknown to me for a long time. My breathing is entirely unobstructed, and I can inflate my chest to its fullest extent without a single sensation of irritation.

A peculiar sort of wheezing, – which gave me more annoyance from its persistency than perhaps any other single symtom – has also entirely disappeared for ten days past. My strength increases daily: and my " Lifting Cure " has straightened my backbone in the most surprising manner.

---

[77] Lanier's wife had asked him to pay another visit to her cousin, Pamela Sherman, and play his flute for her, if the doctor permitted (see note 76, above).

I have felt this improvement for many days: but I have forborne to speak of it too confidently, and have waited until the D'r.'s examination should confirm it.

Altogether, I have reason to thank the Higher Powers for what seems to be a very wonderful recovery; and I know that you will share the sentiment heartily.

Mr. J. F. D. Lanier & Charles have returned to the city, though their families are still in the country. They have shown themselves very cordial to me. Mr. J. F. D. is going to Lennox on Friday, and has pressed me to go with him: but, as Harry and his bride will expect to meet me here that day, I shall remain to see them.

Mr. Day is in Boston: will probably return tomorrow. The weather is perfect: clear, cool, and bracing.

Convey a loving kiss to my dear Sissa and to young Edward, for me. I long to be with you: and am champing the bit very impatiently for my winter's race.[78] I sincerely hope business has improved. Should any chance occur to get me any outside employment that w'd. be consistent with my office-work, I wd. be glad to avail myself of it.

I send my usual daily bulletin to Mamie.

With all love

> Your Son
>> Sidney.

To Mary Day Lanier [79]

> N. Y. Sep. 24th 1870

Janie and I went, at One O'clock today, to hear *Nillson*. She sang, in concert, at Steinway Hall: t'other artists were Vieux-

---

[78] In a fragmentary letter of Sept. 10-13(?), 1870, Mary Day Lanier wrote: " Papa bids me tell you that if your improvement continues uninterruptedly and the D^r discharges you in time he will hope to hear you make 'the maiden speech' (only, *that* was made last year) in your long-postponed ' cotton-case.' "

[79] Previously published, *Scribner's*, XXV, 623-624 (May, 1899); reprinted, *Letters* (New York, 1899), pp. 69-70. Mr. Day had returned from Boston on Sept. 22; Harry Day and his bride, Janie, had reached New York on Sept. 23.

Lanier's posthumously published poem "Nilsson" (I, 196) was probably inspired by this concert. Of the musicians mentioned in the first paragraph (in addition to Christina Nilsson, the Swedish soprana), three were famous in that

temps, the violinist, Wehli, pianist, Brignoli, tenor, Verger, baritone.

Thou fine Soul! Mlle. Nillson singeth as thou and I love.

She openeth her sweet mouth, and turneth her head o' one side like a mocking bird in the moonlight, and straightway cometh forth the purest silver-tones that ever mortal voice made.

Her pianissimo was like a dawn, which crescendo'd presently into a glorious noon of tone, wh. then did die away into a quiet gray twilight of clear melodious whisper. She sang nothing mean, or light, or merely taking. Handel's " Angels ever bright and fair," solo: a duett with Brignoli by Blangini: and a noble solo, a scene from Ambrose Thomas' " Hamlet," (the insane song of Ophelia); with " home, sweet home," for encore; – these were all.

Vieuxtemps was unequal. He fired off innumerable crackers, and fired them very skillfully, – but made no music, save in the mere *tone,* in wh. he was very fine. Wehli is entirely splendid, and played a very beautiful and skillful set of concert pieces. Brignoli was too fat, and Verger too lean: wh. also expresseth their music.

Janie was greatly delighted. Harry was down town and did not go.

Thy little cooing of 20th inst., hath just floated into my heart. — I do not dare to give myself leave to write thee my love. My heart will not endure it. —

I am glad thou art pleased with the pictures. It is declared here that they are not nearly so handsome as thy husband: wh. is true.

Thy father leaveth for Macon tonight. I am to go down presently and dine with him, at six, he leaving at half past seven.

I wrote thee anent Cupid. Kiss Sissa and Father for me. I shall not be much longer out of thine arms. – Aye, May God be near thee, crieth also

Thy

Husband.

---

day: Henri Vieuxtemps, Karl Wehle, and Pasqualino Brignoli—the first two being composers as well as performers. Verger has not been identified.

To Mary Day Lanier [80]

New York, Sep. 26th 1870

Why, My little Sweet, Why, My great Sweet, Why, My tender eyes, my love-stung lips, my heavenly-globed brow, – look ye so lovingly at me from the mute page?

My too passionately Beloved, I devour this eidolon of thy face with a starved man's eagerness.

I did not think there was aught in life, or of loveliness, that might make me love thee more: yet, this picture, meseemeth, doth sublime my love into somewhat of additional holiness, for one reason: – it might well go for *the portrait of my mother* in her youth. Did this strike thee when thou sawest it?

I showed it to Janie this morn, and presently told her the same. " Oh ! " she said, and a great expression of awe came upon her face, " it is the perfect image of y'r. mother, – and I never thought of it till this moment."

So, thou who hast been always the White Star of my guidance through all mazes of love and of life, dost whiten and sanctify thy passionate-sweet ray with touches of her whom, next to thee, I loved best of all in the world.

It is well, My Sweetest Comrade, that thou art like my Mother. So, thou Commandest my soul from all imaginable points.

I am thy knight. – Thou has done me the most grateful grace in all the world, in that thou hast sent me thy face to pore upon. It is my book, My Bible. For me, the Word is most sweetly writ therein: and the eleven great Commandments. I learn my prayers from thine eyes, and my thanksgiving from thy lips. Thy forehead roofeth my Temple, thy heart sanctifieth it, and thy spirit is mine exquisite Preacher.

Thou art full liberal in thy gift. That thou hast proved thy love for me in the way that I desired, among so many things whose difficulty to thee I well know! that thou hast " wounded no one," where sometimes it seemeth almost like a duty to

[80] Written on Salem Dutcher's stationery, bearing the letter-head: " ' The World ' Office/ No. 35 Park Row." The photograph described below has not been found unless it was the one reproduced in vol. IX, facing p. 23.

wound some one ! – this is a noble benefaction to thy husband, and his heart is thereby as a land whereover Spring hath but just passed, dropping flowers and germs of summer. — It is the consummation of life to be great and sweet in sadness. Sit thou forever, My Queen, My Queen, on this far peak where even clouds dissolve, and where small mists of earth cannot come.[81]

Thy brother — " crazy," thou callest him — had directed thy letters containing my Dan Cupid's letter and pictures, to Winslow Lanier & Co's care, where they lay a couple of days without my knowledge, – I not dreaming of aught from thee in *that* place. I got them safely however, and have written thee, thereanent, wh. thou wilt have doubtless rec^d, ere now. Yesterday gave I the crazy man a fearful lecture, and meseemeth he hath bubbled off a little of his wildness today: wh. Janie also declareth to me in private.

Tomorrow thy father will reach thee. Happy, happy father, he will kiss thy very lips !

Will I never stop my garrulous pen?
Kiss thou My father and Sissa for me. My heart is there with thee, yearning over thee in thy pain. Perhaps while I write these words thou art in the fearful anguish. Ah, My little wife, Mutterchen, in each throb of thy pain is pressed also the faithful heart of
thy husband.

To Robert S. Lanier

N. Y. Sep. 30th 1870

My Dear Father:

Your letter of 27th has just reached me.
Each day seems to confirm the improvement, whose substan-

---

[81] This paragraph is in answer to an undated letter from his wife, Sept. (?), 1870. Since her letter is fragmentary, the reference to having " wounded no one " is not entirely clear, but it seems to refer to some adjustments connected with their sharing the home of Gertrude Lanier Shannon. The following paragraph is in answer to the same letter (see also Lanier's letter of Sept. 20, and note 76, above).

tial character I have myself scarcely dared to count on. Dr
Marcy, – whom I saw today,– seems to entertain no doubts on
the subject whatever. He declares the recovery to be a genuine
one, and that I have *nothing* to fear, as long as I am careful
in regard to catching cold. He thinks I can go home with entire
safety, now.

A long letter from Mamie, dated 26th, urges me to stay two
or three weeks longer: and *your* urgency on the point, so supple-
mented, makes it really hard for me to determine to go home,
sooner.

There are, however, some circumstances which render it
quite desirable for me to leave, at least *one* week earlier than
the time you propose, – the middle of October. The chief of
these are: first, that the climate, here, is now becoming a little
unfavorable for me, I think. The change in temperature from
morning to noon: the excessive *difference* in temperature between *sunlight* and shade, the former being extremely warm,
and the latter quite chilling: and the rawness of the air after
sundown all conspire to render it extremely difficult for me to
prevent sudden checks to perspiration; in addition to which,
the drafts in the street-cars on which I ride every day are
becoming more and more likely to produce colds. Secondly,
since I am pronounced well by my physician, I find it entirely
impossible to make myself contented in idleness – wh. was
hard enough while I was sick – and the desire to make some
arrangements for my winter's work – whatever it may be –
makes me intolerably impatient to inaugurate something by
wh. I may earn some money. I do not propose to go to *hard*
work as soon as I return,– wh. May seems to fear –, but only
desire to be where I can do something.

There are other circumstances wh. make me more anxious to
return: such as, for instance, that I find that Salem's sisters are
all crowded into one room, wh. inconvenience I wd. like to
remove as soon as possible.

Of course, if it were likely that I wd. be injured by the
change, these arguments wd. not avail: but I rather think the
climatic advantage is at present on the side of Macon. I do not
find myself hurt by *warm* weather: – we have just had a week
of it, here, intensely hot, in the day time. 'Tis only damp,
raw weather that I fear.

As I telegraphed you, I had thought of leaving for home tomorrow, –Saturday–: but, after getting y'r reply and letter, I put it off until Tuesday of next week, when I think to start by the Savannah steamer. This will bring me home about Oct. 7th, – a week earlier than y'r proposed time. I have been thus explicit that you may not think me headstrong.

I found I shd. need a little more than telegraphed for; and drew on you yesterday, at *twenty* days, for $150.00, through Winslow. L. & Co.

Tell Sissa I was glad to get her letter, and hope to kiss her therefor, in person, before many days.

Accept all love for yrself from

Your Son,

Sidney L.

To Mary Day Lanier

N. Y. Oct. 4th 1870

I do but walk about suffused with a fair sense of *thee,* and whatever of sight or sound is in the world, is instantly transformed into some phase of thee in my soul.

The violins play, – and it is as if thou wert singing to me: the flutes play – and it is as if thou wert thinking in my heart.[82]

Visible Nature is by turns thine eye or thy lip or thy cheek; and all human life, by contrast or by suggestion, bringeth thee to my contemplation.

I am nothing more, nothing less, than simply a

Lover.

We failed to get state-rooms on the steamer of Tuesday, and so were forced to wait until Thursday, – day after tomorrow, when, D. V., we will all start. We have secured our state-rooms on the steamer wh. leaveth that day, being the " General Barnes," a fine side wheel vessel. This shd. bring us to Macon

---

[82] In his letter of Oct. 1, 1870 (here omitted), Lanier had written his wife that he was going to hear Thomas's orchestra that night.

by Sunday night next. Thy brother and sister are well and send thee love. I called to find thy Mrs. Vandervoort today, but she was not in town. We have had wretched rainy weather for some days wh. has kept me indoors: and so I will not be able to see thy Mrs. James or Miss Bean.[88]

Love to father & Sissa.

Thy Husband.

To Virginia Hankins

N. Y. Oct. 5th 1870

Yr. little note, Dear Friend, reached me, and I respond to it with the greater pleasure, in that I am able to say to you that the health wh. I thought, two months ago, to be forever gone, is likely to be restored to me in full measure.

My physician regards my recovery as very wonderful, and declares that he has never seen anything like it, tho' he has treated many such cases.

I had hoped to come by your sweet Castle and wind my horn at the gates thereof: but I dare not travel by *cars* any more than absolutely necessary, and so I am going by sea to Savannah, whence I have but short distance by land to Macon.

That this is a woful disappointment to me, ——— ——— you know.

Yr. letter was from Lexington. What do you in the mountains? I am glad you are there. I made friends with all your Virginia hills this summer, and I love them. Are they not noble? Let us be like them. How little *they* mind wind and rain!

I send my grateful regards to your father and brothers.

To *you* ― ― ― ―

S. L.

---

[88] For the identity of Miss Bean see note 69, above. Mrs. James and Mrs. Vandervoort were probably New York friends of Lanier's wife during her residence there as a young girl.

To Mary Day Lanier

N. Y. Oct. 5th 1870

Thou Sweet enchanted Dream in wh. I move by day and night, I am about, if God so will, to realize thee, and my heart is as the heart of him that seeth Heaven with eyes that live, and heareth the music thereof before his ears be dead.

Sixty six days and sixty six nights thou hast wrapped me in thine etherial presence, and had I not known how exquisite thou wert in the reality of thee, then wd. I never have wished to wake from this Dream.

But in the days so long, so long ago, I remember that I have kissed thine actual lip and rested my head on thy breathing bosom: and this memory driveth me and driveth me, until these shall be mine absolute and tangible glories again.

Till wh. heavenly moment, I pray the wild winds blow a million loves over the waters to thee from thy

Husband.

To Clifford A. Lanier [84]

Macon, Ga. Oct. 22nd 1870

My Darling Clifford:

I'm at home again, and fairly at work: tho' this last has been delayed somewhat by a cold which attacked me shortly after arriving, and used me somewhat hardly for a few days.

Here is come an infinitesimal man out of the wonderful Dimness, to Maydie and me. He hath done nothing but sprawl

---

[84] Lanier had reached Macon about Oct. 9. On Oct. 12 Robert E. Lee had died, and shortly therefter at the exercises in Macon Lanier delivered his address, "Robert E. Lee: In Memoriam," not mentioned in any of his letters and only published posthumously (V, 273).

Sidney Lanier, Jr., the principal subject of this letter, was born Oct. 17, 1870. Apparently it was on the day of his second son's birth that Lanier wrote his burlesque essay entitled "Peace" (VI, 247). For in it he tells how he volunteered to play nurse-maid to his nephew and his son who was "two years, one month and five days old" while their mothers "went out," and his eldest son Charles had been born on Sept. 12, 1868—the figures thus adding up to Oct. 17, 1870. This essay was not published until four years later (see note 95, 1874).

and suck since he came, and I know nothing of his capabilities or spiritual power. He cometh imbued with singular ideas, such as, for instance, that day is the time to sleep in, and night is the time to indulge one's grief in: acting upon which, he sealeth up his eyelids all day long, and waileth away over some private sorrow he hath, all night. Whether his agony be pins, colic, or conviction of sin, I know not: certes, it is persistent and genuine. He hath finally, – viz, at two O'clock this morning, – taken wildly to gin, and now lieth in a disgraceful drunken slumber, having stupefied himself with three drops of the fiery liquid. Such is man!

Are you really going to hang on to that name, for your boy? Mine, in that event, (so the womankind tell me) is to be called Sidney.

Tell me what you are doing. All join me in love to you. Mary is doing finely, and will, I think, come entirely through her after-illness without trouble. I write Auntie today. Love and kisses to Willie, and all the family, from

Your

Sid.

To Virginia Hankins [85]

[Macon, Ga? Nov. 9, 1870?]

Oh Holy Ginna, O Sacrosanct One to whom I scarcely dare to write; — Did you believe I did not write you, because I " had no time to spare," or because — — anything else?

Know that I did not wish to tread with alien feet beside this grave which was yet open to you.

Know that I half hestitated even to throw, with alien hand, a flower upon it!

Know that beside this mound where you mourned and ministered I wished to stand afar off, with uncovered head, and with silent tongue, – until *you* gave me leave to speak.

---

[85] The occasion of this letter was the death of Virginia Hankins's father, announced in a letter by her which has not survived. The conjectural dating has been arrived at from the badly blurred postmark on the accompanying envelope, and the evidence of the entire sequence of letters at this period.

The leave is given, your letter is here, and I send mine to meet it as a flower meets its shadow on the top of the water.

You – – a Starveling, *you!* Great God, who, then, can say that he hungers not? If your life, – which seems to me already to have nearly accomplished what Novalis calls the essential requisite to transcendental conduct, namely Self-death –, if *your* life is not full of satisfaction, – whose life *can* be?

Ah, it is as I always believed. You speak of incantations which generate temperance in souls; My Beloved Ginna, My Little One, there is in a human Soul no temperance. The incantations of men, be they of Spell-words, be they of Magic-rings, be they of "woven poses and of waving hands," – *can* call up but one Spirit. It is the Spirit of Love, and Love is not temperate. He is a very drunkard and a glutton, and He is forever crying out for more of his drink and his meat; which meat and drink are – yearning, yearning, yearning.

And so, do *you* leave temperance to God, it is His prerogative, *we* cannot attain; and let yourself be forever intoxicated with that divine draught of Love which is offered by our Friend Christ; and O Ginna, – honor, with one touch of your lips, that wholly-human cup of Love which is dipped for you from a brimming soul, and is offered, kneeling, by the loyal hands of

Your Friend

S.

To Virginia Hankins [86]

[Macon, Ga? Dec. 3, 1870?]

Dear Friend, Your last communication gives me inexpressible sadness, and I find it difficult to bring my mind to the task of writing about it.

---

[86] Conjectural dating as in preceding letter (see note 85, above). Virginia Hankins's letter to which this is an answer is also undated. In it she had said that her home, Bacon's Castle, would have to be sold; and since her attorney feared the sacrifice of a county sale, she asked Lanier to let her know of anyone coming to Virginia from Georgia who might care to buy or lease such a place: "We could get no one to administer and things are very unsettled. . . . At present we expect to remain here a year. . . . Mark & Leigh [her brothers] want to get situations, but it is difficult."

I have always felt a sense of proprietary interest in your home. It was mine by right of happiness. Joy confers its authorities. The glory of your sweet youth,—when I saw you there among your girlish guests, in those early days – this, and the songs, and lights, and dances and music, and gracious hospitalities,— Ah me, my heart is o'er full, and there are tears in my soul.

But you did not tell me,—what a practical friendship desires to know—of the condition of your Father's estate. Are there debts to pay? Will there be something left for you to go upon? Have you good advisers? Are you obliged, *financially,* (I know why you wish the boys to be out of Surrey, of course) to sell the sweet old Castle? I ask this last because the present is *so* unfavorable a time to sell: and if you *could* hold it, it would be *so* much more valuable in a few years.

Answer me these questions, good Little One.

Meantime, I forget not to cast about for purchasers, nor for a place that may suit Mark or Leigh.

I've been very ill again since coming home: but am recovering. It cut my heart, to pass you, on my way Home from N. Y. *N'importe*: I will see you, again.

Write me, fully, the condition of things. In every matter, I am your.

Friend.

To Paul H. Hayne [87]

Macon, Ga. Dec. 7th, 1870.

My Dear Mr. Hayne,

Your

"——Old world song, whose breezy music pours
Through limpid channels 'twixt enchanted shores."

had stolen on me wooingly, before I received your letter announcing that you were going to send it; and I will not easily forget the

——" Hale, sun-warm atmosphere of song "

---

[87] Lanier's letter is in acknowledgment of a lost letter from Hayne, inclosing a copy of his poem, "The Wife of Brittany," based on Chaucer's Franklin's Tale.

in which it wrapped me. As for your " daring," in treating a
theme of Chaucer's – why I love daring, and the poets are not
all dead yet. The ending of the poem is entirely the sweetest
strain you have ever sung, to my knowledge. I mean:

> " My song which now hath long flowed unperplexed
> Through scenes so various, calm as heaven, or vexed
> By gusty passion, reaches the lone shore
> Ghost-like and strange, of silence and old dreams:
> Far off its weird and wandering whisper seems
> Like airs that faint o'er untracked oceans hoar
> On haunted midnights when the moon is low.
> And now 'tis ended: long yea, long ago,
> Lost on the wings of all the winds that blow,
> The dust of those dead loves hath passed away;
> Still, still, methinks, a soft ethereal ray
> Illumes the tender record, and makes bright
> Its heart-deep pathos with a marvelous light,
> So that whate'er of frenzied grief and pain
> Marred the pure currents of thy crystal strain
> Transfigured shines through fancy's mellowing trance,
> Touching with golden haze the quaint old-world romance,"

and, By Heavens if there were a thousand more lines like it,
and my pen should once get a-quoting them I should never be
able to stop till the end thereof.

Therefore, Good my Friend, ask me not to criticise the same,
candidly or uncandidly. Would you ask a man to dissect his
own sweetheart? Could I carve up these dainty limbs with a
scalpel, and cry, here look you, is a sound organ, and this look
you, is a diseased nerve, and there is a muscle awry, and the
like?

No. I love the poem, just as it is, and you know a man can't
be a surgeon to what he loves. Your poetic power seems to me
to have taken a step forward, – a palpable stride – lately; and
the spiritual growth, so evinced, is a source of great pleasure
to me, for even in my little way, I have discovered the glory
which shines in one's soul where one stands today, upon a
higher peak than one stood on, yesterday, and reflects that he
does so by virtue of hard climbing.

" To him that overcometh." This is the Word, of a man's
life.

I do not envy you the tergiversation (anglice redditum, lying) that you'll have to perpetrate, in your acknowledgement of Mrs. E. P. C's " Autumn Leaves." [88] She is an unhappy victim of the ' Poets' Corner ' of the " Telegraph & Messenger " and one or two other provincial papers, & her nom de plume is Chiquita. I have a speaking acquaintance with her. My lady friends tell me she is a little fast. I am told she is travelling through the land dispensing " Autumn Leaves " to a grateful public at (I forget how much) per volume. Her husband is a very modest, an [un]assuming and pleasant gentleman of this city, and is a physician.

And this is all I know about Chiquita. As for her " Poetry," why – you exhausted that subject; at any rate, I don't feel equal to it today. I think she knows my opinion of her power. At any rate she has not sent in " a copy," for which, Laus Deo.

I would not have waited for your letter, to announce my arrival at home; but I fell sick after leaving New York, and was too desperate to do anything decent.

I'm going to send you some poems [89] in a day or two.

Meantime, I am always Your Friend,

Sidney Lanier.

---

[88] Probably Elizabeth Pettit Cutler, the author of several volumes of romantic fiction and poetry, though no record survives of a volume by her bearing the title here given.

[89] These were possibly two of the " Songs for ' The Jacquerie ' " (I, 189-190) and another installment of the long poem itself, all acknowledged by Hayne in a letter of Jan. 10, 1871 (see note 4, 1871).

On the other hand they may have been the two dialect poems, " 9 from 8 " and " Jones's Private Argument " (I, 194, 24). Both of them are said to have been written in 1870, though they are not mentioned in any of the Lanier's letters and were probably not composed until 1871.

1871

To Virginia Hankins

Macon, Ga. Jany 7th 1871.

I see no chance, Dear Friend, to sell the place here.[1] There
is no tide of emigration from here in your direction; all goes
to Westward.

I continue to look for places to suit the brothers. There are
some; but they would not do.

Dear Heart, My thoughts go to you so often! It is painful
that my feet cannot follow them. If I might sit with you, in
the sunshine of today, and look over Burwells', and forget that
life is life!

Tell me what you write, these days? Is it poetry? Send me
some.

I have ordered that the " Southern Magazine," – formerly the
" New Eclectic," of Baltimore, be sent you. Let me know if it
comes.[2]

I'm greatly overcrowded, in matter of time. My poor Maydie
has been ill a long time, and my small manikin, Charles,
indulges in the croup: so that what with much nursing, and
anxiety and daily work,[3] I need some good words from My

[1] The reference is to Bacon's Castle, Virginia Hankin's home (see note 86,
1870).

[2] On Dec. 21, 1870, W. H. Browne, editor of the Southern Magazine of
Baltimore, acknowledged receipt of Lanier's letter of Dec. 13 (not found)
inclosing his essay " Retrospects and Prospects " (V, 280). He explained that
since Lawrence Turnbull had retired from the firm of Turnbull & Murdoch, he
(Browne), Murdoch, and W. S. Hill had taken over the New Eclectic and
changed the name to the Southern Magazine. As they were unable to pay for
contributions at present, Browne suggested that Lanier might secure subscribers
to the magazine and retain the subscriptions collected in payment for his essay.
Lanier accepted the suggestion, secured a number of subscriptions, and gave one
to Virginia Hankins.

[3] Salem Dutcher's letter of Jan. 15, 1871, quotes a lost letter of Lanier as
" saying how, after many things contrary, all was now well."

One Friend, who is so strong and so pure and so entirely sweet. Life is a high rock, Little One, and you grow in a cleft of it, like the blue Gentian in the Alp. Breathe some of your impalpable blue this way, to

Your Friend.

To Mary Day Lanier

My Darling: [Macon, Ga. Feb. 28, 1871]

       Please send me my Ms. Book, – in wh. the Jacquerie is written [4] –.   Get yourself and the babies into this glorious air, as soon as you can. 'Tis simply delicious.

Yr.

Feb.

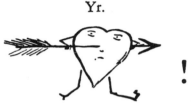

Office. 28/71.

---

[4] The reference is to Lanier's Ledger (Henry W. Lanier Collection, Johns Hopkins University). Several surviving letters written to Lanier during the winter and spring of 1871, echoing lost letters by him, indicate that he was again actively at work on his poem " The Jacquerie." For example, W. H. Browne's letter of Jan. 10, 1871 (answering a lost letter of early January), and his letter of Feb. 17 (answering a lost letter of Feb. 13), both promise to fulfill Lanier's requests for " authorities bearing on the Jacquerie."

Further, in a letter of Jan. 10, 1871, Paul H. Hayne acknowledged receipt of a letter " of the 7th inst " (not found), inclosing extracts from the " Jacquerie " on which he commented at length:

" Once– months ago, I told you how noble a subject it seemed to me you had chosen in ' *the Jacquerie*,' and all the extracts I've seen, prove that you understand the right mode of treating it.

" As for the two *lyrics,* now before me, I think them *perfect*– each after its kind. The *first* is a true mediaeval song, the sentiment, & quaint turns of expression showing your familiarity with antique ballad poetry, and having, so to speak– a *smack* of the old dead Centuries about them; and the *second* is EXQUISITE a thing not [to] criticise, but *feel!* . . .

" Remember too, if you please, that as your Poem ('twill be a tolerably elaborate work I suppose) as your Poem progresses, I would esteem it a privilege to see *fragments* thereof, preluding the completed strain. God knoweth, we have but few poet-artists, South;– shall we not hail them when they appear? At least, the few genuine men of letters in our section (YOU I KNOW are one, & let me humbly *trust* that I may be reckoned another) ought, & must stick together; encourage each others' efforts, and support each other's fame! "

Hayne's letter of Mar. 6, 1871, acknowledged another lost letter from Lanier

To Virginia Hankins

[Macon, Ga? Feb.-Mar.? 1871] [5]

My Dear Friend:

Much sickness in my little family, and some death, (– of an uncle [6] whom you do not know) have prevented me from sending you so early an answer as I wished.

Today is such a marvel of a day. It is like a great woman, rapt in the terrible serenity of some passion that is too intense either for word or sign. The sunlight feels as if there were a sort of quiet lightning in it, which, at a motion, would break forth and envelope all men in an awful flame. — I would I might see you, and sit by you, today.

I enclose two little things, which have been heretofore printed. The long one is what people would call an " abler " poem than the little one: but I like the little one better. Send to Miss Brock, – if you choose – which one of the two *you* like.[7] I would not dream of sending anything to her; for you see

containing another installment of " The Jacquerie," which he asked to keep for several weeks before returning with criticism. His letter of May 6 announced that he was returning Lanier's MS by the same mail, saying: " My Son! you MUST *finish* ' *The Jacquerie!* ' – I tell you, it would be rank injustice to yourself; more, it would be rank injustice to our *Literature* if you failed to do this." Finally, his letter of May 24 acknowledged receipt of another lost from Lanier (" of the 22nd inst ") saying that the MS had arrived safely.

[5] The conjectural dating of this letter has been arrived at from the following evidence: it is an answer to Virginia Hankins's letter of Jan. 9-12, 1871; it is in turn answered by her letter of Apr. 15; and the reference to Lanier's being "twenty-nine years old " places it after Feb. 3, 1871.

[6] Possibly his great-uncle, Sampson Lanier, brother of his grandfather, Sterling Lanier.

[7] Virginia Hankins had asked Lanier as early as Nov., 1869, if he knew " Miss Brock an authoress in N. Y." Again on Jan. 2, 1870, she had written: " You did not say if you knew Miss Brock– you know she is compiling a book to be a representative Book of American Poetry, and she is thoroughly Southern, and I hoped you knew her." But it was only after Virginia Hankins wrote him, on Jan. 9, 1871, that Miss Brock had requested her asistance in securing contributions to her book that Lanier took notice of her desire to have him included in Miss Brock's projected *Poets of America*. The volume was apparently not completed at this time; but a book by the same name was published by her in 1894, including four poems by Lanier, though only one of them (" Nirvâna ") could have been sent by him in 1871. (The editor was Miss Sallie Brock of Madison, Va.—later Mrs. Richard Putnam—who had previously edited an anthology entitled *The Southern Amaranth* in 1868.)

I am so obscure that she has never even heard of me; and I
wd. think it presumptuous, having rec^d, no invitation so to do.
But a request from *you* — admits of but one answer from *me*.
I now say " yes " in advance to every wish that you shall hint
to me in future. Is *that* presumptuous, because too sweeping, –
and will you resent it? – – – – – Permit me so small a boon,
good Friend –

_____

As to the " biographical sketch," – – why, I was born (in
Macon), and I am twenty nine years old.
That is all: – except what *you* know.

S. L.

To Mary Day Lanier [8]

B[runswic]k. March 7th 1871

Ah, Dear Heart, if one could but look upon the face of the sea,
always, and get always that large message wh. comes up out
of this most fair suggestive countenance ! Through this serene
day I have prayed that thou mighs't be with me by the side of
this water, when sun, air and birds were gracious as now. And
thou shalt, D. V. We have a very pretty arrangement a foot,
of wh. thou shalt hear more, – to bring thee and the babies here.
I have found our dear Lily here, and she and I and Janie have
had a most rare time together, today. I have somehow managed
to keep them laughing pretty much all the time; and we prosper
famously, what time Harry driveth the busy wheel of the
Agency.
I find the latter not so busy as formerly. We rode together
up town, this morning, and had some talk of matters generally –.
The town seems improving rapidly: and is quite cheerful with
sound of hammer and saw on all sides –.

[8] Lanier left for Brunswick, Ga., on Mar. 6, 1871, partly on a business mission
but chiefly on account of his health. On Mar. 8, his wife wrote to her sister-in-
law, Mrs. Clifford Lanier: " Sidney has been failing greatly in strength for two
months—and after spending a day or two in bed, from debility and cough, he has
gone to Brunswick, to try the salt breeze, with Janie's and Lilla's nursing. (For
Lilla has been visiting Janie for a month.) He feels already much improved:
indeed, it makes me hopeful that he was rather *worked down* than failing from
any return of disease."

Mr. Wharton – whom I wished to see – is out of town, and will be back tomorrow probably.

Love to my father and yrs. Say to the latter I think there is prospect of disposing of a lot or two.

I send thee my whole heart, wh. indeed is my all, and I wish thee to kiss my well-beloved sons for their father and thy

Husband.

I forgot to say that I am improving, in throat and in general feelings.

To Mary Day Lanier

B[runswic]k. March 8th 1871.

Hast thou seen, My Little One, the down of a thistle let loose upon the wind, and yielding itself to the buoyant caprice thereof, in utter abandon of happiness and carelessness, as if it – the thistle – knew well that God is God, and that He has the world always in mind and the winds always under His instructions? If so, thou hast seen how my Soul floats out day by day over the sea yonder, fearless, hopeful and joyful.

If thou wert here ! To this thought I come back, as I go back *home* in the evening.

Thou wilt be glad to know that I am greatly better. The little change has been of great benefit to me. The climate here is too e[x]quisite for description. During all the dismal rain we have been enduring in Macon, they have had nothing here but uninterrupted succession of cloudless bright warm days. Janie is enchanted with the climate, and seems to have greatly improved.

They live very nicely indeed: and at much less expense, Janie tells me, than when boarding. There is a very nice little house in the same lot, just *twenty feet* from Janie's, with two rooms in it, and a nice kitchen adjoining. It is now occupied by one of Hal's R. R. men, who is to give it up, in a day or two. I think to rent it for a couple of months (it rents at $10 per month) and send thee and the babies down. Janie is delighted with this idea: indeed she suggested it. Her cook will do all

the cooking. Her idea, – wh. she unfolds to me enthusiasti-
cally – is to put her stove into the kitchen of the house I am
to rent: to lay a platform from *her* house to mine, – wh. can
be easily done: and, then, for you to sleep in *her* house, while
the cooking and eating will be done in the other. The children
wd. thrive magnificently. The grass and the noble trees, and
the dry ground, wd. allow them to be out of doors all the day:
and the fine dry air wd. quickly cure those dreadful colds. As
for *thee,* – thou wilt luxuriate in the *freedom* of doing precisely
what thou wishest, and when . Hal and I will have a horse
and buggy for thee and Janie to drive where ye will. Thou
will find several very delightful people here, to visit, and thou
choosest, and altogether tis a good plan. – I do not wish thee
to come, of course, until after my return: but wish thee to
write me at once if thine assent is given to my plan, so that
I may perfect the arrangement.

My love to all. Lily and Janie and I will go to Fernandina
[Fla.] by Steamer this afternoon: to return tomorrow morning.
I am

Thine.

To Robert S. Lanier

Brunswick, Ga. Mch 11th 1871

My Dear Father:

You will be glad to know that I have im-
proved during my stay, here. The sore throat wh. had troubled
me has almost entirely gone; and the fine dry air has been of
much advantage to me generally.

I find the town considerably larger than when I was last here,
and many evidences of improvement present themselves on
every side. If the people wd. but go to work to *produce* something from the soil, and make the surrounding country contribute annually to the actual wealth of the place, I should have
some strong expectation of seeing a city here. As it is, all
are consumers; and, besides the lumber exported hence, and the
R. R. work, there is little to bring money in from abroad.

The car-factory, wh. we are trying to get located on the
Day Tract, is prospering. Thirteen cars, manufactured here,
were yesterday turned out from it and sent to their destination.

The proprietor, whom I wished to see, has been absent, and I have not yet met him.

I find Harry up to his ears in business. The R. R. freights seem to have increased very greatly within the last two months, and, besides these, he has a multiplicity of other calls upon his attention. We have a prospect of selling a lot or two.

Have seen the decisions of Supreme Court in Wednesday's Constitution. Was disappointed in that on the McGloughlin Case: as it left the point on the non-record of the marriage-settlement *in statu quo*.

Write me what new business comes into the Office. It fairly breaks my heart to be absent from my work: but - —— it is useless to repine.

Mamie's letter of Mch 9th has just arrived. I enclose a note for her.

I hope the sale has been made in New Orleans, and at some satisfactory price. Let me know what has been done.[9]

I shall probably remain here until the middle of next week. I wish Mamie to come down, in the hope that the children will get rid of their colds here, and that she herself will be benefited by the change.

Regards to Uncle Clifford,

Yr Son

Sidney.

To Mary Day Lanier

[Brunswick, Ga? Mar. 11, 1871?] [10]

My Poor Heart, Thy letter breathes so sad a tone, that I know how thou art over-wearied with care of those little ones

---

[9] Gertrude Lanier Shannon was in New Orleans at this time, attempting to secure a final settlement of her husband's estate. She was staying in the home of her attorney, Mr. King, whose daughter, Grace King, recorded the visit in her autobiography, *Memories of a Southern Woman of Letters* (New York, 1927), pp. 111-112.

[10] Conjectural dating from the sequence of Lanier's letters from Brunswick and from the fact that this is clearly the note to his wife mentioned as being inclosed in the preceding letter to his father. The superscription, "Kindness of Chas. Day Esq.," indicates that it was delivered, not mailed.

that thou hast on thy bosom, and I am fain to put reproach on myself that this too-heavy work is upon thee alone.

How long and how wearisome is thine illness! Will not the cloud ever break? Good God, Break it! We are so tired.

Thou wilt be glad to hear that I am better. My cold is about gone: and my strength is come back.

There is no dampness on the ground here: the rains dry off almost immediately. I know the small folk wd. prosper, here. But of this I will talk to thee face to face: for, D. V., by the middle of next week I will look into my two gray eyes again.

This afternoon Lily and I strolled into the woods and took captive certain sprays of yellow Jessamine, most fair to see: and Lily, leaping a wide ditch, fell therein, whereby I saw the foot thereof, wh. was also fair to see: and we had much loving talk of thee. Lily is wondrous amiable to me, and is full of all sisterly lovingkindness.

I have been playing for her and Janie all the evening, – 'tis now 11 P. M. – raking up many old tunes wh. I have played in sweet past times, under the inspiration of thy love and thine eyes. Thou will rejoice with me, to know that I played a long time, without fatigue.

The Bk Paper of Friday prints " Jones," [11] with the heading from the Savh News.

Transmit for me some solemn and tender kisses to my two boys, in whom I see the pride of my manhood and the solace of mine age: manhood and age being lived wholly that I may be always

Thine

[11] This is the only mention in Lanier's letters of his dialect poem, " Thar's More in the Man Than Thar Is in the Land " (I, 22), here referred to by the variant title, " Jones of Jones." Though 1869 is said to have been the date of composition and first publication (*Poems*, New York, 1884, pp. vii, 182), the earliest printing that has been found is in the Macon *Telegraph and Messenger*, Feb. 7, 1871, with the statement that it was written for that newspaper, which implies original publication (clipping in the Chas. D. Lanier Collection, Johns Hopkins University). That it was widely copied is evidenced by the reference in the present letter and in note 17, below.

To Mary Day Lanier

[Brunswick, Ga.? Mar. 15, 1871?] [12]

My Dear Sweetheart, I will not see thee tomorrow as I expected. A little matter of business requires that I stay until next day, and so I will not get my kiss from thee until Friday, when, D. V. I will be at thy side.

Tomorrow I am to ride out to the tract with Mr. Wharton, whom we desire to locate his car-works there: and as it is quite to our interest he should do so, I have thought it of sufficient importance to keep me another day, Harry being so over-run with business as to render it quite impossible for him to go. M. Wharton does not seem inclined to make the move: but he may change his mind.

A Mr. Smith is to bring $350 on Monday next, to pay for Ten acres of Demerest's Hammock, wh. we have bargained and sold to him today. This, for yr. Father.

Lily was intending to leave tomorrow morning, but finds that no train leaves on that road until next day, and so she, too, is detained one day over her time.

We are to go over to Armstrong's,[13] tonight, to have some music.

I am considerably improved by my visit, both throat-malady and in general condition. I wish I might hear tonight that thou wert so.

Mr. Coley – Episcopal Clergyman – called on me today, and spoke of having met thee at Mr. Duncan's in Savh. Mr. Way has also called.

I send my love to Father. Thou art to wind thine arms about my wee Seraph and to'ther man, for Thine

Husband [14]

---

[12] The conjectural dating has been arrived at from the opening sentence, since Mary Day Lanier's letter of Mar. 16, 1871, indicates that date as the one originally set for his return.

[13] Lanier's friend, J. S. Armstrong, was now married and still living in Brunswick.

[14] Lanier's wife wrote Mrs. Clifford Lanier on Mar. 23, 1871: " Sidney came home last Friday [Mar. 17], decidedly better. He evidently needs frequent rests; has no cough now."

To Paul H. Hayne [15]

Macon, Ga, March 20th 1871

My Dear Mr. Hayne:

Yr. letter came during my absence from Macon, else I shd. sooner have told you the pleasure wh. I have derived from yr. Ms. " Fire-Pictures."

I have picked out a grain or two of gravel, as it were, and slag, wh. I find scattered thro' your Fire-Product; and I mention them, simply *because* they are small and might therefore escape yr. attention: — wh. being first done, I can then tell you about the pure fire and the rare flame-beauty wh. delight me in yr. Poem.

1st In the second stanza-picture, two of the verbs have the ancient termination . . . *'eth, viz,* " turneth " and " burneth "; while, in the same stanza, the first verb has the modern termination *'s, viz,* " sweeps." W'd n't the critics require all to be homogeneous, either modern form, or ancient form?

2d In the 4th picture, the word " lava's " is intended for the plural *lavas,* and not for the possessive case, *nicht wahr?*

3d In the same stanza, wd. you not desire to make some change in the " *mothers'* frenzied *hand* "; " Mothers' " being the possessive *plural,* and " hand " being singular?

4th In the same stanza, do you not think the *last two lines* wd. be better in the earlier portion of the poem, before you have passed from the *general,* to the *detailed* description of the pictures? Do you not think that a *general* idea, (as contained in
" What strange visions form and start
   Out from its mysterious heart ") makes rather a fall, than otherwise, from the *climax* of a picture whose details, so nobly done, justly sum themselves up in the words . . . " But how near
   Seem the anguish and the fear " ?
                              That is, does not the generalness of " what strange visions &c " blunt the dramatic

---

[15] Previously published, *Letters* (New York, 1899), pp. 229-234. Compare Lanier's detailed criticism of " Fire-Pictures " in his review of " Paul H. Hayne's Poetry " (V, 322), begun the next year though not published until 1875.

point wh. comes to a keen and fine climax with " But how near
Seem " *this* " anguish and " *this* " fear " wh. you have just
been so beautifully describing?   The principle on which I wd.
exclude the two last lines of the stanza, and let it end with
" seem the anguish and the fear " – is the same with that wh.
explains the well-known fact that, to see *one man* with blood
flowing from a wound is a more powerful excitement of
ordinary sympathy than to read in general terms of a thousand
men killed and wounded.   In the *beginning* of a picture the
excluded lines wd. be unobjectionable; but I am confident they
injure the climax in the *end* of one.

5th In the 7th Stanza, the line " Here's a glowing warm
interior " hath no fellow in the matter of rhyme, but is a
widow'd and all mateless line. So, also, the line " with those
hues, rich-toned but homely " in the same Strophe.

6th Is there any authority for the form " Salvator*e* " – of
Salvator Rosa's name? I merely mean to call y'r. attention to
it; and have no means immediately at hand to satisfy my doubt
as to whether that is a permissible method; indeed it is quite
possible that my question is ridiculous, but, – *stet.*

7th In the 8th strophe, " gleams," in the last line should be
gleam, agreeing with " hill-side and meadow."

8th In the 11th strophe, wd. not the line " *And* the heavy
grief-moulds pressed " reveal its grammatical dependence and
connection better by substituting WITH for " *and* "; – or by some
such construction?

9th And lastly,, and generally, wd. not the refrain " Oh the
Fire " be better *without* the brackets in which it is enclosed?

– And now, when I commence to tell you about the charm
wh. yr. Poem has for me, I am greatly at a loss where to begin,
and *wholly* at a loss where to end.

> . . . . Backward o'er its river-courses
> Backward to its mountain-sources,
> While the blood-red sunset burneth
> Like a God's face grand with ire,

is too beautful, and one can say nothing about it better than to
quote it. To this, the
" Oh thus wan faint-hearted fire " in the next strophe forms
an exquisite set-off.

I have already spoken of the Vesuvian picture. With what
a poet's-instinct you have seized upon those accessions of the
Volcano (*i. e.* the temples, the statues, the town, the hill-top,
the mother, the children, the strand) which would make the
picture necessarily *beautiful* at the same time that it is *tragical!*

Ere the flames devouring magic
Coils about their golden splendor
And the tender
Glory of the mellowing fields
To the wild Destroyer yields. . . . is an exquisite stroke of
melody, and tingles in my ears a long time.

In the martyr-picture, I am specially struck with the marvellous marriage of sound and word in the last two lines:
" And o'er those reverend hairs, silvered & hoary,
Settles the semblance of a crown of glory." This is *long*
and *serene*: – as a blissful eternity shd. be!

Yr. Flemish interior is simply perfect. It creates within one
a parlous longing for a tankard and pipe: – and, what ho,
drawer, let them both be of some capacity!

And next comes the (*me judice*) glory and fair climax of
the poem, the sweetest notes, to my mind, and the fullest of
genuine poet's-music, that you have ever sung. I mean

. . . . Fairly flowing
Like a rivulet rippling deep
Thro' the meadow-lands of Sleep,
Bordered where its music swells
By the languid Lotos-bells
And the twilight Asphodels,

(and if flower-bells were church-bells they wd. chime just so!)

Mingled with a richer boon
Of queen-lilies, each a moon
Orbéd into white completeness: –
O the perfume and the sweetness
Of those grouped and fairy flowers,
Over which the love-lorn Hours
Linger, – not alone for them,
Tho' the Lotos swings its stem
With a lulling stir of leaves,
Tho' the lady-Lily laves

Coy feet in the crystal waves,
And a silvery under-tune
From some mystic wind-song grieves,
Dainty-sweet, amid the bells
Of the twilight Asphodels –
But because a charm more rare
Glorifies the mellow air.
In the gleam of lifted eyes,
In the tranquil ecstasies
Of two lovers, leaf-embowered,
Lingering there,
Each of whose fair lives hath flowered
Like the lily petals finely,
Like the Asphodels divinely?

I am quite in friendly earnest, – and you know I *love* music! – when I tell you, dear Mr. Hayne, that I do not know of anything, of the same style, in our language which is so beautiful as this passage. The flow of the melody is unbrokenly perfect: and the interfusing of the exquisite nature-picture with the one-passion of the two *human* hearts makes an *inner* music dwelling in the *material* music wh. enchants me beyond measure. Nothing you have ever done has pleased me so entirely: and I believe the verdict of after-poets will support me.

My letter is so long that I will not go into any more details – than to notice with what exquisite art you have made your poem, at the close, flicker into silence as the fire flickers into darkness. And I w'd. have you to know that if it were *I,* I would not for all the world disturb one line of those last ones about which you have drawn brackets and noted " to be altered "! Do not alter one jot or tittle of those concluding lines: you could not improve them, nor any man. Do not put a sacrilegious pen-stroke through a single word of that Strophe no. 11. You can't paint a rose; no more can you paint a dead leaf; one is perfect, so is t'other: – let yr. dead leaf alone.

I return your Ms., having numbered it, so that you can understand my references: – but won't you be kind enough to send it back to me, *to keep*? I wd. like it hugely, as a remembrance of you.

I'm always Your Friend

Sidney Lanier

To Mary Day Lanier

[Macon, Ga. Apr. 3, 1871]

My Darling Child:

Yr. father seems to be suffering with his cold today: and, tho' not in bed, is confined to his room.[16] I doubt not your presence there would cheer him greatly: suppose you come down and see him?

There is no occasion whatever for alarm: and I only write this, thinking you would like to be with him.

Your

S.

Office. April 3d 1871.

You had better come in the carriage: wh. can wait & we'll all go out together.

To Virginia Hankins

Macon, Ga. April 6th 1871.

Dear Friend, Why do I not hear from you? I wrote, a long time ago, enclosing you a couple of poems for Miss Brock.

I do not know whether you received them: nor where you are: nor y'r. plans for the summer: nor your state of health, wh. some time ago was not good – a fact wh. gave me great concern, for if health shd. fail you, then wd. yr. lot be hard to bear. I do not know what you have written: nor what you are going to write: nor what you think or dream or feel, in the unearthly Spring-days that now are.

After much reflection, I am arrived at the conclusion that it wd. not be well for any of the boys to come here, at present, and have almost ceased to think of getting a place for them, here. The condition of the State is so bad, in matters of com-

---

[16] At the Lanier House. A second note, dated Apr. 6 (here omitted), reported that Mr. Day was improving.

merce, of agriculture and finance, that I do not regard the prospect a cheerful one for a young man just entering life: at least, until political matters change.

Do you get the Southern Magazine regularly? "Retrospects & Prospects," continued from March No. to April No., is mine. Let me know what you think of it.[17]

I hope I may hear from you soon.

Yr.

Friend

FROM W. HAND BROWNE [18]

Office So. Mag– [Baltimore]
April 20– 1871

Dear friend:

To get such a letter from you sets me hankering after my old flute which has not been out of its box for many a day. For when I speak of playing this and that, I have reference rather to what I once could do, than to the present, when my right hand has lost the best part of its cunning. I say " right hand," for I was trained in the Nicholson School – my old master having been a pupil of Nicholson's – which gives nearly all the work to the right hand; taking, for example the upper notes which follow, from the lower notes under them

---

[17] In her reply, Apr. 15, 1871, Virginia Hankins wrote: " I do not read– or write. . . . But when I read such things as ' Retrospects & Prospects,' the old life I had once hoped for myself, a life ever developing & hourly renewed through art, a life devoted to beautiful things, arises before me, & awakens I know not what feeling of longing and pain."

In the same letter she added: "I saw in the [Lexington, Va.] Gazette . . . a piece called ' Jones,' copied from the Macon Tel'ph– & as the editor gave you the honor & glory of its authorship, I am a little curious to know if you are guilty. The boys laughed & said 'twas smart & ' good ' & funny." This reference is to Lanier's dialect poem, " Jones of Jones," later entitled " Thar's More in the Man Than Thar Is in the Land " (see I, 22, and note 11, above).

[18] None of Lanier's letters to W. H. Browne have been found. In later years Browne told Lanier that he had saved the letters of no correspondent except Edward Spencer (see Lanier's letter to Spencer, Apr. 1, 1875). The following letter by Browne is given to indicate the place he took about this time among Lanier's friends, though they knew each other as yet only through correspondence. Later in Baltimore they became very intimate indeed.

(Written as upper notes
(Played as harmonics of lower –
This gives, as you see, the work to the
right hand, which is naturally the deftest. But I am forgetting
that I am talking to one who knows far more about this than
I do.

I never did anything in the way of improvisation. Whenever
I tried it, I have always found myself gliding into some familiar
phrase from something or other; so that I was convinced I had
no talent for it. What little I used to do in composition (and
I never got further than duos) was to invent a theme, harmonize it carefully, but simply, with full chords; treat it as
trio, slow movement, and rondo, with perhaps a lively opening.
Then with my full chords to guide me, I wrote the second flute
part, giving it as much variety and independence of melody as
I could. I then interchanged parts, here and there, so that the
2nd flute would have its share of the melody. It was poor work
enough, I dare say, but my master used to encourage me, and
say that some day, perhaps, I would produce something worth
having. I don't think I ever was so proud as once when he
came to a passage of mine when I had worked the two flutes
up in contrary motion to one bar of unison, and he said " Well
done! that was right good! " Poor old fellow – he had the
patience of an angel with me. I hope he has a solo now and
then in heaven, with 'cello and bassoon accompt.

As for that little motive I sent you, it is utterly worthless as
music. Consider it in the light of an *autograph* only.

I prefer A♭ to any other key. It is very easy, and perfectly
in tune if you take the D♭ (when held) with the two C keys
down – otherwise you get a C♯. The notes in this key seem
to me sweeter and evener than in any other; and you have such
a fine 5th, that will bear any amount of forcing. I don't like B♭
because the dominant is such a weak note, and the sharp 7th
is worse. But on the Boehm this may not be the case.

☞   I shall be overjoyed to get the improvisation you speak
of. I have a great deal of music, both in Ms. & print, from

Nicholson, Bucher, Berbiguier, Kuhlau, Tulon, Fürstenau, Rabboni, Böhm, Forde, Briccialdi and I don't know how many more.

I will tell you what I will do. I have in an old portfolio a number of very rough copies of pieces which were lent me by friends, and copied very hastily. Afterwards I made neat copies, but did not throw all the rough ones away. They are frightfully rough, and have errors which you will see of course. I will send them to you: if there is anything in them you like, you can make a fair copy, and throw away, or give away all the rough drafts when done with. I will also send you, later, when I have looked them over, some choice pieces, which you can return at your leisure. Any pieces that I don't care about your taking the trouble to return, I will mark with your name in the corner.

I do trust that you will come this way and come out and see me. I would furbish up my old flute, and try to get a modest second out of it in any easy duo.

You must have administered some sort of philtre to our Mr. Hill.[19] He says "Lanier is a glorious friend!" (His very words, s'elp me!)

Thanks for the photo. I have none of myself, but when I next have any taken, shall not fail to send you one.

The verses [20] are *good* – fresh. Many thanks.

Glad you like Maga. Ay de mí ! what a magª. we could make, if our people would only encourage us !

faithfully yours

W. Hand Browne

Sidney Lanier Esq.

———. ———

To Mary Day Lanier [21]

Macon, April 28th/71

Thou dear One, Thy face was so too-sweet, and the faces of my two boys were so heavenly, – when I left you yesterday, – that I have had naught else in my mind or my heart, since.

---

[19] Browne's partner, W. S. Hill, had been travelling in the South in the interests of the *Southern Magazine*.

[20] "A Sea-Shore Grave" and "A Song" (I, 214, 213) by Sidney and Clifford Lanier, written in 1866, published in the *Sou. Mag.*, July, 1871.

[21] On Apr. 24, 1871, Mary Day Lanier wrote to Clifford Lanier: "I am about

Thy little note came & cheered me.

I have but time to scratch thee this: as I must hie to the Court House.

I send, this morning, the baby-carriage and *one* chair: t'other I will send when thou writest me which *one* I must send – for in the hurry yesterday, I forgot which of the three remaining ones it was that thou desiredst to be for^d.

Will write again tomorrow.

My love to Hal & Janie.

Thine

To Mary Day Lanier

[Macon, Ga.? Apr. 30, 1871?] [22]

Dear My Heart,   Before thou hadst left me I thought the Spring was come, but now, when thou art gone, I find that thou wert my Spring: and without thee there is only some fine weather wh. is very good, but is not Spring.

Through this fine weather goeth this little Half-of-Thee, inwardly sighing that life, broken in two, is hard.

Otherwise well, however.

Tomorrow I go to Atlanta to argue a case before the Supreme Court. I will get there some hours before Nillson sings: & will hear the same – I will not be happy in said hearing, and will hear but dimly and hardly: for thou art my best sense, – my spirit's ear – and without thee there will be only certain sweet sounds, wh. – if thou wert with me, – would be music.

Wilt thou tell me in what dim corner, or far obscure shade, hath been hidden my pair of well-beloved pantaloons, my gray beauties, my pearl-tinted darlings ?   The closet betwixt the children's and the lumber-room have I searched with critical eye and inquisitive finger: remembering me that the same did

to start, on the 27th, for Brunswick, to visit my Brother & Janie, in their little house: thence to Lilla's. . . . Dear Sidney is not strong but is free from cough & pain– and takes care of himself."

[22] Conjectural dating from the evidence of Lanier's Atlanta trip in this and the following letter.

whilom hang therein: but nothing cd. I find save melancholy dry bottles & the wood-box wherein the long-suffering Leila [23] hath been accustomed to deposit loudly her nightly store of lightwood. Tell me where be these breeches: for other places have I also searched, without avail: and the weather groweth warm withal: wherefore have pity upon the much burdened leg of

Thine.

Much search revealeth not the small pillow whereof thou speakest.

I send a kiss to Janie & my bairns, & Harry.

S.

To Mary Day Lanier

Macon, Ga. May 3d 1871

Thou art *my* Sea-wind and Sea-dream, dear Child: and before thee is my heart ever stretched and strained outward, like a sail, and thou drivest me over the great Deep, and into most sweet harbors. If the fine energies of thy breath shd. grow still, if thine enchanting impulsion shd. fail me, then wd. I lie inert on the bosom of life, or sink feebly to the bottom of death. Grow not still, fail me not, intense motive Breath-of-my-Love! Come to me from afar, breathe me onward, press me forward, swift, buoyant, to some fair bay of Dreams, shored round with Heaven!

I have much concern anent Janie's sickness, of who thy letter, recd yesterday on my return from Atlanta, brought news; both on her account and on thine. I greatly hope for something today to tell me that she is better.

Also, I grieve much to hear of Bro. Hal's indisposition. Thy Father *suspects* that something is wrong. He told me yesterday " that he feared Harry was not at all well; that he had had no letter from Harry in several days: that he had been twice asked

[23] A negro nursemaid who had joined Mammy Lucy in the service of the Laniers.

by different parties *how* Harry was, each of the parties informing him that *they* had heard that Harry was sick." I think thou wert better not mention this to Harry, as it wd. only trouble him. But tell him, from me, (with my love) to write his father, every two or three days, *if only a line or so*; wh. will greatly tend to relieve his solicitude. I do heartily hope Hal will soon improve. Am glad to hear Charley T. goes down: this will brighten him.

Thou wilt be glad to know· I have found my sweet pantaloons, – in my *valise*.

Ellen [24] doeth well: and we get on in quite style, most like two old soldiers of the Hospital *des Invalides,* or a couple of superannuated Chelsea pensioners.

My most sweet Charlie! How hungry are my arms for his fair little body, and my neck for his fair little arms! As for the Seraph, I think not of him, for fear my heart will break with too much longing.

I pray thee, convince thyself that art on holiday, and try to rest thy heart and thy body. I am full of much life, and hope: and I do thrill alway with the intense hope to give thee some suitabler taste of life than God has yet allowed me. I think I will do this: meantime keep thyself fresh and hopeful, – if thou canst.

I am thy
>   Lover.

To Mary Day Lanier

>   Macon, Ga, May 4th 1871

Thou art the Spirit of my heart,– *Cordis Spiritus* – even as the wind is the soul of the sea.

It is 11 O'clock, at night, and I am scratching this at the Brown House.[25] About an hour ago, a dispatch came, to father

[24] Gertrude Lanier Shannon's negro cook.

[25] A hotel in Macon opposite the railroad depot. Aunt Jane, mentioned in the next sentence, was Mrs. Abram Watt of Montgomery.

& me at home, announcing that Aunt Jane was very ill: & Sam being gone, I got a man to drive me here, where I will spend the night, in order to be sure of the five O'clock train tomorrow.

I write this that thou mayst know why, if no letters come from me to thee, in the next day or two.

I wrote thee this morning, and sent by today's train.

Auntie has so often been at death's door that I trust things may not be as bad as Clifford fears.

Thou wilt embrace my two young men, in thy mother's-arms, for me,

As also Hal & Janie: – as also Lucy: – & Leila.

I am

                    Thy Lover

To Virginia Hankins

                              Macon, Ga, May 22d 1871.

I shd. have written you, dear Friend, sooner than this, but was called off to Alabama to visit a friend who was supposed to be dying; – and so prevented.

It gives me great pleasure that you have thought so much of me as to write the sketch for Miss Brock to wh. you allude.[26] *Am* I afraid that my life shd. be in yr. hands? Why, are they not white hands, and most sweet and rare hands? I wd. sooner trust that same life in *yr.* hands, than in my own: – more than this can no man say.

I only wish there were some way of conveying to you the longing wh. I have to be of service to you. And I cannot even tell you how long nor how vainly I have beat my brains, to think of aught that wd. suit you. Help me in both these difficulties. Tell me what you desire: and how I can serve you.

Somebody, not far from my office, has a bird in a cage, who sings away all these summer days as if he never knew what

---

[26] In her letter of Apr. 15, 1871, Virginia Hankins had written: " When her book comes out you'll see your ' biography ' sketched by your friend– Long ago, would we have dreamed of this? I who had such awe of you! (Of course I was too clever to let you see it.) Are you willing to trust yourself to my hands? The truth is, I said very little– for reasons." This sketch has not been found. (See note 7, above.)

liberty was. He does not seem to be mournful in the slightest
measure. He simply melts his captivity, and moulds it into
good music.

Strange that God shd. give the birds power to do it, – and
deny it to man and woman.

Always, somehow, this bird sets me dreaming of you.

I wd. that I might sit on the bay-bank with you, and hear
the waters, again. Perhaps I will, this late summer, or fall.

Yr. letter was very dear to me, breathing friendship. Give
me some more.

You will write, again, some time: and you will *not* lose yr.
taste for the art in which one renews one's life daily. The
apathetic mood: – ah, do I not know it? But it ends.

Yr.

Friend

To Mary Day Lanier

Macon, Ga.
June 4/71.

I did not forget my Sweet T'other Heart, that I was to send
thee a letter by yesterday's train, to reach thee last night: but
'twas made impossible by the fact that the rain poured in such
torrents yesterday morning, that Father and I could not start
for the office until it was too late to get my letter to the train.

Meantime, the " little sore spot " of which thou heards't me
speak, developed itself yesterday morning, in a certain bloodi-
ness of expectoration. It was *not* a hemorrhage; but only an
expectoration of mucus, tinged with blood, about *once* in each
half hour –, I paid little attention to it until afternoon, being
in the office at regular work: but, on consulting Dr. Hall, went
to bed, and have remained there today, feeling somewhat weak,
but not doubting I shall be about again in a day or two. This
is the way of it; and thou art not to be alarmed at all. I find
Sissa has written thee and fear she may have magnified the
danger so as to make thee think of returning.[27] There is no

[27] On June 4, 1871, Gertrude Lanier Shannon wrote to her brother Clifford:
" Our dear brother Sidney is sick in bed, having had a slight hemorrage yester-

necessity whatever for *that*; and thou wouldst probably find me up when thou camst.

Kiss my two men for me: as also Lilly, & the rest of 'em.

I will write thee again tomorrow.

Thy

Lover

To Mary Day Lanier

[Macon, Ga.] June 6th 1871

Thou Loving-Heart, thy letter of 4th, as full as a bee's thighs with sweets, came to me today. I thank thee for thy love's sweet estimate of me: not caring, – Love being the 'countant – that it is surely greatly too large.

I am steadily improving: and will probably be allowed to sit up a little, tomorrow. Indeed, I shall do so tonight, while Sissa makes up my much-tumbled bed.

Dr. Hall thinks my attack principally *bronchial,* from the indications.

I shall be about in a few days –

Thy father is bright and well. Janie is in splendid condition and spirits.[28] She spent yesterday with me, and seemed over-flowing with buoyancy and life. Sissa has a sick-headache today; but is up and about.

If all the butterflies in the world had gathered about one marvellous flower,– then they would be like my fluttering thoughts, which, as I lie here through the long days, do all flap their wings in a little circle around thee.

Having taken my two little men in thine arms, & kissed them: do likewise, then, with my fair Lily, for thine

Husband.

day. He is always greatly prostrated in these attacks & terribly depressed. . . . Poor Maydie is at Lilla's– thinking brother Sid very much improved. . . . She will be nearly crazy poor child, to hear of his sickness." No letter from Gertrude to Mary Day Lanier of this date has survived.

[28] Janie, Mrs. Harry Day, had come to Macon, possibly to consult a physician; Mary Day Lanier and her boys had left Brunswick for Waynesville.

To Mary Day Lanier

[Macon, Ga.] Saturday, June 10th /71.

My heart is like the still sea, and thou art the sheen-of-stars, wh. glorifieth it with a broad and heavenly radiance. Moreover, 'tis a *warm* radiance: whereby love-shine is sweeter than star-shine wh. last hath no heat in it.

There are two certain days in time wh. I do chiefly love: One is this same June tenth, wh. brought thee into the world: and 'tother is the day that brought thee into my heart. Thou camest, dear Child! into a very rank wilderness, on both these days! And when thou dids't leap out of the world-forest into *my* woods, Ah, do I not mind me well what a shiver of compound fear and delight ran through all the leaves and fibres thereof? – whereto succeeded a great calm of quiet ecstasy? – whereto succeeded thy quiet tendance of my wild-growth until the same was wrought into some orderly semblance of a useful garden, wherein nevertheless thou dids't leave, deep in the heart of it, certain wild and bosky spots for a romance-refuge in the hot days?

Thou art the sweetest gardener that ever trained vine.

And all the trees, and leaves and flowers and products of my heart acknowledge thee mistress and exquisite Queen, and love thine eyes as sunlight and thy words as rain.

Cometh a letter from Clifford today wherein he saith Willie is detained by desire to see and confirm her new mother, and also by desire to time her visit so that it may embrace Lou's College-Commencement,[29] they will therefore likely be here in the course of the next two weeks: and thou wilt probably see them after all. Yet, – being greatly rejoiced at reading that thou art *resting* at Lily's – I desire that thou remain there just as long as it may be pleasant for thee. There is no occasion whatever to hurry any of thy movements. The Summer is before us.

[29] Mrs. Clifford Lanier's father, David Clopton, had made a second marriage, to Mrs. Mary F. Chambers. Her sister, Lou Clopton, was attending Wesleyan Female College at Macon.

I sent thy bottle by thy father, who started this morn'g to visit Hal.

I am greatly better, and as yet feel no ill effects from my attack, beyond the weakness, which daily diminishes. I have not the sense of lassitude wh. remained after my last year's attack; and I see every reason to believe that my summer will be far more hearty and pleasant than last. I have been using the Drosera constantly; and it seems to have performed its work with the usual success. I have no cough whatever: and am quite free in the chest.[30]

It is probable that my father will be married towards the last of July: tho' I am not sure that it is finally and irrevocably so decided.[31]

Thou art to put thy hands on my Lily's head, and so convey to her my hearty blessing for all her loving goodness to thee. I feel quite sure that at some future time Life will lend me some eloquence – either in the shape of serviceable act, or beautiful word, – by which I may express the now unspeakable tenderness and faithful love I have for her: but at present, thou knowest, I am the fallow field, I do not produce, I say nothing.

Thine account of the small man-angel giveth me keen pleasure. Put him in among the oaks, and let him smile there, and absorb the wood-loveliness and the ineffable leaf-purities and the fibrous virtues of the great forests. With a pen or a fiddle or a pencil, or summut like, he will reproduce them some day, and make folks in hot cities hear the wind in the leaves and see the dew in the acorn-cups.

Embrace also my sturdy gray-eyes, and convey to him that his kiss has reached papa, and is making him well.

Whereupon crawleth Sister to her door and ordereth me to bed, saying it is late in the night. And, therefore, mourning that mine arms are empty of my love, I send thee the long kiss of a most loving and faithful

Husband.

[30] In a note written earlier the same day and sent by Charles Day, Lanier had written: " I am doing splendidly. Have been down stairs, and feel myself strengthening all the time. My attack did not amount to a hæmorrhage: but was in consequence of a cold wh. I had caught, and wh. settled on the bronchial tubes, and caused the bloody expectoration."

[31] This marriage did not take place for nearly two years (see note 17, 1873).

As also my love to Mammy, and tell her all are well at her house, as per report of Henry, made yesterday during a certain financial transaction betwixt me and him as agent of Washerwoman.

To Mary Day Lanier

[Macon, Ga.] June 14th 1871.

If a bee could extract his honey-essence from the mere *shadow* of a flower, – then he w'd. typify me, who day by day fill my soul with a sweetness drawn from that mere insubstantial *image* of thee wh. is in my memory.

"
―――――
"

Howsoever long thou remainest away from me, my heart is always like a nest wh. the bird hath just abandoned: still suffused with the soft warmth of the bosom that was there, and yet palpitating with the late motions of my bird's heart. Hereby one learneth the divinity and the immortality of love: wh. can preserve a heart-warmth and perpetuate a heart-motion, independently of the heart itself.

"
―――――
"

Thou art a gloriole of clarified light, dwelling always around my head. In the old paintings, the painters put a *nimbus* about the brows of any one who had some particular Divine Blessing. This particular divine blessing, in the picture of my life, hath taken the shape of thee, my Halo, my Beloved, my Wife.

"
―――――
"

My Subtile-Sweet Woman, how tenuous and how real thou art ! I have plainly seen thee in the waving of a leaf; I have had a perfect vision of thee in the exquisite evanescent tremor of a music-tone; I have distinctly caught thy face peeping from behind a beautiful idea in my soul, like Titania half-hid in a flower. Yet I know that thou hast actual lips and eyes and brows; and arms of sweet flesh, wh. have been about my neck in past time.

"

"

This is my morning-service to thee, for the morning of the Fourteenth Day After The Beginning of My Lent:– wh. began on the day when thou didst disappear from my sight.[32]

Thou wilt be glad to know that I am about recovered from my trouble. I write this in the office: where I come daily, tho' they will not let me do any work. Father desires me to run off for a little trip up to *Gainsville,* to see how the land lies thereabout, and to spy out the same, if peradventure it might be a good place to spend a month or two during the summer. I do not think of the *latter* at all; but probably I will take the trip merely by way of a little change.

Thy Father arrived yesterday, a little fatigued. He seems bright & well this morning. Sissa is well: & Father & Eddie. But we are fearfully lonesome without thee and thy blessed little men. Nevertheless, I desire that thou stay, so long as thou art resting quietly: for this is what thou art in need of. Take thine own time about all matters, and do as thine own will moveth thee. My loving regards to all thy friends there, especially my Lily: from thine

Husband.

TO MARY DAY LANIER

[Macon, Ga.] June 19th 1871

Dear Heart, I sent thee this morning, in a letter enclosed to Hal, the $15. referred to in thine of 15th ult. wh- I recd this mg. I hope it will come safely to thee.

[32] This seems to indicate that Mary Day Lanier had been absent from Macon for only two weeks on the present trip. It is possible that the earlier trip to Brunswick and Waynesville on Apr. 27 (see note 21, above) had been broken by a return to Macon, and that this was a second visit to the same friends—a conclusion supported by the fact that no letters from Lanier to his wife between May 4 and June 4, 1871, have been found.

I write this afternoon, to be in time for tomorrow, Tuesday's, mail. I leave tomorrow afternoon for Atlanta and Gainesville, expecting to be absent for three or four days. I long to come to thee; but I think the other trip best for me.

I need a little bracing air: and fancy that a cool night or two would set me up mightily.

Sissa was glad to get thy letter, enclosed in mine. I wrote thee a birthday letter, on the 10th of this month.

When wilt thou come back to me? Yet hurry not: for I wd. have thee be with thy Lily as much as thou wilt.

Thy father is well as usual. Janie is at Mrs. Fulton's, and I have not heard from her in a day or two. Sissa not well: bad cold. I hope my man Charles is better. My love I send to Lily & all thy friends. Tell Mammy all well at her house. It will hardly avail to write thee from Gainesville, if thou art to come on the 27th or 29th. Yet I will write anyhow, when I get there.

Thine
Husband

To Mary Day Lanier

Atlanta, Ga., June 26 1871

Thou Sweeter I, —   I am just come from Gainesville: am abluted, dressed, and made sweet, and sit here, – it being nine O' the clock, evening, – in this exquisite writing-room, which looks into the *suite* of parlors and the wide circle of the promenade, – listening to the clarinetts, violins, a flute, 'cello and piano (wh. play here nightly) swelling and dying, in ever new deaths and resurrections! – and withal meseemeth my heart must needs break if I have not some little word with thee! so I write this, wh. I will carry with me to Macon in the morning, and hand to the conductor on the M & B. train at the depôt, for thee *per* Harry.

I am much improved by my little jaunt. Thy long letter was ford here, and I have just read it. Thy father must have mistaken, as to my absence from thee this summer. I am quite resolved *that* shall not be: save upon some such dire necessity as does not now at all exist.

— I do not believe I wd. have been sick, hadst thou not been absent from me. Dear Beloved, thou hast grown to so integral a part of my life, that I cannot at all live unless thou art by.

This I have discovered, during thy last absence. I *cannot* be from thee, this summer; nor any other time, for long. Think not this is is the passion of approaching meeting, after separation. Wilt thou smile, if I tell thee that it is come upon me like a marvellous revelation, — that I *love* thee? It is very true. Without thee I have no breath. I will stay with thee: unless death is the plain alternative.

Come to me, as soon as thou canst: I am famished for my Love. I cannot think of aught else, now, than this: and so I say no more but that I am verily famished for my

Love.

To Clifford A. Lanier

My Dear Clifford: Macon, Ga. July 10th 1871.

I—and all the rest of us—have been greatly disappointed that your coming has been delayed, and perhaps entirely prevented. We were anxious to see all the babies together. I went down to Waynesville, and brought my wife and little ones back on Friday last. We will be here a week or two: after which I think of taking my family to Griffin (where we get board for $22 per month) and remaining there for the summer.

I find myself greatly enfeebled by the heat, and am compelled to seek some cooler air.

The July number of the Southern Magazine contains two little pieces by *you and me,* wh. I sent to Dr. Browne some time ago.[33] They are not indexed: you'll find them in the last part of the Magazine.

Write us if you can still come. May sends you & Willie a heart full of love: in wh. joins yr.

Bro.

Sid.

---

[33] " A Sea-Shore Grave " and " A Song," both written in 1866.

To Mary Day Lanier

[Marietta, Ga.? July 20, 1871?] [34]

Alas, and woe is me, Alhama ! What have I done ! Here
have I travelled all the way with thy fateful pill-box in my
pocket, wh. I did *not* deliver to Sam, as thou didst request, in
almost thy parting words ! What pain I may have caused
thee by this criminal thoughtlessness, – I fear to think.
Yet, blame me lightly. For, in the moment when I leave thee,
then all my thought is gone to one sole point, and there is only
my Love in my brain.

I have secured rooms for us at Mr. Whitlock's: wh. was by far
the pleasantest place I saw, in Marietta, after riding over the
whole town and inspecting the boarding-places, inside and out.
The McC. place wd. never have done, at all: for reasons wh.
I discovered after being in the house ten minutes, & wh. I will
communicate at other times. I will be at home Tuesday or
Wednesday next: but will write thee again tomorrow. I am
much improved already: and I hope good things from the
Marietta climate.

I am nothing save thine

Husband.

(P. S. Whitlock does not live where he did last summer. He
has a yard of *six* or *seven* acres, filled with trees. Our room
down-stairs.

To Robert S. Lanier

Atlanta, Ga., July 21st 1871

My Dear Father:

      Finding that the Case would not come on until
today, I kept on through Atlanta, and reached Marietta by 11½
o'clock, after a very pleasant journey.

I spent yesterday morning in looking up a boarding-place,

[34] Conjectural dating from the evidence of the following letter.

and finally succeeded in securing one which I think will suit us charmingly.

I bought a Thousand mile ticket, at Macon, for all of us: wh., I state for fear you might buy one.

The R. R. case will come up in a few moments. The other side has the conclusion. Bacon, Hinton, Judge Jackson, & Mr. Anderson,[85] expect to speak on our side.

I found the weather very cool at Marietta, and under the influence of the bracing air, I began to rally almost immediately. I am much better than when I left home. Will remain here until the R. R. case is through, and then go back to Marietta, where I propose to stay until Tuesday, and then return to Macon, reaching there Wednesday, or perhaps Tuesday, as I wd. like a day at home to attend to some matters before leaving for the summer.

Have met many acquaintances here, and the time goes pleasantly by: – tho' I cannot help thinking of you, alone, in yr. hot office, at work, – and this makes me sad.

I write to May by this mail. My love to Sissa.

Yr. Loving

Sidney

To Mary Day Lanier

Atlanta, Ga., July 23 1871

— As I was saying, My pretty Heart, I do not indeed think of aught else besides thee: and the most common place propositions of life come to me expressed (as the mathematico-scientific men say) *in terms of thee.* For example, if I hear that two and two make four, I reply, yes, it is true, my Love hath two eyes and two lips and these be the four sweetest things in all this world:— or if it is asserted profoundly that black is not white, I answer – *aye,* witness the exquisite opposition betwixt the dark eyebrow and white forehead of my Beloved.

---

[85] Probably A. O. Bacon, Lanier's friend; Judge James Jackson, one of the examiners at his admission to the bar; and Clifford Anderson, his uncle. Hinton has not been identified. This letter and the next one are written on the stationery of the H. I. Kimball House, the leading hotel in Atlanta at that time.

Spinoza, who wrote always of God, was called a God-drunken man:– but I am thee-drunken.

Here hath just passed by the wildest storm I ever saw. First came the wind, and whirled such overpowering clouds of dust high in the heavens that the sun was quite blotted out, and was a mere sickly-yellow spot. Then the wind raged more furiously: sheds fell crashing about the town, the air was full of things caught up and carried above the earth, and the long howl of the wind changed to a multitudinous-toned roar.
Suddenly great torrents of rain and volleys of hail swept along, and beat down the cloud of dust and flying missiles, until in a few moments the streets were like mountain cataracts. — And now, the heaven is as clear and serene in the twilight as if this passion had never been. Something, which is to the earth as thou art to me, hath moved along and stilled the heart of the world.

I improve daily. Will reach home Tuesday night. Let the buggy be at Vineville station about eight O'clock. I send my love to Father & Sissa and the dear little ones.

Thine

Husband.

To Virginia Hankins

Macon, Ga. July 31st 1871.

Dear Friend, I've been quite " demoralized " by the warm weather,[36] and am just about to start, with my little family, to *Marietta, Ga,* where I propose to spend a part of the summer, – I do not know how much of it – and then travel to New York. Meantime; – having the keenest desire to see you again in your sweet old Castle, and, fearing (from what you have said in former letters) that you may possibly be going to leave the dear Home; I desire that you write me immediately what will

---

[36] Gertrude Lanier Shannon had written Clifford Lanier on July 27, 1871: " He [Sidney] is suffering from cold now & is not well."

be your motions, so that I may arrange mine to accomplish my desire. Address " S. L. Marietta, Ga."

A multitude of little matters, which I must attend to before starting this afternoon, prevent me from writing more now. Not knowing whether you will have " rendered yourself " at home from Richmond, I ask them to forward to you, if not there.

I hope I may hear soon that you are greatly better; and I shall count the days, My beloved Friend, until I see you.

S. L.

To Robert S. Lanier

Marietta, Aug. 2nd 1871

My Dear Father:

We all arrived safely, and, after a day's experience, are quite delighted with our quarters. The fare is excellent; and we have to draw on the blankets at night, tho' this is declared to be the warmest weather that has yet been felt in Marietta.

We have found a number of friends, whose cordial welcome has contributed to make us well content with our summer abiding-place.

Charlie luxuriates in his ample range; and the baby thrives apace.

Mr. Duncan has called on us: and we take tea at his house tonight.

I intended to go to the Telegraph Office before leaving, and have the paper sent to me here for two months: but forgot it. Will you please call there, and give proper instructions?

Tell Sissa there is to be a County Fair here tomorrow, in which one of the articles of home production to be exhibited is – *babies*. A prize is offered for (among others) the brightest, smartest and prettiest boy-baby: and we are all agreed that if we could " enter " Eddie, he would walk over the Course. Mary declines to put in Charles & Sidney: having certain suspicions as to the capacity of the Judges.

We think of you, when we plunge our faces o' mornings & evenings in the fine ice-cold water.

There's no news. Mary is out visiting, but told me to put in her love, to you and Sissa & Eddie; in which unites

Your Loving

Sidney.

To Robert S. Lanier

Marietta, Ga, Aug. 13th 1871.

My Dear Father:

We were glad to get your letter, and to learn therefrom that the recent derangements in your culinary department had, at any rate, failed to cast anything like the atrabilious gloom of dyspepsia over your spirits.

Mary and I have been a little under the weather for a day or two, having over-fatigued ourselves among our friends. We are now retired into an ascetic seclusion, – tho' our asceticism is of a very mild sort, chiefly displaying itself in a very bitter hatred to beef, mutton & vegetables whereby the latter do suffer much detriment.

We really regret, tho', that we are not well enough for gayety; for we have many friends here, and some good musicians who can do nothing without us; so that we *could* enjoy ourselves hugely.

The children continue in fine condition, and have made themselves greatly beloved in the household by their handsome faces and gentle behavior. Charlie seems to have utterly lost his warlike disposition, and I think he will shortly retire from the army to resume the peaceful walks of life. The fatigues of his last campaign with Edward I appear to have given him an inclination for the gentler arts of peace. His ferocious passions, nowadays, only vent themselves in an occasional sullen menace, of dreadful import to hapless heads of bears; or in asking his mother (as he did t'other day), when she tells him about the Flaming Sword of the Archangel, " ef he would cut off a bear's tail with it? "

We send you our love, and our hope that you will find some solace for the lonesome position in which you are left by children and kinsmen.

I wrote you, some days ago, of Uncle Clifford's stay with us, and of several matters he desired me to communicate to you.[37]

The Supreme Court, I observe, is rushing through the Docket with unexampled rapidity: averaging, for several days past, more than 6 cases a day. I've subscribed for the [Atlanta] Constitution for one month. The Telegraph & Mess. comes duly.

Yr. Loving

Sidney.

To Robert S. Lanier

Marietta, Ga, Aug. 19th 1871

My Dear Father:

We have just recd yrs. announcing arrival of Cliff & Willie, & Sissa, and their intention to meet us, at the Kimball House, on Thursday, next. D. V. we will be there in time: and we anticipate a happy reunion.

Mary is still a little indisposed, tho' improving. I believe I am also geting a little better. The children are in good condition, tho' Sidney's teeth (coming) make him grin a little occasionally.

I wrote Sissa at the Springs: suppose she left about the time my letter got there.

I suppose the Supreme Ct., from present appearances, will likely reach our cases either towards the last of next week or early the week after. What time will Uncle C. return?

Was anxious to hear if there were any further developments in the matter of our R. R. appointment. I suppose not, as yr. letters make no mention of it.

A letter from Mr. Day this morning informs us that he has improved. He was about to leave Saratoga for Chicago and Toledo, near which latter place he has some land to look after.

No news. Weather pleasant. Mary joins me in many kisses for all of you: and we impatiently await our meeting.

Yr. Loving

Sidney

---

[37] The reference is to a letter that has not survived.

To Robert S. Lanier

Marietta, Ga, Aug. 28th 1871.

My Dear Father:

We all arrived safely at our pleasant quarters on Friday night, having witnessed the ball at the Kimball House for a half hour. I have rested somewhat since returning, but am not yet entirely recovered from the effects of my stroll with you & Clifford. Mary is pretty well: and the children in their usual fine condition.

We have had steady rains since Friday: being part of the storm which appears to have prevailed with you and below. Today, however, the sun is out, and I hope we shall have clear weather.

We are distressed at the report of yellow fever in Charleston, and have great fear that the wet season will render other places liable to be infected.

Can you not arrange to come and spend a day with us, here, on yr. way to Robinson? I should so like to see you, and have a quiet talk with you: and I think you would enjoy it. Now that Uncle C. is at home (for I suppose he arrived according to appointment), a day or two more or less cannot be in the way. May joins me very heartily in this request, and sends her love and a kiss by way of underscoring the same.

I send the numbers of our cases in Supreme Ct, remembering that you did not take them.

Swift, H. & Co. .	No. 5
Nutting et. al. vs. Boordman & c.	" 8
O. F. Adams.	" 10
Gertrude Woolfolk	" 13

The *first* case on our Circuit, (the Mercer College Case) will not be argued, having been settled, you remember? So that there are but three cases before our first one. Uncle C. had better come, therefore, at least by Tuesday ev'g train. If he does, please telegraph me the fact and I will send the briefs to him, at Atlanta.

We hope to see you very soon: meantime, dear Father, I am

Yr. Loving

Sidney.

To Virginia Hankins

Marietta, Ga, Aug. 28th 1871.

Yr. letter is come, dear Friend, and I thank you for making me know that my poor unproductive friendship, – wh. has never presented you with anything save that earnest constancy in whose steadfastness I repose as much confidence as in my own immortality – is remembered with pleasure by you.

This same friendship of mine is always like a poet struck dumb, or like a lame musician, or like an armless painter; burning with a heartfull of sweetness, yet forever debarred of expressing that, in visible sign. The word, the tone, the color; the poem, the tune, the picture; – of this friendship have yet to be uttered, played and painted.

But I have a happy hope that what friendship demands almost as eagerly – the sight of its friend – will be mine in some weeks more. Towards the last ten days of September I think to start North; and will go by your Castle to rest me once more within the good old walls that have so happily sheltered me, ere now.

I think I see you at this moment, standing beneath the jet weight of your hair, like a Caryatid under a black marble capital: there, in your porch, with the wonders of the summer fields and trees sailing down your soul like leaves and flowers down a river.

I travel alone; my wife remaining here with the children until the frost shall allow them to return to Macon.

I long for the pressure of your hand. I have no friend at all like you; nor, indeed, in changéd sense, have you any   like

Me.

To Charles Day

Marietta, Ga, Sep. 8th 1871.

My Dear Father:

I have waited a day or two before answering your letter, in order that I might arrive at some definite conclusion in regard to my departure for New York; so that I might answer your inquiry exactly.

But circumstances which I cannot control render it impossible

for me to say, within some days, what time I shall leave.
I expect to get off *about* the 15th of this month: but it is quite
likely, – in view of some collections which I have to make first –
that I may be delayed a week beyond that time.

Although I should be delighted to meet you in N. Y., yet,
in view of this uncertainty, and of the fact that perhaps a little
cotton will be coming into Macon by that time, I think you had
best not depend on me, since my movements will be controlled
by those of others, in some measure.

I shall miss you greatly in N. Y: for, during the first month,
at least, of my stay there, I propose to be very quiet. After
that, if I should gain the strength wh. I expect, I hope to be
able to go among the business men, and do something towards
increasing our firm connections.

We have been appointed attorneys for the Macon & Western
R. R. Of course, we accepted: not feeling it right to decline so
good a position, tho' it might sometimes bring us in antagonism
to our sympathies with the M[acon] & B[runswick]. I hope
however that this will not occur, and that *that* " cruel war is
over."   Our Macon Circuit is just finished, at the Supreme
Court. We gained *every one* of our cases.

My father spent last Wednesday with us. He was on his way
to Montgomery (going *via* the Selma Rome & Dalton R. R.)
to bring back my Sister who has been spending some time in
M'g. They will return the same way: passing next Sunday with
us, here, and going to Atlanta on Monday morning, when we
expect to argue one of the offshoots of the Thatcher Case
before the U. S. District Court. It is the suit we brought in
favor of Thatcher & Co. vs. C. A. Sindall, to subject some $5000
of R. R. stock owned by S. If we succeed,– and we now think
we will – we will get the oldest judgment against S., and will
save at least *that much* of T. & Co.'s money.

It is rumored in Atlanta that some Northern capitalists have
invested largely in the Atlanta and Savannah R. R. and that it
will certainly be built, running *via* Monticello, from whence
two branches will diverge, one to Macon, and one to Milledge-
ville. The rumor seems to be well-founded.

Our boys continue hearty, and constitute a source of infinite
delight and amusement for us. Mary was not so well yesterday
and day before, but is up this morning and seems very bright.

As for me, I hardly know how I am. Altho considerably stronger than when I came here, I am yet quite incapable of any physical exertion. I have no cough: and, as long as I keep perfectly still, feel as if I was in excellent health. A walk of a half-mile, however, wearies me beyond measure. I have strong hope that Dr. Marcy can put me on my legs again, in a month.

Mary sends you many kisses. She was intending to write you this morning, but bids me say that, as I am writing, she will wait a day or two.

We have pleasant weather: tho' I observe they have had a gale at Macon, and wash-up, five miles below, on the Central R. R.

We have nothing late from Harry. At last accounts, he was very well.

Your. aff.

Sidney L.

To Paul H. Hayne [38]

Marietta, Ga, Sep. 13th 1871

My Dear Mr. Hayne:

Yr. letter is received, and I thank you very heartily for the frankness with wh. you speak therein. I shall remember yr. prescription, if the means I'm about to try shd. fail. Truly, it is a somewhat desperate alternative; but desperate

---

[38] Previously published, *Letters* (New York, 1899), pp. 234-235. Two letters written by Lanier to P. H. Hayne in the late summer of 1871 have not been located, but Hayne's replies indicate the nature of their contents. On Aug. 31, answering Lanier's lost letter of Aug. 28, he wrote: " But *mon ami,* the tone of your communication distresses, and a little alarms me. It seems as if under the surface of your careless *badinage,* I am forced to recognize the presence of *pain,* if not of absolute or dangerous illness. Be frank with me; tell me the *whole truth.* Are you threatened, or are you already burdened with the Night-mare, Consumption? and if the *latter* be the case, how far has the disease progressed? . . . I can well understand that in regard to every department of Art, you are now *hors de combat.*"

Then on Sept. 8 Hayne thanked Lanier for a " long and interesting letter," also lost: " The details of your sickness I have read with great attention, and *frankly,* my dear fellow, I'm sorry to see that things are worse than I expected. Not that you ought to be discouraged; for Consumption is not a cureless disease, & moreover, it is certain that, as yet, you cannot be properly said to have consumption.

" Still, all your symptoms point to great feebleness of the lungs; & the

emergencies always present such, and I am not one of those who wd. shirk the situation, and die dilly-dallying.

Yr. treatment of the Macrobian Bow [39] is vigorous, and full of dramatic *verve*. Tis a fearful tale, beautifully told: like a terrible narration issuing from the red lips of a dainty woman. The utter coolness of the cruelty is brought out with great clearness; and the stroke of pain goes to the heart of a reader, straight as Cambyses' arrow to the heart of the page. The accessories, too, – of the " hot, wan morning," the slumbering wave, the stirless tree – all these give a kind of heartlessness-of-atmosphere to the whole scene that frames it perfectly.

I find nothing to suggest, to help the piece; and have made only a few small verbal and *punctuational* corrections, indicated with a ∧.

I will be obliged if you will forward the letters of intro-duction to me, " Care of Winslow & Lanier " 29 Pine St. New York," as I shall probably leave before they could reach me here.

It gives me great encouragement that you think I might succeed in the literary life: [40] – for I take it that you are in earnest in saying so, believing that you love Art with too genuine affection to trifle with her by bringing to her service, through mere politeness, an unworthy worker.

I enclose yr. Ms. Where will you print the piece? Let me know, so that I may see it when published.

If I can do anything of service to you, in the way of *small* corrections of Ms. (at wh. I'm said to be very keen-eyed – a

---

muscular & nervous disorganization you mention, is significant & serious enough. Then, your *average* weight being near a hundred & fifty pounds, you only weigh a hundred & *twenty two*, at present. . . . WHAT should be done in view of these considerations? " Hayne then proceeded to tell Lanier how, at the advice of an eccentric English doctor, he had cured himself of consumption years ago by taking regular doses of morphine.

[39] " Cambyses and the Macrobian Bow," a poem by Hayne, sent in his letter of Aug. 31, 1871.

[40] In his letter of Sept. 8, 1871, Hayne had said: " Well may you refer mournfully to Literature, above all, to Poetry, as the means of gaining one's bread! Bitterly myself do I feel the degradation, when *forced* to manufacture verses for the *Market*. . . .

" As regards *yourself*, I *can't* help believing that if *circumstances* DRIVE you into *Literature, as a profession,* you will *unequivocally* succeed; & I could almost find it in my soul to rejoice if you *had* to become an author. ' *Tis thy vocation, Lucius!* ' "

small hunter for small game, you know) do not hesitate to call on me.

Yr. Friend

Sidney Lanier

To Mary Day Lanier [41]

Astor House, N. Y.
Sep. 21st 1871

Encore, Ma Mie, Je suis á Babylon.

I had a charming journey, in point of weather, and accommodations generally, and the two days of enforced stillness rested me inexpressibly. What I had been doing to be tired, – man were but a patched fool if he should go about to tell: notheless tired I seemed to be, and my forty eight hours of still-sitting was wondrous grateful.

I find the weather here exceedingly cold; indeed it seems *bitter* cold to me, coming out of our warm spell at Marietta. But it does brace one so! Already I begin to feel as if I had some marrow in my bones, and some spring in my muscles.

And I missed your father by just one day! This was a sore disappointment to me. But I suppose he ought to be at home, as the cotton begins to come in. Do give my love to him, and tell him that I came to the Astor House to meet him.

I shall move up town tomorrow: tho' I don't exactly know where.[42] Until I write you my address, you can reach me, " care of Winslow & Lanier 27 & 29 Pine St. N. Y."

I met Salem today. He seems wondrously improved by his marriage,[43] and I doubt not he will become a civilized being, as time rolls on. I am to dine with them tomorrow. He and his wife are keeping house, at the place where I staid with them last year.

[41] Lanier left Marietta Sept. 18 and arrived in New York Sept. 20. His wife returned to Macon shortly thereafter.

[42] In a letter to his brother Clifford on Sept. 23, 1871 (here omitted), Lanier gave his address as: Westmoreland Hotel, 17th St. and 4th Ave.

[43] Salem Dutcher was married to Albina Victoria Dortic. (A note by Mary Day Lanier in the Henry W. Lanier Collection, Johns Hopkins University, says that she was a widow named Mrs. de L'Aigle.)

I am just going out to Theo. Thomas'. There are only two more nights before he closes for the season, and I cannot resist the temptation to drink a little of this Wine-of-Heaven, for my soul is thirsty. Come, Sweet: go thou with me: I feel thine arm, thy hand, thy heart, come on.

I send love and kisses to Father & Sissa whom thou wilt see ere this reaches thee.

I am thy loyal

Husband.

To Mary Day Lanier

[New York? Sept. 23, 1871?] [44]

Dear Comrade, Sweet Comrade, I am all one longing to look into thine eyes, and there will be no satisfaction in my heart nor quietness in my soul until I have again thy hand in mine.

Rememberest thou the men in " Myrza," how presently the only thing wanting was that they wanted nothing more: and how God gave one of them the woman: and how this one, happy with his Beloved for a few hours, suddenly bursts into tears remembering that he must die and leave her, sometime?

That is like me and thee: before God gave thee to me, life was very full, and yet, wanting thee, was wholly empty: and, then when thou camest, straightway come the terrible necessities wh. carry me away from thee, wh. put long dismal leagues betwixt me and the light of thine heart wh. is my sole light in which I can flourish.

When I look back, and see how unutterably good thou hast been to all my sick-man's-whims this long time, – Ah, Friend, how fair and how winning-gentle thou seemest! And yet thou, too, wert struggling with the vile down-dragging of the disease-devil. So: it is well that I go away from thee, for a little. Withdraweth not the painter a little way from his picture, that he may fully take the beauty thereof? And art thou not my one picture, to make my life a worthy one if haply I may put some small touch of completeness to thee?

[44] Conjectural dating from the accompanying envelope.

I pray thee that thou love me very fervently, for I am truest and devoutest worshipper of

Thine.

Having written Father by this mail what Dr Marcy says, and it being just what he said before, – viz, no softening nor tubercle, but obstruction wh. can be relieved – I say no more now.[45] Put thine arms about my two men, and embrace them for their father and thine

Husband

To Mary Day Lanier

N. Y. Sept. 26th, 1871

Thou art the prettiest soul in the world !   For this, thy letter, wh. I rec^d today,[46] declareth it to me, in sweetest and clearest fashion. This is the noblest letter, as a mere work of art and also as the indicative outcome of a heart, that ever I read from woman's pen. Its daintiness, its womanliness, its girlishness, its wifeliness, its motherliness, its perfect culture, its indescribable mingled perfume of gentleness, of love and of deep understanding, – ah, my pretty Comrade, where is another that can put all these things in one letter, – and do it unconsciously, withal – beside thee?

If I had never seen thee, nor aught else of thine, this letter wd. have put me madly in love with thee.

And now, if I tell thee to write me some more like this, – then thou wilt get *conscious* and wilt not be able, n'est ce pas? Perhaps I shd. not have praised thee this time : but my heart,– wh., O my Darling, is so full, so full of thee, today – wd. not let me hold my tongue. ————————

[45] Lanier's letter to his father has not survived. But in a letter of the same date, Sept. 23, 1871, to his brother Clifford (here omitted), he said: " Dr. Marcy has examined my lungs, and gives me pretty much the same account of them that he gave last year. He thinks there has yet been no softening of the lung, and that no tubercle has formed: but says the cells are greatly obstructed, and that the obstructing matter must be at once removed by medicine. He is confident of being able to do this, and I am taking his prescriptions regularly."

[46] Mary Day Lanier's letter of Sept. 20, 1871, to which the present letter is a detailed answer.

How well do I know those *petites* desperations, such as drove
thee to take thy long walk ! Dost thou not divine wherefrom
they arise? It is from *too much restraint* wrongly put (by
poverty or manifold circumstance) upon a nature like thine,
wh. feeling its own desire for the sweet and the good, and
perfectly confident that it could use liberty well and rightly
and healthfully, resents the needless constraint enforced upon
it and sometimes breaks into — having its own will, at what
may, prove a desperate expense. Nevertheless, I am clear that
it is good at such times that *thou* should'st have thy desire, and
indulge thyself: it is good, it is right, and I uphold thee heartily,
and wd. have upheld thee in my heart (even if my tongue had
scolded thee) altho' thou mightst have suffered from thy walk.

Well, if Mrs. Smith [47] hath been made able to walk a mile, then
thou canst be made able to do it: and, thou *shalt* be made able.
I wish thee to correspond with her in detail, and find if the
treatment would likely affect thee as her: then write me, and
I swear by my manhood thou shalt be given the means to try
it. ————
It takes some apprehension from my mind to know that thy
good father will be with thee, and will likely accompany thee
to Macon. ————
My fine Charles ! If thy father's arms were but strong as thy
father's heart, thou shouldst be in them, now and always ! ——
Felon that I am, I did steal thy tooth-brush, and have used
the same, wondering much at a certain dainty flavor wh. I
detected therein, and wh. was not wont to hang about mine
own . ————
I am doing well. I commence the lifting-cure tomorrow.
The Dr. wd. not let me, sooner, wishing, he said, to get me
under the influence of his medicines first. ————
I go, presently, to dine with Charles Lanier at Delmonico's.
His family is in the country still: Mr. Lanier Sr. is abroad, —
in Switzerland, I think, for his health. — Thou shalt be third
at our table, Sweet: and from the Chablis to the Champagne
I shall dream of naught but thee —

[47] In her letter of Sept. 20, Mary Day Lanier had said: " I enclose my news
from . . . Mrs. Smith "—probably their Macon friend, Mrs. Cosby Smith.

I send kisses to Sissa and to Eddie, and to Father, wh. thou shalt deliver, for indeed they are

Thine.

To Virginia Hankins

New York, Sep. 27/71

For no man's-reason, Dear, Friendly Heart, but purely for a true God's-reason, – namely because my health imperatively demanded that I get to this place at the earliest possible moment – did I come past the spot where you work, without running across to press your hand. To say that this was a bitter disappointment to me — — is to say nothing, for I cannot tell you with what eager desire I had looked forward to seeing you.

But if all go well, – and all *is* going well – I shall fill this gap in my life before long.

I hope to leave here towards the last week of October: and then, – with stronger frame, and happily with a day or two more to spend *chez vous* than I wd. have had if I had stopped as at first proposed, – I shall come, O sweet *Châtelaine,* and beg that yr. portcullis may be arranged for my entrance.

Meantime, waft me some little flower-petal of a letter over to this wicked Babylon, so that peradventure, what with the pure and saintly beauty of yr. thought, my soul may not grow faint in the midst of this fierce delirium, this mad *can-can* which is here daily and nightly danced by two strange partners, two antipodes, Luxury and Wretchedness, each of whom makes love in his dance to the other, the first *un*consciously, the last full consciously.

I am convinced that there are but three things wh. I like in N. Y. One is the *beef,* wh. is full of a certain building-up richness that advances my physical interests mightily; another is the fall sunshine, which is simply unattainable elsewhere on this continent in like glory and bracing quality: and last is the skill, in all arts, trades, professions and guilds, wh. here reaches its highest perfection because it here finds its best market and amplest field.

How keenly I wd. like to pace with you down Broadway (wh. I look out upon from my window while I write), this

glorious morning! Never was folly more gloriously pranked. –
But I would still more keenly like to stroll with you down one
of yr. sweet lanes to the mill; until I do wh., I am yr. waiting

Friend.

To Mary Day Lanier [48]

N. Y. [Sept.] 28th 1871.

I am just come from St Paul's Church, where I went at Eleven,
this morning, by invitation of Mr. John Cornell, to hear some
music composed by him for the organ and *Trombone*: not the
old slide-in-and-out trombone, but a sort of baritone Cornet-à-
pistons, of rare mellow yet majestic tone. This was played by
one of Theo. Thomas' Orchestra. The pieces were, a Funeral
March, a Religious Air, and a Concert Piece. Hadst thou been
with me, to hear these horn-tones, so pure, so noble, so full of
confident repose, striking forth the melody in midst of the
thousand-fold modulations (in which Cornell always runs riot),
like a calm manhood asserting itself through a multitude of
distractions and discouragements and miseries of life; – hadst
thou been there, then how fair and how happy had been my day!

For I mostly have great pain when music, or any beauty,
comes past my way: and thou art not by. Perhaps this is because
Music takes us out of prison: and I do not like to leave prison
unless thou goest also.

For thou art my beloved Sweet, in whose smile my life
cometh to life, even as a flower under water gleameth only
when the sun-ray striketh down thereon.

The Dr. saith I am improving and I agree with him. He
thinketh it an encouraging sign that I am not so ill this year
as last, and giveth me hope of entire cure. The lifting-cure
goeth on apace, and I am becoming quite reconciled to cream,
insomuch that I smile a greasy smile over the deglutition thereof.

---

[48] Previously published, *Scribner's*, XXV, 624 (May, 1899); reprinted, *Letters*
(New York, 1899), pp. 70-71. Cornell had played the organ for Lanier two
years before (see Lanier's letter to his wife, May 17, 1869).

I am greatly anxious to know that thou and the children are safely arrived. I will surely hear, tomorrow.

My love and kisses to all. I wrote my father yesterday. Trouble not thyself to write to   Thine.

To Mary Day Lanier

[New York,] Sep. 29th, 1871.

At last, Good-Heart, do I know, by thy note enclosed in thy father's letter, that thou and my two young men were safely gotten home. Yet, that mine open-faced gray-eyed first-born is sick, giveth me grief, and I wait with much impatience to know that he hath won back his sturdiness. Smileth my Sidney as grandly as erst, upon all the ills of life? This boy fairly breaketh down my heart when I think of him, so that my soul goeth wandering afar off into great meditations upon where he is come from, and whither goeth he, and what will he finally be.

I have made an arrangement with Salem to board at his house, where I shall be much more comfortable than at this place, and at about half the price. I move there tomorrow. Therefore when thou writest in future, address me there, viz, at No. 226, E. 49th St.

I improve apace. I think I must have walked a couple of miles yesterday, and was not overfatigued. My lungs begin to feel better and freer from obstruction, and all my system seems to be working more smoothly.

By this time the regular flow of my daily letters must have begun to reach thee, and thine apprehensions whereof thou spokest to thy father have been allayed.

I greatly hope that Mrs. Watt will come hither, and see me. Poor Weary Heart! How many fearful years it hath groaned and travailed beneath the inevitable woe that could not be spoken! Here she cd. repose, and I wd. make love to her all the day long.

Kiss my father & sister for me: also thank thy father for his letter to me, wh. I will answer speedily. I have a letter from

Hal, who saith Janie is in Macon. My love to her. And Oh, to thee, My Darling, My Darling, the perfect love of

Thine Husband.

To Mary Day Lanier

[New York,] Oct. 1st [1871]

at

226 E. 49 St.

———————

Here, My sweet Lady, have I been sitting some long hours, in my high room at Salem's, full in the noble sunshine that streameth in through my window, lazily reading at the "Woman Column" of the N. Y. World, and wondering if such a Column *could* be printed in a great paper of Society if there were many women in the world like thee. And this proveth, by logic intellectual, what my heart hath long known confidently through perfect love-logic, that there is none other in the world so rare-womanly, so gentle-minded, so thoroughly endowed with clear and keen intuitions of the need and nature of a man, so deep-motherly, so enchanting-girlish, so tempting-waisted to a strong and honorable arm, so dainty and so warm-lipped to the kiss of a true lawful husband, so quick-responsive to man's Art and God's Nature, so high of taste, so accurate of perception, so honest of enjoyment, – as thou art.

I would thou mights't know with what serene yet high-mounting jubilation I – calm in the possession of thee and in the unreserved worship of thee – look forth upon all these women that I see here. He that walketh the great Broad highway of this city, seeth many thousands of thy sisters in ten days, of high and low degree. In all these faces, which I have glanced into with curious interest, I have not seen a *thee,* at all, nor anything nearer thee than the space betwixt heaven and earth. Thou art my Very One: and I well know that while God leaveth me thee, Comrade, storm and battle of life have no permanent power upon me.

I have put in some slips, excerpted with my dull knife-blade, that may bring to thy face the smile wh. I most love.

———————

Make my daily greeting to my father and thine, and my Sissa and Eddie, and my men, for

Thine Husband.

To Mary Day Lanier

[New York,] Oct. 2ᵈ 1871

My window, Dear Heart, commandeth insight into sundry of the back-rooms appertaining to the houses in the next square: whereby, yesterday, amidst many domestic scenes whereof I was unwilling spectator, one did fairly bring all my heart into mine eyes. This was the arraying of a small man, nigh the size of my smaller man, in a clean clout about his wee loins: and as the mannikin lay all a-sprawl on the bed thrusting his heels on high with much gyration of toes and general pedal gesticulation, what time the good *Mutter*,– for they are all Germans over there – smilingly swathed him in a fa[ir] white napkin, with many a playful pat upon those portions of his wee body wh. have from of old been set apart as the residence and seat of honor,– then I yearned for my fine Schafchen, with great yearning, wh. wd. not be satisfied.

And for thee, Mutterchen, Thou rare Mate, that hast given loveliness to my children in giving love to me, – for thee my heart cried with an anguish of separation that could not utter itself.

Day by day, I catalogue anew thy distinct virtues, one by one, and then rearrange them in groups about my heart, as rare flowers set about a room, blushing and breathing fragrance and trembling with tender and holy dews of motherhood and wifehood.

Translating the hours into memories of thy separate lovelinesses;– so I make them tolerable.

As for ˣ   ˣ   ˣ   ˣ   ˣ   ˣ   ˣ   ˣ   ˣ [49]
Oh! Ah ˎ *!* Ugh !!! to which add the vowels, he, he, hi-yi, and y = why? – For she is a plaything that *hath been* pretty,

---

[49] The deleted portions in the MS of this letter apparently refer to an approaching wedding in Macon.

but alas, will ne'er be so again, and when he is in his prime,
then will she be in her wrinkles drinking candle and mumbling
mush.

Wherewith, and with my kiss for Sissa and Father, I say only
further that I am, thank God!

Thine Husband.

To ROBERT S. LANIER

N. Y. Oct. 4th 1871.
at 226 E. 49th St.

My Dear Father,

I was very glad to get yr. letter yesterday, containing check for $100,[50] and bringing me news of you all, wh–
I had not had for some time.

It is gratifying to learn that business continues good. O, if
I could only be at work! This is my daily cry.

I will endeavor to attend to the matters desired by Hubbell.
Meantime, please get a blank *Commission,* (for Interrogatories)
and send it on to me; as that is one of the things he asks for.

When you get the State fee, will you please hand Mary
$25.00:– for some winter preparations wh. she will need?

Mr. Hayne has sent me some valuable letters of introduction
to prominent literary men, here: [51] and I am impatient to get
well enough to go about freely, so that I may avail myself of
them.

I have written Aunt Jane, begging her to come here, and rest,
after the many scenes of grief through which she has passed.[52]

---

[50] That Clifford Lanier also contributed to his brother's support during these
periods of illness is evidenced by a passage in Lanier's letter to him of Sept. 23,
1871 (here omitted): " Can you lend me another hundred? If anything should
happen to me, Mary will see that this and the other sums wh. I owe you will
be repaid: and if *nothing* happens to me, – it *will* be repaid, Dear Brother."

[51] Hayne had sent letters of introduction addressed to R. H. Stoddard and
J. R. Thompson, with his letter of Sept. 27. Later, on Oct. 16, he sent a letter
to O. B. Bunce, editor of *Appleton's Magazine.* Only the one to Stoddard seems
to have been presented (see Lanier to his wife, Nov. 8, and note 76, below).

[52] Abram Watt had died suddenly. Mary Day Lanier wrote her husband,
Oct. 3, that by his will he left " *all* to Bob Watt– except Aunty's separate estate."
The will is referred to in later letters by Lanier.

Charles Lanier has been very kind to me. Mr. J. F. D. will sail for America on the 12th *inst.*

I progress well.[53] Dr Marcy has invited me to go with him to his Country-place at Orange, N. J. wh. I will probably do, on Saturday next, spending Sunday there.

My love & kisses to Sissa & Eddie. I write Mamie every day: & so send no messages. Love to Uncle C. also.

Yr. Loving

Sidney.

To Mary Day Lanier

226 E. 49th St. [New York]

Oct. 7th 1871.

This " Charley's cold very bad " of thine of Oct. 3rd giveth me great distress, for I had hoped he was recovered, and I fear these long colds beyond measure. What remedies art thou administering? If he have a cough, I prithee give him Drosera, faithfully. Thou wilt also benefit him if thou wilt him caused him be rubbed with thy hair-glove at night when he is put to bed and in the morning when he is dressed: let him be scrubbed therewith till he is in a fine glow from head to foot. This is very good to prevent that tendency towards congestion of the lung, blood-vessels, which cometh with long colds: which it doth by forcing the blood outward to the surface-vessels. Write me of his progress.

I had not heard of Dr. Bonnel's death, until day before yesterday when I saw a telegram in some paper announcing that one Dr. O. L. Smith had been elected Prest of We. Female College, *vice* Dr. Bonnell, decd.[54] 'Tis a sad blow to the

---

[53] In a letter to his wife, Oct. 5, 1871 (here omitted), Lanier wrote: " The Dr. thinketh my condition better than at this time last year, but I have not asked him how long it will require for me to be cured this time. I have commenced at the Lifting-Cure with about the same weight that I used last year, tho' they are carrying me forward a little faster than then, having increased the weight at the rate of 10 pounds per day, instead of five as then. I now lift 115, tomorrow 120."

[54] Dr. Bonnell, President of Wesleyan Female College, had died Sept. 30 of heart disease (see Mary Day Lanier's letter of Oct. 3, 1871). He was succeeded by Prof. O. L. Smith.

College: for he was worth all the other slow brethren that have hung upon the neck of the institution for so long.

Nor had I heard at all of the disposition of Mr. Watt's property, whereto thou referrest. I suppose it is well enough. I think Bob hath four sisters and a mother whom he hath been supporting out of his slender earnings.[55]

I thank thee for thy flowers, whose dainty balms are floating now about my room, as it were emanations from thee, tired with so long wandering. Sweet languid Essences, it is but four days since ye kissed the fingers of my Love: it is four Æons since I did !

I do well. Write me precisely what sort of shoes thou desirest.

And now God keep thee, and all mine, prayeth thine

Husband.

To Mary Day Lanier

[New York,] Oct. 9th 1871.

Thine of 4th *ult.* is just come, Comrade, and I thank thee for the fair and womanly words that stir my heart as no other words in this world can. Cometh also, today, a letter from father and one from Mr. Hayne, wh. I found at Westmoreland Hotel, where I call daily for letters.

Thine account of my youngest man beginning to fare forth alone upon his little legs giveth me great delight. God prosper all his steps, and keep his walks straight and his port upright.

I have employed some moments when I was forced to be idle, in reading the second of the "Three Guardsmen" series of Dumas, called "Twenty Years After." Here beginneth the noble affection of Athos – Comte De La Fère – for his young son Viscounte De Bragelonne. Between these two are some tenderest scenes of father-and-son love I have ever read. How my heart beats over them with glowing sympathy, transferring each fatherly thought and act of fine Comte De La Fère to

---

[55] See note 52, above. Bob Watt was apparently a nephew of Abram P. Watt. The will caused considerable bitterness on the part of Lanier's Aunt Jane and some strong family feeling (see Mary Day Lanier's letter to her husband, Oct. 4, 1871).

myself, and recognising each stroke of Dumas' noble delineation in mine own heart ! Rememberest thou the history of Bragelonne's entrance into life ? 'Tis a marvellous piece of Frenchiness. I cannot tell it in a letter. Thou shalt have the book to read it. I have tried to find the first of this series; but could not do so.

I wrote to Aunt Jane shortly after my arrival here, but have yet no reply. Poor heart ! The truth in a nut-shell about the matter of the Will seems to me this: 1st I do not see how she could have expected anything else: 2dly nor do I see how she *could* have comported herself in such a way as to *authorize* her to expect anything else,– that being simply beyond human ability under the circumstances.

Meantime thou art my Pretty-Sweet, and I love thee beyond all earthly measures and standards, and am thy true and faithful

Husband.

To Mary Day Lanier

[New York,] Oct. 12th 1871.

There is nothing, dear Wife, that giveth me keener pleasure than to read of the Count De La Fère, the sweet brave gentleman, the valiant knight, the courteous enemy, the trusting-hearted friend, the father with the soul of a mother, the *man,* who having commited a crime repenteth thereof in secret blood and tears which only display themselves to the outer world in an infinitely-tender gravity of demeanor.

This is a noble creation, and the soul that conceived it could not have been despicable.

Wd. not the Count De La Fère ravish thy heart, if thou knewst him?

Tell my hunter of bears how papa went to the Park t'other day, and saw eight or ten bears, – a great grisly, with claws longer than thy forefinger: – and a knot of black bears, big woolly fellows, all tumbled up together, being a very interesting family, composed of mother and father and a lot of baby-bears. Also reveal to him that papa saw three enormous ostriches, enclosed in a wire-fence on the lawn: each being a bird whose head, as we stood side by side, was some two feet higher than mine, and whose legs wd. almost have fitted my pantaloons!

Apprise him further of a troop of deer, elk and antelopes wh. papa also descried, making free of the vast lawns in all manner of gambols and stately strolls: also a *black* swan in a lake: also a multitude of monkeys who sat presenting each other's tails to each other's ears, – or eyes, or mouth, as the case might be – : also a pheasant, with reddish-gold and green-silver feathers that made him show like a sunset turned into a fowl.

And then, My Beloved, My Niñita, My Child, inform thyself that thou art the Sweetest Sweet and the heartsomest Heart and the loveliest Love in all this world to thine adoring

Husband.

To Mary Day Lanier

[New York,] Oct. 13th 1871.

But today, My Maydioléna, My Maydiva, My Mariovuola, the Signor Sun is come forth in his glory, the ferocious wind that howled all night is gone to wail in some other world, the heavens are in a broad and tranquil repose of perfect trans-parent-heartedness, the earth drieth her poor face that was seamed with storms of tears, the sparrows pursue their small avocations with confidence, the air hath a tense and steely spring in it, the drawing of breath is pleasure and mere life is luxury.

But, O Maymettina, thou knowest what Moses saith Eden was, ere God put a true wife *therein*: and what Myrza saith the world was, ere God sent thither the Woman: – therefore, dear Mariañina, thou knowest what the heart of thy poor lover hath been, today, not beating near thy heart.

Here cometh a letter today: from Aunt Janie, writ at Balti-more, wh. ordereth me to look for her in a day or two, and to change my quarters to the Grand Central Hotel as soon as she shall telegraph me, wh. she will do just before departing. This last I do not, until I see her: when perhaps I may, – as she

insists upon bearing the expense of the difference betwixt that
and this. ——————————

As soon as thou wrotest me of thy desire to teach for thy
Church, I replied to thee, the same day, consenting.[56] Thou
shouldst have had my reply ere now.

Ginna's address is " Virginia W. Hankins,
Bacon's Castle
Surrey County
Va."

Art writing to her? I am very glad, if so.

I have gained some four pounds of flesh since I came to
N. Y., and I think I am now making a fair start for 140.

Embrace my dear ones, Father, Sissa and all, for me, and
forget not thy

Husband.

Thou failest to receive my letters. I write thee every day, precisely at the same hour, and mail promptly. Thou shouldst
have a letter from me each morning regularly.

S.

To Mary Day Lanier

[New York,] Oct. 14th 1871.

It is five O'clock, Nina, and Herr Schlangenputz (–it *might* be
his name–) who liveth opposite me and whose back-window
looketh into *my* backwindow, is just come home for his dinner.
Schlangenputz hath a young wife, – she looketh at this distance to be not more than twenty,– there, du Himmel, she hath
clasped her good arms around Schlangenputz' neck, her lips
are glued to his – Schlangenputz' – lips, they kiss, they squeeze,
they linger, they kiss again, they gaze thrillingly each into
t'other's eye, they fall kissing again in good hearty German
fashion, until now finally Frau Schlangenputz is out of breath

---

[56] Mary Day Lanier had written on Sept. 30 to ask her husband's permission
to give music lessons—a single pupil—to raise money for her church. In a letter
to her on Oct. 5 (here omitted) Lanier had replied: " After some struggle, wh.
I care not to recount to thee, I say yes, quite cheerfully."

and sinketh upon the sofa, whereupon Schlangenputz removeth his spectacles and his coat and goeth to the washstand to wash his – Schlangenputz' – face for dinner.

But O, Niñita! where are thine arms, that they are not about *my* neck; and thy lips, that I go unblessed with kisses through many days !

Where thou art: – that is my Beautiful Place, My Home.

I have no news to tell thee. I long to hear that thou hast received the prescription I wrote, for Charley's sore throat, and that he is better thereof: and also that thou art recovered from thy weariness whereof thou informeds't me.

Things do not go on well, here, as between the newly arrived [wife] [57] on one side, and the sisters three on t'other: wherefore rageth intestine war, and the household is to be broken up sometime soon, *i. e.* within a month or so, [Salem and his wife] going elsewhere to board, and the girls also seeking other quarters. Let this be very strictly *entre nous.*

My kisses for all that I love, especially for thee, since I am wholly thy

Lover.

I send thee some French Comic papers. Some of the wit is naughty, but I know thy heart, I !

S.

To Mary Day Lanier

N. Y. Oct. 17th 1871.

O Lili!

My heart and my arms are afire for thy heart and thine arms. This is as pure a fire as ever burnt, and hath within it a

---

[57] Certain words deleted from the MS have been restored in brackets by conjecture. Another reference to Salem Dutcher's marriage occurs in a mutilated letter from Lanier of Oct. 8 (here omitted). This is followed by the sentence: "A Bohemian, he was simply delightful: but now prim Decorum hath him on the hip, and (for only a mixed metaphor could do justice to the subject) he is like champagne whereof the sparkle hath departed,– flat. Some day he may come out of this:– so mote it be."

spiritual puissance that hath quelled many another smoky conflagration which hath blackened over my sky.

How dear thou art, True-Heart! How fair and fine thou art, thou pure Lady, thou Gentlewoman! How firmly thou supportest the fainting of my soul, pretty Comrade!

I would I might have naught claiming my hand save to sit and write love to thee for a month. But tonight I think my heart will surely break if I set thy sweetness before mine eyes any longer; therefore know that

"
————
"

————

————

at four this afternoon, I lying in bed wrapped in my customary doze wherewith I kill off a couple of hours daily after my lunch, came a knock upon my door, followed by the announcement that a lady wished to speak to me. Dreaming that my distinguished personal appearance – for the girls here declare that I am grown fearfully handsome in the last two weeks – had driven some poor maiden to desperate means, and bracing my soul with high resolution to be strong, – I descended, after a hasty yet somewhat elaborate toilet, and found in the parlor – Aunt Jane. She had written me from Baltimore that she wd. spend some days there, and wd. telegraph me when she started for N. Y.: but, with her usual consistency, didn't telegraph. She had come on, taken a cab from the ferry, driven to the Westmoreland Hotel, (where I wasn't) found out my address there by a lucky accident, and posted on here. I entered her *fiacre,* we drove to the Grand Central, I engaged apartments communicating, for her and myself, saw her safely in bed (for she was very tired with her long drive), and am just returned to my room at Dutchers, (9 P. M.) after having had a two hours' chase over N. Y. after Madame's baggage which had been entrusted to an Express-man and by him carried to the wrong hotel through mistake, whence, after displaying a wonderful amount of skill, address, and knowledge of the tricks of Babylon, I rescued it and carried it to my lady, – to the good Checchina! – in triumph. Here, then, I spend the night, and tomorrow morning I pack my luggage, and move.

Arrived here, I find thy two letters, of 13th and 14th *ult.,* stuck in the frame of my mirror.

Having just skimmed over the same, my mind cometh out of them with a confused notion that thou hast fourteen music-scholars, who have each badly inflamed tonsils, to cure which thou hast been giving Mr. Reese large doses of Drosera, and that meantime, Mammy hath been like to perish with famine in consequence of Gov. Bullock's failure to return to Georgia, though thou thinkest that the new parlor curtains together with my wedding-card plate (wh. by the way, thou needest *not* send, as I have had cards printed from another & better one) may enable thee to save up $300 towards our house &c &c [58]

I will endeavor to answer thy questions tomorrow, categorically. Meantime; I have gained just five and one-half pounds " for thee to love " – thou pretty-thoughted One! – in the last three weeks: and, although it is entirely impossible for Dr. Marcy to say when he will be ready to discharge me, still, by the middle of November the climate will be growing too severe for me, and I confidently expect to return to thee by the 15th of that month.

[58] Mary Day Lanier's long double letter of Oct. 13-14, 1871, was filled with a multitude of commissions and queries, most of which are answered in this and the following letter. Concerning her plan to teach a music pupil for the benefit of the church, she reported a recent visit from her rector, the Rev. Mr. Rees: " He . . . said he could offer me a half-dozen or more scholars immediately! and only wished that my strength and inclination *could* prompt me to take the charge of the remaining number for my own purposes. . . . how I did yearn to say ' I'll take them all! ' I have a real love for it, and such a desire *to be doing something to help.* Other women help by domestic labors and million stitches— by nursing their own children– &c. I can do none of this, I *could* do part of the other; and think of putting aside this year– $300.00 to help towards *our home!* "

In March, 1871, Lanier had bought a " lot and premises " on the east side of Orange St., between Bond St. and Georgia Ave. (See Deed Book W, 504-505, Bibb Co., Ga. Information through the courtesy of Mrs. Frank Jones, Clinton, Ga.) Evidence that he was accumulating a fund for building his own home appears in a later letter to his father, July 12, 1872 (omitted), asking that the $150 due him on salary from the firm be used to pay his " dues " to the Building and Loan Association.

By this thou must have received the prescription I sent for Charley, and I hope to hear good accounts of his throat therefrom.

Until tomorrow, then, – and until any other point in time, –

Thy

Lover

Thou mayst take as many music-scholars as thou desirest.

TO MARY DAY LANIER

[New York,] Oct. 18th 1871.

No, Geneviève, thou didst *not* give me a *shoe,* but only the last, wh. I have cherished up to this time; but my doubt was, whether thou saids't one pair of *slippers,* besides the kid gaiters. Make me out the list thou promisest, for I am a poor wittol at remembering things.

When you get Lilla's money, hand it to Father and tell him to get a check on N. Y. for $35.00: then send said check to me. Tell him to have it drawn payable to my order.[59]

As to Lucy's and Harriet's money &c, do not hesitate to ask, when thou needs't it. I wd. save thee the trouble: but, for two reasons, perhaps thou wert better ask, thyself: 1st because if I write, Father, who hath many things to think of, will forget, most likely: and 2d, I fear he wd. be pained to think thou w'ds't not apply save through me (thou knowst some men wd. be) and he regardeth thee his daughter, and hath been so good and tender with me, that I wd. not have him pained, even in so small a matter. And then, O Maida, if God will, it will not be for long, and I will try to recompense thee some day for this suffering thou undergoest on my account.

Do not hesitate, therefore, when thou desirest aught, to ask him. If he hath it, he will give it thee cheerfully.[60]

---

[59] In her letter of Oct. 13-14, Lanier's wife had asked him to make some purchases in New York for their friend Lilla Hazelhurst.

[60] In her letter of Oct. 13-14, Mary Day Lanier had written that she was reluctant to ask her father-in-law for the money she needed to pay Lucy, the nurse, and Harriet, the washerwoman.

I find I have said more about this than I intended. I had not thought of it, at all: and thou must not fancy I am blaming thee for asking through me: wh. is the right way, indeed.

I moved to the Grand Central this morning, and am writing this in Auntie's room, in front of a noble coal fire. Mr. Given is in town, and will dine with us here at six.

Auntie is improving, and I will talk to her of matters yonder, when I see that the time is ripe. Tis a delicate and rare diplomatic business.

I was going to write thy father this afternoon: but packing and moving this morning occupied my Lifting-Cure hours, and I must therefore go there now, ere it is too late.

Auntie, who lieth on the bed, (having eaten ice-cream, whereby she hath taken detriment in the region where compassion resideth) sendeth thee a hearty kiss.

My love to father & Sissa & Eddie, I so long to see them!

As for Thee, Yoland; – I were naught were I not thine

Husband.

To Mary Day Lanier

[New York,] Oct. 21st 1871.

Togliarnolina, Sweet, thy letter of 17th – part written 18th – is come, and thy pathetic appeal that thou might'st lay thy head on my breast and rest thee, together with thy measure of troubles wh. seemeth very full, – quite overcometh my heart so that I am fain abandon all and go back to thee, where I long to be, as God alone knoweth.

Yet a little while, Wife: then I will be at thy side, brimming with love and with loyal worship, whereof thou mayst drink forever, as thou wilt.

Meantime, I pray thee, do thine earnest best to smile thy spirits bright. For after all, what mattereth all? Thou hast the two very best things in the world: towit, the enthusiastic and ever-growing love of a man, who, however he may lack in all things else, yet is surely earnest and faithful: – and the love of God, who surely could never forget that dainty spirit wherewith He hath endowed thee, O thou exquisite Soul.

In thy distress: which I know is great, for do I not understand how thou must suffer, thou who are so fine-tuned and who yet art so environed with all manner of harsh circumstance against which, alas, God hath for a little time numbed mine arm? in thy distress, then, here be two bosoms for thy tired head, the Bosom of God and the bosom of thine husband. Go thou to Him, O Heart that I cherish, and renew thy strength: come thou also to me, O Rare-Sweet whom I worship, and renew thy store of power, thy consciousness of queenhood over me, thy sense of the dignity of thy State.

Pour thy troubles out, to me, without the fear that thou hast had. Time hath been when I was not, and could not be, thy comforter. But I have had a little hour for my thought to work freely: I have penetrated many problems, since I saw thee: I have had strength, I thank God, to pluck out certain eyes that have long offended me. As M. Victor Hugo hath well said, *J'ai grandi.* One of these offenses was, that I could never console thee, in thy time of grief: not that that my heart did not always bleed for thee more than I could utter, My God, no! – but because I was always filled with curses at mine inability to strike down the enemies that hurt thee straightway, so filled that I could dream of naught else, – which, as I now clearly perceive, was but another form of intense selfishness. But this is plucked out. Let me have, therefore, thy whole heart, whenever thou choosest, whether it be light or whether it be heavy: and: always, at such time, thou shalt find *my* heart light: for if thine is, mine *must* be so, and if thine is not, mine will still be so, dreaming that its worship can be of service to thee, My Comrade.

"

————

"

Thou could'st never conjecture where this is written, I am in the bar-room of this Hotel: on to'ther side the great room is the bar-counter, and on this, the writing-desks, newspapers &c. Auntie wishing to sleep, and there being no fire in my room, I have come down here to write. At this moment is a great clinking of glasses and burst of laughter whiskey-hoarse and grating, over-against me: but God is very quiet about it, and therefore I do not distress myself.

Thine account of my brave Charles filleth me with distress. Let me hear of his progress: but, when thou hast other things to do, trouble not thyself to write more than a simple bulletin of health.

I thank thee very heartily, that thou hast written to Ginna: for I know how she will delight in the dainty words that flow from thy pen as odors from a violet.

I will try to arrange thy commissions for Lilla, on Monday. Auntie hath been very sick all day, and I have been nursing her constantly. Should she not be well enough on Monday, I will endeavor to get Miss Julie Dutcher, – who has exquisite taste – to make the purchases. Failing with her on that day, I will get her to do the business as soon as possible, for I wd. not like to ask Saidee,[61] who is cumbered with household cares.

I wrote Sissa Yesterday. My love to all.

And now God breathe a troop of fair dreams into thy soul this night, crieth

Thine

Husband.

To Clifford A. Lanier

Grand Central Hotel, N. Y.
Oct. 24th 1871.

My Dear Clifford:

Yr. letter to Auntie informing her that it will be unnecessary for her to be present in accordance with the terms of the Citation, is recd.

She has been very sick, but is now steadily improving. I called in Dr. Bozeman, who has greatly relieved her. He says she can go out day after tomorrow.

I am progressing well: and shall return to Macon in a little more than two weeks. A frightful Dr.'s Bill admonishes me that I shall have difficulty in paying out: and if you can send me $50.00 without inconvenience, it will relieve me from some distress.

The Lifting-Cure has acted like a charm upon me, and

---

[61] Mary Day Lanier's cousin, the wife of Foster Higgins.

I breathe with a freedom which fills me with a delightful hope of future activity.

'Tis a Tantalus' cup, tho', to be here, in this way; for, for lack of means, I go not to hear any of the glorious music that goes on nightly, nor to see any of the noble presentations of Shakespeare now being given at Booth's Theatre.

Auntie joins me in love to all.

Your

Sidney.

To Mary Day Lanier [62]

[New York,] Oct. 24th 1871.

So: I understand.

And how utter sorrowful, and bitterly indignant thou must have been under *all*.

And how sweet thou wast, not to put it in words, in thy letter.

Well, well. I pray thee, Queen, have patience, yet a little while: have patience, in loving me: for, so help me God, thou shalt come out of all this trouble wh. shd. have no place in thy life. I swear, thou shalt be taken from out of it. Feed thy heart with this hope, if thou canst. It were better I say no more about it, now.

"

————

"

As for Lucy:— [63] it is the progress of things. Let her go:— and let us at least hope that we will get some other whom we will train, and make to love us with better, and less interested, love.

But oh, how this makes me long to be there, that I might take some of the work from thy tired arms! God speed these three weeks, (tho' not quite three, for I hope to see thee ere Nov. 14th) that must still divide me from thee.

[62] This letter is an answer to a lost letter from Mary Day Lanier; the references in the first few paragraphs are not clear.

[63] Mary Day Lanier's letter of Oct. 23 refers to some trouble with Mammy Lucy.

It is but two hours since I kissed a Mary Lanier and held the son of Sidney Lanier in mine arms ! – being the wife and son of my Uncle, of that ilk. They came over to see us this afternoon, and spent some hours. She has grown wonderfully bright and young : and was very cordial. I was asleep when she came: but she pushed through the door of my room, and came and embraced me in bed, and (having never seen me *en* beard before) vowed I was the perfect image of Uncle Sid. Her children are noble boys, and I made great friends of them in a few minutes.

Auntie is improving, and the Dr. says she may go out day after tomorrow. She is greatly taken with the idea of the Atlanta water-cure, of whose success she had heard from other persons, and thinks she would be very glad to join you there in the spring, fearing it wd. be too cold for both of you in the winter. I think much of this. To see thee rosy ! That wd. be Heaven.

I do sincerely hope that Miss Julie will succeed with the commissions tomorrow.

I am doing well. They are carrying me on by a somewhat different system at the Lifting-cure. They increase my weights more slowly: but make me lift eight times a day, instead of six as formerly. I think it works better. At any rate, it is giving me extraordinary sense of freedom and fullness in the lungs, wh. I enjoy with delight unspeakable, and which fills me with noble visions of the possibility of an active and useful career.

Thy good news of Charley's improvement gives me great pleasure, and I pray God he may regain his health entirely. It wd. break my heart to see " those noble legs " grow slim. I showed Aunt Molly his pictures, naked and clothed, this afternoon over wh. she had some little ecstasies.

"

"

And now, Iphigenia, who hast sacrificed thyself for me ! continue to love me very dearly, for I am so utterly a dreamer-upon-thee, that if thy love should faint then my Dream would fail: and this dream is my Life. Send me some love with thy good pen, me who am thy faithful

Lover.

To Mary Day Lanier

[New York, Oct. 28, 1871] [64]

Oct. 27th (or –8th, is it?) 1871.

O, Pretty, I have just been talking, for an hour steadily, with a bride! A thin-skinned, delicate-textured, blue-eyed, *petite* wife-of-three-days, with a thousand blushes a minute travelling over her face, sparkling, warm-hearted, an admirer of Tiger-Lilies,– she hath put me dead in love – – – – –with *thee!*

This morning, as I sat at breakfast with Auntie, came sauntering down the breakfast-room a face that was evidently endeavoring to look as sober as it could under the circumstances, – the circumstances being this pretty little wife just behind – and which I thought I had seen before. Upon ransacking my memory, I concluded it must be Northrop. So, I finished, went to his seat, and, after a curious stare, at my beard, he recognized me, whereat we had a hearty hand-shake. After dinner tonight, he asked me in the parlor, whence I am just come.

The world hath evidently prospered with Northrop; he is Editor of the Syracuse Courier, and seems to have become a man of substance in the land.

This afternoon I took the boys, Sterling and Russell,[65] to Central Park, to see the animals, and we had a great time among the bears and monkies. Russell, the younger of the two boys – has fallen so in love with me that he could hardly be persuaded to leave. Aunt Mollie says he has talked of nothing else but Cousin Sid since our first interview.

---

[64] Conjectural dating from the evidence of a preceding letter, dated Oct. 27, 1871 (here omitted). The couple described in the opening paragraphs are Milton H. Northrup and his wife. In her letter of Oct. 17, 1871, Mary Day Lanier had referred to the receipt of invitations to his wedding. He had become editor of the Syracuse *Courier* in 1870 (see Vol. N, Obituary Notices, Syracuse Public Library).

[65] Lanier's cousins, the sons of his Uncle Sidney C. Lanier. Their mother is referred to variously as Mary and Molly. Sterling, born June 24, 1860, became a prominent business man of Birmingham, Ala.

I forwarded thee the box of gloves early this morning. I then went forth to match the blue silk and the Empress Cloth; but could not succeed. All the clerks say these are last year's shades, and that it would be by a mere accident that I could get it matched. We tried, to strike the accident, if possible; but nothing would suit at all. I think it more likely they might be matched in Macon, where the style of shades is not kept up to so closely, and where perhaps some of last year's dying might be lingering. I enclose the samples. Thou wilt express to Lily my grief that I could not do better.[66]

Tonight thy letter is come enclosing the check. I will take out what I paid for the gloves, and return the balance to thee immediately. If the other package should arrive by express before the money reaches thee, just get Father to advance the amount necessary to take the charged package from the Express Office: it will only be some $13 ^{00} to $15 ^{00}.

I wrote thee that I had found thy shoe.[67] I wd. thou hadst seen the fervent kiss which I pressed thereupon: thy foot had been there, and I loved it.

Canst thou tell me exactly what day I *should* arrive in Macon? There is in this question a whole world of meaning. Meditate, thereupon, and answer.

Auntie improveth rapidly, and will be about next week.

I grieve that thou art so overworked. Save a little strength, to kiss me wherewithal when I come.

To this point, now, all my dreams, my thoughts, my actions, my loves, converge. When I come! O My God, that meaneth, when I rejoin thee, when I have thy hand to clasp, when I have thine eyes to pore upon, when I have thy voice to flute love and consolations and dear solaces into mine ears. Until then, then, and after then, forever, I am

Thy

Lover.

---

[66] See note 59, above.

[67] Referring to his commission to purchase shoes for his wife, Lanier had written in his letter of Oct. 25 (here omitted): " I have carried the same to one Dunham who hath made some fair and shapely *bottines* for Mrs. Salem [Dutcher]."

To Mary Day Lanier

[New York,] Oct. 31st 1871.

Tonight, my Sweet,   I can only say a few words to thee.

By reason of the fact, partly, that I yesterday ate some English Walnuts at lunch: whereby, about six O'clock, arose the most enormous inflation in a certain portion of my system, insomuch that I doubt not Auntie believed I was preparing for a balloon-ascension. Suffice it to say, that betwixt the hours of six and twelve last evening I was in great discontent, and wrote thee not, as usual: winding up, at twelve, with a fit of vomiting wh. out-vesuviused Vesuvius. This morn, altho' very sore and weak from previous performances, I was compelled to fare forth down town, in negotiations concerning Auntie's policy, in the payment of which we had apprehended some hitch: and I have been going backward & forward on this behalf all day, having finally succeeded, late this afternoon, in collecting the money, and winding up the whole business for her.

I am therefore too tired to write thee further: and, what I more regret, I have not had time to get a check for the balance of the $40 00, to return to you.   This I will do tomorrow.

I have thine describing the fair,[68] and thine envelope enclosing list of commissions, wh. I will execute . −

If I but might lay my tired head on thy bosom tonight.

But, weary or fresh, I am thy true

Lover.

To Mary Day Lanier

[New York,] Oct. ⸺ (wh. I mean *Nov.*) 1st 1871.

Again, My dear Twin, can I only say a few words of love to thee. My little attack was more puissant than I thought, and I have been feeling badly all day, tho' better than yesterday.

[68] Mary Day Lanier's letter of Oct. 26, 1871, contains a detailed description of the Georgia State Fair, held at Macon.

I saw Dr. Marcy this morning, who telleth me that the bile was stirred by my vomiting, and hath given me medicine to remedy the same. I think I shall be all right to morrow.

I have been too uncomfortable today to go down town for the check to send thee, and I hope sincerely that the delay will not occasion inconvenience: wh. I suppose it will not, as the money could not have arived anyhow in time for Mr. Mac [69] to carry it back with him.

I trust I will be able to go down tomorrow. Today was wet, and the Dr. told me that as he was giving me medicine to produce perspiration, I had better stay in the house after going to the Lifting-Cure.

Checca [70] waxeth strong and fat, and simultaneously therewith, saucy. Her breakfast this morn was a sight to see, consisting of *imprimis,* a dish of stewed oysters, 2nd a broiled pigs-foot, 3rd another broiled pigs-foot, 4th a fried (in butter) pigs-foot, 5th lamb chops, and 6th a glass of pure cream, together with accompaniments of bread &c.

My little attack particularly vexeth me just at this time, when, as the eve of my departure approacheth, I had planned to make many calls, and do many things.
Thine of *23rd* came this morning: tho' I have had letters from thee written four or five days later.
O my Sweet, lovest me very dearly? I prithee hold me in thy sweet wifely longing: I am all sick-hearted for a kiss of thine, for thy gray eyes, for thy fair broad brows: and I do charge thee have thy treasury full of kisses and all manner of love-coin, against the time when, if God will, I shall be thy

happy
Lover.

Checcina, spectacles on nose, dressing-gowned and loose as to garters, sitteth near me, reading Scribner's ! and crieth much love to Maydie.

---

[69] The money was for Lilla Hazelhurst, who was in Waynesville. "Mr. Mac" was a relative—perhaps a brother—who was visiting in Macon, and who was to be the bearer of Lanier's purchases and hence of the unspent money.
[70] Nickname for Lanier's Aunt Jane.

To Robert S. Lanier [71]

Grand Central Hotel, N. Y.
Nov. 2nd 1871.

My Dear Father:

Your letter advising me of draft &c drawn on
Mr. Depuy, is just rec[d], and I thank you for yr. prompt reply.

I suppose the disposition given the Thatcher case by Judge
Erskine won't hurt our side at all, and I'm glad you obtained
the judgment against Sindall.   I had not heard of the Armory
Suit before.

I'm waiting curiously to see something further of Gov. Bullock's resignation, of wh. I've been able to learn nothing, so far,
except the mere telegraphic announcement in the papers. I
suppose it must precede some rare developments.   Somehow,
this isn't a good day for thieves.   Wouldn't it be a curious and
refreshing phenomenon, if Tweed, Hall, Bullock, and that ilk,
should all continue in the service of the State, – only changing
the scene of their labors from the Office to the Penitentiary? [72]

Mary sent on some money to me for Lilla Hazlehurst, only
a part of wh. was used, and I desire to remit her the balance,
but have been prevented for three days from getting a check.
Finally, not wishing to delay longer, I have concluded, since
getting your letter today, that the shortest and safest way will
be just to get you to pay over to Mamie the balance due, and
I will deduct that amount from what I was to use of the $500
draft.   The amt. is $31.[60]: *less* what Mamie *may* have called on
you to advance before this reaches you, to pay for a C. O. D.
Express package I had sent her, for Lily.   Will you please hand

[71] Excerpt previously published, Mims, p. 115.
[72] R. B. Bullock was the Reconstruction governor of Georgia, 1868-1871.
After two years of misrule, charged by the Democratic press with every known
form of rascality and fearing criminal indictment, he resigned on Oct. 23, 1870,
and fled the state.   He was not arrested until 1876; tried then, he was acquitted
for lack of evidence, but historians agree as to the corruption of his carpet-bag
regime (see C. M. Thompson, *Reconstruction in Georgia,* New York, 1915).
Lanier's poem " Those Bonds " (I, 199), written in Dec., 1871, deals with
his alleged embezzlement and flight from the state. The opinion in which he
was held is evidenced by Lanier's linking him in the present letter with A. O.
Hall, Tammany Mayor of New York in 1871, and Wm. Marcy Tweed, " Boss "
of the infamous Tweed Ring.

it to her (Mamie), as soon as you get this? I've written her of it.

I've been somewhat unwell from a fit of indigestion for a day or two: but am much better today.

Auntie is in fine condition.

My love to Sissa and Uncle C.

Your Loving

Sidney.

To Mary Day Lanier

[New York, Nov. 2, 1871]
Oct. (Hang it, thou knowest
what I mean) 2d 1871.

This morning, dear Twin, I was much better, and Checca and I, having breakfasted, did fare forth upon Avenue 6 a-shopping. I purveyed for thee the gloves thou didst name on thy list: to wh. I did add two most dainty pairs, pearl-colored, of sweetest texture and of double-price, and these I do long, Ah Saint of Music that fashioned'st thy hands ! – to see upon thy good fingers, too strongly to tell thee the strength thereof. Also did I negotiate thy silk at Stewarts': luckily finding the match to thy cross-barred piece. Checca leapt into the maze of cheap things on that wonderful Avenue precipitously, and thereamong did she rage and disport like any wild lioness in a jungle. I finally left her, popping from one shop into another, to gang my ways. Such a purveying as she hath wrought in one day, man were but a patched fool if he should go about to recount. I came home at four and found her fatigued. Since that hour, the door of her apartment hath been continually upon the hinge, vibrating to the touch of an eternal procession of shop-boys fetching in the goods: whereby her apartment, where I now sit at this hour of eight, evening, showeth like the Bazaar of Bagdad in the days of Haroun al Raschid, being heaped with fabrics of Eastern looms and products of the West, ranging from garters, nay, lower, from hose (mammoth hose, for dear old Grandmother, of such giant girth in the upper segments thereof as I did not think any mortal leg could fill) through bustles, to caps and head-gear.

Also did I arrange the matter of young Charles's hose. I was so taken with the general appearance of those of wh. I send thee a pair, that I disobeyed thine order, wh. was for white, and purchased a half-dozen of them at 35¢ per pair. An thou likest them, write and I will purvey a half-dozen other pair for him: for they seem to me very warm and cheap. But an thou likest them not, write, and I will still purchase the white ones.

A letter from father today advises me of money to be collected by me, part of which I am to appropriate, and remit balance, or rather deposit balance for him. I therefore write him to pay thee the amount of balance due Lilla, from me,

$$\left. \begin{cases} 7.65 \\ .75 \end{cases} \begin{matrix} \text{for gloves} \\ \text{``} \quad \text{Express} \end{matrix} \right)$$

which is $31.⁶⁰ (being $40. less = 8.40 pd. by me), and I will remit that much more to him. If he shd. have advanced thee the amount due on the *black silk* package wh. was sent by Express C. O. D., before this reaches thee, then the amt. to be paid thee for Lilla will of course be $31.⁶⁰ less that.

This is the shortest and safest way to get it to thee. I went down this afternoon, a long journey, clear to the P. O. to get a Money-order, thinking to send it thee that way, – and found the Money-order office closed ! – so, not wishing to delay longer, the above method occurred to me.

I fear I cannot manage a rocking-horse for Charley: for the freight wd. make it too expensive. What shall I do? It cutteth me to the heart that he shall expect it when I come, and be disappointed.

Father writeth that thou art not well for two or three days. O Comrade! Canst thou not find some little rose to put in thy cheek somewhere? – But I think I have found a way to compass a Lifting-Machine, to have at home, for mine own: and with this, I do firmly believe, I can make thee strong and well as thou has never been before. God speed it so !

I send kisses for Sissa & father & the little Ones.

To thee, turneth all the life of thy

Lover.

To Mary Day Lanier

[New York,] Nov. 4th 1871.

Straighter and swifter, – because shot by love wh. is truer-eyed and stronger than vanity – straighter and swifter than that arrow from the Macrobian bow to the heart of Prexaspes' son, cometh thy love-letter to *my* heart.

——*"*—— I have caught a violet thrown from afar. Sweet hands that waved it my way, do ye not feel my tears and my kisses raining my return?

"

"

I wish thee to make whatever arrangement seemeth to thee best in the matter of a nurse. That wh. thou proposest appeareth likely to be good. Consummate it whenever thou desirest.

As for *l'odeur*: why, perhaps we can drown it out with water. Art sure, however, thou wilt not interfere with the present employer?—Tho' I doubt not thou hast been careful of this. And now I think of it, she is but returning to us who had her first.

——*"*—— Je te comprends, tres-bien. "*Attendre*," – mot terrible, mot diabolique! Ah, ne le connais-je pas? Je ne reviendra pas a toi jusqu'a le 19me Novembre. Alors, ——.

——*"*—— Judge Herring and family are in customary health. The Judge is fearfully broken, tho': and his memory exhibits its failure, in constant repetitions of remarks made but an instant before. He seems absent-minded, too: though he was very cordial to me.

– I have purveyed for thee some of the loveliest collars! at Stewarts'. As for the gloves I had bought them, both finer and cheaper ones, before thy letter came. Thou canst take Lily's colored ones off her hands (!) though, still, if thou desirest.

——*"*—— Checca is kicking. She goeth home Monday – day after tomorrow. Will not wait for me. Is afraid of getting sick here again.

I note thy father's and thy commission for medecines.

Embrace my boys, and my father & Sissa for thy true

Lover.

To Virginia Hankins

Grand Central Hotel,
N. Y. Nov. 4th 1871.

I am glad I cannot tell you, dear Friend, the wearying succession of disappointments which has kept me dallying here, and away from you, until now: for they would surely make you suffer with me.

But *Laus Deo!* they seem to be coming to an end: and I now confidently hope to see you by the fifteenth of this month.

I have been somewhat apprehensive that you did not receive my letter, written early in October [73] from here, inasmuch as I have received no reply; but I trust you may have just delayed writing in the expectation of soon seeing me. I sincerely hope you did receive it; otherwise my failure to come to you might have seemed careless, or for less grave cause than was actually the case.

Ah, Friend, how I long to pace the broad fields with you, and to drink some wine of the sky-and-air, at your hands!

Till I do, and always thereafter, I am your   faithful

S. L.

To Clifford A. Lanier

N. Y. Nov. 5th 1871.

My Dear Clifford:

Yours containing check for $50.00 is received.

I ————I've tried, but I can't say a word more about the money. You know, or rather, you don't know: for which I devoutly thank God.

I sincerely hope the old Exchange [Hotel] will come out of her dull ways. Have you leased it? Let me know what you have done.

Auntie leaves tomorrow morning for Montgomery. I am obliged to stay here until the 13th.

An unexpected loan from Auntie, together with yours, will,

---

[73] Perhaps Lanier refers to his letter of Sept. 27, 1871.

I hope, enable me to purchase a Lifting-Machine to carry home. After much investigation and experience, I am quite convinced that this is the only thing that will save my life.

I will take Willie's dress home with me, and send it from there to Montgomery. It was not done in time for Auntie to carry it. Embrace her and your little ones for Yr—

Sidney

To Mary Day Lanier

[New York,] Nov. 6th 1871.

Well, have I not muddled, distorted, twisted, cuttle-fished, bungled, and thrice and utterly confounded the Lily Commission business! Here is thy note in Sissa's wherein thou sayst the package hath been two days there and thou hast not been able to get the money to take it out of the office! And I had thought and planned and every way tried so hard to get as much of it smoothly and speedily done as possible!

Well, it were well I say nought.
But thou shalt come out of it.

Chécca departed this morning: whereby I have succeeded to her room, wh. is twice as large as mine and hath a good grate. At this present writing, nine P. M., I sit therein before a glowing Anthracite fire, listening anon to the vile music of many political bands who blare forth seductive invitations to the voters to vote early and often tomorrow – (there is a " Michael Norton Association Headquarters " just across from my window, – Michael Norton being a candidate for something or other – where, from the great rush of wonderfully-ragged men and fearfully-bloated boys up the steps, I fancy whiskey and funds are being liberally dealt forth tonight), and then dreaming that thou wert sitting here by me, with thy great eyes aglow and thy hands in mine: whereupon rush over me such agonies of tenderness that I am fain forget all the world and fly to thee.

But life saith no, and life is king of me, now, for life

meaneth, to work and strive that thou mayst be a queen upon a pleasant throne.

The bitter cold weather has prevented me from doing anything that requireth long rides, and I have been forced to limit my excursions simply to those of health: viz. Dr. Marcy's and the Lifting-Cure. I have had some cold, too, wh. obliged me to be doubly prudent.

Kiss Sissa for her letter.

Now may God look into thy heart with loving and lighting Eye, crieth thy

Lover.

To Mary Day Lanier

[New York,] Nov. 7th 1871.

Tes bottinès are just come in. M. le Cordonnier hath unrolled them upon the floor with the pride of an artist. As soon as he hath gone rejoicing with his *honorarium,* I have seized the same, one by one, and administered thereupon the fervent kisses of a love wh. hath been a weary long time without aught to kiss. Besides thy boots, I ordered a third pair, of shoes, – I know not the name thereof – shaped thus,

– I prithee believe not *exactly* thus – being a compromise betwixt thy slipper and thy boot:– . . which are dainty and delicious, and O that I might kiss feet in these fair habitations !
——"⁄⁄—— I lunched with Saidee [Higgins] today. All were at home save Foster, and were exceedingly cordial. Their quarters are very charming indeed, and I enjoyed my visit very greatly. Auntie – I mean Foster's mother – seems in splendid health and spirits, and smacked me right heartily in the mouth when I met her. They talked most lovingly of thee and of thy

father; and tried to get me a room in the same house, or rather, in one of the three co-operative houses, where they live, but all were full.

My cold improveth somewhat. The weather is still very wintry, tho' bright and sunny.

I dine with Mr. Lanier tomorrow. I shall be very busy all this week: as I have many commissions to execute, and also wish to make the acquaintance of some literary men to whom I have letters.[74] I have not yet been able to read any at the Astor Library, even ! And this, too, I wish to do.

And as for thee, My Darling, My Darling, thou art the crimson of my blood: thou art the dainty quality of my life whereby that is a flower which were else but a weed: yea, thou art a sweet white Fire in the heart of thy

Lover.

To Robert S. Lanier

Grand Central Hotel, N. Y.
Nov. 8th 1871.

My Dear Father:

I went down to Winslow & Laniers' to-day, to inquire for the expected letter enclosing draft &c from Mr. Depuy, but found nothing there. Yr. letter was dated Oct. 30th and stated that the draft was drawn at 10 days from date: so that it would fall due tomorrow. I infer there must be some hitch in the matter.

Inasmuch as the weather here is getting very cold, it is quite important for me to leave soon: and I had calculated on starting next Tuesday, intending to pass a couple of days in Virginia, and to reach home on Sunday 19th.

Suppose I wait until Monday night, for the Depuy draft: and if it is not recd by that time, draw on you for $170 through Winslow Lanier & Co. at ten days?

This I will do, unless I receive a telegram from you meantime suggesting otherwise.

[74] These were the letters to R. H. Stoddard, J. R. Thompson, and O. B. Bunce, sent by Hayne.

I regret the trouble very greatly: but I think it very important for me to get to a milder climate at an early date.
I am doing very well. Have had some cold, wh. I had to fight pretty hard, and wh. I think is now being conquered.

I've just come from Mr. Lanier's where I dined and spent a pleasant evening. He is very cordial, and they all seem specially kind to me.[75]

Everybody is exultant over the Tammany defeat yesterday. Boss Tweed was elected in his own District, but he stands in a position of melancholy solitude. The election, – as is usually the case when a great deal of trouble is apprehended – passed off very quietly. One of the precincts was just under my window: and I didn't even see a man drunk: tho' there was an immense amount of huggermuggering going on, and with little or no attempt at concealment.
Embrace all my dear ones, for

Yr. Loving

Sidney.

To Mary Day Lanier

[New York,] Novr. 9th 1871.

It may be thou art at this moment looking upon thy two sons asleep: buds from thee, thou Rose ! O, that I might love thee with mine eyes, as thou standest there: for when the mother-passion is upon thee then thou art lovely as Heaven. T'other day I found this in some story or other:

> " Sleep, Baby, sleep.
> Thy father watcheth thy sleep.
> Thy mother shaketh the dream-land tree.
> And a little dream hath dropped on thee.
> Sleep, baby, sleep."

Sayst thou not, that is perfect?

---

[75] In Lanier's letter to his wife, Nov. 8, 1871 (here omitted), he added: " 'Twas a marvellous fair dinner, served with perfect elegance by a melancholy gentleman in white vest and white gloves, who seemed to have lost all hope in life save the melancholy solace to be extracted from his own dainty grace in handling the silver and pouring the wine. The Claret was simply delicious; and I did imbibe thereof freely, yet without any but the pleasantest result."

—"— Wings, wings, O My Master, put some wings on Time, and feather them with broad feather, and let him have strength to beat them lustily, that so I may come quickly to my Darling. For my heart is sore with longing, and I would fain clothe with sweet flesh the dreaméd arms that my yearning fancy perceiveth ever about me.

—"— Ah, how fearful a cantle is this cut out of my life! Sixty days have my lips been dry of my Love's kiss, and my eyes in dark bereavement of my Love's eyes.

A note from Foster desired me to dine with them today: but, expecting Mr. Stoddard,[76] I had to decline. I saw Foster this afternoon. He seemeth well, and was very cordial. Just at dinner-time came a note from Mr– Stoddard saying he was too ill to come: so I spend my evening alone. I am to eat birthday-dinner with Kate Lanier tomorrow at Delmonico's. My cold improveth.

—"— But I cannot write anything save that I love thee. Wilt thou get tired of so much love-talk? Indeed, I cannot help it. I am truly thy

Lover.

To Mary Day Lanier

[New York,] Nov. 13th 1871.

Thy little love-letter of 8th is come, and is put in **my heart** as twere a rose in my button-hole.

Thine is the most delicate soul in the world, and I love thee as the first Man loved the first Woman.

     "   "

     "   "

I have been quite unwell for a couple of days, and have kept my room. Dr. Marcy saith it is the culmination of all my trouble, and that I shall in a day or two, be better than I have

---

[76] In Lanier's letter to his wife, Nov. 8 (here omitted), he had said: " I called on Richard H. Stoddard, the poet, today, and was pleasantly rec^d. He has halfway promised to dine with me tomorrow."

been in a long time. I think he is right. The attack is very much like that I had five years ago, when a dangerous spell of Bronchitis went off in erisypelas: [77] only nothing like so severe as that was. Yesterday morning came on a fever and headache, which put me in much pain for a time, but promptly yielded to Dr. M.'s remedies. Today I am in a gentle perspiration, and greatly better in all respects. I expect to start home tomorrow, or perhaps next day. If, when I get to Portsmouth, the weather should be very pleasant, I may go to see Ginna: but, unless all things happen exactly right, I shall give it up, as I cannot risk catching another cold. [78]

Aunt Molly and little Russell came over today, and spent most of the day with me. Thou shouldst have seen the small man take his luncheon! I judge he fareth not well in Brooklyn: and the pickled oysters, the tongue, the sardines, the cold chicken, the glass of milk were absorbed with a gusto that was heartsome to see.

I cannot trust myself to write thee any more love. My heart burneth. About me seemeth nought but sand and a merciless sun, until I see thee, my Palm tree and my cool Spring. Dost thou not wish a little to see again

Thy Lover?

TO MARY DAY LANIER

[New York,] Nov. 14th 1871.

O My Twin, tomorrow night, (or, if the weather should be very inclement at 8.30 the following morning), I put myself in God's hands, that they may bear me to thee.
In the presence of this thought I dwell cheerily, as if it were a fireside on a winter's night.

I go not to Ginna's, observing from the weather reports that general rains prevail down the whole land.

I should therefore see thee, if God be willing, either on

---

[77] Lanier probably refers to his illness of Mar.-Apr., 1865.
[78] In Lanier's letter to his wife, Nov. 11, 1871 (here omitted) he had said: " If, when I get to Portsmouth, the weather shd. be inclement, I will be forced to pass by Ginna: as it is a ride of six or seven miles to her house from the boat-landing, and that wd. be too much risk for me in cold weather."

Saturday morning at 11.30 or on Saturday evening [Nov. 18] at 8.30: as I will probably go by the E. Tennessee route, through Atlanta. Should I decide to change my route, I will telegraph thee from some point on the way: and will do so at Atlanta, if I do not change, telling thee which train to send to.

How can I write more?

I am improving.

Embrace my father and Sister, and my lovely ones

for Thy Lover.

To Virginia Hankins

N. Y. Nov. 14th 1871.

Dear Friend, The great God Almighty saith " No! ", and there's the end of it.

I have been ill a long time. The Climate has not agreed with me. I must crawl home by the easiest way, and shortest: and have not strength to make even the short journey from the boat-landing to thy Castle.

Dear One, what heart can I have to write more?

It is the heaviest blow I have known — this failing to see thee and to grasp thy little hand — since, — since my Mother died!

Once at home, I will write thee again.

The Soul of God is large, and therefore It must needs be merciful. I doubt not He understands this matter: but I do not.

Unfailing, unforgetting, and steadfastly true,

I am Thy

Friend

To Clifford A. Lanier

Macon, Ga, Dec. 2d 1871.

My Dear Clifford:

I send by Express today Willie's dress, and hope same will suit her. It shd. have been sent earlier but for my illness wh. has prevented me from doing anything until the last three days.

Enclosed please find also check for $20.⁰⁰ wh. father desires me to transmit to you; being amt. advanced by you, I believe to Sissa.

I improve in this milder climate, and hope to be able to work during the winter.

What are you going to do anent the Hotel business? Let me know.

Tell Aunt Jane I have her letter.

Family pretty well. Write. Love to everybody.

Yr.
Sid.

Father says he has been trying to write you for some time, but has been prevented by pressure of business.

S.

To Virginia Hankins

Macon, Ga, Dec. 6th 1871.

Yr. expressions of yr. friendly regret at not seeing me, dear Heart, at once re-open *my* wounds and pour balm into them.[79]

What a pure an dainty thing you are!

— You will be glad to learn that I am somewhat improved since coming home, and that it wd. seem that God intends, for some purpose or other, that I shall live a little longer.

As for me, I am very grateful that this is so: for there are some things I had set my heart upon doing, in this world, and it may chance I shall compass them, after all.

One of them is:— to see you.

I pray you, dear Friend, give me detailed particulars of this " plan " you mention. Where will it carry *you*: and where the boys? Will my fair and dear old Castle be sold or rented?

---

[79] In her letter of Nov. 17, 1871, Virginia Hankins had written: " Tonight— I thought to be with you. . . . I have kept fresh flowers in the house and looked for you ever since the ' last ten days of September.' I thought the fall was more beautiful, because you were coming. . . . I thought–, to be here, might benefit you. I got great oysters & everything to suit you. I said, when you were tired you should rest, & I would read you to sleep, from my Book.– I gathered fresh flowers today– and *now*, were spring-time here, I'd not gather a single flower that bloomed."

In either event, to whom; and how will this leave you financially? You are to quit Surrey: where go you? And how will you dispose of your boys?

Answer me these questions, categorically.

And believe, Good Little One, that all your words to me are like sweet white hands that reach down from some higher place, to help me upon a nobler level.

One finds so few women in the world, My dear! And one gets tired of the wire-figures that display the costumes of *Les Modistes.* What do I care that Madame Thus-and-so has builded a dress intricately? I like a passionate soul of a woman, cunningly hid away behind some large eyes and a wonder of dainty flesh.

If you but knew how I hover about you with a tender solicitude that knows no bounds! I do not doubt that sometimes, when you think the wind is blowing at your window, or lifting your curtain or your hair,– that is *I,* moving about you.

If I confided less in the heartiness of your friendship, I might think it necessary to fan the fires thereof, by recalling myself to you more frequently in letters: but I never like to write you aught less than a poem: and life does not leave me time to construct these often: so that I content myself with trusting you.

But you will likely have time: and I would be proud and glad to know, through your frequent letters, every trouble and every dream that crosses your soul.

Let me do so: for I am in truth

Yr.

Friend.

From Virginia Hankins

Bacon's Castle [Surry Co., Va.]
Dec: 13th 1871.

My dear friend.

I was so relieved to get your letter; *so* glad to learn that you are better. You do not know *half how* glad I am. I think when one has experienced a great joy one should make it a religion to be indifferent to the " cares of the world," – so, since you are getting strong, I will not fret over *some things* that my heart cries out against and will try " to keep my calm sublime." The fear for you overcame in a great measure, my disappointment but I still say, if you only could have come! Everything was so lovely just then, the whole land lay in a glory of mellow light and my old castle seemed so doubly " fair and dear " to me. *Then*, — now it is mine no longer. Here I will answer all your questions. I think our counsel was either inefficient or indifferent; at any rates, everything seems to have been badly managed and we knew nothing about law. Mark, who is very energetic, had been off in business six months, came home and we tried to make arrangments to buy the home-stead, we did not want the whole plantation. The time came and we lacked $2000. to make up the sum required. The place was put up for sale & no one bidding, Mr. White who had a mortgage on it for $6000. bought it in for his debt. Imagine! the place is valued at $35000. After the sale a cousin hearing of the desire of the children to retain the home, offered the loan of the money. We then endeavored to repurchase it but Mr White refuses to part with it, and we are to leave the 30th. You ask who it is that has taken our places here. Mr White was a common carpenter but is now a large money lender. He looks like a beggar in his dirty homespun clothes and milks his own cows. Himself said after he had gone over the house: " What will the world come to? Two hundred years ago this was owned by Nathaniel Bacon [80] & is now owned by such a man as old Edwin White! " I had an idea of making an appeal to the U. S. court. In many cases it has set aside the sale of land at such a great sacrifice, but law-suits are so wearying – and we cannot bid high enough – you know how that is, Mr. Lawyer. And – I almost feel as if a higher voice called us hence. I have had a weary time, dear friend, since my brother died.[81] I have lived as if on a fearful precipice, day & night. Never for all these years have I felt free. Ah! it would be so easy to leave it all behind – if I could only see God's will in it and not human hands. *This* is the great want of my life. I cannot realize change nor comprehend Life. — As for my

[80] The leader of " Bacon's Rebellion " in 1676. The historic Castle, still standing, is said to be the earliest example of Tudor architecture in America.

[81] See notes 58 and 62, 1866.

boys; – John & Legh do not know what they will do nor where go. The little boys are at school, Willie & Mark are engineers on the Chesapeake & Ohio R. R. with Jimmy & Johnny Douglas, on wh: road cousin Henry Douglas is Chf: Eng^r. I am going first to Richmond for the winter. The bitterness of my home-leaving has been greatly softened by the desire my friends have shown to have me with them. Every mail brings me the sweetest, kindest letters from friends & relatives asking me to go to them. I have for a long time wanted to give myself a holiday, when I might warm my heart in the homes of some dear friends, but [it] has been impossible until now. If all goes well I shall next year " take mine ease "; and hope that the petting & goodness which I know is in store for me will reestablish my health & spirits. Little Mary, of course, goes with me. I expect to make of her the daintiest lady in all the land. — — —

— *Is* the world really coming to an end that I have filled a letter to you with figures of dollars & cents? – Believe, I would not have done it if you had not said, " I pray you, Friend answer my questions." And I will not deny any prayer of yours.

Remember me lovingly to Maimie & tell her I rejoice *so* truly with her over your returning health. Let me hear how you continue to be. You understand how I felt, in the poem,[82] and you like it? Wherever I go I remain faithfully your friend.

G. H.

To Mary Day Lanier

[Macon, Ga., Dec. 1871?][83]

Dr. Wife:

The Dr. will come at Three, as thou desirest.

Get thyself into this most sweet air and sunlight: it is the resurrection, and certain dry bones of flowers and dull roots of grasses take sense of it and shiver with such thrills as loving people know,

Think lovingly upon

Thine

[82] See note 51, 1869.
[83] This little note, written from the office, seems to belong with two other

To Joel Chandler Harris

Macon, Ga. Dec 28th 1871

J. C. Harris Esq
    Savannah.

Dear Sir:

Enclosed please find the poems referred to in yrs. of 21st *inst.*

I will be glad to know when the 2nd Ed. of Mr D.'s book
is out.[84]

Very Truly Yours

Sidney Lanier

notes, one fully dated Dec. 12, 1871. Lanier had once more taken up the practice
of law, but he seems to have put himself under a regimen of rest and regularity
prescribed by his wife, whom he now addresses as "doctor."

[84] No second edition of J. W. Davidson's *Living Writers of the South* ever
appeared; hence the poems here referred to—probably some that had been
published previously—cannot be identified. But Lanier's Ledger (Henry W.
Lanier Collection, Johns Hopkins University) gives evidence of his renewed
literary activity at this period with its drafts of two poems dated Dec. 23 and
Dec. 24, 1871: "The Carrier's Appeal" and "Those Bonds" (I, 197, 199).
Another poem probably written in 1871, but not mentioned in any of Lanier's
letters, was "The Homestead (I, 25), published in the *Southern Farm and
Home,* Aug., 1871.

Further evidence appears in the correspondence of W. H. Browne, echoing
lost letters from Lanier. Browne's letter of Dec. 18, 1871, accepted for publication at $2.00 a page Lanier's essay "Nature Metaphors" (V, 306), which
though composed somewhat earlier seems to have been revised at this time and
submitted to the *Southern Magazine* early in December. In his letter of Dec. 30,
1871, Browne remarked in criticism of a passage in Lanier's essay dealing with
Greek metres:

"The recent investigation of German scholars, such as Westphal, Schmidt,
and others, founded upon common sense, and a thorough knowledge of the
principles of rhythm and music, have shed a flood of light upon and almost
revolutionised the study of Classical measures.

"I have had thoughts of turning the same principles (which I consider
universal) upon English rhythm, and preparing a new system of English prosody
which should be rational, intelligible, and musical. I have the materials partly
in my head and partly in condensed notes; but shall never publish, because (1)
I shd. never find a publisher, (2) I shd. not have ten readers." It is possible
that this is the germ which fruited nearly a decade later in Lanier's *Science of
English Verse.* Lanier continued to discuss metrics with Browne for several
years, as is indicated in Browne's letters of Feb. 26, 1872; Oct. 23, Nov. 9,
Nov. 30, 1874.

1872

Macon, Ga, Feby 12th 1872

Dear Friend, I have striven to write you since your good friendly letter came: [1] but a great multitude of other-people's-businesses have kept me bound in what is to me the most galling of bonds.

— I am better:— for you were good enough to say that you wished to hear so.

— Furthermore, your poem went whistling through my soul, very much as a wearisome wind in winter through a rift in a ruin: and I have been trying to collect myself, in order that I might be tranquil in the face of this – to me – unintelligible distortion of circumstance, whereby you have no home.

Was this sale an administrator's sale? Had the mortgage been foreclosed at law, *before* the death of your father? If not, was there a proper order obtained from the Ordinary, – or such Court as you may have in Virginia, taking cognizance of estates of deceased persons? If said order was obtaind, was the sale advertised according to law? Was it a fair sale; – free from collusion or combinations to suppress bidding?

I am so indignant about the whole business that I have no words at all in which to talk about the matter.

But if, as in any of the questions above, you see reason to suspect the *bona fides* of the sale, let me know it.

———— The poem was a good poem: low on the chilly earth, liest thou, Sweet Friend, Pretty Friend? I deal in no mock consolations: 'twere easy to tell thee, thou hast a dozen homes in as many faithful hearts: – but that is not the one

[1] On Jan. 12, 1872, Virginia Hankins had written Lanier expressing her concern for his health, since she had received no answer to her letter of Dec. 13, 1871, telling of the sale of Bacon's Castle. The present letter is apparently his first reply. (No letters by Lanier to any correspondent have been found for Jan., 1872, and only one each for the next five months.)

Home.[2] One *near* one is too far, quo' Master Browning: and it is a fair saying.

— Commend me, O true Heart, unto thyself, as one who rejoices, with a quiet, restful and unnameable joy, in calling himself thy

Friend.

To Paul H. Hayne

Macon, Ga. March 2d 1872

My dear Mr. Hayne:

If you only knew in what a swirl of business I've been tossed (*"Jactatus undis"*) for the past thirty days and nights, – professional business, *i. e.* business of other people wh. they pay me to do, & which therefore I'm obliged to do before anything else – you w'd. not, as I fear you have, suspect me of unfriendliness in failing to acknowledge yr. kindness in sending me " Legends & Lyrics." I have, – without resorting to that exaggeration wh. long usage has rendered almost pardonable in letter-writers – really been *unable* to write you as I desired: and I wd. not, because I cd. not, consent to fob you off with a line. And yet it comes to that, almost, now: for I'm afraid you'll think me unmindful of yr. goodness and insensible to yr. beautiful things in " L. & L." if I *don't* write: – *hinc illæ lachrymæ.*

I expressed, some weeks ago, to Mr. Randall, a desire to review your book: and I will do so, either in the " Telegraph," here, or elsewhere.[3] I desired to make a more elaborate review of it than wd. be suitable for a daily paper: but I fear the time is not at my disposal. If it shd. be, I shall so devote it.

I know nothing in " L. & L." wh. gives me more pleasure than the Mocking Bird piece,[4] wh, ends

---

[2] The reference is apparently to a poem by Virginia Hankins, which has not survived.

[3] On Feb. 15, 1872, Hayne had written saying that Jas. R. Randall (editor of the Augusta, Ga., *Constitutionalist*) had told him of meeting Lanier in Macon recently. In the same letter Hayne had asked Lanier to notice in " ' The Telegraph ' – or elsewhere " his new volume of poems (*Legends and Lyrics*, New York, 1872), a copy of which he was sending by the same mail. The request eventually led to Lanier's article, " Paul H. Hayne's Poetry " (V, 322), which was not published, however, until Jan., 1875, in the *Southern Magazine*.

[4] Hayne's sonnet beginning " Of all the woodland flowers of earlier spring."

" A Star of music in a cloud of fire! "

There is a certain effulgent outpouring of warmth, of light, of melody, in this little poem that gives me keen pleasure. The gold of the woodbine & the gold of the setting-sun strive together: and the swaying branches and vines, and the powerful-thwarted bird hid in among the flowers, work a strange influence upon me as of various senses melting together and approaching through each other; as if a man should *see* the music, and *hear* the sunlight.

I observe that Margaret Preston [5] notices the book very heartily in the March No. of the Southern Magazine. Do you know her by the way? I do not, but wd. like to.

There is prospect that my press of busines may be over in a few months: probably by May: and then I hope to cultivate you a little. Meantime, if I don't do justice to your kindness, by answering you as soon as possible, dream not that I am any less

Yr. Friend

Sidney Lanier

To Paul H. Hayne [6]

Macon, Ga. April 17th 1872

My Dear Mr Hayne,

It would seem that Fate does not desire me to write a review of " Legends & Lyrics," — just as the old hag did not desire me to negotiate yr. poems you sent me in New York; [7] for now — as then — I had written the first page of a review, when I was stricken down with illness, from which I am just beginning to crawl forth. The review of " L. & L." was particularly near my heart: for I was keenly desirous of pointing out, and dwelling upon, a certain rare and lovely feature in your writings, wh., in these days, gives me a world of pleasure. I mean the entire *absence,* in every thing you write, of *Trade* in any of its forms. Utterly *uncommercial*: that is glorious, my dear Friend, and that is the spirit of your writings.

[5] Margaret Junkin Preston (1820-1897), a Virginia poet.
[6] Previously published, *American Literature,* I, 35-36 (Mar., 1929).
[7] On Oct. 24, 1871, Hayne had sent two of his sonnets to Lanier with a request that he try to place them with a New York religious magazine.

Trade, Trade, Trade: pah, are we not all sick? A man cannot walk down a green alley of the woods, in these days, without unawares getting his mouth and nose and eyes covered with some web or other that Trade has stretched across, to catch some gain or other. 'Tis an old spider that has crawled all over our modern life, and covered it with a flimsy web that conceals the Realities. Our religions, our politics, our social life, our charities, our literature, nay, by Heavens, our music and our loves almost, are all meshed in unsubstantial conceal-ments and filthy garnitures by it.

But your poems are not. Here the brooks wimple down the burn in order to be beautiful, and not in order to make money by turning mill-wheels: and the trees wave, and the birds sing, and sweet human emotions come into the woods and blend therewith: and no money-changers sit in the still leafy temples.

It is not necessary for me to explain, to *you,* what I mean by these hasty metaphors. You know what the commercial spirit is: you remember that Trade killed Chivalry and now sits in the throne. It was Trade that hatched the Jacquerie in the 14th Century: it was Trade that hatched John Brown, and broke the saintly heart of Robert Lee, in the 19th.

As soon as I get so that after my day's work, — which is continuous and exhausting every day — I can think at all, I propose to write my review. I read aloud to my wife, t'other night, the last strophe of the poem " To Sleep ": and we agreed — and my wife, mark you, hath an ear in her soul, and a soul in her ear, of the delicatest apprehension in the world! — that there is not a sweeter piece of melody in the language.

Let me know what you are doing; and believe me

Your Friend

Sidney Lanier

To Virginia Hankins

Macon   May 1st 1872

It is true, dear Friend, life *does,* in a sense, glide away. But when you said that, you were sitting (you tell me) at yr. window, looking at the river.

At the SURFACE of the river, Little One!

You only saw the top of it: – but the innumerable lives beneath the surface, the hopes, the fears, the struggles of small powers against greater powers, the waving sea-grasses and ferns at the bottom, the strange shelled creatures, the marvellous freaks and glories that exist in the depth of sea-water; – do *these* glide away?

And then again: the tide goes out, and life seems to dwindle away into the sea: but in six hours the tide comes in again, and then life is full.

As for you: – why, the flood tide has not commenced to make, yet.

——"——Tell me, succinctly, what are yr. plans for the summer, I will likely travel: and it may hap that I can look you up. To say how the hope of this shakes my heart – would be to tell you how I yearn over you continually with solicitude: – and how can I tell you that?

I have a mind to hear some gossip about the people whom I have associated with the old fair time. Write me of the Wrenns, the Crumps, the Wilsons, the Pegrams, and all the rest. Is the land given over to peanuts still? How beautiful, kind Heaven! must that fair bay be, in this Spring weather! O, to pace the sweet sandy shore with you,— dear friend, will not this grace come to me once more? I know that it will.

You will be glad to know that although not a strong man, I am better, and that I am working hard at my profession, and that I hope to be, [some] [8] day, a lawyer, and mayhap also a poet; tho' I can never be aught I hold higher or sweeter than

Your

Friend.

To Virginia Hankins

Macon, Ga, June 18th 1872

My Dear Friend, Where are you? I have written you, months ago, to care of Milhado & Ricks, Norfolk, Va; [9] giving you some most sage and valuable lectures upon things in general: but I do not hear from you, and I fear you are sick.

[8] One word, torn from the MS, has been conjecturally restored.
[9] After leaving her home in Dec., 1871, Virginia Hankins spent the next

Let me hear from you; tell me where my good
friend, my sweet Spring in the woods, my unfailing pure-of-
heart, my lucid-soul, My little One-in-whom-I-have-always-con-
fidence, – is, and how she fares, and whether life is as tender
to her as would be her

Friend.

To Virginia Hankins [10]

Macon, Ga. July 2nd 1872

It is like a wave from the fair blue Southern Ocean of a
far-off happy time, – this wave that swells with round ripple
and delicate murmuring to my strand, and lays thereon a
serrated leaf and a lock of green sea-hair, taken from the spot
I love.

I thank you for them, dear Friend: and I " remember," full
well, the sweet surprise of that sacred morning, and the laugh
of the child that made me dream for a moment that my ears
were turned into eyes which the sunlight broke upon. [11]

There are things one does not forget. How serene must be
the bay-shore, these days, curving about the waters! And how
utterly mournful! As long as I could think of *you* as the
indwelling spirit of the Bay, I could recognize that it still had
some *life* that connected it with the Past; but now you are gone
from it: and only a dream-of-you will forever hover over my
dream-of-*it*.

Ah, Burwell's Bay, why did you let her go?

If I had been Burwell's Bay, I would have lured you in
among some of the big rocks and bound you with a powerful
spell of sun-sparkles, green waters and water-voices, and held
you so, in my sight, and out of all others'.

---

year visiting friends: the winter in Richmond, the spring in Norfolk, and the
summer in King William Co., Va. The winter of 1872-1873 she spent in
St. Louis.

[10] Excerpt previously published, *Southern Bivouac*, II, 761 (May, 1887).

[11] This seems to be a reference to the first meeting of Lanier and Virginia
Hankins in 1863. She had apparently made a visit to Burwell's Bay (see the
following paragraph), near Bacon's Castle, and sent him a token of remembrance in a letter that has not survived.

—— I am very much surprised at the conduct of Burwell's Bay in allowing you to escape.

///

Next Monday, D. V. I start for the Allegheny Springs, in Montgomery County, Va. to spend a month: being ordered so to do by certain authorities who are supposed to have charge of my physical welfare. I go with my sister, and an Aunt from Alabama, who will be in my charge, and whom I will not be able to leave, save for a short time, without escort: nor will I be allowed to absent myself from the healing-waters for any length of time. But, dear Friend, I cannot be in Va. when you are also in Va. without seeing you. Can you not plan a visit to, (say,) Lynchburg, or some other place *th*ereabout? Have you no friends in that section, whom you would like to visit? You *must* have: it is not in nature, or in the fitness of things, that you have not: – then will you not visit them? May – my wife – declares that if I do not see you this summer, and bring her news of you obtained face to face, she will not forgive me.

Set therefore, O cunning woman! thy's woman's-wit to work, and answer me, (directing to me at " Allegheny Springs, Montgomery County, Va ") where I may haply find you, and when.

What – in the name of all that is mysterious! – will yr. little hands find to do in St. Louis?

Write me, as being always

Your Friend

S. L.

To Mary Day Lanier

Marietta, July 8th 1872

So, my Sweet, here am I again, not with thee.

By heaven, a mountain has become to me a symbol of Sorrow: for it has so happened that when I have left thee I have always gone amongst mountains.

Loneliness; unmatedness: desolation: that is what mountains

have come to mean, to me: – and yonder is Kennesaw, full in
sight, over against my window.

"

"

I have been quite on the run since I arrived. Gussie and
Jennie,[12] – on whom I called immediately – do not seem to be
in the best of spirits. Gussie has had much trouble with the
baby: and Jennie says the cars, which pass by their door – jar
the house, and shriek, so unmercifully that she can't sleep.
She consoles herself however with the glorious reflection that
she has lost flesh by it. They seemed greatly delighted to see
some one from home.

I played the organ at Church yesterday; and saw hosts of
people all of whom inquired about you tenderly. Every one
seems rejoiced that we are coming back to Marietta. I dined
at Mr– Whitlock's yesterday and today. Mrs. W., as well as
Mrs. Hége (?!) and Mrs. Leak, seemed exceedingly anxious
for your return and vowed you should not stay at any other
house in Marietta.

Which brings me to say that I have made the following
arrangement, after much discussion & negotiation. We are to
occupy the same room we had last year, at Mrs. Earle's: the
children in the Granberry room adjoining: & take our meals
across street at Mr. Whitlocks. This suits us admirably: and
combines many advantages over any other practicable arrangement. The rooms at Whitlocks are small & low, and the house
is much warmer than the other. He has wonderfully rejuvenated
things though, and the bright fresh paint, inside and out, with
new matting, furniture &c, and the airy, cheerful appearance of
things generally, make it a very attractive place. We will have
the fine old shady yard for Sidney & Charlie to disport in: wh.
anticipation gives me great pleasure. Whitlock seems to have
a pleasant party of boarders: most of the present company
being from New Orleans.

I have seen Mrs. Wallen, and had a long and very sweet
interview with her. She sends many loving messages to you,
and awaits your coming with anxiety. Mamie [13] is wonderfully

[12] Augusta Lamar Ogden and Virginia Lamar Bacon.
[13] Mamie Boifeuillet was the niece of Mary Wallen; both were Macon friends.
The (William) Duncans mentioned in the following paragraph were relatives
from Savannah.

lovely, with a perfect milk-and-roses complexion, and is getting more and more stout every day. Her acquired flesh seems, too, to be good, solid flesh.

Mrs. Duncan, whom I called on yesterday afternoon, is as good and pretty as ever, and made many kind inquiries of you. She seems somewhat worn with watching. I did not see Mrs. Screven, who has not yet come out of her room, tho' able to sit up occasionally. Mr. Duncan opened fire on " Patty " yesterday afternoon, and got well bombarded for his pains. He seems very hearty; and wished very much for your support during the battle betwixt him and the Spouse.

I am better since I came here: and am overwhelmed with the cheerful consolations of the virtuous man. I have smoked nor chewed no cigars since Friday night last.

Embrace my two young un for me. – Oh, my bairns!

Kiss father. I'll write him from Allegheny. I leave here at six this afternoon: expecting to connect with Montg'y train, at Dalton, at ten, tonight.

"
_____
"

To thee, sweetheart, I send my heart, which indeed is but *thy*

Heart.

To Mary Day Lanier

Montgomery White Sul. Spgs. Va
July 9th 1872

Dr. Wife:

I found Sister, Jimmie & Auntie,[14] at Dalton a little after ten O'clock, on Monday night. They were all a-bed, in a Silver-Palace Sleeping-car: and might have been very comfortable, but Auntie had, in that excess of gastronomic enthusiasm wh. frequently comes when one begins travelling, overeaten her capacity as to a certain ham wh. they had for lunch:

[14] The reference is to Lanier's sister Gertrude, his Aunt Jane Watt, and probably his cousin James Eason of Charleston, who had been accidentally injured by his cousin Clark Lanier during the previous summer and had not yet recovered his health (see Clifford Lanier's letter to his brother, Aug. 27, 1871).

and consequently was in great pain. She entertained a car-load of people throughout the night, and part of next day, with spasms of vomiting: in the intervals whereof she seemed possessed with a strenuous desire to either stand on her head, or to tie herself in a true-lovers' knot: and, in her indecision as to which of these postures she preferred, she frequently came as near as the human conformation will permit, to doing both these feats at one and the same time.

Seriously, she had a very hard time of it; and as she was unable to go on to Allegheny, we landed her here, where her doctor had ordered her to stay and drink the Sulphur waters for two weeks before going to Allegheny. She is greatly better today.

We arrived here yesterday (Tuesday) afternoon about half-past seven. I shall go on to Allegheny Springs (which are about six miles from here) this afternoon, and if I make a favorable report Sister will come over there immediately: if not she will stay here a week or so with Auntie & Jimmie. We find that board here is much cheaper than at Allegheny: forty dollars pr. month here,— sixty there. There are, I suppose, about two hundred and fifty people here: and, we are told, about half that number at Allegheny.

Sister and Eddie are in fine condition.

I am doing well. The air here is too damp for me: the place is in a deep valley, and completely shaded by trees: moreover the rain falls once a day, in a mountain-shower. All send loving kisses to father and you: to which I add mine.

"

———————

"

But, O my Heart, thy love is to my soul as the wings that are on the feet of Mercury, and thereon I fly into a quiet heaven whenever I desire: quiet, as to all earthly noises, and filled with all thy fair faiths in me, thy dear tendernesses to me, thy gracious veilings of my default, O, with a myriad sweet phases of thine immaculate and blessed wifehood wherewith as with two milk-white arms thou hast purely encircled thy

Lover.

To Robert S. Lanier

Alleghany Spgs. Va.
July 11th 1872

My Dear Father:

I came over here yesterday, arriving about seven O'clock after a magnificent ride of three miles from the depot.

I am as much pleased here as I was disgusted at the Montgomery White. A different spirit reigns over everything: and the natural advantages of this place are far superior to those of the other. I telegraphed Aunt Jane & Sissa this morning to pack up incontinently and come over here: and look for them this afternoon.

I have met some friends here from all parts of the Country: and am pleasantly situated in all respects. I am told that Major Dent, of Macon, is here: but have not yet seen him. He is suffering great agony from a huge carbuncle on his neck.

I was introduced to the resident physician this morning, and found him a very pleasant and intelligent gentleman. He thinks the waters will be beneficial to me, and has given me full instructions how to use them. He made an examination of my lungs: and gave an account of them which coincided well with that of Dr. Hall. He thinks I have no reason to fear at all, and that my disease is a chronic bronchitis which can be counterated by open air and active life.

The air here is very delicious to me: and the mountains are continual inspirations of fine dreams.

Aunt Jane was very much better when I left her yesterday: and was moving actively about.

I've met here MaCaw[?], – an old College-mate–, now a wealthy Cotten-broker, of Mobile: who has taken me in tow, and in the course of this morning has made me acquainted with pretty nearly every man on the grounds.

Kiss my dear wife & children for me: and believe me always

Your Son

Sidney

To Mary Day Lanier

Alleghany Spgs. July 11th 1872.

I sit, dear Child, at the back door of my room. Three steps lead from this door to a grass-plot, which presently becomes a broad meadow. In this meadow they have been harvesting the hay all day: and the great round hay-cocks are like hundreds of globes of sweetness, as the just-perceptible breaths of air blow across them to me. Across the meadow – a couple of hundred yards from my door – there is a sudden bold and round upswelling of the earth into all manner of globular hills and mountains, some of which are clothed with the foliage of innumerable trees, and others with a vestiture of inexpressibly soft green, which is at once tender and brilliant, as if it were velvet woven of green silver. A few feet from my door runs a clear stream across the meadow, and presently falls into the Roanoke River, which winds about between the hills. This little stream has a quiet yet tinkling murmur, which is as if the velvet-grass yonder were done into music. It is six O'clock: and the sunlight falls – no, it does not fall, it lies quietly over the meadow, the grass and the hills, like a visible manifestation of perfect contentment. A small bird is chasing a grasshopper from one hay-cock to the other, uttering little cries in which are blended the eagerness of the chase and the irritation of disappointment: and the keen monotone of a cricket comes up out of the meadow-grass. The Spirit of quiet has possessed himself of men as well as of nature: for hardly a sound can be heard from any part of the grounds.

The sky is of a marvellous still blue: and the few light clouds that are in it do not float, they pause and remain motionless over head. – If I did not *know*, O My Darling, My Darling, that thy love was utterly mine, this heavenly-sweet picture would be insupportable to me. But I well wot how thy large eyes would gaze, – if thou wert here – first at me and then at this beauty: and therefore, in a great serenity of soul, as I can not now bring thee to this fair vision, I send its *eidolon* to thee, as this day's offering at thy beloved feet from thy

Lover.

To Mary Day Lanier [15]

[Alleghany Springs, Va.,] July 12 th 1872

How necessary it it, Dear Comrade, that one should occasionally place oneself in the midst of those more striking forms of nature in which God has indulged His fantasy !

It is very true that the flat land, the bare hillside, the muddy stream, comes also directly from the Creative Hand: but these do not bring one into the sweetness of the heartier moods of God, – in the midst of them it is as if one were transacting the *business* of life with God: whereas, when one has but to lift one's eyes in order to receive the exquisite shocks of thrilling form and color and motion that leap invisibly from mountains and grass and streams, then one feels as if one had surprised the Father in His tender, sportive and loving moments.

To a soul, then, weak with the long flesh-fight, and filled with a sluggish languor by those wearisome disappointments which arise from the constant contemplation of men's weaknesses and from the constant back-thrusting of one's consicousness of impotence to strengthen them, – thou, with thy nimble fancy, canst imagine, what etherial and yet indestructible essences of new dignity, of new strength, of new patience, of new serenity, of new hope, new faith and new love, do continually flash out of the gorges, the mountains and the streams, into the heart, and charge it, as the lightnings charge the earth, with subtle and heavenly fires.

A bewildering sorcery seems to spread itself over even those things which are commonplace. The songs and cries of birds acquire a strange sound to me: I cannot understand the little spontaneous tongues, the quivering throats, the open beaks, the small bright eyes that gleam with unknown emotions, the nimble capricious heads that twist this way and that with such *bizarre* unreasonableness.

Nor do I fathom this long unceasing monotone of the little shallow river that sings yonder over the rocks in its bosom as a mother crooning over her children: it is but one word that the stream utters: but, as when we speak a well-known word

[15] Previously published, Mims, pp. 112-114.

over and over again until it comes to have a frightful mystery in it, so this familiar stream-sound fills me with indescribable wonder.

Nor do I comprehend the eloquence of the mountains, which comes in a strange *patois* of two tongues: for the mountains speak at once the languages of repose and of convulsion,– two languages which have naught in common.

Wondering, therefore, from day to night, with a good wonder which directs attention not to one's ignorance but to God's wisdom: stricken, but not exhausted, by continual tranquil surprises: surrounded by a world of enchantments which, so far from being illusive, are the most substantial of realities: – thou knowest that nature is kind to me.

– Indeed, O My Sweet, O My Wife, my heart would utterly break, here, for lack of thee ,– were I not so " in-the-spirit " that I can hear *thy* heart beating, across all the miles betwixt us: and, with that sweetest rhythm pulsating softly in my soul, I can lull for a little time the overmastering desire that thy true eyes might look on this beauty at the same-time with mine. Somehow, I do not doubt they *will* do so, some day: and this faith, too, gives me a little patience.

—— Ah, my God ! how my thoughts do rise up and close about thee fast and tenderly, as these mountains enclose this valley: thou, My Soul-of-a-vale, deep, delicious, warm, steadfast, musical with glittering springs of pure love and passion, fertile in manifold rich tendernesses, beloved of the dews, the stars and the sun !

Breath upward some faint exhalations from thy flowers, that they may float on and wreathe about thy

Lover.

To Mary Day Lanier

July 13th 1872

Thou couldst never guess what I breakfasted on this morning. — On thy letter, a mountain, and a mutton-chop.

Twas a *carte* for a God's meal: and I did linger over it in a long protraction of luxury.

"
————
"

That x x x x x [16] I thank Heaven: I have been
afraid to write thee of it. Well: God is great, and there is
but one God.

"

———————————

"

Thou art right: — what a nose thou hast for smelling out
the *truth* in difficult moral problems! — the man and his true
wife should be together mind to mind, as well as heart to
heart, otherwise something lacks. Thou canst not dream with
what keen anticipation I crave the time when thy dear tongue
shall again form for me the quaint French syllables, beneath,
as thou sayest, the waving leaves. And I am infinitely glad
that here, alone, I can in silence bring my heart to be at such
ease with itself that I may plunge whole-mindedly with thee
into these sparkling French pools.

"

———————————

"

Pollard, author of the " Virginia Tourist " [17] is here. He has
Bright's disease of the kidneys, and gets about the grounds
feebly, leaning on a stick. He seems not long for this world.
I have not made his acquaintance: and do not feel any inclina-
tion to do so, by reason of his gall and bitterness. The Dr.
White, of whom he speaks, is a very pleasant gentleman, and
I have had considerable talk with him.

"

———————————

"

As to the Congress Water, do, I prithee, precisely that which
seemeth good to thee: also as to the trunk. I will endorse and
defend in advance any action thou mayst take in the premises.

"

———————————

"

[16] Several words have been obliterated in the MS at this point. Since Mary
Day Lanier's letter to which this is an answer has not survived, no conjectural
restoration is possible.

[17] Edward Alfred Pollard (1831-1872), author of a guide book, *The Virginia
Tourist* (Philadelphia, 1870), a copy of which survives in Lanier's library, Johns
Hopkins University. He was better known for his volume of reminiscences, *The
Lost Cause* (New York, 1866), to which Lanier is probably referring at the end
of this paragraph.

I did *not* interview the men of leather anent the shoe-bill: and I beg thou wilt do so when thou happenest in town.

Neither did I order the Macon paper: but ordered the Atlanta Constitution, which has commenced to arrive, and is a source of great solace to me.

''

''

Wagest thou still thine entomologic war? Smite, and spare not: until thou hast driven the enemy from Aroer even unto Ammon. 'Tis a foul bug. I do verily believe it was known in the time of the evangelists, and that it is the origin of the idea of hell. I make no doubt St. Mark had slept beneath the roof of some unhousewifely parishioner, on the night before he penned those fearful sentences anent the worm that dieth not and the fire that is not quenched.

''

''

I will transmit thy messages to Sissa, who is yet with Auntie at the Montgy White. They had been comfortably fixed by the proprietors, and as Auntie was desired to drink the waters there for two weeks before coming here, they have concluded to remain there for that time. This is a good enough arrangement: particularly as board is said to be a little cheaper there than here.

I think I improve in the matter of digestion, and I make no doubt the water will be of advantage to me in that respect. I do not as yet take much exercise: having been so long over-tired, a week or two of perfect rest is not unacceptable.

I am sorry to hear of father's indisposition, and hope he is by this time quite recovered. My love to him, and to thy father, – who I am glad to know has been staying with thee.

Embrace my bairns, for their father and thy

Lover.

To Charles Day

Allegheny Springs, Va.
July 14th 1872

My Dear Father:

Mary will doubtless have told you ere now that
I am here: and will have given you such little items of news
as my grudging love allows me to put into the love-letters that
write themselves from me to her daily.

I think I can begin to detect some good influences of the
water, distinct from the benefit which any change into more
bracing atmosphere always brings me. I find the water quite
unlike any mineral water I have ever before seen. It is remarkably clear, & cool; and is almost tasteless. Indeed the only
flavor I can distinguish is like a faint suspicion of Epsom Salts.
My quantum is half a glass, three times a day, an hour before
eating. It has had a slight aperient effect on me: and has produced a quite sensible toning-up of the digestive organs.

From present appearances, there seems to be no prospect
that the place will be crowded inconveniently. About three
hundred people, I think, are on the grounds: — a party large
enough to keep things from seeming gloomy, though I believe
two hundred more could be well accommodated.

The proprietors seem to be *au fait,* as to all matters connected
with hotel-keeping: and I have never seen better success attained
in respect of attentive servants and perfect cleanliness in dining-
room and bed-room.

John S. Preston,[18] of S. C, and E. A. Pollard, of Va, are here:
besides them, I believe, no persons of more than local note.
I have met some old friends: and made some very pleasant
acquaintances.

I suppose, however, there be a little Satan in every Paradise:
and, so I find myself often disquieted with a sense of selfishness,
in midst of the infinite delight that flows in upon me out of
the mountains and the forests — when I remember, as I do each
moment in the day, that my dear ones are not with me.

[18] John Smith Preston (1809-1881), secessionist leader and Confederate
general.

I suppose that by this time Janie is on her way to Virginia. If I knew exactly what train she left Atlanta on, I might ride to the depot and see her for a few moments.

I hope, dear Father, that the summer heats do not enfeeble you: and that some way will open itself for your annual visit to Saratoga.

Don't take the trouble to answer this: which is but a scrawl to remind you of the continual affectionate remembrance of

Your Son

S. L.

To Virginia Hankins

Allegheny Spgs. July 15th 1872

My Friend, permit me to observe that you *are* a cool one.

As they say in horsemanship, you have a firm, and at the same time, a light, hand over heavy ground.

As for example. — I had written you again yesterday, urging all the inducements I could fancy, as likely to open a way to bring our two hands together. This morning, your letter [19] was handed me. I recognized the chirography of the address, I would not open it, I carried it with me up-stairs where I was proceeding to breakfast, I placed myself in a chair so situated that a beautiful long stretch of mountains revealed itself through the opposite window, I ordered my favorite breakfast, I arranged my other letters and papers on one side, and then luxuriously opened your envelope.

Just Heaven!

" It *is* altogether within the range of possibilities for you to be in Virginia and not to see me, since were you many many miles nearer than you are, I would not, for any condition, have you come to this County—! "

A sort of dazedness seized my eyes at this point, I dropped your letter, I fell violently upon an egg and devoured it with the greatest ferocity, I stabbed my beefsteak, dismembered a

[19] Virginia Hankins's letter of July 10, 1872, to which this is a detailed answer, is the only one from her during the summer of 1872 that has survived. Lanier's letter to her of July 14, 1872, is here omitted.

piece thereof, tasted the same, then pushed away the whole with a gesture of contempt,—and resumed your letter.

" The malaria " – you proceed to observe, – is fearful, and whilst *you* are somewhat accustomed to it, yet you fear for your little sister &c, and yet you had promised to visit &c, and finally you conclude this topic with some modest asseverations as to yr. knowledge of geography.

— My Friend, when I had reached this stage, I declare to you that I was wrought up to such a degree that I could have danced about you with a stick in my hand and beaten you therewith and uttered the most frantic yells of joy at every stroke. For here have I been giving reasons why I could not come to see you, and why *you* must come to see *me*, – and you demurely declare that this cannot be, that we cannot meet, —and you assign, as cause therefor, what is the very best reason in the world why I should not come to you, and why *you* should come to *me!*

— Kind Heaven, is not this one of thy perverse women-creatures that drive men to drink and to suicide?

"

———————————

"

You next proceed to observe that you do not know anyone in Lynchburg. — Now if this is not too exasperating for any human heart to endure without breaking, – I wd. be glad to know what is. True, I said Lynchburg, in my letter: but then I presume that betwixt Wytheville and Petersburg, there are forty other places that might answer as well: and I only used Lynchburg as an example. But you, O woman-without-a-vestige-of-conscience, – you demurely remark that you know no one in Lynchburg: – as if that exhausted the subject.

"

———————————

"

Well: you continue with some very remarkable animadversions upon my solicitude for you, in particular: and upon the course of destiny, in general. From these, I select the following sentences as samples of the whole, upon which I desire to be indulged in a single observation:

(1) " Be content and let the rest of the world go, since Fate so wills it: "

(2) " It is useless to combat the ordinances of life – it is worse than folly to hope for anything that the Future may hold: "

(3) " One endures simply what is inevitable: " and

(4) " It is better to be cold than bitter."

In regard to no. (1), I have to remark that " Fate " is dead this two thousand years, – and therefore cannot " will " this or aught other thing:

As to no. (2), I beg to cite the beautiful words of Emilio Castelar: [20] – " The human race forever cools its brow and dries its tears in the breeze of Hope ":

Upon no. (3), I observe that " the inevitable " is a phrase which has no meaning save in the minds of certain imaginative persons who dwell in France and who write the most entertaining and untrue novels in the world: while, with respect to no. (4), I declare unhestitatingly that the doctrine is a lie, and he who taught it you is a liar.

—— O, my dear little Child, over whom God knows that I watch with a solicitude which is known only to lovers, to mothers and to true friends, and wh. almost seems to me to combine all these three—You will forgive me if, having commenced to write you in *badinage,* I end in prayer — in prayer that whenever it shall so happen that Life shall approach you with " the cold " in one hand and " the bitter " in the other, and shall put you upon the mournful election of one of these, – you will seize the bitter and reject the cold.

I hate cold, the cold man is dead before he dies, he has neither heaven nor hell in his future, he has no right to live and less right to die.

But bitterness, – dear, there are worse things than bitterness: bitterness has in it a vitality which, in some hearts, as time flows on, turns it to an exquisite Sweet.

—— Finally, how can I persuade you to let me see you? If *your* health does not require it, will not at least your little sister's health demand some stay in the higher regions, somewhere in this neighborhood?

[20] Emilio Castelar (1832-1899), the Spanish statesman and author of numerous political and historical works. The particular quotation given here has not been located.

Give me the pleasure of shaking your hand, of looking into your eyes, of hearing your voice. Life is short: an opportunity is an invitation from Heaven: an hour of friendly talk with you wd. be an event in my life. Let me have it, Ginna: arrange it: you are cool, you are strong, you are resourceful, you are a woman. Arrange it, and write quickly to your

Friend.

To Mary Day Lanier

[Alleghany Springs, Va.,] July 16th 1872

Last night, I promenaded the long piazza with Miss Kirchoff, of New Orleans; and presently we began to speak of German matters: and thereupon in a few moments, with soft and mellifluous tongue she did begin to repeat whole German poems to me, trippingly and yet feelingly: especially the Song of Thekla, – dost thou remember? –

> Fater, rufe dein Kind zurück,
> Ich habe gelebt und gelieben.[21]

And this morning, we met, by appointment in the parlor, and thereupon she played me a noble largo movement from Beethoven, then the *Traümerei* of Schumann, rememberest thou? –

that we heard at Theodore Thomas' concert? and then what but thy Mendellsohn's Capriccio.

Not having thy soul, she could not breathe any of these airs, as thou canst: many times the expression of the master went by, uncaught, many times it was mistaken, many times attempted but unconquered for lack of the spiritual genius thou hast residing in thy finger tips: and yet, O my beautiful Spirit. the tones of the piano and a certain liquid softness of voice gave my soul help to bring thee before me, and I sat and listened and gazed upon her and saw her not but saw thee and worshipped.

[21] Inaccurately quoted from Schiller, *Die Piccolomini*.

Dost thou know the German word *Sehnsucht: i. e. sehen* (or seh'n), to see, and *sucht,* longing – the see-longing, or sight-yearning?

So does my sight yearn for thee, who to all my sense and all my spirit art the One-Satisfaction that bringeth Heaven to thy

Lover.

TO MARY DAY LANIER

[Alleghany Springs, Va.,] July 18th 1872

The Dr. having declared that I was given over to moping and to solitude, and having insisted that I should go more into company, with a view to better digestion: I – ah – ahem – I last night plunged into the giddy mazes of the dance, and accomplished the Lancers, as also a set of quadrilles, as also a flying schottische wherein my fair partner cried out in fear and terror at the unearthly strides wherewith I did gyrate down the room. In short, dear Comrade, I have been capering like a young kid upon the mountains: thou canst fancy thy poor long-faced sheep served with caper sauce.

For long-faced he remaineth: – in spite of my greatly-increased strength, I gain not an ounce of flesh. Perhaps this will come later: I am certainly greatly improved: tho' I cannot definitely say that the water – whose effect, I thought I noticed definitely for a day or two – continues to show any decided influence. They have a remarkable alum-and-iron spring here, which the Dr. wishes me to commence using in a day or two: the water thereof being considered much stronger than that of Rockbridge Alum Springs.

I am glad to have read thy message, wh. comes to thee from Heaven through thy friend and well-wisher Mollie White.[22] Perhaps by this time the good woman has found thy mother and told her how gray thine eyes are and how heavenly-sweet are thy lips and brows.

[22] In her letter of July 12, 1872, Lanier's wife had sent him a note from a Macon friend, Mrs. Gardiner, delivered by her daughter, Mollie White. Mrs. Gardiner had died between the writing and the delivery of the note.

— I did not leave any boots; nor any *camisa* that I knew of, nor vest: at any rate I have had no need of either.

— That thou art not so well, – is great pain to me: but I rejoice that thou hast thy father's loving heart, to be at ease upon. I fear thou doest not prosper, in the hot airs of this July. I long so for that happy first of August which shall bring me to thee, and both of us to the sweet mountain-winds of our Marietta. Then, my pretty, thou wilt straighten stem and be fresh-petalled: God keep thee till then, thou Tuberose!

My love distribute thou betwixt thy father and mine, and my two young men.

It is but twelve days ere I start, for thee and my bairns!

I desire that thou trouble not thyself in the least degree to write me. Let it not be upon thy mind, save as a pleasure, when thou hast plenty of time and of strength. I know that thou art my True-heart, Wife: and that I am thy

Lover.

To Virginia Hankins

Allegheny Spgs. July 18th 1872

Dear Friend, I don't believe in special providences: and, if I did, I wouldn't believe that Providence would ever do anything special for a lout like me that isnt worth even a general providence: — but today I had a talk with Mr. Ricks, of Norfolk, yr. cousin, — to whom I was casually introduced – who is here with his wife, and with Mrs. Milhado & Miss M. Now why couldn't you run down, – or up? – here for a day or two and be chaperoned by them?

And how a ride through these blessèd mountains with you, would be one of my glories!

Friend, Friend, do I weary you with importunities? If I do, forget not, it is the pleading of a

—— Friend –

To Mary Day Lanier

[Alleghany Springs, Va.,] July 19 th 1872

Lord, what a silly thing is man!

— The gentleman who waits on my room is a colored gentleman. His name is John Brown : but his principles are not John
Brown. He is tall, slim, erect: and his head runs up to a point
like that of the traditional Bones. He is Dignity, Affability,
Humility, Discrimination, Sense and Deftness combined : and
he has an eye single to the due and plentiful distribution of
towels.

On the first morning after my arrival, this blessed Combination fell in love with my pantaloons, which he had carried out to brush, and which he brought in, tenderly hung
over his arm, and restored to me with lingering glances and
expressive phrases of commendation; – a passion somewhat
surprising, since John Brown is a middle-aged man, not given
to the gew-gaws of life at all, and therefore I regarded it as
at once a tribute to John Brown's taste in admiring and to my
own in selecting.

On the next day, – when John Brown "had come to know
me well", – he did me the honor to extend his affection beyond
my pants to myself, and he has since displayed his attachment in all manner of attentions, insomuch that I can really
say I was never better cared for by any servant in my life.
This attachment is also shared by Matilda, John Brown's female
coadjutor, a spruce and sprightly chambermaid, who refuses to
let John make up my beds of mornings; flatly informing him
that he cannot do it nicely enough.

Now this morning, to me lying lazily in bed and meditating
whether I should get up or snooze away another fifteen
minutes: John Brown, having entered by my window (as is
his habit; to save me the trouble of getting up to unlock my
door, when he desires access to my boots: and I wd. give a
pound of flesh if you could see, of mornings, at the invariable
same time, this good creature's long foot, followed by his
long leg, slowly inserting itself into my window, and carefully
feeling it way to the floor, – so as not to awake me –, to be

followed by the long body, writhing in serpentine convolu-
tions through the all-too-small space, – the whole done with
inimitable gravity, dignity and softness, such as nearly chokes
me as I lie covertly watching in the bed where honest John
thinks I am asleep !) remarks, seeing me awake, that a phenomenon totally unaccountable to him arrests his attention
every morning, towit: that, although I walk about over the
wet walks, yet he never finds a particle of mud sticking to
my boots, when he cleans them of mornings: adding that he
has waited upon a great many gentlemen, but that I am the
very nicest one in all particulars that he has ever served.

All this I take with a kind of lordly air, – as if mud really
had too much respect for me to stick on my boots–, and John
retires, with the air of a man whose mind is easier after a
deliverance of opinion. — – Now, wilt thou believe it ? I have
daundered about the grounds all day, swinging my cane, in such
a mood of intense complacency and self-satisfaction as rarely
falls to my lot: and, coming to bring myself under examination,
at dinner-time, I, after rigid self-scrutiny, cannot discover the
slightest cause for this complacency, except John Brown's
remark this morning: nay, I am convinced the flower grows
from that root alone.

—   One is not only not indifferent to the praise of the
humblest human being: but one even accepts the flattery which
one knows to be simply absurd, and unconsciously places it in
one's button-hole, as if it were a reward of merit !
Therefore I say, what a silly thing is   Thy

Lover.

To Mary Day Lanier

[Alleghany Springs, Va.,] July 22nd 1872

For two days, Comrade, I have not sent thee any of my little
mountain-flowers. On Saturday I went over to see Sister. I
found her in bed with a genuine attack of croup. She had been
suffering with a severe cold for some days: and as usual had
done nothing for it. The croup-attack was beginning when I
got there. I promptly sallied forth to forage for physic: and
went to work on her with quinine and carbonate of Potash.

These succeeded admirably and yesterday morning she was up and well.

I got back here last night and tried hard to have a letter for you in the mail, but could not yet get it in, in time.

I was unable to write you, from there: Mrs. Watt,– who is in great health and rages about the grounds devouring everybody – occupied much of my time showing me round to the people: and I found there, very unexpectedly, Tench Schley and Sallie,[23] who had stopped on their return from Baltimore. Tench was to leave last night for Memphis. Sallie remains for a month.

Sissa & Auntie are to come over here tomorrow, for a day's visit. Henry J. Lamar and daughter, and Mrs. Bibb, are here.

Give my love to father, and my thanks for the papers he sent me, wh. I received this morning. I rejoice to learn from thy two letters, that thy father remains with thee.

I am glad thou hast written to Ginna. I have another letter from her wh. thou shalt read, when I have answered it.

"
———
"

It is late in the afternoon, the air is cold, brilliant, tense as a bent steel bow, and invigorating as life itself, the shadows extend themselves at great length along the grass as if they were all lazily a-stretch, from the top of a high tree a locust sings his long monotone, just outside my window a dog stands lapping the water with red tongue, yonder under his favorite avenue of Maples lazily strolls Pollard, hump-backed, bent, gazing upon the earth, here come two on horseback, Franceville of Mobile and pretty Mrs. Barney, and clatter off up the road, here sit I – thy lover – bound by an entrancing yearning for thee, and the mountains enclose us all, with a sort of quiet smile upon them as of a great aged wise man who understands it all and knows the end and meaning of it.

I pass my days simply in longing for thee, in building hopes for thee, in execrating the hard moments in which I have been with thee without the power of worshipping thee as I desire, in exquisite bodyings forth of the kiss I hope soon to win from

[23] Sallie Lanier Schley was a Montgomery cousin; Mr. Lamar and Mrs. Bibb, mentioned in the following paragraph, were Macon friends.

thy lips. Thy lovers [letters?] come, like Glory, to sit upon the
brow of thy

Lover.

To Mary Day Lanier

[Alleghany Springs, Va.,] July 23rd 1872.

Last night my partner in a Lancers was Mrs. Manly, of Columbus, (née Doughty, of Augusta). As we stood up, she said:
" I once saw your wife, at a concert, not long before you were
married. It was at a time when the hair was accustomed to be
frizzed and generally complicated with all sorts of puffs, rolls
&c. Your wife's was brushed plainly back: and she had a string
of pearls wound round her head. I thought she was the loveliest
human being I ever beheld." – Thus, thou pretty Comrade!
when I had been forced temporarily to put my unceasing Dream
of thee into the background of my soul in order to collect my
forces to entertain my partner, – thus did this good creature
give me *carte blanche* to bring thee forward, to talk of thee,
to contemplate thee. For this unconscious grace she did me,
I do love her much: and therefore have I already caused
Monsieur Manly – who has but possessed this lady some six
months and is not, I suppose, as yet quite firmly seated in the
saddle – to cut his eyes round at me.
—— Ha! by all the Wiggletails, who, nay *what,* is this which
comes oscillating from side to side, and which slowly moves,
by a marvellous composition of forces, down the ball-room?
It is concealed in vast quantities of draperies. If an earthquake,
or a boiler explosion, should shoot the lay-figure in a milliner's
establishment through successive shelves of clothes and string
the garments thereon like partridges trussed upon a spit, – that
wd. be like this — phenomenon. It has white slippers, and it
appears to move upon tremulous springs, like those glass pea-
cocks which were toys when I was a child. Yet no less is its
head on springs: and its eyes are worked by vigorous wires:
for it languishes, ogles, smiles, smirks, snickers, giggles,
trembles, shivers, shrugs, all in a moment.
  It is going to dance.
  It dances.

It dances doubly. It dances behind, and it dances before: and its behind-dancing is no more like its before-dancing than wriggling is like capering.

Ye spirits of the Chamois, of the Wild Goat, of the Kangaroo, of the Dromedary: Ye Wild Phantoms of the Wiggletail, of the water-moccasin, of the tadpole, hear my prayer, protect this fair young Devotee, who is made in Your image, who follows in your way, who faithfully worships you: guide her footsteps, have watchful eye upon her front and her rear: which I ask, for that she is my countrywoman, she is my compatriote. She is Miss Tharpe, of Macon.

I am Thy Lover

To Mary Day Lanier

[Alleghany Springs, Va.,] July 25 th 1872

A quick fierce shower has just rushed across our valley and gone careering into the mountains yonder, and – as if they were thereby frightened out of their lairs – a troop of strange griffin-shaped mists is flying up the gorges in disorderly succession. The mountains have grown dark and iron-bound, with a stern blue cloud contracting about them: but yonder on the left this cloud has broken into a splendid sheet of rain, which is as white and soft as a lace veil, being illuminated by rays of the low sun that come slanting through a gorge which opens out westward. Behind this water-veil, a great round mountain dimly outlines itself: and it is as if one saw a new world forming itself into a globe and about to roll forth presently into space. Through another gorge come rays which light up our meadow and lawn. They are all a-glitter, green and silver, grass and raindrops.

From a stand hidden in among the trees higher up the lawn, come strains of harmony: the brass band is playing there. These wandering chords float about over the monotone of the river,– which is now louder and more vigorous since the rain – very much as yonder light cloud-wreaths linger about the sides of the steadfast mountains.

"
———————
"

Child, Child, amidst these shifting phantasmagories of clouds, of suns, of mountains, of streams, of rains, of music, of trees, of grass; while all sweep over me in a dim shock of delight and of yearning, I do not shape to myself any definite thought, save one: it is that I love thee infinitely, being naught more, nor less, nor else, than

thy Lover.

To Virginia Hankins

Allegheny Springs, Va
July 26th 1872.

—— First, however, I must tell you something wh. I doubt not will make you laugh.

Some days ago, I concluded, after mature deliberation, and in full view of the possible consequences (for, as the personage whom I am presently to introduce to you afterwards remarked to me, " where there's strange washerwomen, you know, Mr. Lanier, things will get mixed ") – to send some linen into the laundry. Now, the gathering up, the counting, and the classification, which are involved in operations of this description, have always been, to me, matters to be postponed to the very last moment, and to be altogether avoided, if possible: for they always bring me into a most low-spirited and melancholy state of helpless heat and perspiring perplexity (the alliteration is quite irresistible: you teach me you know, not to struggle against Fate.).

Fortifying myself, however, by a few moments spent in private meditation upon a certain heathen maxim which is to be often found in the Copy-books of the period, as also upon a saying of St. Paul from which I do often draw much courage when I am about to begin any arduous undertaking which requires a forgetfulness of the past and a hopefulness of the future; I pressed on, and, – after a season of toil such as could be realized by only one person in all history — that person St. George while he was slaying his dragon, & only by him provided he slew in the summer time –: not to mention a condition of bewilderment which well-nigh rendered me unable to distinguish a sock from a handkerchief, and wh. I cannot

illustrate more effectively than by referring to the construction
of this sentence –; I finally enjoyed, – if I could be said to
"enjoy" anything in my condition at such times – the satisfaction of banding to Matilda Chambermaid a bundle, whose
departure gave me a lively realization of the sentiments of
Christian when his pack fell from off his back – and hang the
rhyme. (I am obliged to pause here, a moment, in order to
avail myself of what is probably the only opportunity I shall
ever have to transmit the praises of this Matilda to succeeding
ages: and I do aver in brief, and will maintain the same against
all comers, that in the matter of the making up of a bed she
has daily afforded me the sublimest example, not only of self-
sacrifice in respect of muscle and of breath, but of modest
humility, in accomplishing deftly and quickly and successfully
what I have always regarded as requiring perhaps as much
foresight, delicacy, strength, endurance, spinal elasticity and
moral courage as any other human undertaking: and the favor
she has shown me in the daily distribution of fresh towels, – in
which her kindness to me has been lavish to the degree of reck-
lessness – has impressed me profoundly with the conviction
that (*a*) either she has been touched by that attitude of chivalric
politeness which I am always careful to assume to this class of
persons who are the arbiters of our happiness – for suppose they
don't come to "make you up" till five O'clock in the afternoon! – and who hold our lives in their hands, – for suppose
they leave needles in the beds! – : or (*b*) that she regards me
as a person who needs a great deal of scrubbing!)

Soon after Matilda had disappeared with my pack, she returned to me, all a-smile, bearing in her hand a paper (of which
the enclosed is a *fac-simile*, being indeed a duplicate, in all
respects, *verb. lit. punct. print.* paper, and all), which she
handed me, with the request that I wd. read the note written
on the back thereof. Reading, I found what you see on the back
hereof. I responded "yes, I know them well": whereupon she
flitted away, and in a few moments returned, still more broadly
a-smile, and informed me, with an air of mystery, that "the
lady in charge of the Laundry Department desired to make my
acquaintance, and requested that I would meet her in the hotel
parlor the same evening at nine O'clock."

Upon inquiry, I was informed that "the lady" was unmar-

ried: was from Richmond: was nice ": beyond which items
Matilda could not enlighten me, nor could she give me any
intelligible account of her name.

Having gathered these particulars, I observed to myself that
here seemed to be the beginning of a very pretty adventure,
indeed: – a nice, unmarried lady communicates with me upon
the back of a Washing-List, and then mysteriously desires me
to meet her at an appointed hour, in a crowded parlor, whose
crowd wd. be our solitude.

It so happened that when the fated hour arrived I was in the
ball-room under engagement for a dance (well, open yr. eyes,
if you like, *I* don't care, I'm not dead yet); and when I proceeded to the parlor my fair *Incognita* was not to be found.
Thus matters remained until the day before yesterday: when,
as I was putting on my coat to fare forth on the lawn, Matilda
appeared in a state of breathless agitation and announced
through the window that the Lady was then on her way, coming
to see me. I hastily completed my toilet: tho' meantime the
Lady had arrived, and I had begged her, through Matilda, to
be seated,—handing out a chair through the door.

Presently, I emerged, in gorgeous array, prepared to kill and
utterly devour any presumptuous female who shd. throw out
any challenge to flirt.

I was confronted by your Cousin, Miss Cornelia
Winston. — Matilda Chambermaid hovered about, with sparkling eyes.

After a second of stiffness, succeeding her announcement of
her name to me, – for you must know my face is so elongated
that few people have the temerity to venture upon a joke in
my presence – the comicalness of " the situation " struck us
both so irresistibly, that we laughed till our sides ached, while
she related to me her manifold troubles. A crowd is here:
this crowd is well-provided with clothes; these clothes had been
flowing in upon poor Miss Winston in such multitudes that she
had utterly lost all reckoning: and scenes of worry, of distress,
and of ill-humor were daily being enacted in her *sanctum* which
wd. melt the hardest heart. Among multitudes of sufferers, —
for probably never before on this earth was there collected in
one spot a more miscellaneous assortment of male and female
wearing-apparel awaiting identification by the owners thereof

— I was *parva pars*: whereat Miss W. was greatly distressed: and after in vain endeavoring to prevail upon me to accept a white vest of a gentleman who she said she was sure, had gone off with mine, she finally made an attack upon me in the matter of socks,—a particular in which I was also loser–: and fairly threw me into a spasm as she told me with a tear half-starting into her eye and with tragic bated breath: " Mr. Lanier, *please* come up and look over the socks: I'm sure *you* can find 'em; I've got at least a peck of 'em that nobody can't recognize; and lem 'me tell you something" she added, half crying and half laughing, " I'm so mixed up about socks, a thing happened to me this morning that I don't remember ever to have occurred to me before: I got a pair of stockings out of my trunk, — a pair of my own stockings, Mr. Lanier – and when I put 'em on, I found they were odd! "

"
_____
"

I *won't* teaze by pretending I don't understand why you cannot come.

Indeed, Friend, I do not think that I've been doing anything more, in all I've said, than simply going through a trick in wh. I've often caught myself, towit: the trick of fighting off, and fighting off, a conclusion to which I do not like to come.

It is true, you *are* a woman: and that *is* the reason, in the last analysis, why we cannot meet this time: and, verily, that *being* the reason, I can " forgive God " for not allowing us to clasp hands until later: for, indeed I would not have you a man, for a world of fair women.

Well, well, Little One, I am of the sort that never give up a thing: – and the summer is not yet over.

On Monday, I must return to Georgia, where I have some engagements I cannot well neglect: meantime write me at *Marietta,* and keep me advised of yr. movements.

Yr. two letters, of 20 th & 24th, have reached me. I will not attempt to express to you the delight wh. I have drawn from them: for I could only do so in such extravagant terms as might not be seemly.

I am much improved since I came here, by the waters: but the climate is too damp for me, and I must hurry out of it.

As for the good spirits: why, I am in good Spirits' hands, here. Out of the beauty of this exquisite place: out of the mountains, the trees, the wonderful grass-blades, the streams, the rain-storms, the sunshine, the stars, — there exhales continually a sacred Serenity into my soul: whereby my heart grows to be " at rest with itself," insomuch that I am able, as any strong or complete man should be, to lay hold of life with a firm hand and mould it to my mood, be that humorous or earnest.

—— But Ah, you Fine-Heart, you Faithful-Soul! – how I did long to gaze with you upon these distant blue hill-sides and wander with you upon the near ones, and wonder with you at these long graceful swaying grass-blades which I love!

– However, as I said, the summer is not over –: and it is impudent to forestall God's management of His world, by saying that a thing will not be. — I cannot but believe that your Spirit does visit me, from out the winds of day and night; and I dwell with inexpressible emotion upon the eloquent sweet words wh. you send me in this behalf. That this coming to be about one so poor as I am — is a pure grace of yours, I well know: and there is no acknowledgement can be made thereof, save a reverent kiss printed on each footstep you make.

———— Write me at Marietta.

———————

To Mary Day Lanier

[Alleghany Springs, Va.,] July 26th 1872

Rain, and early dark, have come on and surprised me while I have been writing a long letter to Ginna, and one to my father: and I have but time before the mail goes off, to acknowl-edge thine of 23rd wh. came this morning, and wh. refers to thine " of last night " wh. I have not recd. I did not know thou hadst been ill, lately. Thou pretty Sweet! I am about to return to thee.

First, the climate is too moist for me: and Second, I can be with thee at Marietta and derive as much benefit from the water as here: for it loses absolutely nothing by transportation.

Sissa will not marry before winter: thou needest not therefore

to weary thyself now with packing to move. She will not speak
to father of it yet awhile. But of this, more anon.[24]

I wish thee to get out of Macon, to change thy life, to drink
some Allegheny Water, to gain some time to give thyself over
utterly unto loving thy

                              Lover.

I leave here Monday morning about nine O'clock: but cannot
learn exactly what time this will bring me to Macon: it will be
either Tuesday eve, or Wednesday morning.

                    To Robert S. Lanier

                              Marietta, Ga. Sept. 18th 1872 [25]

My Dear Father:
                    I was glad to learn from yr. letter to Sister that
matters were going on smoothly, and that you had enough to
keep you so busy.

[24] Lanier's wife had written, July 23: " Yet, I am persuaded that Papa [R. S.
Lanier] or Sissa, or *both* will shortly marry, and that our effects ought to be in
good order for removal, and systematically, (not entomologically) packed." For
the past few years the Sidney Laniers and R. S. Lanier had been living in the
home of Gertrude Lanier Shannon.

[25] Lanier had returned to Macon at the end of July. But he had left shortly
thereafter—presumably on Aug. 1 according to plan (see Mary Day Lanier's
letter to him, July 23, 1872)—to spend the rest of the summer in Marietta with
his wife and boys. No letters by him between July 26 and Sept. 18, 1872, have
been found; but apparently his health had not improved, and his father was
already thinking of Texas for him. On Aug. 19, he had written:
" Councillor Wright handed me the other day a copy of N. O. Med. & Sur.
Journal which I send, containing a communication from *Boerne*, Texas, as to
climate &c. which you will find on p. 39. It is so in accordance with the
thoughts that I have been seriously digesting for sometime past that I send it to
you – not waiting till I go up – that you may consider the matter beforehand, &
give me your views when we meet. Boerné, as you see, is situate in the mountains. I have just been examining the locality with Bob Jamieson, on a map at
the Bank. It is about fifty miles above San Antonio, near Braunfels. Jamieson
says he has been at the latter place but not the other. He says it is a beautiful
country. Boerne is near to or on a branch of the Guadelope river. He says the
route is to go to N. O. then by steamer to Galveston, then by Rail to Columbia
about 100 miles, then by Stage, equal to Rail (magnificent roads & teams &c) to
San Antonio. My notion is that you & Mary both need a different climate from
any you have been in, & that the climate referred to is what both of you need.
I think you should go there and spend the winter with your family, & if you
improve remain there one year, if you continue to improve remain two years,
& if then you have toned up your systems to robust health, return here & resume

Saw Bacon on Saturday, who told me that law-business was dull. He seems to have a good case for the Telegraph Company.

Our lives here are so uneventful, and one day is so much like another, that there is really nothing to support a correspondence. Sister [26] and Mamie went to Atlanta today on the twelve Oclock train, and returned late in the afternoon. They seem to have done a good deal of shopping.

Sister keeps well: and Mamie is beginning to improve very rapidly. The children all have slight colds: otherwise well. Weather very delightful.

I looked anxiously in today's Constitution for the Sup. Ct. decision in the Thatcher case, but didn't find it. I suppose probably another batch of decisions will be published tomorrow:

Sister tells me she has written you for some money. Please include, in the check you send her, twenty dollars ($20.00) for me; as my cash on hand is quite inconveniently low.

I ride horseback faithfully twice a day: and in all respects am improved, tho' for some unaccountable reason I've been suffering a great deal of pain from an unlocate-able and indescribable misery in my chest for several days.

I'm beginning to get very restive in idleness, and hope to get to my work before long. Let me hear from you whenever you get time.

Your loving Son
Sidney.

To Mary Day Lanier

Macon. Oct. 16th 1872.

Here came I safely, praise to the God of travellers.[27]
Perhaps at this moment thou art in midst of thine agony.

the practice, & meantime you can practice there, or otherwise engage yourself as circumstances & your health will permit. I have a strong conviction you will get into good health there. (Bro. Sid has told me about the effect of that climate on him. . . .) If you remain here I do not think your health will be such as to enable you to work. I had rather increase my own activity & do your work for you than to see you try under the circumstances. I have an *immense* desire to see you take rank as your capacity entitles you."

[26] Gertrude Lanier Shannon and her son had joined the Laniers at Marietta on Aug. 22.

[27] From the available evidence, Lanier seems to have remained in Marietta from

My heart is there throbbing with thine, and praying that out of thy keen pain may come rest, even as out of the rough moss-rose-husk cometh the perfect bud.

Father and Uncle Clifford are off a-lawing, the one at Twiggs and 'tother at Sumter. Both will probably return this afternoon.

I have been sitting in the office this morning, where thy brother and father have held talk with me. Thy father hath found a gentleman here, who left here some time ago and spent some time in San Antonio for his health. He was entirely restored, and is now living here in active business. He had hæmorrhage from lungs. This encourageth all parties. Thy father seemeth well: so Cubbie.[28] This latter will go down tomorrow morning, leaving the wife of his bosom, who will follow some time next week. Sissa hath a cold, and cougheth in season and out of season, – but groweth better. She had things very bright for me, – warm coffee, blazing fires &c, – and what with over towering piles of blankets on my bed did make me sensible of Empedocles his feelings when that he lay with Mt. Aetna atop of him. All seemeth to fare along quietly in ye domestick world. Mistress L. did not receive ye important letter containing ye propositions of alliance, until just as she was settynge forthe on her journey homeward, by reason of her absence from N. Y. at Morristown where she was gadding. She is just arrived here.[29]

This is alle the Newes I know. Herewith I send thee Appleton's, which I in vayn did look for in Atlanta: allsoe a certayne most comicalle-tragicalle book 'cleped Tom Thumb, which my little Sydney can suck spiritually even as he doth physically suckle his material thumb.

"

———————————

"

Aug. 1 to Oct. 15, 1872 (see Mary Day Lanier's letter of Oct. 15). Though without any real improvement in health, he returned to Macon and to work on the latter date, leaving his wife and children in Marietta until the end of the malarial season.

[28] Harry Day, Lanier's brother-in-law.

[29] The reference is apparently to R. S. Lanier's prospective second wife. Lanier's use of the older spelling may have been prompted by his recent reading of Sir Thomas More (see his letter to Mary Day Lanier, Oct. 17, 1872, here omitted).

And now, Wife, the thought that I can trust thee to the Love of God is all that bringeth aught of rest to the anxious-hovering and fiery-solicitous love of thy

Husband.

Allsoe herewith I enclose the key of my P. O. Box wh. after all I find I have brought away with me.

To Mary Day Lanier

Macon, Oct. 18th 1872

Thy note is come, and bringeth me a world of pleasure, in that I know thou art better and little Nimble-wits is well.

Thy love droppeth upon my musty law-life even as a rose-petal droppeth on the dust and glorifieth the same with the warm red thereof. Yet task not thy fingers and thy brain: for I know at how great disadvantage thou wieldest the pen.

Art able to sit in the sun? I hope thou feelest him, warm upon thee.

By reason of stress of time, I say no more. After tomorrow, I propose not to work any more in the office.[30] Father and Uncle C. both at work today, and both well.

I do well: and thy father, whom I saw this morning, and will see again at dinner-time.

I send thee a letter of Ginna's, just come, for thy delectation.

I am irked that thou hadst not my book for the little mirthful Soul in time. There was no reason but negligence of the mail-people why thou shouldst not have had that any my letter yesterday.

As one that liveth underneath a star, so, walking alway beneath the bright thought of *thee,*   liveth

Thy Husband.

---

[30] By this date Lanier had apparently decided to go to Texas (see his letter of Oct. 21, below), though it was nearly a month before he finally left Macon.

To Mary Day Lanier

Macon. Oct. 20th 1872.

I have but time to send thee a quick husband's-kiss, having unadvisedly put off my letter until it is nearly the hour that we fare homeward.

Sister hath written thee today.

I stop work from this out. 'Tis so dusty that I like not to stay in town, where the irritating particles do fill the air and insinuate themselves into all the apertures of the human frame.

I do well, and find my weight somewhat increased.

I hope that I may be able to come back and spend some sweet days with thee, ere thou comest down: which latter event I do not wish thee to hasten.

Thy father is well. Commend me to my young men: for whom mine eyes thirst and mine arms hunger. Also to thyself, for whom breaketh my

Heart.

To Mary Day Lanier

Macon. Oct. 21 st 1872

So: I have thy letter announcing that thou hadst celebrated little Soul-o'-mirth's birthday by walking over to visit our dear friend: and that thou hadst again walked across. I rejoice that thou hast been able to do these things: yet grieve for thy weariness in the doing thereof.

x   x   x   x   x   x   x 31

This matter keepeth my soul continually upon her knees: for God is great, and this *one* thing I do know, towit, that in bitterness my soul findeth no rest, whereas in love I am upborne upon a vast Content even as the eagle upon the still air of the world. Let the Will of God be done.

″
———————
″

[31] Parts of this letter, apparently referring to the condition of Mary Day Lanier's health, have been cut out. A few conjectural restorations have been made on the second page.

It is settled that I will go to Texas; but no details are arranged: nor will I arrange any until I see thee.   I could not sell the lot to Mr. Roberts as I had proposed: everybody here is avoiding investments in real estate, on account of the Taxes, wh. are very large. I hope to sell to Mr. Huff: and am to have a definite answer from him this afternoon.[32] I wrote that I wish thee to stay in Marietta just so long as seemeth good to thee: and I add that I do not wish thee to come here yet awhile.   However it is now [my] expectation to return to thee in Marietta a[n]d spend some days with thee there before I bring thee back here. This is *certain*, unless something unforeseen [s]hould happen.   Meantime nothing will [be] arranged, about Texas, until I see thee: [and] there will be no progress for me to re[port] to thee save the selling of the lot, [a thing] I hope to accomplish, but which is [most] uncertain, for reasons aforesaid. Things go on well and smoothly at [hom]e. I have – broken off work, entirely, and am my own man. Uncle C. has talked with me about Texas. He earnestly advises me to go there, as the clearly wise course.

"

————————

"

I have been revelling in certain sublime sonnets of Michael Angelo, whose powers I knew not before.   I will send them to thee. He is peer to our Sir Thomas [More]: and cometh nearer to thy heart and mine, being an Artist, – wh. Sir Thomas was not. I know nothing more intense, more pure, more sorrow-fine, than some of these sonnets.

"

————————

"

God take thee in His arms, Lady, and thee hold fast from all mischance and all sorrow, prayeth thy

Lover.

[32] In his effort to raise money for the Texas trip, Lanier was trying to sell his Orange Street property, bought the previous year (see note 58, 1871). It was finally sold to his father in May, 1874 (Bibb Co., Ga., Deed Book X, 248).

To Mary Day Lanier

Macon.   Oct. 23rd 1872

If I have done aught this day-and-night since I wrote thee, save think upon thy saintly face, revel in thy sweetness, pray for thy strengthening, and glory in hopes of being by thee soon, – may my sins be as little as that aught.

O my Love, how very utterly am I thy lover!
To me, Time is what time thou art by: and Life is whatever sweet subtle force that may be that preserves thine eyes gray and wifely to me and thy lips sweet and red to me : and Death is that which hideth me from thee.

"

"

Here we have welcome rain, and a ceaseless wind: tho' the air is warm and balmy enough. I have kept me away from the office all day, fearful of that no-breaking-off-place which maketh always a hard task to stop a piece of work once begun. My cold is greatly better. There is a case of ours in the Supreme Court, of no great importance, wh. likely will be called this week, towards the latter end thereof. It is probable I will go to Atlanta to argue it: and thence to thee, to remain until I am willing for thee to come down. Matters be all smooth, here. I have no news of bargain-and-sale to send thee, not having seen Huff today.

"

"

God get thee to sleep tenderly this night, My Child, My Darling, – crieth

Thine.

To Robert S. Lanier

Marietta, Ga, Oct. 28th 1872

My Dear Father:

         I arrived safely yesterday morning, and found a rejoicing family awaiting my arrival.

Mary is still very much under the weather, but improving.

Dr. Dunwoody has initiated a new course of treatment for her, from which I have reason to hope the best results. I cannot yet tell exactly what day we will return: but will make it the earliest day when it is prudent for her to travel.

The weather is simply perfect. The clear, sweet air is a noble tonic to me, and the mountain seems like a great coal of fire, so brilliant are the flaming tints with which Autumn is consuming the foliage. There is a spring in the air that makes me feel as if life were not quite all gone.

I have met here a Dr. Steiner, – brother of Dr. Steiner, of Augusta– who lived twenty years in Texas, at Austin mostly. He is an invalid. He thinks the climate of Texas very fine: but says that there is a fine dust at San Antonio, which renders that not so desirable a point as some others.

I shall go down to Atlanta tomorrow, and attend to the Thatcher matter.

The children are in fine condition, except that Sidney has some cold which reduces his merriment to some extent.

Mary sends a great deal of love to you and Sissa & Eddie.

Your Son

Sidney L.

To Virginia Hankins

Macon, Ga. Nov. 9th 1872.

So: you are in exile.[33]

How dear is Home, when it is receding from one's view?

God weaves another bond betwixt me and you, Friend. In a week, I, too, will be in exile. I do not get well, here. The climate is atrocious. It makes me stop my work too often. I've been ill, – and enforcedly idle, all summer. It is decreed that I cannot live in this air. Behold me therefore about to depart, for Western Texas, where they say a man can breathe and be full of life. I go to San Antonio, first: and then roam, till I find some spot that suits me, where I settle, to practice my profession, – if I live, wh. is likely.

---

[33] Virginia Hankins was spending the winter in St. Louis, probably employed as a governess (see her letter to Lanier, Oct. 13, 1872).

Thus doth Misfortune kick his football. Perhaps, this next time, Fortune, who affects high strokes, will get a fair kick, and lift me in air. This, – only because 'tis the comical view: I am not a pagan: Fortune is a heathen God: and the heathen Gods are all dead and I don't believe in them. I believe in God. He understands His world. Let Him do His will. I fear not but it will be well done.

You say rightly, it is not well to keep one's friend in ignorance of one's life. Advise me, therefore, quickly, what make you in St. Louis, city of bacon, of iron, of trade? Are you turned Cook, – or Author? Do you teach the little tongues to gabble French, do you wash, or lecture on Woman's Rights, or, – heavens! what a range of guessing your silence as to yr. occupation leaves me!

And who is he that " is anxious for you to enjoy y'rself," and conveys you hither and thither? Aha! What manner bells be these that tinkle in my ear, from far? And who is this I dimly see, in white, floating along the aisle o' the church?

Answer me these, thou!

Write me here, until you hear from me further. I'm keen to know what you are doing. You're " a deep 'un," as somebody says: and you keep your counsel well, till act-time comes: which is great, and good, and makes me glad that I am

Your Friend

S. L.

To Mary Day Lanier

Montgomery, Ala. Nov. 14th 1872 [84]

So, thou Sweet *pro tem*. Widow, am I so far on my way to the far countree, without other hap than being delayed an hour on the road at Auburn by the breaking of some valve of our engine, – and a crick in my neck wh. hath given me that degree of discomfort that I have postponed my letter to thee all day (in the hope of being better and of giving thee a longer epistle) until now it is ten o'clock at night and I so tired that

[84] Lanier had brought his family home from Marietta early in November. On November 13, he left Macon for Montgomery on his way to Texas.

I am fain lay my head on thy love, as it were on thy bosom, and go to sleep: first, only, announcing to thee that all here (including dear Grandmother who came over to meet me this morning) are well and do cover me with kindly cares so that I lack not for aught of possible comfort: secondly, begging thee say to my father that this same crick hath estopped me from writing him today and that I will do so tomorrow, D. V.; thirdly, conveying through thee my love and blessings to Sissa and Eddie and my two young men of my house: and fourthly and lastly transporting to thy lips, by the dear Angel of Kisses, the most reverent tender salute of thine

Husband.

To Mary Day Lanier

Montgomery, Nov. 15th 1872

Well,   Well, *J'ai grandi* : the things wh. did please my youth, please me not now: it is thou that hath wrought this change: for thou art delicate, thou art as it were silken-souled and thy heart is of lily-petal texture, and in being much by thee I have had to cast out what was gross in me.

Nearly all folk offend me, but thee ; and mine apprehension is become so nice that it layeth continual burden upon my charity, in compelling the ceaseless manufacture of excuse and allowance and extenuation.

This moral should come at the *end* of a fable : but my fable were better remain unrelated.

"
——————————
"

I found Aunt Jane, Cliff and Willie waiting for me at the depot when I arrived night before last, hopped into the carriage with them, supped hastily, plunged into my black suit, and fared forth with 'em all to the Theatre where Auntie had secured a box in honor of me. From this box we saw Mrs. Bowers play Mary Stuart,[35] and did while away some two

[35] Elizabeth Crocker Bowers (1830-1895), who had made her debut as early as 1846, was at the peak of her career at this time. The play was an American version of Schiller's *Maria Stuart*.

hours in alternating tears for the wrongs of this unhappy queen (wh. were personated with some force), and jokes upon some most farcical-tragical acting of the Star's so-called " support." Then we fared back, and I quickly to bed, being crook-necked and greatly way-worn. Yesterday I passed in pulling at this same crook, and in lounging around grandmother's and today we have all been nursing Auntie, and indoors all day, the weather having suddenly changed to bitter cold.

Thus thou hast all the outward facts of my life : there being but one inward fact, wh. is thyself.

"

"

So: thou learnest to take no thought for the morrow of pain? It is the prettiest lesson of our life. An a sparrow shd. pass over, in her small fancy, the multitudes of wing-flutterings, of keen hopes, of heart-breaking disappointments, of frights, of distresses, that she must needs know in the matter of crumb-getting during the little years of her life, I make no doubt she wd. be fain creep under the dead leaves and pray for the hawk to come quickly and have his will upon her. To crowd into one day, by sad fore-brooding, the sorrow of six months, is as it were to over-eat oneself of sorrow: wh. must needs be terrible, when a surfeit of even a good thing is known to be full of hurt.

God hath the same care of our heart-growth which he hath of the earth-growth: and sendeth sorrow, as rain, not in torrents, but in drops, so that the slim grasses and the violets take no harm.

Our life, verily, is ordered, not in a heap, but as thou well sayest day-by-day: and thou art a sweet Christian sage to discover this and to act upon it.

I kiss thy letter wh. is just come to me, enclosing Whitlock's: to wh. latter I will reply fairly, as I think thou wdst. like me, healing, if I may, what wound may have been given.[36] Continually over to thee passeth the fervent aspiration of my

Love.

[36] This is apparently in reference to a misunderstanding over Lanier's board bill in Marietta (see Mary Day Lanier's letter of Nov. 14, 1872).

To Mary Day Lanier [37]

Montgomery, Ala. Nov. 17 th 1872.

" . . . . Hire eyen grey as glass;
Hire mouth ful smale, and thereto soft and red;
But sikerly she had a fayre forehed.
It was almost a spanne brod, I trowe.

. . . .

Of smale corall aboute hire arm she bare
A pair of bedes, gauded all with grene;
And thereon heng a broche of gold ful shene,
On whiche was first ywritten a crowned *A,*
And after, *Amor Vincit Omnia* : "

              and verily thinking upon thee
(for Dan Chaucer was fore-dreaming of thee when that he
wrote of this most sweet " Nonne ") I am become also as the
yonge squier, whereof quoth Master Geoffrey

" So hote [1] he loved, that by nightertale [2]
He slep no more than doth the nightingale."

      "

––––––––––––

      "

[1] *Hot.* | | [2] *night-time*

Yesterday Mr. Clay called on me (C. C. Clay) and we had
a pleasant talk of old times. I think you wd. not know him.
He is grayer than yr. father, and beareth much mark of the rude
face-fillips of debt and poverty. He was exceedingly kind and
cordial; and proposed to give me a letter to his brother-in-law,
Col. John Withers, who is a banker at San Antonio, Texas.
He reporteth Mrs. Clay in magnificent health.

I enclose thee a P. O. order for $25 wh. thou canst get cashed

---

[37] Lanier seems to have acquired a copy of Chaucer in Montgomery and carried
it to Texas with him, for there are numerous quotations from Chaucer in the
letters of this winter, 1872-1873, including several that have been omitted from
this edition. The extracts in the present letter are from the prologue to *The
Canterbury Tales.* The footnotes to the text are by Lanier.

Lanier's discovery of Chaucer may have grown out of his correspondence with
W. H. Browne (see, for example, Browne's reference to the " Nun's Priest's
Tale " in his letter of Dec. 18, 1871).

at the Post Office, on presentation. I wish thee to wear the
merino undervests and hope thou wilt forthwith purvey thee
some. Get them ready made, and of best quality. I love not
to think of thee, shivering: and Willie here declareth she hath
never known greater comfort than since she began to wear
merino undervests. I am feeling greatly better, this morning,
than in some weeks before. The weather has been bitter cold:
thermometer ranging between 30° and 43°: but today is dry
and sunshiny.

"

———————

"

They desire me down-stairs and I leave thee, my heart being
not so strong as for to leave thee thus. Commend me to thy
father, and my sister. I write my father today. I am always thy
true

Lover

To Mary Day Lanier

St. Charles Hotel, N[ew] O[rleans,] La.
Nov. 18th 1872

Over a multitudinous uprising of black slate roofs, wherefrom a thousand ragged-topped chimneys arise, each spouting
his smoke as high as he can; past many keen spires and quaint
towers; through the grace of masts and the ugliness of smoke-
funnels, on, across the river, to where the sunlit smoke blots
out the distant trees and houses with a silver blindness; – so out-
spreadeth my prospect, framed by a large square window in
this Number Two hundred and sixty nine, wh. is on the third
floor of the St. Charles. Through this window cometh a liberal
warmth of sunlight, save when the wayward smoke of a certain
high chimney flutters betwixt the sun and me.

Come on, my Sweet, through the smoke and the light, betwixt
the steeples : come on : for do I not see thee there in the distant
glittering haze, smiling to-me-ward, and drawing my heart forth
with thy large eyes, there as thou hangest, swaying and floating,
upon the air ?

"

———————

Cometh a time when the true lover seeth – through all things whereon he looketh, and beholdeth at the bottom, through the transparency thereof, but two, namely, his God, and his Beloved. O God, thou who, for all men, dwellest beneath all things, have charge, have charge of My Beloved who, for me, dwelleth also beneath all things.

"

"

Albeit I had but a rude night of it between Montg'y and Mobile – there being no sleeping car by reason of the failure of a connecting road to bring the same – yet I find myself tolerably well, and without other hurt from travel than some fatigue.   Tomorrow I go, at 7 ½ A. M. by rail to Brashear City, where I take steamer for Galveston.   The steamer leaves about One O'clock, and arrives at Galveston next morning; making the trip in less than twenty four hours.

Tell thy father I called on Mr. Lafitte this morning. He received me very cordially, and spoke kindly of thy father as one of his oldest friends. He is to call on me this evening, and bring me some letters for people in Texas.

The weather hath been cold, here, without precedent. A flake or two of snow actually fell here, yesterday, so 'tis said. To day is pleasanter, and I hope for a fair sail tomorrow.   I have not yet seen McDaniel.

Thou wilt next hear from me at Austin, D. V. Until thou hearest otherwise, write me there; I will leave instructions for forwarding letters.

Kiss my father for me: also Sissa, and the young men.

I write no more now, desiring to rest: being, whether I write or not, thy true

Lover.

To Mary Day Lanier [38]

Austin, Texas.
Friday, Nov. 22 d 1872

Thou shalt know my life.

At New Orleans, o' Tuesday night, having written thee, as one that hath said a prayer. I go to bed, tired, snuffling, with dusty

[38] More than one hundred letters by Lanier have survived from his three and a

sensations in the nostrils. Through the night I wake often, with sound of a hundred bells ringing all at once for the half-dozen fires that occur through the hours betwixt midnight and dawn. I am waked at six o'clock by the porter knocking on my door: it is time to go to the ferryboat wh. takes us to the Brashear City Railroad. I open my eyes, my square window reveals to me a dull pink haze in the East, into wh. the sun will presently arise, as it were Love entering into a heart. I think, *O sweet East, bring up the Day full fair and warm upon my Beloved, that sleepeth nearer thee, by many miles (heigh-ho!), than I*: and, mine orison being thus said, I gingerly snuff the nipping air and am shrinking back into the cover, but with sudden resolution leap from bed, dress, lock trunk, descend, breakfast, get to stage, and in a few moments find myself in midst of a motley crew of city folk, emigrants, indians, and hoosiers, grouped about the deck of an enormous ferry-boat wh. beareth on the bow the baggage and express cars of our train. The river is all in a thick cloud of mist, through wh. our boat drives steadily forward, the sun glaring strangely thereupon. After some two miles, we draw to wharf, there is a great rush up a long strange-looking wooden way to the long train that stands waiting under a great shed. At the entrance of this shed standeth a man who, at my distance, — I am in the rear end of the crowd, I hurry not — seemeth utterly demented, throwing his arms hither and thither, in a wild way: but when my section of people arrive, I perceive he is separating the emigrants from the first-class passengers, as it were a rock in a stream, sending two currents where one was. This he doth with a dexterity as marvellous as it is unceremonious, for he seizeth the goats as it were by the beard – distinguishing them instantly, in the hurrying herd, from others – and sendeth them off to the left, in the same motion courteously waving the well-dressed sheep to the right. In a sudden fit of perversity, as well as of inquiry, I dash into the emigrants' line, and enter one of the cars into which they are crowding. Herein I ride with them: I wish to observe them, to learn their hopes and plans: they are going to Texas.

half months stay in Texas. Over half of these have been omitted from the present edition, only those being included which were essential to the narrative of his life.

The emigrant, (I discover long before we reach Brashear City) is not a lovely person. These men and women are mostly from Kentucky. There are five or six women. They have each a stick protruding from their mouths, wherewith they are rubbing snuff : except one, the youngest of them all, a young mother, with a child in her arms, who is chewing a large and wonderfully elastic mass of sweet gum, with such rolling thereof beneath her licking tongue, and such unceasing to-and-fro of her big-toothed chops, as is altogether marvellous to behold. The men are mostly hogs. There are boys, young men, old men. One hath a great flask-shaped bottle of a villainous whiskey that is red as fire. Hardly is the train in motion ere he taketh a huge swig: then he beareth it about, and serveth it out to old and young. He offereth to me: I shake my head and tell him it is a little too early in the morning for me to start a-drinking : whereat he smileth a ghastly smile and passeth to the next man. They all eat, frequently: and chew great quids of tobacco betwixt their frequent victualling, expectorating non-chalantly in whatever direction it happeneth by fore-ordination of Providence they shall be looking at the time being : spitting, as it were, *pro re nota.* One is a very cormorant. He hath procured him, from some bag or other wh. he carryeth, a hunk of cheese bigger than my fist, and some dozen crackers: he sliceth off, with a big pocket-knife blade, pieces of cheese as large as one of Rhina's [39] biscuit, pretty nearly : which he then marrieth to a cracker, and straightway plungeth the twain into that mow of death, his mouth, where, with one or two cruel sawings of his savage teeth, all is over: and time for another. All the jaws work alway. Apples, oranges, candies; – each hath one or t'other. Presently a train-boy comes in with a great basket of pies and cakes. Instantly the whole hive is in commotion. They crowd up to him, they buy rampantly, they bite incontinently: the train-boy selleth out well-nigh instantaneously, and is gone for more.

By this time, one, an old man, who hath been pulling at the whiskey-bottle many times and oft, is quite drunk. His drunkenness taketh the maudlin road, he smileth upon the company, he grinneth upon the cypresses and the sugar-cane

[39] Rhina was the Laniers's cook in Macon.

fields flying past the window, he loveth his neighbor, he beareth
in his hands a pie wh. he hath bought from the train-boy,
whereof he lovingly and tenderly partaketh at intervals, with
the air of doing the pie a wondrous favor.   He, also, who
handed about the bottle, is now quite mellowed by much
absorption of the liberal warmth thereof.   *His* drunkenness
goeth on the amatory road. He standeth up before his wife,
taketh her by the arms and giveth her a vigorous shake, with
a smile and a wag of the head: then he floppeth down into the
seat beside her, extendeth his long arms to Eastward and
Westward, as if he would enring all earth, and suddenly
casteth them about his wife; – whom they do almost wrap
twice-round, for she is but a slim and cadaverous wife, and
her face, albeit she is beyond doubt a young woman, is wrinkled
and sallow with care and tobacco.

   Withal, these emigrants make little noise. They have not
much to say to each other. They are somewhat stolid, and dull.
They do not chat, at all.

   By this time it [is] half-past eleven: and presently the train
dashes out from the cypresses and pulls up at a vast wharf, on
the shore of a wide bayou, whose beautiful waters sparkle in
the sun. We see six or seven fine iron steamships lying along-
side the wharf, all belonging to the " Morgan Line."   One of
them, ycleped " the Josephine," sendeth smoke from the funnel:
to her we all rush. As we reach the gang-plank, " Deck passengers, all, stay on wharf till further orders! " crieth a burly
voice that hinteth of much crabs and oysters and fat sea-fish :
and herewith I lose my emigrants : for we cabin-passengers
walk lordly aboard and are met by obsequious waiters who
strive for our satchels and wraps and march before us to our
state-rooms. My room is No. 41. Berth No 1: I enter: a short
square built gentleman, with a broad forehead and a blonde
moustache is depositing his satchel in berth No. 1 : " Ah," I say,
in my courteous tone, " you have berth No. 1 ? " and I pull
out my ticket and show him that *I* have berth No. 1, whereupon
he taketh out *his* ticket and showeth me that *he* hath berth No.
1 also; then we laugh, and arrange it, betwixt ourselves: first,
however, repulsing an attack from a tall, lank and rare sour-
faced gentleman who cometh in upon us and saith *he* also is in
Room No. 41, but whom we finally consign to the purser of

the ship, nor hear of him afterwards. Presently I go stand on
the bow of the ship, and gaze down the long hazy distances
of the winding inlet, and am growing dreamy in the warm
sunlight: when my room-mate ,– whom I have noticed to be
standing near me – addresseth me some courteous remark, and
we fall a-talking. In a few moments, to my entire astonishment,
we are discussing Beethoven, and Wagner, and the music of
the future: and after cantering rapidly across many fair fields
of music, we leap a hedge over into the Painting road, and
away, past many pictures, we go: and then we emerge into the
open glades of literature, we commence at Chaucer and come
down to Tennyson, then turn back to Rabelais and come down
to Victor Hugo, then back again to early Germans and come
down to late Germans, then our horses take wings and we fly up
into Scandinavian Mythology, (my companion is a Dane, as he
hath early informed me), and so we fare till dinner, and having
dined so we fare till night, sitting on the after deck, the Steamer
flying swiftly over the smooth gulf. After ten, we go to bed,
I with a great cold. I fall asleep quickly: and awake not
until day-light. I turn, shake myself, my cold is gone, the
warm airs of the gulf have spirited it away, I lie complacently
and look out through the state-room window which gives me,
when the ship rolls down, a flying view of green waves, and
sky flecked with orange-colored clouds. Presently it groweth
lighter. Past my window runs a narrow strip of the deck.
Along this strip, the emigrants, who have been on deck all
night, are passing and repassing: and the faces as they slowly
file past my window are too ludicrous to grieve over and too
pitiful to laugh over. For alas, the emigrants have had but a
sorrowful night : I now perceive that the wind *hath* risen
during the night, and that the ship *is* rolling deeply: wh. I
have rather dreamed, before, than perceived (in my sleepy
complacency) : – perceiving the same, now, vividly, in the
wretchedness of these faces that move slowly past my window.
O how mournful, how without hope, are these mouths, how
limp along the lips and how down-dragged at the corners,
these mouths that carried it so bravely but yesterday ! For every
mouthful of yesterday's sweetness, have they been compelled
to render unto the sea a double mouthful of bitterness and of
bile. Here cometh one, and old man and a grizzle-bearded,

whom I did specially mark yesterday for that he was so valiant and lusty at his feeding. But woe, woe is me: how hath he suffered a sea-change! His stubble-beard is prickly upon the folds of his wrinkles, like pines upon distant sandy ridges, and his mouth is askew in a manifold sort of pout that seemeth to protest at all points against this shameful loss of so much good victual, that rageth violently around.

I arise, presently, and dress, performing during my toilet many marvellous feats of dexterity in posturing. I sally forth into the cabin, and perceive about me many grave and serious countenances. I note, also, a wide-spread indifference to breakfast, wh. is now ready. I conceal my astonishment that I am not sick: it is without any precedent in my experience : I feel perfectly well, and buoyant: I discover that we are within an hour's ride of Galveston: I resolve to go and lie on my back and read, fearing that I may yet grow sick and spoil my rare immunity. I re-enter Room 41. My Dane is awake. Alas, it is easy to perceive, he is but poorly. I lie down, read " The Nation," get interested forget all about sea-sickness, and rejoice in the long glorious swing of the ship. Presently, my Dane disappeareth. I have strong reasons to suspect that something is rotten in Denmark. When he returneth, this suspicion becometh certainty. It is quite unmistakeable that the viking hath been paying tribute to the yeasty surges of the sea. To any wicked suggestions in connection with breakfast, he replieth only with a melancholy smile in which a tender longing (for my Dane is a valiant trencher-man, and the fare aboard ship is fine) is blended with a touching resignation. I arise, I minister to him, I place [him] in my berth on his back, I give him a little whiskey from my flask, I then considerately leave him, and go forth upon deck, where I stand and take delight in the far green gulf, the distant smooth beach, the white lighthouses, the gulls, the nearing city.

Presently, we are ashore, we discover that we have three hours before the train starts for Austin, we repair to the restaurant of Monsieur Biron, we seat ourselves, the warm tropical air blows upon heads through open doors and windows while we read the paper and lazily discuss our oysters, people are breakfasting around us on iced claret and porterhouse steaks, the life of the city goes on without noise over the shell-

paved streets, all is dreamy, all is like a plunge into another
land when we think of the bitter cold we had yesterday at New
Orleans. Finally we finish, My Dane being still qualmish and
having eaten very lightly: he goeth off upon his business,
(he is Agent of a firm at Saratoga that owneth the *Excelsior*
Spring, and is travelling pretty much over the world to introduce Excelsior water everywhere), I stroll about and wonder
at the magnificent stores of this new city, and at the size
thereof; until the Dane and I reassemble, and seek the depot
on a street-car. Here amid a great crush of emigrants: our
Kentucky delegation having been reinforced by some hundred
Swedes, Norwegians, and Germans, who have just come from
aboard an emigrant ship and marched through the streets, in
the queerest of costumes and the strangest shuffling of gaits,
to the depot. Finally our baggage is found, and checked for
Austin: and we start, across the seeming-interminable plains.

And here, I must leave thee: being somewhat tired and
sleepy. I have not yet explored Austin: but will tomorrow.

Meantime – till I write thee again – give kisses for me to
Father & Sissa & my two young men: – with the two former
of whom thou canst share this letter, an it like thee: in view
of which I will write no further sentimentalities than to declare
that I am thine unfailingly faithful and true loving

Husband.

To Robert S. Lanier

Austin, Texas. Nov. 23rd 1872

My dear Father:

I arrived here yesterday, after a somewhat
fatiguing trip from Galveston.
I've spent today in looking about the city. The whole land is
so utterly unlike anything I have ever seen before, that I constantly ask myself whether I am dreaming. From Galveston
to Houston (50 miles) and from Houston to within fifty miles
of this place, the route is over the vast prairies. The sensation
of loneliness which these create in me is simply indescribable.

Except the solitary frame-building at each station on the
road, no human habitations are in view for miles and miles:

and the occasional specks of cattle dotting the great expanse only serve to heighten the lonesome effect: very much as the cricket's note in the night makes the silence more intense. Through this we travelled until I went to sleep on the cars night before last. When I awoke the scene was greatly changed, tho' equally as strange to me. We were gliding through what is called the rolling prairie: the road being built along the backbone of a sandy ridge, which divides the valleys of the Colorado and the Brazos rivers. This ridge was covered with a growth of scraggy oaks, gnarled, stunted and crooked in all fantastic shapes: and the frost, which covered the earth like a light snow, glittered under a cloudless sky and a brilliant sun. It was like an indefinite expansion of the top of Chilhowee mountain [40] (without the rocks): and the " feel " of the air combined, in the most singular manner, the springy briskness of the mountains with the balmy softness of the Gulf of Mexico. Presently we stopped at a station six miles from Austin, in the midst of the rolling prairie proper, where the soil is of indefinite depth and great fertility. From the platform of the car, my eye ranged over vast fields of cotton and corn, belonging to three great plantations which were commenced here some years ago by three judges from Alabama. The fields were noble: but the houses seemed infinitely desolate to me: for they stood out, bare and unshaded by trees(with one exception), and instead of making me think of homes and refuges, they rather gave me the desire to put my arms around them and shelter them from the winds and suns. I had never dreamed that the absence of trees could make homesteads so unfarmlike and unhomelike. You know I have always loved everything that belongs to the tree family: but now, since I have seen this tree-less land, I could fairly throw my arms about a good honest Georgia oak, and hug it and kiss it.

Of course there are trees, (so-called) along the banks of the streams, and occasionally in other spots: but they are trees to whom existence is a battle, and who seem to say, with Thomas Tulliver,[41] life has been too many for me.

Arrived at Austin, the general strangeness of things continues in full force. Austin is a white city. The main street leads up

---

[40] Near Montvale Springs, Tenn. It is frequently mentioned in *Tiger-Lilies*.
[41] A character in George Eliot's *The Mill on the Floss*.

a hill to the Capitol building, much as Commerce Street in
Montgomery, Ala : the Capitol – which is an insignificant
structure, of no pretensions to architectural beauty of any sort –
is white, the buildings, as far as the eye can reach, are white,
the street itself is white, the rocks lying about the hills are
white, and the dust in the air is white.   It is a real relief to me
to look at the Mexicans sitting about at the street corners selling
tomalas and pecans (great pecan country is Austin): for they,
(– the Mexican, not the pecans: tho' really it's the same thing
for present purposes, since they're of precisely the same color)
afford an agreeable change to the ghastly hue that prevails.

As I stroll along the street, this afternoon, it is full of anima-
tion. Crowds of wagons, some with twelve big-horned oxen in
team, stand about the stores: an auctioneer selling old furniture
and " things " has drawn a large crowd around him, of negroes,
Mexicans, half-breeds, country men, Germans, and Jews: a
fellow that runs a Merry-go-round is being driven slowly around
in a one-horse wagon, wherein he sits and grinds the most
strident, the most remorseless, the most utterly maddening and
soul-and-body-parting hand-organ, and eke the largest – it's
pretty nearly the size of the Presbyterian Organ – that ever I
saw: a horse auctioneer is riding the horse that he is selling,
up and down the street, and getting bids " all along the line,"
which he cries in a voice that I would give a thousand marks
for, – an I had a thousand marks: yonder is a drunken Mexican,
a dirty, pitiful creature enough, about whose neck another has
thrown his arm to hold him up, while his wife walks beside,
with distressed face, bespeaking momentary dread of the police:
crowds of Texan farmers, young and old, in all manner of
country rig, move in and out the stores, filling their wagons and
emptying their pockets: the German merchants are in great
force, and the air is fairly husky with gutteral *ch's* : here comes
a man on horseback driving before him a native steer, – a great
beast, standing about as high as I am, and humped up over the
fore-shoulders as if he were first cousin to a buffalo: now a
negro, just from the country, – a tall, lean, lank brother, with a
foot that is a perpetual moral lesson, (for it's so long, it makes
me think upon eternity) – steps into the clothing-store in front
of which I am standing, and inquiries if dey got any finger-
rings for sale: and so they chaffer and buy and sell, what time

the sun is warm, and the white stores shine, and the breeze blows like as on a soft day in spring. Most of the buildings are of white limestone, wh. is quarried here in great abundance: and the rest are of bricks made from a whitish clay.

From the Capitol hill is a very pretty view of distant hills and of the valley of the Colorado: but it does not begin to approach the prospect from the Bond [Street] hill in Macon. The Colorado winds round the town. Most of the bed of the stream is now dry, and looks like a steep, wide stretch of seabeach. When this bed is full, the Colorado must be a mighty river: it is now a little larger than the Ocmulgee at Macon.

Altogether, I don't think much of Austin. It gives me the sensation of a new house before the plaster is quite dry in the rooms.

I'm booked on the Stage-slate for San Antonio in the morning. We leave here at eight: reaching San Antonio (wh. is here universally called San Antôn') at ten o'clock tomorrow night.

I am doing well, in point of health. My cold is almost entirely gone: and I have a pretty good appetite. As soon as I get to my destination, and ride a horse, I shall bound upwards, I think.

I long to hear some word from home. Wrote Mary a long letter yesterday.

Direct to me at Fredericksburg, Gillespie County, Texas: for I shall only stay in San Antonio a day or so.

I pray God bless you, My dear Father, and am

Your Son,

S. L.

To Mary Day Lanier [42]

" Menger Hotel."
San Antonio, Texas.
Nov. 25th 1872

With many fair expressions, I parted from the Dane at Austin, and took stage yesterday at 8 ½, A. M. for this place. We arrived last night at 12 ½: being a steady ride, through the

[42] Many of the facts in Lanier's Texas letters from this point on were incorporated in several articles which he published. For example, the stage-coach

great round waves of the " rolling prairie " of sixteen almost unbroken hours. But we had a queer stage-load of nine passengers: a milliner, of Michigan: an army officer, from away out on the frontier: a miner from Chico, California: a substantial burgher from Indiana: and a much-travelled lady who is at present combining the important avocations of landlady and Milliner at San Marcos: and what with gathering a whole hive-full of honey for future use from these most diverse flowers, all in the summer atmosphere of a long dream of you, I whiled away the time marvellous smoothly, and am not nearly so tired today as I have the right to be.

San Antonio is charming. The hotel at wh. I am stopping is of stone, with a fine paved court in the rear, after the manner of the Cuban hotels, and fair broad pavement in front where we sit in arm-chairs and look out upon the Alamo plaza. A few yards off is the Alamo: and I walked over just now, and stood in the angle of the wall where Crockett made his desperate stand and where he was slain. 'Tis a quaint old building of a bluish-gray stone, with carven pillars at the entrance, and niches on each side for saints to stand in.

As I strolled down the main street this afternoon, I found myself in midst of a most *bizarre* exhibition of such sights and sounds as might be supposed to arise from the rushing conflux of Americans, Mexicans, Germans, Frenchmen, Swedes, Norwegians, Italians, and negroes: but things are more decently done, life is less crude, civilization is less new, than at Austin, and this variety, which was there grotesque, is here picturesque. Presently, I stood, before I knew it, on a bridge over the San Antonio River which flows directly through the City: and my surprised eyes ran with delight along the lovely windings of the green translucent stream, flowing beneath long sprays of

passengers mentioned in the first paragraph were used in " The Texas Trail in the '70's " (one of three " Letters from Texas " first published in the New York *World*, Dec., 1872-Mar., 1873). Again, the accounts in the following paragraph of the semi-legendary politician, humorist, and soldier David Crockett and the celebrated battle of the Alamo during the Texan war for independence in 1836 were expanded in Lanier's " San Antonio de Bexar " (an article first published in the *Southern Magazine*, July-Aug., 1873). Since all of these are included in the present edition (VI, 187-246), no further parallels will be cited.

For further facts concerning Lanier's residence in Texas see J. S. Mayfield, *Sidney Lanier in Texas* (Dallas, 1932).

weeping willows and playing unceasingly with the swaying stems of the water-grasses. Many enclosures of dwelling-houses run down to the stream, on each side, and afford ample field for pretty summer houses and lawns. I found also some churches which, as compared with anything else in Texas, are simply magnificent: indeed there is nothing in Macon which can at all compare with the new Episcopal Church now being built here, or with the Catholic Cathedral.

This morning after a lazy and long-drawn breakfast, I sauntered out on the pavement, sat me down, – and began to dream away in the balmy summer air, thinking what an accomplished flâneur I would soon be, in such a languishing company of breezes as played softly about. Presently I had occasion to go indoors for a few moments: and when I returned, to my astonishment the air was cutting, the breeze whistled shrilly, I laughed involuntarily at the absurdity of my ten minutes by-gone dream of summer, and incontinently stepped off, in anything but the sauntering pace of the flâneur, for my overcoat.

It was the beginning of a " Norther," which has continued all day: tho' it is, I believe, a mild species of that fierce genus, and I have found no difficulty in keeping warm.

I called on Col. Withers [43] today, and was received with the greatest cordiality. He was at Richmond during the war, being Asst. Adjt. Gen. of the Confederate States: was an officer of the old army: and is now conducting the San Antonio National Bank, upon a career of great prosperity as I am informed.

On the whole, San Antonio is the only spot in Texas which has not greatly disappointed me: and I think I shall spend a few days, here. 'Tis a place of eighteen thousand inhabitants: and is full of life and activity. Address your letters to me at " The Menger Hotel, San Antonio, Texas." If I should leave, they will be forwarded. Tell your father I have met here a young Mr. Frazier, grandson of the partner in the old house of Frazier Trenholm & Co. of Charleston. He is book-keeper in the bank of which I spoke, and seems to be a pleasant young gentleman.

Distribute, I pray you, a host of kisses for me, betwix't my father and yours, my dear Sissa, and my little men. I dare not enlarge upon loving messages to them all, tonight: for I feel

[43] Col. John Withers, brother-in-law of C. C. Clay.

myself upon the very imminent brink of a deep sea of home-sickness, into which I must not plunge. Know that I am in better condition than I have been in two months past: and have drawn some delightful free breaths that give me great buoyancy, and a thankful soul to God.

S. L.

True-heart, Sweetheart, with what impatience have I penned these preceding words – wh. thou wilt allow to be read by other eyes, as being a " family letter " — in order that upon this different page I may put forth my very, bare heart unto thy most dear loving eyes, to the end that thou mayst look me through and through and see if there be aught in my soul but thee-worship, and thee-love, and thee-longing.

O, from this out-land and these outlandish souls, I do rise into the lovely vision of thy love, as one that floateth out of the grave up into Heaven.

Thou delicate Soul, thou fine white slender-stemmed lily, thou subtle-lighted star, thou floating essence of the balm of love, thou up-breathed spirit out of God's finest Thought, thou, My Wife, my holy-darling, O how fain, O how fain, for thy kiss, for thy word, for thy daily love, for the flutter of thy garment, for the spectacle of thy mother-ministration, for the ecstasy of thy near-being, known not until I have it not, – is

Thine Husband.

To Mary Day Lanier

San Antonio, Texas.
Nov. 26th 1872

Today, at twelve O'clock, my " Norther " perished – as may all such cold-souled invaders of a happy land! – the clouds took panic, their leader being dead, and abandoned the field in a shameless rout, the sun came forth, the loveliest of blue skies shed a calm solace downward, the river resumed his peaceful way like a good citizen returned from the wars, and the time of the quiet *régime* of dreams returned again upon the land.

Again, therefore, I am relapsed into the *flâneur*.

Having done some work upon a magazine article I am con-
cocting,[44] at two o'clock I saunter into the dining-room. Fritz,
my waiter – the waiters are all German boys and young men,
in shirt-sleeves and slipshod slippers – quickly hastens to me,
with my soup. What this soup is made of – – – – but that way
madness lies: into this unfathomable mystery I will not venture:
it is a German soup. While I slowly absorb it, I take the opportunity to observe my waiter more closely. Fritz is a slender
Teuton, about twenty one, with a complexion of perfect milk
and roses, blonde hair roached backward in what may very well
be called a combing wave, a tender blonde moustache, and a
generally sentimental air. He removes my soup-plate, places
himself at my side, assumes a bending attitude as if he were
about to say his prayers, and in a devout tone of voice which
would quite upset me if I were not too utterly lazy to laugh at
anything, he slowly recites this rubric: " Rust Peeve " (*Anglice,*
roast beef,) "Rust Vainzin" (Roast Venison) "Poiled Mud'n"
(Boiled Mutton) " oout Shtewt Gwaile " (& stewed quail)!
I choose Vainzin oout Gwaile; which he brings me, along with
a waiter full of vegetables, out of which I select asparagus,
tomatoes, and potatoes. These I discuss; discuss thoroughly,
turning them over, and viewing them leisurely and deliberately
from all points: for that is the only way in which any subject
can be well digested. After an unconscionable time, I signal
Fritz: he removes the débris, and brings me a salad of lettuce,
real lettuce, crisp, white lettuce, goldenly suffused with my
favorite sauce, – a sauce which I have never before seen out of
New York, and which I am resolved to learn the secret of, even
at the expense of inviting the steward to beer. Over this salad,
I linger: it is, as it were, the approaching sunset of dinner,
which will presently flame out into gorgeous pastry, and then
go down in a night of *café noir.* Soon, this darkness comes on:
it covers up my cheerful dinner: howbeit, it is not a starless
dark, for bright memories of the quail and the asparagus
twinkle silverly. I complacently tee-ter to the pavement in front
of the hotel: and, being but human, I smoke a cigar. After
this, a siesta: after the siesta a stroll to the bridge, where I stand

[44] This was Lanier's article, " San Antonio de Bexar " (VI, 202), published
in the *Southern Magazine* in July-Aug., 1873.

and gaze upon the pleasant pale-green water, the queer canvass-covered bathing-houses, of which each riparian owner seems to have one, – and upon the long swaying tufts of a grass which grows in the middle of the stream and lies along the surface and laves itself forever in the smooth fresh current. Returning, I sit beside Mr. Frazier at tea: who introduces me to young Mr. Berg, of Savannah, Ga. Berg resides here, but travels much along the far frontier; and tells me some interesting things. As I come forth from the supper-table, I observe much commotion among the waiters. There is to be a ball tonight: Fritz, Hans, Dietrich, and all of 'em, with honest German glee are pattering back and forth, removing the tables from the dining-room to make place for dancing. It is to be a fine affair: the army, – there are many officers in town – is to be out in great force. I have an invitation to go; but I am too tired from my stroll, and I decline. I come to my white-walled cuddy of a room, and scribble this letter, which must seem infinitely trivial and absurd to you poor laboring people who have something to do and a sharper winter air to spur you to it. While I am now writing, some lovely long-drawn notes come floating up stairs, from the flute, the horn, the violin and other instruments, which are getting themselves in tune: – a preliminary spreading and shutting of wings, as it were, before a long flight.

Such then is the poor record of my life up to this moment: save the brief times when the home-longings spring upon me from unsuspected places, and tear my soul with remorseless fangs: whereof I write not, for it is my duty to struggle against them, and this I cannot do if I tempt myself to dilate thereupon.

It is ten days since I had any word from home ! Of course, I know you've written: and I'll only enjoy the letters so much more when they come.

Dispense my daily dole of kisses and loving messages to all my dear ones: and hold me in your heart as being your true, loving

Husband.

To Mary Day Lanier

San Antonio, Nov. 27th 1872

Acting upon good reasons gathered from observation of my own, and many conversations with others, I resolved this morning to stay here a month: and forthwith proceeded to search for some cheaper quarters. After some explorations I succeeded. I have moved, unpacked, and settled myself: and am at this moment in as comfortable environment as one could wish. My apartment is in the " Vance House ": a new place, just fitted up. I have a Brussels carpet on my floor: a pretty set of French furniture, and a merry little stove, wherein at this moment, – for the night air is cool – flares a cheerful fire, built of the roots of the *Mezquit,* a bush which abounds hereabout. On one side of my wall I find hanging prettily framed photographs, of " Geo. Washington & family," " R. E. Lee," " T. J. Jackson," and – – " Gen. U. S. Grant & family "! On the other is a quaint old picture which calls itself " Girolamo Savoldo, eine Venezianerin : " being a beautiful woman, enveloped to the head in thick drapery, and crouching in the angle of a stone wall. A few feet from my two deep-embrasured windows, the river ripples swiftly along, laving stone buttresses and willow-sprays. The whole room is immaculate, with recent paint and whitewash: and the fare – I have just taken supper – is admirable. When I registered my name, mine host stood near: as he saw it on the page, " What," he cries, " why, I knew your Grandfather and uncles, well: I saw your name in the paper, among the arrivals at the Menger Hotel: and I was going to call on you, thinking you were the Sidney Lanier I used to know, to ask you to come down here and show me how to keep this new hotel that I am fitting up. Sir, your Grandfather was a hotel-prince ! I remember your uncle Sidney: he was the handsome one : you are very much like him." (–Ah, ha !) Mine host is a great, tall, portly, swashbuckler, with a huge-brimmed hat, a clean-shaven face whose translucent complexion reveals a blushing blood that transfixes me with envy, and a fine blonde moustache. He says he came here twenty years ago, after several hemorrhages: now, By the Mass! – a most fit oath – he weighs two hundred and fifty pounds, I shd. say.

He is of French descent: born in South Carolina: and is cleped Bill Tobin.

It gave me pain to part from Fritz: but he was a luxury too expensive for me.

Behold me, then, in complacent ease: and happy, as one can be that is a thousand miles from his beloved ones. I progress favorably in all respects: and have great reason to be thankful to God for the encouraging signs which my state discloses.

Address me at the "Vance House," until further instructions. I think I will rent a P. O. Box tomorrow: in which event, I will transmit to you the number thereof.

I send my constant love and remembrance to all my dear ones: being to them true brother, son, uncle and father: and to you true

Husband.

I send a page that will show the most notable places in San Antonio, but they have not put in the river, wh. is to me the notablest of all.[45]

Confidential !

''

_____

''

Thus far, for the family: now, Queredita, now, Alma, now, Wife ! for thee.

When I am at distance from thee, it is as if thou wert one point of a bow bent, and I the other. How constant-intense is my love, that bindeth me to thee, as the bow-cord ! How it draweth, draweth: with thrilling-sweet urgency, with quiet constancy, with awful tension ! Hath there been any heart, since Adam's did first throb, that hath cleaved to another as mine to thine ? This sublime, subtle, unending, ever-growing intensity would make me shiver with fear, were I not so confident of God !

That I love thee better than myself,—is nothing: for thou art so infinitely more loveable than myself that I cannot otherwise.

I know well what thou art: thou art of the kind of woman that hath made some wild chapters in history : large-eyed, wide-browed, intense-hearted: but thou art more gentle-sweet, thy

[45] The reference is to some pictorial stationery, several specimens of which survive in the Charles D. Lanier Collection, Johns Hopkins University.

lip is softer, thy soul is finer and more silver-flaming, than any
before. O, I know thee :– how I do thank the dear God, that
I also know that I am thy

Husband !

To Mary Day Lanier

San Antonio, Texas.
Nov. 28th 1872.

Today hath been simply and purely heavenly: with just enough
of crisp cold in the air to gar a man hold his head up and step
out lively, and at the same time with a glorious out-pouring
of divine sky-blue and generous sunlight and living breezes
and noble warmths.

It hath been also very Thanksgiving, to me: for early after
breakfast, the Post-master, God bless him! handed me thy letter.
Herein learning that thou art well and active, and art cherishing
my memory by eating doubly for thee and me: and herefrom, –
drinking the fair words in wh. thou say'st thou lovest me: so
am I fervently grateful to God for His mercy.

It seemed also to be foreordained that I shd. have some
semblance of " Thanksgiving-dinner." I sat me down to table,
alone: but before I had finished my soup, comes me in a certain
Mr. Marshall to whom I had before been introduced, attended
by two friends: and, espying me, comes to my table and seats
his friends about us. In a moment I perceive, – as they indeed
tell me – that they have been making a sort of New Year's day
calling expedition: and they are marvellous genial and hugely
polite. Presently appeareth a waiter bearing Claret and Champayne: the Master of The Feast doth straightway proceed to
fill each of our four glasses two-thirds full of claret, and then
poureth in champayne upon each till it brimmeth: wh. they
tell me is the fashion of San Antonio: and thus accoutred, we
bow, and plunge. We make a long, leisurely dinner: I let off a
few pyrotechnics, poor, wet-powdery squibs enough, wh. the
other quite fuddled into graciously applaud as wondrous fire-
works, even stars: and when we have arrived at the coffee, in
comes Col. Withers, who has been to the other hotel in search

of me. I make him take coffee: whereupon we adjourn to my room, and quickly dim the radiant sunlight with blue curling clouds. Here occurreth some most wonderful conversation on the part of them that have been made maudlin by much wine: in which I perceive the maxim *in vino veritas* to have much truth, for I discover some solid goodness of heart wh. I had not suspected.

When they are gone, I take my siesta: then a delicious springy walk: then, tea: and as I am coming from the tea-room, a great, burly, shaggy-browed old farmer, in a hat with foot-wide brim, accosteth me, and inquireth if I am not from Georgia; I *am* from Georgia: and we straightway fall into a long talk, when I have seated him comfortably in my pleasant room by the cheerful stove, wherein he telleth me how he built his mills by the San Marcos river and how the same arose and washed away his hard-earned twenty five thousand dollars in a little while: and how he plucked up heart again, and made much money, wh. he still hath: and he telleth me of the wild taking of San Antonio by the Texans, and of the bloody retaking thereof by the Mexicans: and then we talk of old Georgians, whereof he remembereth well Charles Day, of the land-firm of Day & Butts; and so on for some hours.

And he is just gone, and it is far into the night, and I cannot detail, — as I wished, for it would bring a many smiles upon thy face — my maudlin men's talk, nor my sensible man's talk, for my tallow-candle worketh great detriment to my poor eyes.

Of course thou wert right to read Hayne's letter: read then all: my soul is thine. As for the board at Ford's [46] I think it well: pursue thine own wish and judgment, freely.

Now, Lady, God hold over thee His power, as I hold my love over thee, then wilt thou be as safe as thou art dear

to thine

Husband.

---

[46] Since Gertrude Lanier Shannon was soon to be married to Joseph Carr Gibson and the Vineville home was to be broken up, Mary Day Lanier was making inquiries about a boarding house for herself and the boys (see her letter to Lanier, Nov. 24, 1872).

To Gertrude L. Shannon [47]

San Antonio, Texas,
Nov. 30th 1872

My Dear Sissa:

How often do I think of you, and of all your kind ministrations to me and mine, —in this far-off place, which is so genuine an out-land, and where all is so thoroughly outlandish, that one feels thrice as far from home and thrice as stranger like, as one should!

Today has been as lovely as any day can ever hope to be this side of the Millenium; and I have been out strolling, morning and afternoon, far and wide, ever tempted onwards by the delicious buoyant balm in the air, and pleasantly surprised at finding what a distance I could accomplish without over-fatigue. This afternoon, attracted by a large tree with great wide-spreading branches,—being about the only really large tree that I've seen since I've been in Texas – I walked across a pretty stretch of prairie to get to it: and on arriving, was agreeably surprised to find it a Pecan-tree. I incontinently purveyed me a stick: and in a few moments I was cracking and eating nuts as fast as a pet monkey. How I wished for the boys! The nuts were delightfully rich, fresh, and sweet: and I made a long and meditative meal.

Commend me to Master Edward: and tell him I met a small boy this afternoon, on a fiery pony which he sat like a young Centaur, capering along the river-bank and dashing across the grassy prairie, after a fashion that wd. have made the agile Eddie scream with delight.

I suppose May has by this time gone to Waynesville.[48] I've been writing her there for two days. Her letter written from Macon Nov. 21st reached me two days ago; it is the only news I've had from home since I left Montgomery. Write me what you're all about:

address " S. L.

P. O. Box 94, San Antonio,

Texas."

[47] Excerpt previously published, Mims, p. 117.
[48] In her letter of Nov. 24, 1872, Lanier's wife had written that she was going to Waynesville for a visit on Nov. 29. Her letter of Nov. 21, here referred to, has not survived.

Kiss father for me: and give my love to Mr. Day when you see him

Yours truly,

S. L.

To Robert S. Lanier [49]

San Antonio, Texas.

Dec. 6th 1872

My Dear Father:

After several days of waiting, which were beginning to overcome me with something very like homesickness, my suspense is relieved this morning by a couple of letters from Mamie, the last of which gives me news of all of you up to Nov. 28th. I hope my letters homeward are not as eccentric as Mary's have been: I write her every day, and either you, or Sissa, or Mr. Day about every other day.

As soon as I can get such facts and statistics as are necessary to give any solid value to such a communication, I'll write the Telegraph a letter about San Antonio. I w'd have done so before: but I didn't quite feel that I wd be authorized to do so, in view of the fact that my stay here has been so short, and consumptives reading my letter might act upon what would be only my first impressions, and therefore necessarily unreliable.[50] I'm getting up the mortuary reports of the City: and I'm waiting to see a genuine "Norther": and then I'll be prepared to talk. I am working at a more elaborate paper on San Antonio, which will be accompanied by several very interesting drawings of points of interest here and in the vicinity: wh. I shall send either to Harper's or Appleton's.[51] I have also managed to advance very largely my conception of the Jacquerie, through a history wh. I procured from the library of the "Alamo

---

[49] Excerpt previously published, Mims, p. 118.

[50] In a letter of Dec. 4, 1872, to Charles Day (here omitted), Lanier had written: "The climate has been admirable, so far. There has been but one day that had a tang of winter about it: the rest have all been either lovely fall days, or warm spring days. . . . I don't think any two consecutive days have been of the same temperature, since I've been here. Yet, the climate seems to have a genuine,– and marvellous– medicinal effect on diseased lungs. My own have been greatly benefitted."

[51] See note 44, above.

Literary Society ", – a flourishing institution here, wh. is now building a hall to cost some thirteen thousand dollars, and of which I have become a "library member." This history (Michelet's) [52] gives me the essence of an old book wh. I had despaired of even seeing, but which is the only *authority* extant, – save Froissart and a few others equally unreliable– : it is the chronicle of the "Continuator of Guillaume de Nangis." I believe I can get along, with it alone.

I've not yet talked with any of the lawyers here: but from what I have learned, from others, I fancy it is not a very lucrative profession, being mostly confined to investigating land-titles and defending cattle-thieves. This, however, is a mere first impression, wh. may be changed when I get the facts from some good lawyer, as I shall do soon.

I enclose you an article which I have cut from my "Texas Almanac," by Henry C. King, – a brother of Mary's friends in Waynesville,[53] to whom I have several letters of introduction. The article will interest you, not only with its account of sheep-husbandry, but also with its remarks upon the climate of Bœrne, where Mr. King lives. I find that King is a man well-known hereabout: he has just been elected to the State Senate. I doubt not you will be astonished to learn,– as this article intimates, and as I have frequently been told, here – of the insecurity of property, and sometimes even of life or liberty, caused by Indian raids throughout all this section of country. In a morning paper a day or two ago, was printed a letter from Laurie Tatum, – a Quaker Indian Agent at Fort Sill – to a gentleman here, announcing that he held a little boy who was captured and carried away by the Indians three years ago, from within a short distance of San Antonio: and several others from about Boerne, and neighboring sections: all of whom were found among a lot of squaws and children captured by Col. McKenzie in a fight with the Indians two months ago. It is true, the loss of property, or of life or liberty, has not amounted

[52] Jules Michelet's *Histoire de France.*

[53] Some time before (June 15, 1871) Lanier's wife had written him from Waynesville of going with her friend Lilla Hazelhurst to spend the night in the home of a neighbor, James F. King. Then on the eve of her husband's departure for Texas, on Oct. 17, 1872, she had written to Henry C. King, brother of James F. King, for information about the climate at Boerne, Kendall Co., Texas, where he lived. His reply, dated Nov. 15, was inclosed in her letter to her husband of Dec. 13.

to much in these neighborhoods of late years, (though very great further out on the frontier): but to think of children being carried into captivity by Indians, *in the year 1869,* and within a few miles of a town of near twenty thousand inhabitants![54] How far removed we all are, from even the remote appreciation of such a thing, at home!

I've been disappointed, in finding the Livery Stables here very exorbitant in their charges for horse-hire: entirely too much so for a purse depleted by as expensive a journey as it is from New Orleans here! I've had to forego all idea of riding, until I can make some arrangement with a private party, to hire a horse for his feed, or something of that sort. The Stables charge twenty dollars a month to feed and take care of a horse: which I might afford, for a month or so, if I had the horse. But whereas I thought that I wd. be able to buy me a cow-pony (as they are called,) or Mustang, for something like twenty or twenty-five dollars, I find that it will take seventy five or a hundred to get any horse that one would take any sort of pleasure in riding: which is quite too large a cantle to slice out of my resources.

I wrote Sissa a day or two ago: and Mr. Day yesterday. I'm doing well. A little stitch in the back, between the shoulder-blades, has kept me somewhat under the weather for a day or two: but that is much relieved this morning.

Convey my love to Mr. Day, and to all my dear ones: write me, to " P. O. Box 94, San Antonio, Texas ": and believe me always,   My dear Father,

Your loving
S. L.

To Mary Day Lanier

San Antonio, Texas
Dec. 9th 1872

Today is cold and rainy; with a furious wind that whistleth round the house-corners as one that, having blown over the bare prairie freely, taketh much dolor from the vexing obstacles of

[54] An Indian raid actually occurred during Lanier's residence in Texas, Jan., 1873 (see " Letters from Texas," VI, 193).

the city. I say *cold*: 'tis not the cold, somehow, that makes me cold, or gives me a cold, as at home: not the bitter, remorseless, malicious cold, that insidiously lieth alway in wait, like the devil, and creepeth up a man's back even while his front is nigh to a blazing fire: not a cold that rougheneth the skins of small colored people so that a scratch leaveth a white mark thereon; not a cold that putteth one's heart at enmity with God and man.

I pray thee convey always my warm remembrances to Big Mama and her young ladies: as well as to Mr. Hazlehurst and Mr. Mac: as also a fervent kiss to my dear Lily, about whom, as her time of trial approacheth, my heart hovereth anxiously: [55] and, finally, to my young men the daily out-stretching of arms that long for some sweeter filling than even the sweet dreams of them, that come leaping towards their father, who is also thine

Husband.

To Robert S. Lanier

San Antonio, Texas.
Dec. 11th 1872.

My Dear Father:

As I get no letters, I take my revenge by writing them constantly. My last news from home was a letter of May's, of date Nov. 29th: twelve days ago. The mails seem to be very irregularly served, somewhere between here and Macon: I know there must be letters on the way, for me: and I've received letters on the same day written four days apart.

We have been enduring a long spell of severe weather: that is long, by comparison. A day or two ago we had heavy rains: and yesterday and today have been very cold and damp. I have kept myself housed pretty much all of each day, only going to the Post Office or on short brisk walks. So far, I have suffered no ill effect from the bad weather, save from want of exercise. The mud, here, in wet weather is not a thing of beauty. It is a sort of limestone cement. It sticks on when you first put your foot in it: and this clump continually grows by constant adhesive

---

[55] Lilla Hazelhurst had married a Dr. Burroughs and lived at " Valeria," 32 miles from Waynesville (see Mary Day Lanier's letters to her husband, Dec. 4 and 8, 1872).

additions until one's load becomes a burden. Scraping it off is
a matter requiring both skill and manual labor.

I have about finished a letter to the World, (of N. Y.),
which, if they accept it, I hope can be made the fore-runner
of others.[56] I am also preparing a more elaborate article which
I shall send to some illustrated Magazine, and for which I have
accumulated a good many facts.[57] I enclose you a tabular statement given me yesterday by Dr. Pettersen, with whom I had a
long talk. It will give you a pretty good idea of the meteorology
of San Antonio.

Please hand Mary twenty five dollars. I presume she is with
you, by the time this reaches you. If not, hand it to her when
she comes.

I send love to Uncle C. & kisses to Sissa and Eddie. I long
to hear something of yr. business &c. Don't forget to address
P. O. Box *94*.

Your Son
S. L.

To Mary Day Lanier

San Antonio, Texas,
Dec. 14th 1872

Still lieth the quiet dust in my poor box at the Post Office,
undisturbed by in-thrust of any letter: still do I go there
and furtively glance again, if mayhap one may have been put
in the wrong box and been just restored; – to no avail: and all
day long the rain saith drizzle, drizzle, drizzle: and the passers-
by my window have a rough and crouching look like a bird
that ruffleth his feathers to shut out the world: and Tobin,
mine host, sitteth in the bosom of his family and scrapeth

---

[56] Lanier's first letter from Texas, " The Texas Trail in the '70's," was printed
in abbreviated form as " The Mesquit in Texas " in the New York *World,* Dec.
27, 1872; it was dated " San Antonio, Dec. 11," and signed " Otfall "—a pen-
name he had used before. Just how much of the letter as printed in the present
edition (VI, 187) was written in Texas and originally sent to the New York
World cannot now be determined. It is clear, however, that after being cut by
the editor of the *World,* it was later rewritten in expanded form, for the surviving MS is dated " Marietta [Ga.], Sept. 1, 1873."

[57] See note 44, above. The article includes a discussion of the meteorological
tables of Dr. F. v. Pettersén, mentioned in the following sentence.

dolorous jigs upon a most complaining fiddle, what time the younger of his numerous progeny do pensively bawl and wail and yell in accents that make infernal

> . . . " respondence meet ";

and all this wd. go near to make a man sad, if [I] did not remember me how too-sweet thou art, and how content I should be simply to be thy strong, constant and patient waiting

Lover–

To Mary Day Lanier

San Antonio, Texas
Dec. 20th 1872

Each morning when I open my eyes a certain airy carrier doth place before them a sort of paper which I call my " *Home Journal*," – being, as it were, a court-sheet principally filled with news of my Queen regnant, and the Royal Family. This morning I did read therein the following account of

THE BANQUET

In honor of M. D. L. & S. L.
On the Occasion of the Fifth
Anniversary of their Wedding.

This brilliant affair (quoth the Local Reporter of the Home Journal, – who, I violate no confidence in telling thee, is no less a personage than young Bright Ariel Esqᵉ –) came off last night, in one of the halls of the Valhalla, which the Committee of Arrangements were fortunate enough to secure for this purpose. Precisely at the hour of eight P. M. the guests appeared and took their seats.

Love, as Chairman, occupying the head of the table, M. D. L. on his right and S. L. on his left. Next to them were seated two very Young Men; next, Titania & Oberon: and to these succeeded a host of brilliant persons, whom, at the late hour at which we go to press, we can not now take time to specify by name.

As the reporter took his seat, he glanced round the hall, and observed that the Walls were exquisitely wreathed, – with smiles–, which (the Committee having had the foresight to cause them to be plentifully sprinkled – with tears–) were marvellously fresh and fair.

The guests having bounteously regaled themselves with the feast that had been spread by that prince of caterers, Monsieur Fanci, and the wine – which, by the way, was of splendid quality, being a rare wine, of the vintage of | 62 , wh. did throb upward in the glass like blood in a heart, and broke into foam at the brim with a sound as of many faint kisses — having circulated freely – the Chairman rose, and having thrice rapped his glass upon the table, announced to the Company the first toast – and toast of honor – of the evening, towit:

" The day we celebrate – *Mary* Day ! "

A multitudinous clinking of glasses applauded: wh. having somwhat subsided, The Lady, amid a very pretty confusion of smiles and lovely blushes, yet with a certain woman's-dignity born of much love and much faithful pain and much tranquil joy, arose, and said, – as nearly as your reporter could catch it – as follows:

" Mr. Chairman: Inasmuch as man needeth little help in oratory, God did not fashion the woman to be his help-meet oratorical: therefore, when that I have plucked and rendered — as I do now pluck and render– the fairest thanks that grow in my heart, to you, Sir, and to these fair ladies and brave gentlemen who have honored this my poor festival, I do humbly entreat that I may be held to have done my full devoirs, and that I may so be absolved from saying further than this final word: that it is now five full-happy years since (and here the Lady broke into a ravishing wave-on-wave of smiles) since The Day you celebrate did quite evanish and utterly melt away into her Knight! "

When the applause, which shook the hall as it had been an earthquake, subsided, the chairman arose & announced, as the second toast of the evening:

" The Knight that followed the Day we Celebrate ! "

We observed that as he rose, amid great tumult of glasses, to respond to this toast, Mr. S. L. appeared to be struggling with an emotion which he could scarcely control, and about his eyes there shone that light which pierces through tears.

" Mr Chairman " (he said) " I dare not, for too-fullness of

heart, endeavor more than tossing back some mere rose-bud of sentiment for the rose of your honor: I dare but protest that whereas She, My Soul-of-Sunshine, hath with a tender modesty phrased her wifely loyalty, yet hath she not wholly been absorbed into her lord, but rather we, – this Knight and this Day – have mutually blended into one tranquil twilight, lit by two Little Stars," he concluded, pointing to the two Very Young Men. When the goblets had ceased ringing together, the Chairman announced, for the third toast of the evening:

" The First Little Star that glided from the Unknown into that twilight – May a thousand lovers make love by his light ! "

The First Little Star arose to reply, but his head could barely be seen above the table-cloth: wh. had nearly upset both the company and his little gravity, till Titania, who sate next him, gloating upon him with a fervent countenance suffused by rosy Mother-love, adroitly lifted him upon the table, where standing, he said:

" Mis-ter Chair-man : I'm not 'zactly a Little 'Tar, but I *am* Little 'Tarlie ! And my Papa says, a little bits-o'boy can have a dreat big ole Heart ! And I'm got a Heart big as a . . . a house ! And I loves Papa and Mama and Buddie with *most* all of it and I s'anks you with the balance! "

Hereupon the small man was seized by Titania and kissed, and from her snatched by another and kissed, and so was re-kissed from one to another as he had been a foot-ball for lips : which having in some degree been quieted, the Chairman read the fourth Toast of the evening:

" The Second Little Star that glided from the Unknown into that Twilight — May all the Mariners of Time sail truer for his shining! "

Oberon was ready, and lifted the second Little Star, – so rapidly that he passed even like a shooting-star – high upon the topmost round of a many-ledged pyramidal fruit-cake: where he poised himself on one foot, like Mercury

" New-lighted on a heaven-kissing hill," [58]

and said distinctly, eyes a-shine and hands on high:

" 'Tar-'tar ! "

Instantly this small man had nearly shared the destiny of the

[58] The line is from *Hamlet*.

fruit-cake, for he was well-nigh devoured with eager and tumultuous caresses.

When finally he had been rescued, the Chairman arose and announced to the Company that the regular toasts of the evening being now happily disposed of, it was in order to listen to any less formal sentiments that might be proposed by any lady or gentleman present: and, (he continued) in order to start the company, he would beg to offer the following sentiment:

" To her, who never having hitherto appeared to mortal eyes save on a Midsummer Night, does now confer the singular and most gracious honor of leading the wedding-revels of this Mid*winter* night – Queen Titania ! "

Here, by a preconcerted arrangement, twelve grand yet mellow horns of the band joined in with the tumultuous applause, playing that indescribable one of Schumann's Nachtstücke which presents the dignities, the jubilations, the passions and the obscurities of Night, all mingled together, in a few notes full of the harmonies of joy and of the terrors of the Unknown –

When this was ended, Queen Titania floated upright, and said, with an arch expression that enchanted all the Company: " Mr. Chairman; It is true, as you have said, that I did ne'er before come forth out of my warm hidden flowers upon a Midwinter night: Nay, Sir, you might have added that I have not danced at a wedding since Theseus did marry Hyppolita: but I was drawn to avail myself of this particular invitation, tonight, in honor of these two, because . . . . because I was once myself in love with one *S. L.,* that is with one Es-el, or Esel, which is German for, . . . an Ass ! "

This sally fairly threw the company into anarchy, and it was a long time before the uproarious laughter changed into loud cries for S. L.

Presently, to still the clamor, that gentleman arose, and having secured silence, in a faint voice declared that Queen Titania had, as it were, called for the Previous Question, and cut off all further discussion: for (he protested) she had gone to the very Bottom of wit !

This reply was so well received that the entire company then and there declared that further speaking would be but inevitable anti-climax; and the band, straightway catching the spirit of the moment, breathed forth a ravishing waltz: and the company parted into couples that swayed and floated, and separated to reunite into other couples; and so, until gray morning broke, (as your reporter is bound by ancient precedent to conclude)

> Eyes looked love to eyes that spoke again
> And all went merry as a marriage-bell.[59]

I *did* keep the feast last night, My Child: being too poor to buy wine, and too nice to drink beer. I purveyed me a cigar — a rare luxury in these times — and locked my door and placed thee at my little table over against me and said a thousand sweet sayings to thee in praise of thy loveliness and of thy perfect wifehood and motherhood.

I have today thy three letters to San Antonio: and the Sun hath also shone all day !

Thy letters will I answer tomorrow: being until then thy faithful

Husband .

To Robert S. Lanier

San Antonio, Texas
Dec. 22nd 1872

My Dear Father:

Yrs. of Dec. 1st, and Sissa's letter of Dec. 5th with yr. appended note, reached me yesterday, having been forwarded from Fredericksburg. I had written that Post Master,— in anticipation that letters wd. be sent me there — to forward them here: but cd. get nothing out of him until I had stirred him up with three several letters on the subject. I suppose these two must be all he had for me: but was surprised that there were not more, from some other correspondents of mine.

I was very glad to get yr. letters, old as they were. They gave me pleasant news of yr. business matters, and of all home affairs.

[59] Inaccurately quoted from Byron's *Childe Harold's Pilgrimage*.

As for publishing in the Telegraph & Messenger, I believe I wrote you that I was endeavoring to make arrangements to write for the N. Y. World: and inasmuch as the two letters already written wd. be worth but little by themselves, perhaps it wd. be better to wait and see the result of my negotiations with the World.

By the way, the work of Olmsted, to which you refer, wd. be of very great assistance to me.[60] I had in vain looked for it, here. It will be a material help to my pending Mag. Article on San Antonio, and I will be greatly obliged if you will forward it to me immediately by mail.

All that I see and hear convinces me that I have made a wise choice in remaining here, instead of going to Fredericksburg. The latter is fine in spring, summer, & fall: but San Antonio is better on many accounts in winter.

We have had a fearful long spell of bad weather. For fifteen days, it has been miserably cold, wet, windy and disagreeable. Yesterday morning I thought we were at last free: and up to eleven o'clock the weather was too lovely for description: but at that hour a sudden norther came raging from off the hills, and in a few moments the temperature was bitter cold. This wind blew furiously all day yesterday: this morning the little pools were all coated with ice, and to-day has been exceedingly cold, though the wind is much less violent.

During all this bad weather I have not been so well as usual: the confinement being very unpropitious to me. Dr. Pettersén, who is my weatherwise man, declares we will have a pleasant season as soon as this norther has subsided: wh. I impatiently await. Meantime, I hug the stove:– let no one be jealous.

Write me, when you find time. Convey my thanks and kisses to Sissa for her good letter. It is matter of keen regret to me that I cannot see her married,[61] – but I don't dare allow myself to begin sighing about anything.

Love to Uncle C.

Your Son

S. L.

---

[60] F. L. Olmsted's *A Journey through Texas* was used as an authority by Lanier in his " San Antonio de Bexar " (see note 44, above).

[61] Gertrude Lanier Shannon's wedding to Joseph Carr Gibson of Verbena, Ala., had been set for Jan. 15, 1873 (see Mary Day Lanier's letter to her husband, Dec. 11, 1872).

To Mary Day Lanier

San Antonio, Texas
Dec. 23rd 1872

Today I had my first horseback ride, – for an hour this
morning–: and by consequence, My Lady Health, who hath
been somewhat coy of late, hath proven more kind, and I feel,
comparatively, as brilliant as a bridegroom.

This afternoon, Lieut. Dimmick,– a Federal officer who hath
been rooming next me for some days and who hath been very
kind for a scraped acquaintance – came for me in his ambulance,
and we drove out to " The Springs," about two miles from our
hotel. Here the San Antonio river gushes out, full grown, in
three magnificent springs of crystal water, from under a long
white-ledged rocky hill-side. These Springs are owned by a
German, Herr Dürler, who has spent a great deal of money in
all manner of improvements, and has made a very beautiful
spot of it. He has a fine collection of birds and beasts: bears, a
coyote, a wolf, all in one stone pit, in the center of which is a
tree-trunk, up which " Macky," the largest of the bears, doth
shamble when Herr Dürler calls to him, and hold out his mouth
and fore-arms in a spasm of affection which is to me not less
touching than grotesque. He hath also a Cougar, or American
Lion, a magnificent beast, who cometh to his cage-bars for
Dürler to scratch his head: and a parlous row of owls & eagles,
and a Lynx and Opossum, and a Civet-cat that rolleth himself
around his head and covereth himself with his tail and goeth
off to sleep quite snug and comfortable (as Sairy Gamp [62] wd.
say) and white mice, and a happy family of doves, pigeons,
red-birds &c; these, scattered about very pretty grounds, under
old mossy Spanish Oaks, amidst pretty rustic buildings, small
lakes, and great clumps of huge Cactus, what time the pellucid
river ripples in ecstasies of quiet content among his grasses and
flags. Our little men wd. quite lose their reasons here. How
I did long for them, and long for them !
Albeit the day was gray and cold, I enjoyed the visit very
greatly.

---

[62] A character in Dickens's *Martin Chuzzlewit.*

The Norther hath subsided: and just as I write (we have but now returned from our ride) the sun hath broken a breach in the clouds, and giveth a rosy promise of fairer weather tomorrow.

Ask father to examine the law and see if Rena,[63] being now more than fourteen years old, cannot choose a guardian, (in spite of the fact that her mother is living): a thing wh. wd. the more recommend itself to the court in view of her step-father's bad reputation for violence. I think she *can* do it: and if father concurs, ask him to initiate proceedings immediately in the Court of Ordinary, and have himself, or thy father, (either will do) chosen her guardian. This being done, I think the annoyance and uncertainty caused by her father's conduct will be effectually stopped: for when he learns from his lawyer that he cannot possibly have any control over Rena,— nor her mother either — the entire hopelessness of the business will probably cause him to abandon any further efforts to get her back home. It distresses me to think that thou hast this trouble.

I do pray that the young men are better. Thou poor little Mutterchen ! – But God will be thy Friend for it all : and so will thy

Lover .

To Mary Day Lanier

San Antonio Texas,
Dec. 24th 1872

This morning when I recd father's telegram from the office, – thou shoulds't have seen my hand shake as I opened the same !

But it gave me great joy to know that thou wast safe at home, and that all were well: and I answered today by telegram, sending my merry Christmas to all.[64]

Yesterday I thought today wd. be warm & pleasant. But last

---

[63] There are frequent references in Mary Day Lanier's letters of Nov.-Dec., 1872, to difficulties between Rena (nurse-maid to her children) and her step-father.

[64] Lanier's telegram has survived (Charles D. Lanier Collection, Johns Hopkins University): " Splendid, merry Christmas. I feel as frisky as a young Buffalo this morning."

night, early, a huge Norther started up again, and raged all night. This morning the pools were all frozen over: and up to two oclock the day hath been gray and full of wind and sleet and bitter cold. But now (three O'clock Afternoon) the sun is shining forth with all his might in a clear sky, and though the temperature is still very cold, all things look far brighter.

Spite of the weather, I feel gloriously today. A kind of young *coltish* feeling is upon me: I long to stand at a fence and put my long nose over it and gaze seriously at a passer-by, (after the manner of horses) as if I were going to preach him a sermon: then suddenly, head down and heels up, and away, flinging my tail this way and that, and menacing the clouds with my hoofs.

"
————————
"

May thy Christ be born in thy heart tomorrow, dear Wife, and may His Star brood thereupon, and may the Wise Men come there, and leave gifts, – prayeth thy fervent

Lover

To Mary Day Lanier

San Antonio, Texas
Dec. 25th 1872

Today the Sun hath disported himself in a boundless range of clear blue sky all day: and the thermometer hath been twenty degrees above zero ! Yet the cold hath been my good friend: ah, what wine-of-strength it hath been to me all day !

And this afternoon, I mounted a fine little half-breed mare, and capered forth over the prairie: and so have I been riding, riding, for hours, through a sunset that, disdaining gorgeous piles of color, did revel in ineffable hints of pale green and rose and sanctified blue: then through a long, long twilight in which those colors died and rose again in more spiritual phases of themselves, – the angels of blue and green and pink–, and floated about the large flame of sacrosanct Venus: then home, past long broken piles of convent buildings, round the convent-walls winding by the river, along the shining stream; and here sit I, just off my horse, vowing that I cannot go to tea – wh. waits – until that I have told thee how that thou hast been worshipped all one long afternoon, and loved, and kissed, and prayed – to, and prayed for, by thy

Lover .

To Robert S. Lanier [65]

San Antonio, Texas.
Dec. 26th 1872

My Dear Father:

I had, this morning, a letter from you, one from Mr. Day, and one from Dr. Browne of Baltimore; and so I feasted, after my long fast, with a good conscience and an enjoying soul.

Yr. telegram,– wh. came to me promptly on the morning of the 24th and wh. I answered so as that the reply shd. have reached you on the morning of the 25th — surprised and delighted me.   To know that you were all well only twelve hours before, – more especially as May's last letter gave poor account of the little men – was simply charming: and I enjoyed my quiet Christmas day with a great content and a fine calmness of soul wh– does not often fall to my lot.

Yesterday the thermomenter was twenty degrees above zero, and today it has been thirty: a keen wind has been blowing, too, wh. even intensified the cold: but the air has been a veritable wine of life to me. I have ridden out twice each day, feeling always as if I could not get enough of the dry crystalline fluid. I feel today as if I had been a dry leathery carcase of a man, into which some one had pumped strong currents of fresh blood, of bounding life, and of vigorous strength. I can not remember when I have felt so *crisp,* so springy and so gloriously unconscious of lungs. My little half-bred mare improves greatly on acquaintance, and jumps about on the prairies like a rabbit.

---

[65] Excerpt previously published, Mims, p. 5. The letter from W. H. Browne, mentioned in the first paragraph, acknowledged a lost letter from Lanier, in which he had apparently discussed in considerable detail the treatment of a number of authors in *English Literature. A Historical Sketch . . . from the Earliest Times,* a handbook by R. M. Johnston and W. H. Browne, a copy of which Lanier had obviously taken to Texas.

By the way, tell the boys I started one, day before yesterday:
one of the " *Jack-rabbits* " of the country, with ears pretty nearly
as long as a mules', sticking straight up from his head. And
how he did run ! It was like steel and india-rubber on a frolic,—
the way his legs bent and sprung and bounced.

I think I have material for an interesting article on San
Antonio. I have commenced it and am now on the historical
division of the subject.

It gives me great pleasure to hear of yr. prosperity in the
matter of " big cases ": and I hope they will be happily
delivered of fine bouncing fees.

I have just written to Aunt Jane, and will write to May
presently: wh. is enough for tonight: for somehow or other
my sword-arm (*i. e.* the one that wields the pen) has not
worked well of late, insomuch that eight or ten pages at a time
gives me considerable discomfort.[66] This interferes very greatly
with what I *wd.* do in the way of home letters, if I cd. write
with my old freedom: for I'm fairly reeking with all manner
of " quips and quiddities " wh. I yearn to spread for the delectation of such a partial set of people as a home-set always is.
If this don't get better, tell May I'll have to make love to some
girl or other and honey fugle her into acting as amanuensis for
me. Kiss Sissa and Eddie for

S. L.

To Mary Day Lanier

San Antonio, Texas
Dec. 30th 1872

Day before yesterday, long icicles hung from all points when
I arose in the morning. Today all is mud, mist, rain, slushiness
and warm breaths, like spring. Both have been sufficiently disagreeable; as any weather is wh. keepeth me in. To dream of
thee, to write the history of San Antonio de Vejar, to pace my
room to and fro, to gaze from my window upon the little river

---

[66] Mary Day Lanier had suspected this. In her letter of Dec. 24 she wrote to
her husband: " Thou hast not said a word of thy health in six or seven letters,
and I like not the look of thy handwriting."

which in cold wet weather always sendeth up all day a great cloud of mist so that from where I stand it seemeth like a long fissure that letteth out the smoke of sub-terrene fires;– this hath been my life.

I have had but a rude initiation into the Texas climate. If I were not assured by intelligent persons here that what I have seen hath been wholly exceptional and that we are soon to luxuriate in fine weather, I should be greatly disposed to regard the " dry air of San Antonio " as an unfathomable joke. Certainly, since I have been here, " irrigation " hath seemed very like a wild sarcasm: and as for temperature, while some days have been perfectly lovely, yet no two consecutive days, and scarce any two consecutive hours, have been alike, and the thermometer hath bobbed up and down in lawless capers that have ranged all the way betwixt ten degrees above zero and eighty. In spite of all this, in looking back, I see that I am unquestionably better than when I came here: and I continually meet or hear of people who have been either cured, or enabled at least to lead an active and useful life.

So: now write me of *thy*self. I wonder if thou art in pain today ! Whether so, or at rest, may God, who is thy soul's Father, breathe into thy sweet ears some comfortable, warm, whispers of His Fatherhood, answering, so, the unceasing fervent supplication of thy

> Lover .

To Mary Day Lanier

San Antonio, Texas
Dec. 31st 1872

I did so rejoice in thy little strength thou hadst by reason of " The x x x " [67]   must thou now lose it? I had figured thee walking and walking, thy power increasing, thy cheek reddening with the fresh airs of wh. thou cdst. never get enough.

My poor Comrade ! What dost thou not suffer, *through me* !

---

[67] A word has been torn from the MS at this point. The reference is probably to some treatment or some physical improvement that had been reported by Lanier's wife. There are several references in her letters of Dec., 1872, to her probable pregnancy.

Thou talkst of working for me, as Lily doth ! [68]

Hast thou not, in giving me thyself, given me more?

No, no, no, I do not wish thee to be one that can keep house rarely and mend deftly. let every man have his mind, I quarrel with no one, but as for me, I choose my dainty One, my awkward one for Use, my skillful one for Beauty, my long lithe fingers that express themselves upon the piano rather than upon the sock that is to be darned, my uneasy heart through delicacy and through love of that perfection which others dream not of and therefore miss not from their lives, my exquisite soul that hath caught the innermost glory of nature and of art and of culture, my sweet worshipful gracious one whom I can love to very verge of madness, my large-eyed One from whose light high Faith and Truth and Honor and Constancy and Simplicity and Manhood and Womanhood die not away. My broad-browed One to whom I can say something beautiful every day with full anticipation of quick and ample recognition thereof. My girlish-Mother that trembleth with a thousand terrors at future pain of child-birth and, having borne, receiveth the son into her heart with mother-passion and mother-blessing and mother-watchfulness; – ah, pretty Comrade, shall I give this, – thee–, for a housekeeper? God be praised, it is to thee, and not to one that sweepeth and dusteth that   I am

> Husband.

---

[68] In a letter written to her husband from " Valeria " on Dec. 4, 1872, Mary Day Lanier had said apropos of the industrious and economical housekeeping of her friend Lilla Hazelhurst Burroughs: " O, Sweetheart! why was I not made such a wife for thee? Thou needest it more than this favored one. How full might have been thy purse, and how consequent-free for high emprize thy bright soul and magic pen with the road thus cleared for thee."

1873

To Mary Day Lanier

San Antonio. Texas
January 1st 1873.

So: this last mile, tho' main rough in the travelling, hath yet been a short one, for *thou* hast been my Comrade, and thy heavenly companionship and sweet eyes have beguiled my heart's time away rarely: the mile-stone that hath *1872* thereon is already behind yonder: here is another mile. Stretchest thou, O quick-turning road, by hill or valley, fen or mountain, rocks, caverns, or lonesome moors; endest thou in the sea, or givest thou into another mile; – what mattereth, so my Sweet and I journey together?

God arrangeth the skies and the scenery upon this mile, as He arranged them upon the last : and God is thy Father and mine, Little Comrade. Could thou and I but arrange the way for them to whom *we* are mother and father! Thus thinking, my heart is brave with steadfast sense of God's Fatherhood. I fear not.

Thou art ill, thy lover not strong: thy life is hard and poor and bare, thy senses scantily fed, thy spirits heavily burdened,– (Ah God, Thy Scourge is keen, – that I can have no velvet luxuries to wrap my dainty Beloved in, nor even no fit food for her body or her Soul!) : thou hast not even the clothes thou shouldst have, – O my God, O my Father, dost Thou hear? – and my heart is alway nigh breaking with excess of tender yearning to put under thy feet all that this world can yield to any of its queens. Yet, I fear not. Therefore, give me thy hand, dear Wife, and let us fare forth, if even bathed in salt tender tears, still without ultimate fear, seeing that above is God The Father, and below, thou and thine

Husband

305

To Robert S. Lanier

San Antonio, Texas
January 1st 1873.

My Dear Father:

A Happy New Year, to you, and to Sissa, and to all my dear ones!

Albeit, the Clerk of the Weather ('tis a female clerk, I'm confident: judging from the caprices, the hysteric glooms, the inordinate smiles, that lawlessly succeed each other!) is making anything but a happy start, in this part of the world. For three days we have had nothing but rain, air saturated, the solid earth turned to a fluid, the fluid streams turning into visible vapors: today is warm, enveloped in a great thick fog that seems to be in process of being converted into a sort of fog-cheese by the sheer weight of the superincumbent clouds. I have to keep my stove going tho' : for I'm compelled to dry the air of my room as if it were a wet sheet.

For several days I've been fighting a sore throat. Finally, today, after some vigorous treatment with iodine and glycerine,– which I learned from my wife – I've got it under, and feel entirely relieved this morning.

I hope you have rec^d by this time the letter in wh. I asked to have the work of Olmsted [1] sent me by mail. I only mention it again for fear that letter *shd.* have miscarried. I shall soon have finished my article on San Antonio: and desire to read all I can on that and kindred subjects before I finally close it.

Love to Uncle Clifford, and to Mr. Day. I have to husband my writing-energies: hence, brevity.

Your Son

S. L.

[1] See note 60, 1872.

To Mary Day Lanier

San Antonio, Texas
Jan. 2nd 1872 [1873]

" Te, Dea, te fugiunt venti, te nubila cæli
Adventumque tuum, tibi suavis dædala tellus
Summittit flores, tibi rident aequora ponti
Placatumque nitet diffuso lumine cælum.
Nam simul ac species patefactast verna diei
Et reserata viget genitabilis aura favoni,
Aeriae primum volucres te, Diva, tuumque
Significant initum perculsae corda tuâ vi." [2]

Thee, O Goddess, (singeth my Lucretius) the winds fly
before. When thou comest the clouds of heaven vanish, unto
thee the suave antique earth submitteth her flowers, the waves
of ocean laugh for thee, and the pleaséd heaven shineth suffused with light. For straightway when the vernal countenance
of day hath expanded, and the unlocked breath of the fruitful
West-wind swells stronger, then the airy birds first salute thee
and hearts stricken with thy power give token of thine on-
coming. — — —
Thus singeth my heart to my Love alway : and Thus also singeth
to the weather-God, for the rain is over, and the sun is come
forth. When the world shall have dried a little, – if the heavens
hold as at present – nothing more cd. be desired in the way of
weather for the temperature is perfect.[3]

O my Comrade, how my heart lingereth about thee ! What
dost, this day, – And I have not heard from that interview thou
wast to have in thy last letter.

God light thy heart, so that thou mayst be comforted with

[2] Lucretius, *De Rerum Natura*, Book I.
[3] In a letter of Jan. 4, 1873 (here omitted), Lanier reported: " Yesterday was
clear and windy. Last night at two o'clock came a sudden swift storm of rain,
thunder, lightning and wind, as one does not often see out of the tropics. Wow!
how it rained. This morning opened in a great fog, and full of huge languid
clouds. This afternoon hath been clear as thine eyes; and the wind in a great
ecstasy of fury, whistling and groaning: the temperature being that of a pleasant
summer day at Marietta! This is not a climate, at all: it is all the climates under
heaven in succession."

seeing the majesty and the glory of Love, – whereof thy heart is so finely full—crieth this day thy

Husband

To Mary Day Lanier

San Antonio, Texas
Jany 5th 1872 [1873]

Today hath been perfect. The sunlight was so large and friendly, the air was so brave and brisk and cordial, that one felt as if one were among boon companions, only by being out of doors. I longed to go to some service, and worship with the people: but the Churches are so damp and cold, that I feared for health, and so went not in doors. This afternoon I have taken a long ride horseback, and am just returned. I found a long high ridge, with a hard sandy road running along the top of it, wherefrom on the one side I saw the city lying in the plain, and, on the other, the fair blue mountains that rise beyond Bœrne and Bandera. O how ravishing sweet and soft were these noble forms of the hills reposing far away, wrapped in a calm majesty of sun-lit dreams! These enchanted visions that keep the mountains so still, must be visions of God and of Love. Thou knowest that thou didst ride with me, that thou didst lend the loveliness of thine eyes to the loveliness of nature, and that I worshipped thee, out on the wild ridged plains, as fervidly as ever was lady worshipped by

Lover.

To Mary Day Lanier

San Antonio, Texas
January 6th 1872 [1873]

Yesterday afternoon, when I came in from my ride, I found Mr. Henry C. King's card awaiting me. I was sorry to have missed him, for I had a thousand things to talk to him about. So this morning I betook me to the streets, and wandered about, figuring to myself what manner of man Mr– King must be.

Finally I passed on the sidewalk a gentleman whom I inwardly resolved to be my man, and having gone beyond, I turned me back, met him again, and said, " Sir, are you not Mr. King ? " " I am " says he, " and I had just concluded, when you passed me, that you must be Mr. Lanier of Georgia ! "

Pretty good, wasn't it, for two men that had never seen each other, nor heard any sort of description of each other?

He's a tall slim man, in an enormous pair of jack-boots, with a keen dark eye, and a high forehead. As we walked along the street, I found him to be a great man in the land. Everybody stopped to shake hands with him, ('tis the first time he has been to San Antonio since he was elected Senator) and to say pleasant things to him. He came and dined with me: then to my room, where we had much talk. I liked him exceedingly; a man with not an ounce of the trader in his whole composition ! He told me he had thy letter in reply to his.[4]

God, that draweth this night on over the fair world, set a special star in thy heart to light thee, dear Lady, – supplicateth

Thy Lover.

To Mary Day Lanier

San Antonio, Texas

Jany 7th 1872 [1873]

Today I have four letters – from thee, ranging from Dec. 23rd, to Dec. 31st : also thy four newspapers, and a letter from father.

So: it must be, then.[5] – I will take a day or two to think of it. I find I had begun to hope that it was otherwise.

[4] See note 53, 1872.

[5] Of the four letters from his wife which Lanier answers in this letter, the first has not been found. It was probably the letter referred to in this sentence and must have contained a confirmation of her pregnancy, with confinement in June.

Thy questions shall have categoric answer, as far as such can be given, in the order thou askest them.

I do not cough at all, save the one cough after breakfast, in which, and in the expectoration following which there is no perceptible change since we were together at Marietta. Once, while I have been here, the bloody expectoration commenced, with its usual attendant, – great weakness: but it yielded in about four days, and has not since returned.

I think I have gained a couple of pounds in weight, since Marietta.

The " sore spot of yore " is much less troublesome than when I left thee, and on some days it disappears altogether.

I have fair appetite. On the point of dyspepsia, – I can speak in unqualified terms of admiration of the performances of my *apparatus.* I have never in my life enjoyed greater immunity from stomachic consciousness.

I have been taking Möller's Cod Liver Oil regularly three times a day for a month. I have reduced this pleasing formality to a scientific acme of ease. Immediately after each meal I turn the bottle up into my mouth, disdaining spoons, measurements, and even peppermint. I expect soon to arrive at that pitch of pulmonary perfection – which a consumptive friend of mine here has reached, *quoad* Cod Liver Oil: he says, *pshaw, Mr. Lanier, you wont do anything till you get so that you cry for it.* In addition to C. L. oil, I take from three to six doses of pure whiskey, (the best, by the way, that I've ever seen) every day.

I walk not much, but am certainly more puissant in this particular than when I saw thee last.

I ride every day, weather *volente.*

I am *not* reading or writing too steadily, – tho' I think I rather overdid it during the bad weather.

My buttons stick to me closer than a brother, I have lost none since that I left thee, Providence hath watched over me marvellously in respect of buttons.

As for nether garments. I did purvey me two new pairs in Montgomery, – Canton-flannel, with a most sweet long nap inside, wherewith I am swathed an it were a new-born babe in his flannels.

Thou are *not* to keep my light brown overcoat, thou art to dispose of the same in the way of traffic to any forlorn brother

whom misfortune may have brought to that piteous pass that
he needeth such a coat.

I have *not* need of the buttonwood-syrup recipe, I have discovered that a certain preparation called "Burton's Tobacco-
Antidote" is largely composed of the same, and I get all the
medicinal effects thereof by chewing that.

I have not heard from P. W. A. about the lands: nor put in
the advertisement.[6] The latter I have purposely omitted,
because it wd. be folly,– as I now see plainly from my experience – for me to think of *travelling* through Texas in the
winter-time: and I can not yet do anything in lands without
travelling.

I have not heard from Wysham,[7] nor from Ginna: nor from
Charles Lanier to whom I wrote before leaving Macon, nor
from Foster Higgins to whom, ditto.

I believe this about satisfieth thy catechetic maw. By way
of good measure in filling up the same, I will add that I
waked up this morning with my old enemy the crick-in-the-neck
fastened upon me with such violence as I have never before
known, and that I have been in parlous pain therefrom all day:
in other respects being strong and bright, and managing *malgré*
ye crick to take a ride on horseback this morning.

I think, dear Soul, that I have not omitted any precaution
nor any observance known to science or experience, since I came
here, – that wd. go to make a man well. My desire to get out
of this is grown so fierce and so intense that it has all the
wisdom of patience and the inspiration of genius. I think that
on the whole I can say that I am clearly better than I have
been since last March.

[6] On Dec. 24, 1872, Mary Day Lanier had written: "Hast heard from Mr.
' P. W. A.' about Mrs. Shorter's lands?" Also, she had reported that Mr. J. C.
Gibson, Gertrude Lanier Shannon's fiancé, had suggested that Lanier advertise
in the Montgomery newspapers that he would handle Texas land claims.

[7] On Dec. 24, 1872, Mary Day Lanier had written: "Hast heard from yr.
Wysham since leaving?" Henry Clay Wysham, a Baltimore lawyer who was an
amateur flutist, was soon to become an intimate friend. Lanier's description of
an evening spent with him in Baltimore in his letter of Sept. 19, 1873, was
labelled by Mary Day Lanier in later life as the account of their first meeting.
No further evidence of the beginning of this friendship has been found. It
seems likely that their acquaintance until that date was entirely through correspondence, possibly initiated by W. H. Browne, who frequently wrote to Lanier
on the subject of music as well as of poetry. (See also note 83, below.)

— But thou ! thou sufferest, and art to suffer. — Give me a little time to think of this – for I am thy trembling, all loving, yearning solicitous

Husband

I write father by today's mail to hand thee $40.⁰⁰.

To ROBERT S. LANIER

San Antonio, Texas
Jany 7th 1872 [1873]

My Dear Father:

Yr. letter of Dec. 31st was received this morning, and brought me a mingled freight of joy and sorrow.

Uncle Tom's death gave me great pain. I write to Aunt Mina by this mail.[8]

From the number and size of new cases you mention, your business seems to be excellent: wherein I rejoice exceedingly, for labor such as yours shd. have its reward.[9]

I had a long and pleasant visit from Mr. King, yesterday, which wd. have been longer had he not been compelled to hurry away with a physician for a sick friend at New Leon Springs. He seems to be a very popular man in this district,– for which he is Senator. He is going to Austin next week, when the legislature assembles, and promises me all manner of assistance if I will come over there.

I wrote, about two weeks ago, to the Ed. of the World, sending him enough " copy " for a couple of initiatory letters, and offering to write up the Texas Legislature, and Texas generally. I ought to hear from him in three or four days from now: and, if he shall propose satisfactory terms, I will go over to Austin to spend a couple of weeks or so. I shall then get acquainted, through Mr. King and other friends, with people from all parts of the state: and find out about Sherman,

[8] On Dec. 31, 1872, Lanier's wife had written that his Uncle Tom Eason (husband of R. S. Lanier's sister Wilhelmina) had died three days before.

[9] R. S. Lanier's letter to which this is an answer has not survived. But on Jan. 5, 1873, Lanier's wife wrote: " Did Papa mention that they had taken in about $16,000.⁰⁰, cash receipts, since Jan. 1872? And for December $1500 worth of new business taken in."

Grayson County, with a view to the party you mention as about to locate there.[10]

Will you please hand Mary, as soon as you receive this, forty dollars, and send me by check on N. Y. Seventy five ?

I am doing well, tho' suffering very much today with a crick in the neck.

I'll write Sissa tomorrow: meantime my love and kisses to her and to yourself.

Your Son

S. L.

To Mary Day Lanier

San Antonio, Texas
Jany 12th 1873

As long as there were mails, one felt as if one were at least upon the same planet with one's beloved at home: but now since the epizootic hath disabled all the horses,[11] we have had no mails at all, the Post Office is as still as a grave, and yawneth like a great chasm betwixt me and thee. Probably it will be a week yet before we get any letters.

The streets, moreover, seem deserted. Everything, and everybody, goeth here on horseback or behind horses, or some of the horse-tribe.

I wd. not write thee of this pitiable melancholy that thy poor lover is struggling through as best he may: – were it not, that by the time thou receivest this letter it will be *over*, – recollect! for by that time I will probably have heard from thee.

I have several times desired to ask thee, – if thou wert not so love-worship-compelling! – if thou knewest Capt. French, of

---

[10] The party here referred to may possibly have been the one mentioned in Mary Day Lanier's letter of Dec. 31, 1872: " Papa speaks of a Mr. Pope, partner of Gov. Brown, who has moved to Texas; thinks it might be a fine opening for a partnership for you."

[11] In a letter of Jan. 10 (here omitted) Lanier had written to his wife: " all the equine world cougheth and dribbleth pathetically: . . . the stage hath stopped running betwixt here and Austin." The epizootic, a kind of epidemic influenza among horses, was sweeping the country; Mary Day Lanier had reported it in Macon as early as Nov. 24, 1872, and the New York *World* daily chronicled its progress westward.

the Federal Army, a son of one of the instructors at West Point?
Or Gen. Augur, – in command of this dep't? Or Col. Prinie,
commanding the post? Or Maj. Russell (not Sam. Russell),
Adjt. Gen'l?

———— Since I *know,* I wish to be with thee so much that
I am almost on the point of going home to thee. 'Tis hard to
be *waiting* here for the climate to get better! The truth is, I am
growing sceptical of this, as a *winter*-climate. In the late
spring, in the summer, and in the fall (the dying days of which
were so beautiful when I first came here) this is a noble climate
for people like me and you, unquestionably: and the shortness
of the winter, if one were *living* here, wd. render it very
tolerable. But, if I am coming home in the summer, as I have
hitherto, (without having thought out matters) expected, query,
(as Jno. Rutherford saith) were I not better return now, escape
these wretched Northers, and come back here in the summer?
I am going to think of it.

But I wd. like to have thee at Marietta, if I shd. return:
I do not care to go back to Macon, to stay during any winter-
months; for I have a fancy to winter it in Marietta, once: my
experience of the *very cold* nipping weather such as we had at
Christmas (when for a couple of days I felt gloriously) leadeth
me strongly to desire to try the winter-winds of the Kennesaw
country.

These ideas are not formed: I do but entertain them: I will
sift them gravely and thoroughly before I adopt them: but if
I shall then think them right and dutiful, I will come.

God save thy loveliness, dear, lovely Soul to whom I am

Lover.

To Mary Day Lanier

San Antonio, Texas
Jany 15th 1873

No, I will have none of the tri-weekly business: [12] I *will* continue to write thee daily: I tell thee again that, to the Artist,

---

[12] Lanier's wife had written on Jan. 3 that she and both her father and father-
in-law felt that he was writing too much and urged him to write tri-weekly
letters instead of daily ones, to spare his arm and his lung.

MARY DAY LANIER IN 1873

Charles D. Lanier Collection, Johns Hopkins University

to possess a fair womanly Soul to whom he can send daily some
fervent breathing of worship, in the confident knowledge that
no most delicate-hinted inspiration therein will ever miss instant
and loving recognition, – that is a pinnacle and spire of pleasure, high, keen and glittering.

– But it is thou that art writing too much ! Here I have this
morning two letters from thee, long sweet showers out of the
fine heaven of thy heart that set me all a-quiver as it were a
rain-beaten bush.

Surely, dear Lady, my heart will quite die in a great yearning,
an I kiss thee not ere long!

And last night I dreamed of thee, a full calm, quiet, blissful
dream of thy pretty comradeship.

The pictures thou sendest are very fair. This last picture of
thee wd. have been *so* good, had the painter not daubed thy
sweet cheeks with such a blowsy red, whereas thou must have
been but a pale Darling at that time.[18]

I grieve over this last trouble whereof thou writest: but I
have hope that it may yet be well there.

I have, this morning, a fair old-time-y letter from Salem
Dutcher, which I enclose today to father, asking him to hand
to thee: and now asking thee to return same to me. I do not
know that I will go to Austin, to undertake the letters spoken
of, from there: the compensation is trifling: but I *may* conclude to go, in view of two things, first that I wd. acquire
through Mr. King a valuable acquaintance with legislators
from all parts of the State, which wd. be at least facilitated
by the *name* of World Correspondent: and, secondly, it might
be well enough to put this entering wedge into the good graces
of the World people in view of possible future literary ventures.
I will think it over a day or two.

Meantime I prithee let thy " soft pitous herte " graciously
receive the far-off worship of thy

Lover.

[18] In a letter to his wife, Jan. 11, 1873 (here omitted), Lanier had said:
" What happy inspiration led thee to send me that picture, with the hands clasped
in front– thine old gesture! " This is apparently the tinted ferrotype reproduced
on the opposite page.

To Robert S. Lanier

San Antonio, Texas
Jany 15th 1873

My Dear Father:

I was very glad to get Olmsted, and have enjoyed a rapid run through his book with much zest.

I enclose a letter received this morning from Salem Dutcher. The brute of a night-editor had no right to mutilate my letter,[14] for I had not offered it to them unconditionally, I had only sent it as a sample of my wares, asking what they were willing to give. I would immediately write the World Editor my free opinion of the proceeding, (for they had no right to publish the letter at all, much less, garbled, until I had signified my acceptance of their terms) if it were not for Salem's friendly offices in the matter, in view of which a sharp remonstrance from me might seem ungracious.

I don't know whether it will pay to go to Austin to undertake the letters from there: a letter once a fortnight won't amount to anything pecuniarily: but for reasons stated to Mamie in a letter written her today (which, to save my poor right arm, I will ask you to learn from her) I may conclude to go.

I ought to have written you before why I have not pursued the land matters, advertisements &c : but I was waiting to get some assured ideas of a Texas winter – God help a poor devil whose movements depend on the weather! – and to see some part of the season that was not exceptional. I think I have learned enough to know that for *me,* at least, (and every consumptive is pretty much a " law unto himself " in these matters) travelling in Texas in the winter wd. be simply committing suicide: and no extensive business in lands cd. be done in this part of the country without travelling.

I have however reason to hope that I have made a favorable turn in the matter of strength of lungs: and, with *patience,* and by observing all the appliances known to modern science for improving the hygienic condition of the animal man, I honestly think there is great chance for me to live a life of length enough, and of much activity. I underscore " patience " as well for *you*

[14] See note 56, 1872.

as for myself. Do not expect too much, in a short time. Whilst
some days, as at Christmas, I feel literally as frisky as a buffalo,
yet I have a badly hurt lung to nurse, and it is a long business,
and a slow, with frequent set-backs (– of which I do not write,
because I understand them perfectly, and it is no use from this
far countree, to pain you with news of what is probably over
when you are reading of it) which require much courage to with-
stand and much pains to counteract. I am not yet even *sure*
about Texas: the table of Dr. Pettersen's which I sent you shows
very conclusively that it is an error to call this a *dry* climate:
and even when the rains are over, one is often kept from one's
horseback exercise for many days longer by the marvellous mud.
Far from all consumptives who come here are benefited: and
the Northers, (to which *I* wd. add the *Southers, i. e.* the warm,
sickening, relaxing, moist airs that come up from the coast and
which make a terrible alternation with the Northers) are certainly sources of great danger. San Antonio is as subject to
malaria as Macon: and quinine is in as much demand. The
swamp-moss (sure child of moist air!) grows on the trees
around San Pedro Springs, a mile from here. Moreover, residence in this part of Texas is rendered repugnant by the
constant liability, slight, it is true, and yet always a genuine
liability, to have one's child or one's self, if a mile away from
town, picked up by Indians or by bandits under that name.

You will say, doubtless, when you read this, that I happen
to be feeling badly, and am temporarily discouraged. But not
at all so: I am merely stating to you the evidence on the *other*
side, which I have to revolve in my own mind, and upon which
I am endeavoring to form a grave and just conclusion. Indeed
I wd. not write you of it *now,* when you probably have yr. mind
full of business matters: were I not solicitous that you may not
think me dilatory in making, or at least initiating, some business
arrangements: and you will see that until these preliminary
questions are finally established beyond doubt, it is quite impossible to set on foot any business enterprise.

The only work, meantime, wh. I *can* do, is writing: and that
I am doing in as full measure as health will permit.

Mamie writes me in earnest terms of your kind and thoughtful care for her: and for this, I thank you much more than
I will attempt to put on paper.

Please hand Salem's letter to Mamie, who will return it to me.

I suppose little Sissa is off today.[15] I woke up early this morning thinking of y'r. commotion: and have yearned all day to know that all passed well.

Write me when you have time. Love to Uncle C: and congratulations on the great speech that won the Duffield case.[16]

Your loving

Sidney L.

To Mary Day Lanier

San Antonio, Texas

Jany 16th 1873

Today is a good day: last night there came up what is technically called a " dry Norther," swept back the relaxing Gulf airs, cleared the heavens to a limpid blue, crisped the atmosphere, and purified the land of malaria. 'Tis not by any means, considered merely as weather, so pretty as some phases: the birds, for instance; will have none of it, they sing not, and the wind ceaselessly howleth away the river-lisping : but *quoad* consumptives, 'tis the best weather I have seen here.

—   I think I am resolved upon one thing: that is, that I will not finally pitch my tent in Texas, until I have first tried Denver City, Colorado. That is high above the sea: it is a safe land: it is in a country full of life, of energy, of prosperity, of an assured future. San Antonio is not *any* of the aforementioned things. Moreover Denver is cold: that is, quietly and moderately cold: which San Antonio almost never is : indeed this very good air that exhilarates me today, comes, one may safely say, from about Denver.

Thou must not fancy me wavering, nor discouraged, nor ill, when I write thus, I only take thee along with me in the process by wh. I shall arrive at some conclusion.

I wrote my father a long letter yesterday, wh. I hope he will

---

[15] The wedding of Gertrude Lanier Shannon had actually taken place the night before (see Mary Day Lanier's letter of Jan. 14, 1873).

[16] In a letter of Dec. 31, 1872, referring to this case—a suit for $30,000 damages—Mary Day Lanier had written: " Uncle Clifford made perhaps the most brilliant speech of his life."

receive. I know thou wilt enjoy Salem's letter, wh. I enclosed therein: and wh. I shall answer fairly, in satisfaction of certain sneaking hankerings wh. I have sometimes had after my old Scarabæus.

As the glitering heavens and the strong wind rule this land, so do the light and the energy of thee-love rule thy

Lover.

To Mary Day Lanier

San Antonio, Texas
Jany 27th 1873

None but the exile can know the exile's feeling; and well, that it is so: for it is a main sad and dun-colored sensation. Laugh not, that I say "exile": here one *is* an exile, from *any*where: one is in no country in the world: one hears no good honest tongue, of any sort, spoken, but a wretched many-toned lingo.

If I were to compare this town to any *one* thing in the world, I would liken it to boarding-house hash: wherein one can detect a little beef, a little pork, a good deal of pepper and salt, and a vast quantity of an unknown substratum which *may* be yesterday's cold roast-beef, and *may* be dog.

— Thou wilt straightway declare that this is a bitter change of my tune: and I am free to confess it: but it is a matter of today only, and will pass away by tomorrow: today I am indeed angry with any place that does not hold *thee*: for thou art my Comrade and my Sweet, and thou art my Other-Heart, and I am fain, fain look in thine eyes.

They say we will likely have a mail tomorrow: and perhaps I will then receive these famous letters.[17]

Dearest Lady, I am so in love with thee today that I fear to talk with thee, at this distance from thine eyes and thy lips, lest I make myself more conscious of thine absence, and so come to be thy *too*-unhappy

Lover.

---

[17] Mary Day Lanier had sent her husband a telegram (received Jan. 22) stating that after he had received her letter of Jan. 20 he should answer his father's letter of Saturday (Jan. 18). Both letters contained the news of the sudden second marriage of R. S. Lanier to a widow named Mrs. Morgan.

To Mary Day Lanier [18]

San Antonio, Texas
Jany 30th 1873

Last night at eight O'clock came Mr. *Scheidemantel,* a genuine lover of music and fine pianist, to take me to the *Maenner-chor,* which meets every Wednesday night for practice. Quickly we came to a hall, one end of which was occupied by a minute stage, with appurtenances, and a piano : and in the middle thereof, a long table at which each singer sat down as he came in. Presently, seventeen Germans were seated at the singing-table, long-necked bottles of Rhine Wine were opened and tasted, great pipes and segars were all a-fire, the leader, Herr *Thielepape* (pron. nearly *Teelypapper*) – an old man with long white beard and moustache, formerly Mayor of the City – rapped his tuning-fork vigorously, gave the chords by rapid arpeggios of his voice, (a wonderful wild high tenor such as thou wouldst dream that the old Welsh harpers had, wherewith to sing songs that would cut against the fierce sea-blasts) and off they all swung into such a noble, noble old German full-voiced *lied,* that imperious tears rushed into my eyes, I could scarce restrain myself from running and kissing each one in turn and from howling dolefully the while. And so, O my Heart,– I all the time worshipping thee with these great chords and calling upon thee to listen and to love with me –, we drove through the evening until twelve O'clock, absorbing enormous quantities of Rhine Wine and beer whereof I imbibed my full share. After the second song, I was called on to play – and lifted my poor old flute in air with tumultuous beating heart for I had no confidence either in that or in myself. But, du Himmel ! Thou shouldst have heard mine old love warble herself forth. To my utter astonishment, I was perfect master of the instrument. Is not this most strange? Thou knowest I had never learned it: and thou rememberest what a poor muddle I made at Marietta in playing difficult passages: and I *certainly* have not practiced : and yet there I commanded and the blessed notes

---

[18] Previously published, *Scribner's,* XXV, 624-625 (May, 1899) ; reprinted, *Letters* (New York, 1899), pp. 71-73.

obeyed me, and when I had finished, amid a storm of applause, Herr Thielepape arose and ran to me and grasped my hand and declared that he hat never heert de flude accompany itself pefore !   I played once more during the evening: and ended with even more rapturous bravos than before. Mr. Scheide-mantel grasping my hand this time and thanking me very earnestly.

My heart, which was hurt greatly when I went in to the music-room, came forth from the holy bath of Concords greatly refreshed, strengthened and quieted, and so remaineth today. I also feel better today than in a long time before. Moreover I am still master of the flute, and she hath given forth to me today such tones as I have never heard from a flute before.

For these things, I humbly thank God !

I had yesterday two papers sent by thy father, wh. were very acceptable, and for which I beg thee to thank him very heartily. No letter is yet come from my father.

I will not write thee further today. Thou art my dear Sweet, and I am thy faithful humble

Lover.

To Robert S. Lanier

San Antonio   Texas
Feby 1st 1873

My Dear Father:

I have just received yours of Jany 18th, con-taining check for $75.⁰⁰, for which I thank you.

I note with grave interest what you say in relation to your approaching marriage.[19]   Surely, in such a matter, there can be but one question; and that is whether the move is for your best happiness: and since you declare confidently,– you, who only *can* judge, upon such a point – that this one *is* for your happiness, I can assure you, both for myself and for mine, that

---

[19] The phrase is somewhat puzzling, for Mary Day Lanier's letter of Jan. 20-22 (receipt of which was acknowledged in Lanier's reply of Jan. 30, 1873, here omitted) stated that R. S. Lanier's wedding was definitely set for Jan. 23—now one week past. It is possible that in spite of the specific information gained from his wife's letter, Lanier was pretending to a knowledge of only such tentative plans as were announced in his father's letter of Jan. 18 (not found).

nothing will be omitted to advance in every way your pleasure
and your welfare in your new condition of life. I pray very
fervently that in your married life you may realize the very
fullest measure of quiet happiness, and of that calmness of soul
which arises from the sacrifices of mutual devotion.

I think it best for Mary to secure quarters at Marietta, and
go into them immediately upon leaving Harry's.[20] Among your
numerous weddings, there, I suspect she has had a great deal
of over-fatigue: the summer-move to Marietta will require
still more, in packing &c: and, in view of what is to be with her,
I desire her to get all these fatiguing matters over and done
with, and, safely esconced at Marietta, to abandon herself to a
long period of repose. To postpone her removal up there, wd.
involve packing at a time when she wd. be ill able to endure it.

I have not been so well, of late: though much better during
the last two or three days than for several weeks before. I
manage to keep very busy reading and writing, and exercising
when I can: and time does not drag with me at all.

I await anxiously some definite news of yr. marriage: and
meantime am

Your Son

S. L.

TO MARY DAY LANIER [21]

San Antonio Texas

Feb. 2nd 1873

Here cometh this morning th[y letter] of Jany 27th, – same
havi[ng] reached me in about five [days] and a half since thy
mos[t] dear fingers folded it. [Five] days and a half, from thy
[dear] hand ! I can not kiss it enough.

How I wish I c[ould] talk with thee ! There are [so] many
things to be said to [thee] that thy letters suggest [and] then,
thou knowest, I am of old such a wooden-head fool about

---

[20] Upon the breaking up of the Vineville home, Mary Day Lanier was
apparently planning a temporary residence with her brother in Brunswick (see
Lanier's letter to his wife, Jan. 30, 1873, here omitted).

[21] The MS of this letter has been mutilated, and Mary Day Lanier's letter of
Jan. 27, to which this is an answer, has not been found. Conjectural restorations
have been made where possible.

these arrangement-matters: and I am i[n a] tremulous condition of app[rehension] lest I have said, done, omitted to say
or do, something I ought not.

Well; to business. *The last of May,* to *Marietta,* quotha !
Dear Beautiful, I am going, God willing, to kiss thee surely by
the first of next April; it may be, some weeks sooner: and I
desire that thou and I be alone, then ; and I know not where
else we can compass that with so many advantages as at
Marietta. If thou canst suggest anything better, in God's name
do so : thou canst beat me out of my hair, a-planning : and
I am wedded to no ideas in this matter save to one, that is,
that I will live with thee, x x x x x x x
Thou and I, thou and I: God hath married us, let us live
together. I do not well without thine eyes and thy voice
and thy bright intelligence and the lovely spectacle of thy
motherhood.

— It is closely in this connection that I tell thee what follows.
There is abroad a recent theory that there *is* an antidote to that
blood-poison which is called consumption: the same being
whiskey, used in a certain way. I need not detail to thee all
the care I have [em]ployed in investigating the matter, it has
been [ver]y great, close and scrutinizing: I will but mention
that perhaps my most constant visitor here is a gentleman who
hath actually lost about half of both his lungs ,– being rarely
sunken-chested, and yet who is perfectly erect, engaged in active
business, and always moving: and he accounteth for [it] all
upon the whiskey-theory wh. he hath faithfully followed:
another is here who hath but one lung, [if] at all, yet he writeth
day after day, is fat – hale and hearty, and dischargeth the
duties of Clerk of the Court faithfully, – all from the whiskey-
theory: and I believe that out of all the consumptives here
the most strong are without exception those who have adopted
this course. Those who have *not,* quickly yield, in this climate,
to death: thou wilt see in the marked Mortuary Report, in the
Newspaper I send thee today, that five consumptives died here
last month. Among them was the poor fellow of whom I wrote
thee, when I first came, as being a fellow-passenger and as
having looked so much better soon after he came. *That* was
the mere stimulus of the rest from travelling. He soon fell
back: and now God hath taken him and spared me. – But to

go on with my whiskey tale. Having deliberately resolved to give a fair trial to all theories in connection with this disease: and being at the time (a week ago) in a very weak condition, from my chill, and other set-backs, I went to work with the whiskey : the idea is simply to take a good solid dose of it about every hour and a half during the day (the every-three-hour theory is a mistake) : and, although the weather has been, and still is, as bad as the very worst Macon weather ever is, I have steadily improved in strength and in all sensations, and I can say, now, that (while in some particulars I am by no means out of the woods) I feel more like a man upon a sub-stantial basis than in a long time before, except about Christmas time when the intense cold weather made me crackle clear like an ice crystal. – At the same time with this inauguration of the whiskey, I commenced a celebrated remedy wh. I have never tried before: The French " *Sirop d' Hypophosphite de Soude.*" Perhaps this may have helped on the whiskey's benefit.

At any rate, I am greatly encouraged: and all the more so, that my improvement has been in *spite* of the wretched weather: wh. leadeth me to believe that I can in this way live and work in Georgia, (not in Macon) but in a climate whose cold shall brace me, like Marietta. This idea delighteth me: and if God will let me, I am going to test it.

Therefore it is, that I have written Father that I desired thee to go to Marietta as soon as thy visit to Harry was over: I have not said anything to him of my return: not desiring to give any cause of disturbance to him at this time when, in God's name, if he *can,* let him, be happy. I will write him, in a day or two, about the trunks and the furniture. I think in view of Marietta, thou wert better keep the furniture: I will try, in a week or two, if God will prosper a little project or two of mine, to have the $45 for thy father. Nevertheless, thou art on the spot, do exactly as it liketh thee, with furniture and all: trouble not to write me reasons or details, but only give me thy desires and commands in aught that I may do, to help thee, dear Wife. I dare not allow myself to think of thy dear father's trouble: but I only thrill and thrill with strong prayers to God to continue carrying me towards health : for if I were but in health, I cd. erelong pull us out of the mire.

I wish thou wdst. write me ,– if I have omitted to tell my

father anything I ought, (for saving of trouble to thee) to tell him ,– thy instructions.

Do thou bestir thyself, therefore, and look out for a couple of rooms at Marietta: and calculate not upon staying at Hal's more than six weeks. All this, – unless anything better may occur to thee.

Thou shalt receive the $60. I will *never* get a chance to write thee of thy wonderful letter of 14th Jany, anent the small Soul !

I shd. not write any more to thee now, I have some other writing, wh. is *for* thee, if not *to* thee.

I have a fair letter from little Sissa today, in reply to my wedding-letter to her.

God reveal to thee, dear Wife, the faithful worship of thy

Husband.

To Clifford A. Lanier

San Antonio, Texas
Feb. 8th 1873

My Dear Clifford: Your letter came to me this morning, and was as a fair invocation to some good saint in the beginning of the day. I ought indeed to have written you, ere now, – if for no other purpose, at least, to tell you why I *can't* write much. I have been working on a quite elaborate Magazine Article upon " San Antonio de Bexar," wh. has required a good deal of reading and of pottering about in search of information; besides this, I've sent some letters to the World,[22] and have been engaged in the troublesome task of collecting material for more: besides this I have been putting some fire under one or two other pots wh. I don't intend to say anything about until I see that they are coming to a boil: and then, you know, I send some little adoring breath to my worshipful sweet Mary every day,

[22] Lanier's second published letter to the New York *World* (Feb. 6, 1873) is dated Jan. 23 and entitled " An Indian Raid in Texas." In his letter of Feb. 8, 1873, to his wife (here omitted) he said: " I have to write for the World about the Mexican business which is already put off too long, and ought also to write about the Texas legislature &c." His third published letter to the *World* (Mar. 13, 1873) is dated Feb. 17 and entitled " The Mexican Border Troubles."

and a letter reporting progress to father about twice a week, in addition to an unconscionable amount of fortuitous correspondence wh. *will* drop along somehow spite of all I can do; – and, to make matters worse, my hurt lung has begun to protest very loudly during the last three or four weeks against my writing at all, and now spites my heedlessness of its earlier protestations by giving me so much pain in my right arm as to make me incapable of writing more than a little at a time. I particularly regret this, for the reason that it seems to me I was never in my life so full of all manner of poems and books nor so confident of being able to succeed in this way of life.

I've had, too, for a month past, a good deal of trouble with my disease, and an amount of my time wh. seems simply astonishing until one actually goes through it – has been spent in various ways and means of repelling and fortifying against these attacks.

All of wh. is said, not as one complaining, – for with much suffering I grow firm and clear in the faith that God understands His world and that all things (including my little hurts) do fit into some wise administration whose polity is deeper than death wherebeyond man sees not – but only to let you understand how joyfully I wd. keep myself in full and frequent communication with you, if I *cd*.

I believe there is entire peace betwixt father, and me and mine. I wrote him, as soon as I heard of his last intentions, offering to do all in my power to forward his wishes in that behalf: and wrote my fair wishes again immediately on hearing of his marriage. I have a very cordial and loving letter from him dated a week after the event.[23] I unite with you full heartily in yr. wish, in that regard.

The spectacle of dear little Sissa's happiness gives me great pleasure. Joy has long been her debtor: and I hope she will draw without stint while he is in an honest humor for paying his obligations. Commend me to our new brother, as one who will look full warm-heartedly upon whomever our dear little girl has seen fit to love.

---

[23] In a letter to his wife of Feb. 8 (here omitted) Lanier remarked apropos of this letter from his father, which he inclosed: "I infer that these must be Halcyon days. I pray God they may so continue, and that the uncertainty which hath so long disturbed that life may be dissolved in the home-atmosphere and settled round of duty wh. will now supervene."

I think to return by the first of April, perhaps earlier. I am, in the whole, disappointed in the *winter*-climate here; though I doubt not the fall-climate, whose dying days so delighted me when I first came – is very fine. Again, I cannot go out on the plains to rough it, without either subjecting myself to the danger of murder by Indians – a danger altogether greater than I had ever supposed before I came here – or else attaching myself to some party whose movements are uncertain and who might keep me out a great deal too long. Moreover, I want to go to Denver, Colorado: wh. from all accounts has a far finer climate (finer for *me*, I like *cold*) than this, and wh. is in the great line of Western advancement. San Antonio, I think, is soon to be a dead place, in all business. Its previous prosperity has been mostly due to the want of railroads: and as soon as some projects now under weigh are completed, it will collapse like a sucked orange.

Please find herein Invoice I Lot Kisses, Extra Family; wh., when they arrive, distribute among all those dear ones that need a love-reminder from

Your

S. L.

To Mary Day Lanier

San Antonio, Texas

Feb. 12th 1873

Well, thine, explanatory, of Feb. 5th, is here, and let us say nothing more of these hateful matters. I think thou hast been very fine and high through it all, and I am quite satisfied with thee. I do not know, I have never known, any other woman who *could* be so large and honorable and Christian and delicate and womanly.[24]

Today is perfect spring. Such of the birds as have not gone

[24] Mary Day Lanier's letter of Feb. 5 has not been found. The allusion is possibly to a discussion of the change in living arrangements she was making as a result of the marriage of R. S. Lanier and of her own feelings about her new step-mother-in-law, of whom she had written in a mutilated letter of Feb. 2: "Also, poor woman, is it likely that the gentle prompting of *pity* will unite us in a manner, if she continues to be as ladylike and as gentle as she now is."

entirely wild with delight are whistling and trilling with a tranquil passion that is like an ecstasy of religion: but most of them are quite lunatic, and their little throttles are all a-quiver with a miscellaneous mænadic shrill jubilation which maketh the intense blue of heaven seem all a-throb with contagious enthusiasm and the swift water runneth among its grasses like a maiden faring wildly over the earth with locks blown and far-trailing.

Enclosed is a letter from Salem, and a travesty wh. will make thee laugh, and as 'twere " harrow " thine " intercostal spaces." Also I send thee a " programme " of one who heard me playing in my room some evenings ago, and straightway had himself introduced, and came declaring that I was an artist such as the world hath not seen, and making overtures to me to go a-concerting with him: but he knoweth not much of music and he is not of our kind.

Apropos, my hardest cross is in this behalf. I cd. make *so* much money with the flute, in the great cities, – if I cd. but draw breath in them !

But no more complaints – from thy well-pleased-at-thy-picture-of-thy-tranquil-life

Lover.

To Mary Day Lanier

San Antonio, Texas
Feb. 13th 1873

Dear Lady, an thou do not call me back to thee soon, thou wilt have but a white-haired old man for a lover! Brushing my hair just now, I discover that with much grief for want of my comrade, I am turning gray as the old towers of Mission Concepcion.

Dost thou mark what Mrs. Dutcher saith, in the lettter of Salem's I sent thee? She saith to me, " Go home! "

It is really, literally true that with pining for thee I am hurt, and hindered in fighting my lung.

Life seemeth so empty without the satisfactions thy large fellow-soul bringeth daily to mine: and speech seemeth so vapid when I do not hear thy full-hearted and earnest-sweet talk: and music seemeth *so* crude, that *thy* fingers do not make.

> *Rufe dein Kind zurück !* [25]

To-night I go to a little musicale at Col. Withers', with my flute.

Today is also sweet spring. The grass springeth green out there by the river. This morning as I walked along the street, a heavenly fluting fell upon my ear from above, and looking upward I saw that the martins were come. The little gurgling love-notes nearly broke my heart with sudden inroad of the memory of thy sweetness, time agone, when the martins also sang, recollectest thou?

When wilt thou go to Marietta with me, canst thou not, by the first of April, meet there thy

Lover?

TO MARY DAY LANIER [26]

San Antonio, Texas
Feb. 14th 1873

Today I have two papers from thy father, – for which I beg thee thank him very heartily, and tell him I will write my own thanks in proper person as soon as I can clear away some persistent ghosts of unanswered letters wh. take advantage of my lame arm to lie restless in their graves.

I arrayed me last night and went to the party at Col. Withers'. I found a very elegant looking company of ladies and gentle-men, – among the most so, Gen. Augur,[27] and his daughters – already assembled–

First came some very good concerted pieces for violin and piano, then piano solo, then a song. Then they called for the flute. I had not played three seconds before a profound silence

---

[25] From Schiller's *Die Piccolomini,* previously quoted in a letter of July 16, 1872.

[26] Previously published, *Scribner's,* XXV, 625 (May, 1899); reprinted, *Letters* (New York, 1899), p. 73.

[27] Christopher Columbus Augur (1821-1898), brigadier-general in the Union Army. He was in command of various western military departments from 1867 to 1885.

reigned among the people; seeing which, and dreaming wildly of thee, and feeling somehow, in an eerie and elfish and half uncanny mood – I flew off into all manner of trills and laments and cadenza-monstrosities, for a long time, but finally floated down easily into *La Melancholie,* (which, on the violin, ran every body crazy, here, some weeks ago at a concert) which melted itself forth with such eloquent lamenting that it almost brought my tears: – and, to make a long story short, when I allowed the last note to die, a simultaneous cry of pleasure broke forth from men and women that almost amounted to a shout, – – – and I stood and received the compliments and congratulations that thereupon came in, so wrought up by my own playing with thoughts of *thee,* that I cd. but smile mechanically and make stereotyped returns to the pleasant sayings, what time my heart worked falteringly like a mouth that is about to cry. — I wd. there were some other chronicler to tell thee of this success,– for I cannot but seem to blow mine own horn therein ! – but I know it will give thee pleasure, and therefore, failing others, I tell it thee.

We had a superb supper: marvellous French boned Turkey encased in its own transparent jelly, a noble salad, and good Champagne,– wh. latter I did punish fearfully, tho' not to detriment of thine old " No. 1 " [28] wh. I played after supper amid universal bravos.

— Wherefore no more now, from thy horn-blowing, yet thee-desiring

. Lover.

To Mary Day Lanier

San Antonio, Texas,
Feb. 16th 1873

Dear Comrade, A letter of Mr. Hayne's enclosing MS. of a poem [29] he had just written, declaring that he was disgusted with it and begging me to " put it into artistic ship-shape," –

---

[28] Presumably a reference to a musical composition which has survived in MS (Charles D. Lanier Collection, Johns Hopkins University), entitled " Song Without Words: / ' The Widow Sang the Child to Sleep ' / For Flute and Piano / By / Sidney Lanier. / Op. 1."

[29] " In the Pine Barrens – Sunset." Receipt of the corrected MS and of Lanier's lost letter of " the 16th inst " is acknowledged in Hayne's letter of Feb. 27, 1873.

has been lying on my table for several days, and I have just replied, having re-written the piece and a letter beside: and now, the night being advanced, and my arm tired, I will put thee off, – as the laboring-man not seldom must do – with but one little adoring prayer that God may give thy dreams in charge of His daintiest Angel this night, and that thou wilt remember, in some humble sweet interval thereof, the name of thy far-off longing worshipping

Lover.

To Mary Day Lanier

San Antonio, Texas
Feb. 20th 1873

So: Clare thinketh that with these, absence is not so insupportable after all, doth she? [30] Or in other words, hast thou been showing her my letters, Vile, Perfidious Sweet?

I care not if thou didst: did she not think them very pretty? How cd. that be else than beautiful, wh. hath been inspired by love so white-hot and worship so humble-faithful as mine for thee !

Last night, came Scheidemantel, and we went to the *Männer Chor* together. The music was noble: and after the singing was over, I fell into a prodigious discussion with a fine scholarly German on Shakespeare's sonnets (he was a Shakespeare-worshipper as most modern Germans are), wherein we did continue with frequent excursions off into German literature, for long hours, consuming marvellous quantities of Hallgartner, and parting reluctantly. I did not carry my flute.

This morning *Zauberflöte* was in the most ravishing mood, and I played myself fairly into a sacred frenzy. My God, if I never make another note of music, I thank Thee for one perfect Artist's-hour !

Thy Charlie's-letter is simply too good; thou hast hit off his talk so that the sentences carry with them the intonations of his

[30] On Feb. 12 Mary Day Lanier had written: " So many good rich letters from thee! Well! as Clare [de Graffenried] says– ' after all, *with these*, absence is not so insupportable.' "

voice and the movements of his red lips and the sublime honesty of his gray eyes.

Thou art very gracious to thy poor

Lover.

To Mary Day Lanier [31]

San Antonio. Texas
Feb. 24th 1873

Were it not for some circumstances wh. make such a proposition seem absurd in the highest degree,– I wd. think today that I am shortly to die, and that my Spirit hath been singing its swan-song before dissolution. All day, my Soul hath been cutting swiftly into the great space of the Subtle Unspeakable Deep, driven by wind after wind of heavenly melody. The very inner spirit and essence of all wind-songs, bird-songs, passion-songs, folk-songs, country-songs, sex-songs, soul-songs and body-songs, hath blown upon me in quick gusts like the breaths of Passion, and sailed me into a sea of vast dreams whereof each wave is at once a vision and a melody.

Thou, Mate, thou, dear Love, ridest by me, Thank God; an it were not for the gracious Company and Comfort of thy perfect Comradeship, I wd. surely pass on out of life.

Exquisite Soul, I do thank thee humbly that thou deignest to sit, friendly, consoling, rare, dainty, supporting, inspiring, loving, rewarding, by the side of Music-driven

Lover .

To Mary Day Lanier

S[an] A[ntonio, Texas,] Feb. 25th 1873

O, had I but the touch of thy consoling hand upon my head this day!

Ineffable poems, — of music and of words — torment me, I have not patience enough for a pen, who is there that in the

---

[31] Previously published, W. H. Ward, "Memorial," *Poems* (New York, 1884), p. xix.

ecstasy of the kiss of his Beloved could simultaneously drudge down the cold word-translation thereof?

And this,—— for three pathetic strange days I have felt the kiss of Art, whom I love next to thee.

But if I had the comfort of thy gray eyes, and the sweeter sweetness of *thy* kiss, and the love-made-manifest of the tender pressure of thy hand which claspeth for all the world as a soul loveth, and the immediate sure guerdon of thy smile and thy praise, ————— then I wd. be stronger and more tranquil, then I wd. have courage to unloose the arms of Art from about my neck and to freely address myself towards communicating to the world some hint of the glory and the grace that lie out of daily sight.

To thee, alone of all women in the world, wd. I write such a thing; for thou, alone of all women in the world, wilt fully know the pain and the bliss that need to speak thus some-times,—pain and bliss of one who, for thy dear and most sweet sake, doth continually yearn and humbly strive to be at once a man, an artist and a

Lover.

To Mary Day Lanier

S[an] A[ntonio, Texas,] Feb. 26th 1873

Thine of 16th is come. Thou dear, suffering Soul, I do so long to tend thee and minister to thy feebleness !

Here let me ask thee to do something wherein I have great faith. It is evident thy system is so feeble, that thou art prey to all manner of diseases that choose to fasten upon thee. Now I have been lately studying the latest and most authoritative writers on Medecine, – two, especially, one American and one European –: and (without going into details which I have not time to write), I beg thee to procure immediately some Lager Beer, or some good home-made wine, – I think the *beer* will be better for thee – and straightway commence to take a small quantity thereof every hour in the day. Also, purvey thee some pleasant crackers or "Albert Biscuit" or the like, and eat one or two with thy beer before thou gettest into bed. I beg thee, dear Wife, *very earnestly,* to do this: I think I can guarantee that in a week's time thou wilt be free from chills. from dyspepsia, and all, without medecine of any sort. Wilt thou not strictly try this, for my sake? Let the quantity of beer thou takest at each time be quite small, – say a wine-glass-full: or,—if that produce any unpleasant sensation, such as fullness of head— less: yet, if thou canst take more without unpleasant sensation, take it: in short, take as much as thou canst up to the limit of fullness of pulse or of head. Commence this *immediately*: thou art so feeble that I am frightened for thee: if any serious acute disease shd. attack thee, what resistance cdst. thou offer! Let me not lose my Comrade, dear Lady, – of whom, remember, thou art in charge !

No, Friend, not " coming back with a new dream of love," but only with mine old dream purified by great winds of lonely anguish and burnt drossless by great fires of lonely passion. I am not afraid to find thee else than my Love.

"

―――――

"

I will write Mrs. Nisbet. This death giveth me sorrow. I ever loved him, for a hearty-souled good gentleman.[32]

I will probably start homeward in a few days: and I do greatly long to hear, *first,* that thou art safely esconced at Brunswick.

Lily is slow.[33] Go thou and hurry this laggard, – thou that art a month ahead of thy contract!

Pray, Child, that I may soon be by thy side, and be thy happy

Lover.

I find I forgot to speak of the boarding-arrangements at Marietta. I feel pretty well convinced that we wd. be *freer* at Groves' than at Winters'. Winters is Whitlock's partner, you know: and a very clever gentleman: but somehow I have taken a fancy to those *end* rooms, at Groves, so far away from the family, so convenient for all the little household cleanings up &c through the room opening into the back-yard, so retired yet so close to all places where we care to go. Thou knowest how very different good Miss Delia[Roberts]'s standard of a

[32] An unidentified kinsman of Judge E. A. Nisbet, whose death two years before had been commemorated by Lanier in an address (V, 277).
[33] Lilla Hazelhurst Burroughs was expecting her first child.

" BLACK-BIRDS," UNPUBLISHED MUSICAL COMPOSITION BY LANIER, 1873

Courtesy of Henry W. Lanier, New York

" nice " place is from ours ! The very things we most desire
(*some* of them) are the things she most dislikes, or thinks
not of. Then the fine play-ground for the boys! No, I decidedly prefer the Groves': and am quite willing to engage with
them immediately. Art not thou? I fancy Winters' wd. be a
fearfully stiff place: and the house is built (very differently
from the Groves' house) so that we have to be near, say across
a passage, some body else.

I prithee let us go to Groves' !

To Mary Day Lanier [34]

S[an]. A[ntonio, Texas,]. Feb. 28th 1873

Yesterday I did not write thee, having a letter to the World to
finish wh. I had already delayed too long.[35] 'Tis a monstrous
poor business, this newspaper letter writing: each communication is a mint of trouble, and one has to make a dozen inquiries
to each fact: and then the pay is simply absurd. I'm going to
quit it.

But thou shdst. hear thy lover play the flute ! I have writ
the most beautiful piece, – " Field-larks and Black-birds," [36]
wherein I have mirrored Mons. Field-lark's pretty eloquence so
that I doubt he wd. know the difference betwixt the flute and
his own voice.

O dear Wife, how my heart pleadeth to be taken straightway
back to thee ! I wd. flee to thee instantly: but I have a project
wh. looketh fair to yield a little money, and which, -*bête* of a
project that it is – cannot be put in execution before the middle
of April.[37] Yet again, on the other hand, I half fear to stay

---

[34] Excerpt previously published, *Scribner's*, XXV, 625 (May, 1899) ; reprinted, *Letters* (New York, 1899), p. 74.

[35] This is possibly Lanier's third published letter (see note 22, above) ; but
since that letter has the date-line " Feb. 17," the reference here may be to a
fourth, that was rejected and has not survived in MS.

[36] No musical composition by Lanier with this exact title has been found;
but one called " Black-birds " has survived (see specimen, p. 2, of the MS,
reproduced on the facing page) ; also a fragmentary music MS entitled " Mem.
Introd. to ' Blackbirds ' " (Charles D. Lanier Collection, Johns Hopkins
University).

[37] The nature of this project, not elsewhere referred to, has not been discovered.
It was apparently abandoned.

here so long: and so from day to day I am tormented with a terrible indecision, wavering betwixt coming home with empty pockets ,– and bringing thee some fair products of my skill, to lay at thy dear feet.

— It is more than likely, tho', that I will come soon, and leave my project, –which can be carried out at other time –: for I like not to dream of thee, sick, without my tendance; and, thank good God, I am strong enough to wait upon thee very helpfully.

God bear thee across this night, as one beareth his Beloved over a river; so prayeth thine

Husband .

To Mary Day Lanier

[San Antonio, Texas] March 1st 1873

Well, then, thou shalt ride with Sir Stephen; [38] for, O My Sweet, I am coming.

To Mary Day Lanier

Montgomery, Ala. March 8th)73

'Tis a bitter rain without, all day: but in my heart a thousand birds are whistling, a thousand flowers blooming and odors exhaling and radiances glowing,—for, O Wife, O wife, dear wondrous-faithful Heart, I am near to thee, the wild waters and the stolid wastes no longer stretch betwixt me and thee, 'tis but a little twelve hours—so little compared with this age that lieth behind!—and I have thy worshipful hand in mine.

---

[38] On Feb. 22 Mary Day Lanier had sent her husband a poem by Rose Terry (Cook) entitled " Best," the first stanza of which read:

" Love is better than house or lands:
So, Sir Stephen, I'll ride with thee! "
Quick she steps where the courser stands,
Light she springs to the saddle-tree.

It is to this poem that Lanier alludes in this the last of his letters from Texas. He probably left San Antonio the same day, Mar. 1, for he was in Montgomery on Mar. 8 (as the following letter shows), and the trip out in Nov., 1872, had taken him a week.

—"— Here have I been petted all day, and have played for them tonight, Big Joseph lying on the bed by Sissa who is sick with cold, Cliff with Willie in his lap curled about him like a vine about a tree, and Eddie, Willie Jr. and Cliff Jr. asleep in various situations about the room. Big Joseph hath quite won my heart, with his worship of *thee*. "You ask Alexander," quoth he, "if she did'nt look like an angel that night!³⁹ And then she organized everything, *did* everything, and, in fact, she was *the man* about that house": and thereupon Sissa chimeth in, with the wonders that thou wroughtst:—and thereupon I am in agony of passion to kiss but the hem of thy garment, and I quit the flute and betake me to the piano, and manufacture some adoring modulations wh. do cause Clifford to kiss me as he saith fervent good-night. Thou art mine inspiration and thou art the very vital breath of mine art and without thee I cannot be an artist.

—"— I grieve that thou art detained; yet not as much as I ought,—for I will see thee sooner:—since of course thou wilt now wait for me, and we will go down, after I spend a couple of days at home, to Harry's together.

Ah, My God, together! Therein lieth the reward, the hope, the past, the future, the All-of-life of thy

Lover.

I think to come on to thee Monday, 10th; but might stay here till Tuesday.⁴⁰

³⁹ The night of J. C. Gibson's marriage to Gertrude Lanier Shannon, Jan. 14, 1873.

⁴⁰ No letters by Lanier between Mar. 8 and Apr. 16, 1873, have been found. Apparently he spent most of that time in Brunswick with his wife and children. Significant evidence of his renewed literary activity and of his maturing plans for the future may be gleaned, however, from echoes of lost letters contained in the replies of Paul H. Hayne.

On Mar. 27, 1873, Hayne acknowledged receipt of a lost letter of Mar. 12 submitting to him for criticism a poem entitled "June Dreams, In January" (I, 29). The MS of this poem, containing Hayne's marginal annotations has survived (Charles D. Lanier Collection, Johns Hopkins University); its autobiographical content suggests that it was written during the past winter in San Antonio. At some time during April Lanier submitted "June Dreams, In January" to W. D. Howells, editor of the *Atlantic Monthly*, who rejected it. Commenting on this rejection Hayne wrote: "If I can dare to *advise*, I should tell you to put by for the nonce your longer poems– as far as the *Magzns* are concerned–, and to elaborate with immense care a series of *short lyrics*,– 'swallow-flights of song'–, &c. Put all your richness of fancy, and all your

To Mary Day Lanier [41]

Macon, April 16th 1873

I send thee a hasty note, dear Comrade, wh. will make thee aware that I am safely here, after a night wherein, for want of the thee-presence, I did sleep but little. I went to the Lanier House, and, after abluting, fell-to upon the steak and eggs fearsomely, thy father sitting by the while. On coming to the office I find both Lanier and Anderson out of town, – Uncle C. in Savannah, and my father at Jeffersonville. The latter is expected back today.

Thy father seemeth pretty well. He will likely carry this, as he thinketh to go down tomorrow morning. Ye must keep him till I come.

All are well here, – saith Sam,[42] whom I have just seen.

Thinking that enclosed was from Mrs. Wallen, and that it might have some later news anent lodgings &c, I opened it, – but find it is from thy redoubtable relative, and so transmit, with powder – wh. may Heaven render vigorous and searching and altogether effectual!

Did Hal find the check wh. I mysteriously left in the parlor, as I started? – But how coulds't thou expect me to have my head, when there thou sat'st, thy gray eyes greatening, and thy lip furtively trembling!

Thine.

gracious art into these efforts,– and my word for it–, they'll bring you substantial results both in *repute*– and– greenbacks!!" (See Hayne's letter of May 2, 1873, acknowledging another lost letter from Lanier sent from Brunswick on Apr. 11.)

Again, referring to Lanier's lost letter of Mar. 12, Hayne commented: "Good news it is to hear you say, that your strength has *measurably* returned, and that henceforth you intend devoting much time and energy to ART! . . . I hail the determination you express to *snub Law* for *Literature* with *real* delight!!" And in a follow-up letter Hayne added: "What do you mean . . . by saying, that the '*moderate degree of strength*' you have attained, will be devoted chiefly to '*artistic labors*,' since 'it seems *fated* that you are *not* to practice your profession of the *Law*?' *Why* fated?– Because while your physical '*strength*' admits of moderate '*art-labor*,' it is insufficient for the exacting duties of the Lawyer? Is *such* the *case*?" (See Hayne's letters of Mar. 27 and Mar. 29, 1873.)

[41] Lanier had left his wife and children in Brunswick while he went to Macon, planning to go on to Marietta for the purpose of engaging lodgings for the summer.

[42] Office-man and driver for R. S. Lanier.

To Mary Day Lanier

Macon. April 18th 1873

The weather is so cold that I will not go to Marietta: a certain scrapiness of the throat admonishing me that the dust of travel is not as balmy as it might be to the laryngeal integument.

Tomorrow will be a field-day: I will move the plunder: and on Sunday I cannot, alas! fly back to thee: hold, is there not a train on Sunday? if so, I *can,* and will, fly back to my dear Mate,—if not, on Monday.   We will stop at the hotel in Marietta until I can secure thy quarters; or, if thou like it better, thou and the Children can stay at the Kimball House [43] while I run up and make arrangements.

Father and Uncle C. are both at their post, and well.

I have not seen any of thy friends. I am somehow not in heart to say anything further to thee now than that I am thy steadfast

Lover

To Mary Day Lanier

Macon, April 22nd 1873

Thy letter, dear Dorothea,[44] hath brought a prodigious world of comfort to thy poor Casaubon, all a-dust with searching, in musty nooks and by filthy streets, for the key to All Mythologies:—wh. indeed, in my poor case, is a kind of magic key, that is forever hid, and yet forever just before mine eyes: for 'tis Money; wherewith I feel no sort of doubt I cd. unlock all the Mythological crypts and closets that Time ever shut.

——   How prettily thou writest of these misadventures! God save thy lovely fancy, it playeth about this poor atrabilious business like the sweet sea-wave about a dismal coast.

Moreover I do heartily thank God that, for all, and amid all, that thou hast suffered, thy soul hath not ever yet undergone these vile torsions and contractions and spasmodic diminutions and sombre rigidities.

---

[43] A hotel in Atlanta.
[44] Dorothea Brooke and Mr. Casaubon are characters in George Eliot's *Middlemarch.*

I wd. thou mightest keep thy father with thee until I come: wh. happy event will be, I hope, on Thursday next. 'Twas very difficult to keep my heart from quite breaking when I discovered I wd. be compelled to remain here so long: but 'twas unavoidable as any decree of Fate.

Thine enclosure—from the " World "—reached [me]. I cd. not attend to the " account of the crime " part of the business: it being too late to send to the place for facts, and there being no sources of information here. Of wh. I was glad: for I *wd.* not have done it, anyhow; being clearly convinced that to play pander to that morbid Cruelty and cold Criminality wh. delight in reading such accounts, – – is a lower and meaner thing than what Pandarus did: and, so help me thy Gray Eyes,—whose single glance of less respect than thou now hast for me, wd. blight all my life!— I will not do it, not for " The World," the Flesh and the Devil combined.[45]

My Father & Uncle. C. both absent.

How I long to see thee! I shall be happier when I come back to thee: and will have thee & Charles forth, a-fishing. Keep thy father: and God keep thee, crieth thy

Casaubon.

To Charles Day

Marietta Ga. May 15th 1873 [46]

My Dear Father:

I write a note, more to enclose a couple of slips which I have cut from the Atlanta " Daily Herald " of this morning – than for any other purpose. The reading-matter of these slips will, I doubt not, interest you: and *Harry,* particularly, – as showing that his friend, Gen. McCrea, seems to keep up his talent for getting things into hot water. Of course much

---

[45] This seems to refer to a fourth letter for the New York *World* which was either rejected or not completed by Lanier.

[46] No letters by Lanier between Apr. 22 and May 15 have survived, so that his movements during these three weeks are uncertain. Presumably, after about a week in Macon, he returned to Brunswick without having been able to carry out his plan of going to Marietta to engage lodgings at this time. The present letter implies that they had just arrived there about the middle of May and established themselves in their " old quarters "—i. e., the rooms at Mrs. Earle's which they had occupied in 1871 and 1872.

of what appears here is to be set down to the sensation-loving imaginations of the editors of the Herald; but the *letters from Scofield*,– one asserting and the other reiterating his charges against Gov. Brown–, would seem to indicate that the row is based upon *some* sort of foundation.[47]

I have not yet had an opportunity of seeing Gov. Brown about the coal lot. It is now likely that I will go back to Macon on a short visit, in a few days, and I hope to have an interview with Gov. B. at that time.

I have had much trouble in effecting a comfortable arrangement for our " daily bread." I thought I had matters all settled with Whitlock, our old host, for feeding us: and had commenced getting our meals from him: but found trouble, (through the uneasiness and opposition of *Mrs.* Whitlock), so I promptly cancelled my agreement there, and after an immense amount of diplomacy and negotiation, succeeded in an arrangement with Mary's old hostess, Mrs. Smith, who lives opposite us. This works well: and we are very comfortable and cosy in our old quarters, having our own set of furniture, and taking our meals in our rooms; these last being brought us by our faithful manservant, Warren.

Mary seems remarkably well and bright, yesterday and today, and appears to enjoy our *modified housekeeping* hugely.

She joins me in sending a great deal of love to you: as well as to Hal and Janie; with thanks to Hal for his letter, just rec! Do forgive this abominable scrawl (we haven't unpacked our writing-things yet), My dear Father, from   Your   Son,

Sidney L.

To Charles Day

Marietta, Ga. May 19th 1873

My Dear Father:

I write a note to enclose slips from the Atlanta " Constitution " and " Herald " of this morning, which

---

[47] The reference in this paragraph and the first paragraph of the following letter is to the controversy over the redemption of the fraudulent state bonds issued under the corrupt regime of Gov. Bullock (see note 72, 1871).

For the sale of the coal lot to Governor Brown, mentioned in the next paragraph, see Lanier's letter of May 29, 1873, below.

present the next installment of the Brown-Scofield controversy.

The "Herald" people are atrociously personal: and the card of Abrams seems absurdly untrue on its very face, as well as desperately melodramatic.

My little family are in usual health. We have very cosy meals in our rooms, and things move along smoothly enough. I have been quite under the weather with a cold which was certainly the worst I have ever had, but which luckily has not yet gone to my weak point. I take some encouragement from this last circumstance; though my cold still keeps me wretchedly uncomfortable, having assumed the form of a Catarrh.

May has been called for twice during the afternoon (by parties whom we met at the Hotel), to take carriage-rides. She accepted one invitation, and appears to have enjoyed the ride. The country hereabout is lovely beyond description in its spring dress, and I only wish my plans for the future were settled enough to admit of my enjoying the beautiful things without stint.

Mary puts her arms about yr. neck: and joins me in love to all the others who are with you. We were both greatly gratified by the cheerful account of Harry's leisure, and his & Janie's good health, in your last enclosing a note from Hal.

Trusting you may all continue well;– and particularly insisting on our regards being conveyed to Mr. James Holt; [48] I am alway, Dr. Father,

Your Son

Sidney L.

To ROBERT S. LANIER

Marietta, May 19th 1873

My Dear Father:

I had intended to start down to see you tomorrow: but Mary's condition is now such that she may be confined any day: and I can not be absent from her when that occurs without seriously impairing her chances of happy and safe results. Nor is it well for me to be away just now, even if I could go and come before that event: since my absence

---

[48] Charles Day's negro servant.

would render her subject to apprehension, at least. She has not spoken of this at all: but has conversed with me in reference to going without alluding to any objection.

Again, my cold, – which has been one of the very worst I ever experienced – has now become a catarrh, and gives me great pain. This would be indefinitely increased by the dust of even a short railroad journey.

Thinking over the matter tonight, these reasons seemed to me to be strong enough to make me delay my visit, as I gather from your last letter that you did not expect me at once.

— I am obliged to raise fifty dollars by Wednesday next. Please telegraph me tomorrow whether it will be possible for you to send me that amount by that time. The miscarriage of some of my projects has rendered this demand necessary. It is not necessary for me to say that I regret it.

My family are in usual health. Mary joins me in much love to you and Mama & Pringle.[49] Charley and Sidney are asleep.

> Yr. Son
>
> Sidney L.

To Clifford A. Lanier

> Marietta, Ga. May 24th 1873.

My Dear Brother:

Your letter floated into our hearts a few moments ago, like some warm and fragrant emanation from that same glowing Heart-of-Spring which has wrought all these roses, these woods-breaths, these pungent balms of hickories and noble expirations of the oak-trees that seem to breathe hard in the supreme stress of growth.

– And verily, never was there more wintry need of some Change of Season, than ours!

But I will not detail our distresses to you: for that would not help either of us: and I begin to learn not to do *anything* that is not *help*ful. Suffice it to say that my draft on you was the necessity of an emergency which I had not foreseen. The drawing of it gave me so much pain that I did not even have

---

[49] Pringle Morgan, the son of Mrs. R. S. Lanier by a previous marriage.

the courage to write to you about it; though I tried to do so several times.

I ought to say to you: – that I have been straining every nerve to remain with my dear Comrade until next week when she expects to be confined, since (although she would not urge me thereto) I feared the effect of my absence from her at such a time, for she appears to lean on me all the more in consequence of our often and long separations: and I thought I had made arrangements to enable me to do this; but a sudden and very unexpected letter from father (who appeared to have been completely upset by the apparition of Sissa; and the " dreadful account " which she compelled him to render) quite overturned me, and I was forced to bestir myself. Part of this bestirring was my draft on you. The thought of making this diminution of your resources, at a time when I knew you must be losing money, put a climax upon all my other distresses, and I fell ill, insomuch that I *couldn't* go off to work, nor even stay and write Mag. articles. –And here, dear Friend, dear Brother, let me interject, Never get " blue," – never dream that you have any right to feel discouraged–, as long as you're healthy and can go to your work every morning. When you get sick and live upon Charity for a while, *then,* you can talk of " the blues " with at least some *color of title!* – But (to return to my (beef and) muttons) I'm getting a little better, now; and if I can by any possibility tide over until my Dorothy is free from danger, I propose on that instant to go to Atlanta (or, failing that, to any other place where I can get work) and seek for some employment that will furnish daily bread to my darlings: working thus only until I can consummate some dispositions I have in train to get to New York and go at my true labor. For I will never be at rest at all until I so arrange my life as to get myself leisure to write some books that now burn in my heart: I *must* write them: it is the command of God; and I seek in vain for any other method of giving myself free days which I can consecrate to writing, save by making my support with the flute at night. 'Tis marvellous weary, – this waiting; but it seems the only path towards my Hope, my Delight, my Dream, my Glory: which is, to make but the humblest support, if so be that I can live the life that I love, with the dainty comrades that I love, doing the work that I love.

This is a fearsome diatribe, and writ wholly without malice prepense: for I commenced my letter intending only to thank you for *yr.* letter (which was simply too sweet, and drew a long breath from Dorothy Casaubon (née Mary Day) when she finished; yes, – for I *will* tell you – she said, " well, 'tis *better* than a fortune, to have a brother like him; isn't it? ") and to speak to you of Middlemarch. My Comrade and I read it several weeks ago. While we were reading it, we were in such a delight that, as to the outer world, neither of us was fit for anything: though, since we have finished it, both of us have certainly been, as to the whole world, much better for everything. We appropriated the book so thoroughly, that my wife, when she is in a good humor, calls me Will Ladislaw, (forsooth, la, now) and when she is in a bad, addresses me as Mr. Casaubon: while I intitule *her* always Dorothea, wh. she *is,* to a marvellous similitude.

The book is a noble, good book, a very marvel of the quiet English philosophies which have borne so consummate a flower as George Eliot (Mrs. Lewes). She has solved one very difficult problem, among many others: – to be at once large and keen, at once broad and incisive. In our strange modern world, it is becoming one of the very hardest things to do, – to expand one's ideas with genuine culture, and at the same time to preserve one's enthusiasm in life. Have you not felt this? As one grows older, if one *grows* at all one continually perceives that there are many sides to all questions, that partisanship is vulgar, that advocacy of any particular tenet is generally heated just in proportion as that tenet is *narrow*; and this perception of the evils of narrow-mindedness is peculiarly apt in modern times to grow into a calm and cultured neutrality as among the conflicting hopes and passions of the mass of men. The endeavor of culture to make up a fair and honest opinion upon any given state of matters by looking at *all* the sides, is often so overwhelming from the very multiplicity of facts, of opinions, of circumstances, of prejudices, that even an honest seeker after the Right is liable to come to regard, after a while, *all* opinions as amounting to about the same thing, and as not worth the vast trouble of separate examination and of careful comparison. A recent poem called " Olrig Grange," [50] (–a very clever thing,

[50] By Walter C. Smith.

too,, as times go) remarks that its hero might have been " a *stronger,* if a *narrower,* man "; and many persons of great culture really believe that it will not do for a man to try *too* hard to see all sides of questions, since that will abate the strength and the enthusiasm which he wd. have if, shutting his eyes to all sides but one and blindly fighting for that one, he becomes a hot, fanatical and narrow partisan. Now what I particularly like about Mrs. Lewes is that she is, as I said, *at once* broad and incisive: she has as much learning, as much true culture, as much desire to look at all sides, as any woman of the day: but she has at the same time a soul full of splendid enthusiasm for all things, she has never grown *neutral,* she has never evaded the responsibilities cast upon our reason by the enormous complexities of modern life, she appears to have made her judgments, fairly, openly, impartially, faithfully, and to have preserved a desire to keep herself in relation to, and in sympathy with, everything and everybody. Her logic cuts out conclusions like bold rocks, on a mountain, clear and sharp against the sky: yet one feels that underneath these there trickles many a pellucid enthusiasm that will nourish all manner of flowers, and even water a kitchen-garden for a poor family, if need be.

I'm glad you have read the book. I think it about the best product of the times. I wd. like to see Wm Hand Browne's review of it. Somehow I missed the no. you speak of.[51]

Sometime, I'll explain to you why I don't stay in Macon. These *explanations* are so hard to me, that sometimes I prefer to rest under misconceptions rather than worry others with them. I hope you will believe now, however, my simple statement that it was quite impossible for me to remain there.

It is possible I may again draw on you, for a small sum, say $25 or $30: if I do, pay it, and pray for me to get well quickly.

Mary has been begging me to sell our *Silver* set, and purchase a Silver Boehm with the proceeds, and start for N. Y.!

— Finally; yr. letter was *so* good, dear Brother Clifford; I pray you keep clean from this same Avarice; buy thyself straightway, a copy of Chaucer, and read that part of the Parsone's Tale which relateth *De Avaritiâ,* also the *De Superbiâ*: thou hast too

---

[51] W. H. Browne's review of *Middlemarch* had appeared in the *Southern Magazine,* XII [o. s.], 373-380 (Mar., 1873).

fine a soul, I cannot think of it as being smirched with these things, bah, an' I should ever see thee growing thin-souled with these things I wd. be sorry, as now I am right glad, that I am thy

Brother.

To Paul H. Hayne [52]

Marietta, Ga. May 26th 1873

My Dear Mr. Hayne:

The gracious odor of yr. " violets " [53] has reached into my soul, and I have been loth to send them back to you. Stanza No. III is unalloyedly delicious: and the closing line, —" Breathing of heart-break and sad death of love," — is simply ravishing. This sings itself over and over in my heart: and this; —

" Some with raised brows, and eyes of constancy
Fixed with fond meanings on a goal above."

What a tender music these two lines make! Are you, by the way, a musician? Strange, that I have never before asked this question, — when so much of my own life consists of music. I don't know that I've ever told you, that whatever turn I have for Art, is purely musical; poetry being, with me, a mere tangent into which I shoot sometimes. I could play passably on several instruments before I could write legibly: and since, then, the very deepest of my life has been filled with music, which I have studied and cultivated far more than poetry. I only mention this in order that you may understand the delight your poetry gives me. It is so rarely *musical,* so melodiously pure and silvery in flow: it occupies in poetry the place of Mendellsohn in music, or of Franz Abt, or of Schubert. It is, in this respect, simply unique in modern poetry: Wm Morris comes nearest to it, but Morris lives too closely within hearing of Tennyson to write unbroken music: for Tennyson (let me not blaspheme against the Gods!) is not a musical tho' in other respects (particularly in that of phrase-making) a very wonderful writer.

---

[52] Excerpt previously published, *Critic*, VIII [o. s.], 89 (Feb. 20, 1886) ; reprinted entire, *Letters* (New York, 1899), pp. 236-238.

[53] In his letter of May 2, 1873, Hayne had sent Lanier a MS poem with this title.

While at Alleghany Springs last summer I loaned to Miss Julia Foster, of Augusta, my copy of yr. " Legends & Lyrics," on condition she should return it. I've written her since about it; but my letter probably failed to reach her, as I knew not her address save that she lived in Augusta. Having a copy from you, I didn't want to lose it: and if you have another by you, I wd. be glad if you wd. straightway write yr. name therein and mail to me.

I do not know the man Williams, you mention.[54] I have been greatly amused at some strictures upon you made by certain Knights of Mrs. Westmoreland, in condign punishment for yr. critique on Mrs. W.'s. book. I have not read that production: but from all I can hear, 'tis a most villainous poor pitiful piece of work; and, so far from endeavoring to serve the South by blindly plastering it with absurd praises, I think all true patriots ought to unite in redeeming the land from the imputation that such books are regarded as casting honor upon the section. God forbid we should really be brought so low as that we must perforce brag of such works as " Clifford Troupe " and " Heart Hungry ": and God be merciful to that man (he is an Atlanta Editor) who boasted that sixteen thousand of these books had been sold in the South!

This last damning fact (if it be a fact, — and I sh'd not wonder) ought to have been concealed at the risk of life, limb and fortune.

I'm glad to hear you're going to travel; but you are starting too soon.[55] I hope to get to New York City about the 1st of July. If you should be there any time between that and the middle of October, let me know, by a note addressed to care of " Winslow, Lanier & Co. 27 Pine St. N. Y." — an address which will always reach me.

I return yr. " Violets " : and I hope that when you go to

[54] In his letter of May 2 Hayne had asked Lanier if he knew " a young man, named Fred: Williams, a lawyer of Augusta " who had asked Hayne for his candid opinion on a volume of his verse. For that candid opinion, put " as kindly as possible, . . . that his verses, (generally) were insufferably bad! " and for a similar opinion of the novel *Clifford Troup* (New York, 1873) by Maria Jourdain Westmoreland, Hayne had been taken to task by certain newspaper editors for his disloyalty to the South.

[55] In his letter of May 2 Hayne had written that he was leaving about the middle of the month on a trip to Philadelphia, New York, and Boston.

Heaven you'll be wafted there on the sighs of just such another bunch!

Yr. Friend

Sidney Lanier

written at *Marietta.*

To Virginia Hankins [56]

Marietta, Ga. May 27th 1873

I did not know, My dear Little One, but that in some muddy and most fearsome eddy of that turbid Western life, thou hadst been caught and drowned: sunk, perhaps, in a steamer, or crushed on a railway, or killed by a falling building, or even stabbed by a frantic lover: and I will not disguise from thee that I have sometimes fancied I heard thy death-cry.

But, *Laus Deo!* These were but distempered fancies: for here is a letter from thee bearing date from Scotland Neck, (dear Scotland Neck, do I not remember that sweet moonlit oasis in the desert of the North Carolina campaign,[57] and thee, with the big round straw hat, seated on the steps, and the fair peaceful trees, and all?) and all alive with *thee*-ness, — with thy solid-hearted sense, thy marvellous incisive penetrations into things, thy womanly reserves and sweetnesses, thy generous forbearances, and, – to me best of all – thy still-enduring friendship for *me.*

I take so much delight in believing, dear Friend, that thou art come safely out of that Babylon, – – – that I will not push upon thee the friendly interrogatory wh. I have already asked thee a half dozen times and wh. thou hast as many times willfully and feloniously refused to answer, – towit, what *didst* thou

---

[56] Virginia Hankins had spent the winter in St. Louis, Mo. In a letter of May 13, 1873 (acknowledging a lost letter from Lanier, written from Macon earlier in the spring), she had written that she was at Scotland Neck, Halifax Co., N. C., visiting an old friend, Rebecca Alexander, now married to a Mr. Smith of that place.

[57] In Jan., 1864, Lanier had participated in a brief expedition against Newbern, N. C., with headquarters at Weldon; Scotland Neck was on the route of march. A surviving fragment of a letter written by Lanier from Weldon to Rebecca Alexander on Jan. 11, 1864, seems to imply that she and Virginia Hankins were visiting in the neighborhood at that time.

in St. Louis? I will now, in token of my joy at recovering my
sweet Prodigal, freely forgive and absolve thee from recounting
the husks whereon thou has lived, while thou hast been far from
home: wh. is, in the spirit, to kill the Fatted Calf for thee.

My dear Wife acknowledges thine inquiries with answering
heartiness. She is in but feeble health: and we are thus early
come up to Marietta for the summer, where among the lovely
mountains, and trees and grasses and streams, we begin to draw
stronger breaths. I will likely be here for a month, and then hie
away to N. Y. Where will be my friend? It may hap I will see
her this time! Post me, *quoad* thy movements.

———— It is likely that I will be driven into Art, exclusively, for
livelihood. The necessity to abandon my profession appears to
have at last become not only imperative but immediate: and I'm
going to try and live with a flute and a pen. 'Tis a dreadful
blow to quit my beloved Law: but of course, health is all:
and I have no alternative.

Write me whatever you know of Emmett Robinson's family.[58]
I'm curious to know what is become of them. Read " Middlemarch." Convey my regards to whatever friends you're with.
Preserve yr. friendship for me ——— These are the commandments of yr.

Friend.

To Charles Day [59]

Marietta, Ga, May 29th 1873

My Dear Father:

I write to enclose a letter received this
morning from Gov. Brown. I copied the principal parts of
the report of Prof. Hall, and sent it to him: and this letter is
in response to mine.

---

[58] Friends of Lanier's in Petersburg, Va., whom he had not seen since 1864.

[59] The signature of this letter has been cut out and words on the obverse of
the sheet mutilated. Restorations have been made on the basis of the letter from
Governor J. E. Brown to Lanier, May 28, 1873.

I scarcely know what to think about the Governor's tactics. His letter certainly reveals the fact that this Company is continually acquiring new coal lands: and I think that the lot could be sold to them for a small sum. The Governor talks almost too much. For, (for instance) in the last part of his letter, he says: " There are several lots contained in our [lease] much more accessible, & hav[e more] coal in them than we [will] work out during our lif[e time]." (And yet in the [very ne]xt sentence, he con[tinues].) " We have lately bought two lots . . . . at $200 each &c &c." Now why on earth should the company have bought these " two " other " lots," if they had already more than they could work in a lifetime, and if (as stated in the early part of the letter) there is no possibility of competition by adjacent coal-owners? Nay, – if what the Governor says be true – why does he consider that the market-value of lot 35 is more than $200, or is anything at all?

I only mention these points in order to show that the acute Governor is not strictly reliable: I really don't know whether he wants to buy the lot or not, but write to find out what you and Harry desire me to ask him for it. Let me know by return mail what your *ultimatum* of price is: as I expect to see the Governor on Tuesday next, when I shall have occasion to be in Atlanta.

Have just this minute received a telegram from Ogden, asking if I can get rooms for them for a week, and stating " Baby very sick."

We are all in tolerable condition, tho' none of us are as bright as some people I have seen. We've changed our arrangement for boarding, to an arrangement that works charmingly, so far.

I'm glad to know that Hal is not overworked, and that your time is passing so pleasantly. Mary joins me in a letterfull of love and kisses for you all.

My cold is better, tho' not yet well. It has not seriously hurt my lungs.

Your Son

[Sidney L.]

To Paul H. Hayne [60]

Marietta, Ga. June 10th 1873

My dear Mr Hayne:

I'm always inclined (I observe) to think that the *last* is the *best* (of your poems); but I really think I like " The Wood Lake " [61] at least as well as anything I have ever seen from your pen. The " shy romance " of its mist-wreaths, its lights, its ripple-pulses, its morning smiles, its mocking-bird, its looks, — is so delicate, so rare and so alto-gether sweet, that the poem seems to be, itself, a lovely exhala-tion out of the heart of the lake it describes.

I've read aloud to my wife (–a most rare subtle recognizer of good poetry, she !) yr. " Midsummer In the South," and she declares it to be a piece of genuine good music, particularly,

> " Fills with divine amenities
> The bland blue spaces of the air: "

and,

> " Who built yon transient spires in scorn
> And reared towards the topmost sky
> Their unsubstantial fantasy ":

and,

> " . . . . Midsummer uplands, free
> To the bold raids of breeze and bee: "

and

> " . . . Cloudland's misty foam
> Whose wreaths of fine sun-smitten spray
> Melt in a burning haze away: "

and,   – – – and so on, — quite too much for a letter.

" Frida " is a fair and pathetic rendering of the immortal loveliness of love; indeed, do we not all *die,* — die to a thou-sand worlds of error and pitiful selfishness — ere we live again in the purer and higher light of this truth, – the divine preserva-tion of our best by Love?

Apropos of what you say about music, — my wife bids me

---

[60] Previously published, *American Literature,* I, 37-38 (Mar., 1929).
[61] Renamed " The Solitary Lake." This and the other two poems discussed in Lanier's letter had been sent by Hayne in his letter of May 27, 1873.

say to you, that you *are* a musician, and a good one: and that you have need of no other instrument while you play thus with your pen.

I really don't think it worth your while to break any lances against these Westmoreland people. I think it was Schiller who said: " The Gods themselves are powerless against Stupidity." Even if you could pierce Its hide, I think no blood would come. I at first thought of cracking a crown or two, myself, in your behalf: but, By all that's pitiful! they seemed so cracked already, and the whole business appeared so absurd that I simply couldn't. I can easily see how *you* must be tempted to get nettled: but, My Dear Friend, I take the liberty of begging you to resist the temptation. Why should you notice these folk? Your music will still be good music long, long after the world has forgotten the tepid inanities of Mrs. Westmoreland and her valiant knights.

I entreat you, forget not to send me a copy of " Legends & Lyrics " straightway. I can't find it, here.

I send back " Frida: " and with her, by way of escort, the continuing friendliness of

Yr. Friend
Sidney Lanier

To Robert S. Lanier

Marietta, Ga.   June 13th 1873

Dear Father:

Yrs. containing check for $91.^{00} came to hand.

I went to Atlanta yesterday at midday, on some business, and found Uncle Clifford. He came back with me at six O'clock, took tea with us in our room, and returned to Atlanta at 10.

—— I find several circumstances which lead me to believe that Gov. Brown, in offering $400 for our coal-lot must have some reasons for making the offer which are not known to me. It is possible his railroad runs across our lot; or he may have mined over the limit of his lot upon ours; or, (as is rendered likely by all my information) it may be that a much shorter road can be built from our lot to *Whitesides* on the Nashville & Chattanooga R. R., than that now running from Gov. B's

mine to Shell-Mound. I am so strongly impressed with these
facts, – or rather surmises – that I desire to go up there, and
personally inspect the situation before closing a trade with him.
As soon as Mary is safely over her trial, I shall run up to
Chattanooga and see for myself. The trip can be made in
thirty-six hours.

None of us are very well: May and I inclined to be bilious,
and the boys both suffering from bad colds. The weather has
been exceedingly rainy – and we all sigh for some dry days.

All send love to all.

Your Son

Sidney Lanier

To Charles Day [62]

Marietta, Ga.   June 17th 1873

My Dear Father:

Mary had your letter this morning, and one
from Harry yesterday. We are glad you both continue in your
good lazy habits: but sorry that Janie is not so well as usual.

I have been for some weeks working at a plan for utilizing
your famous *sap*-pine trees at Brunswick. It seemed too
shadowy, at first, to write about: but begins to assume some
form and substance now, and therefore I unfold it to you.

I have the opportunity to get a contract for furnishing
Charcoal to an iron furnace in Bartow County, some twenty
miles above this place. The Contract will be for fifteen hundred
bushels of Charcoal per day, for the next two or three years; –
or even for five years, if I want it. The price offered, now, is
eight cents a bushel: but my friend assures me I can get ten. I
have seen the Superintendents of all the railroads leading from
Brunswick to Altoona (the Station at which the charcoal is to
be delivered): and find that I could transport it from Brunswick at four cents (probably a half-cent less) per bushel. The
cost of manufacture, together with incidentals, &c. should not
exceed two cents per bushel, according to my information: and

---

[62] This letter and several others during the summer of 1873 are written
on the stationery of the Georgia Military Institute. There is no evidence of any
connection between Lanier and this preparatory school.

this leaves a profit of two cents per bushel: which is thirty
dollars a day, on a contract of fifteen hundred bushels. I can
probably get some other contracts, if this one prove feasible.
The furnace for which the charcoal is desired, is McNeil's;
it has been in operation successfully for a year or two past, and
McN. is said to be a responsible party. If the charcoal *can* be
manufactured at Brunswick and brought here, it will doubtless
soon become a large business. The difficulty of getting a proper
coke has been very great, and it is yet by no means demonstrated
that the bituminous coal will make good iron with McNeil's
ore in the large furnace which he is erecting, near the small one
in which he proposes to use our charcoal. The large one is
being arranged for bituminous coal: but if that should prove
unsuitable, he would have to alter it to a charcoal furnace, and
in that event would be obliged to have five thousand bushels of
charcoal per day, besides the fifteen hundred bushels now
needed.

I have thus told you pretty much all that I am able to ascertain
definitely at *my* end of the line: it remains for you and Hal
to find out precisely at what price you can manufacture the coal
at your end. In pursuing this investigation, the following *data,*
will help you. It requires three cords of ordinary good pine
to make one hundred bushels of charcoal. The place for you
to manufacture is at whatever point your pines are thickest and
closest to the railroad, as the charcoal should not be hauled at
all, until we deliver it to the furnace-owner who will himself
haul it some distance to his furnace, and it does not bear much
handling because it breaks up too easily. I am told that the old
process of manufacture by heaping up and covering with dirt,
has been much improved upon: and that a brick kiln can be
constructed for the especial purpose of manufacturing charcoal
by which the process is rendered much more certain and less
tedious, as well as cheaper. The point of danger in the manufacture by the old plan is in the want of vigilance of the colliers,
and the consequent firing of the mass of wood, so that it is
consumed instead of being *Charred*. The clay from your Clay-
ground would probably answer admirably for building a char-
coal-kiln. At first, of course, it would be advisable to manufacture on the simple old plan: and I suppose that, by that plan,
the items of expense are:

1st cost of cutting the wood: ———————

2nd " " colliers, watchman &c, ⎫

    who stack up the wood, fire it, ⎬

    and carry it through the process. ⎭   ———————

3rd cost of loading cars   ———————

The *method* of *transportation* has given me more trouble than any of the other preliminary points about which I have thought. I am told that it is successfully transported in other states, by hoisting, with a derrick, the wagon-bodies containing the coal directly upon the flat-cars: and unloading, in the same way, by taking the wagon-bodies off with a derrick at destination. This would not suit us, for the reason that these wagon-bodies (which are built for the purpose, with a high, light railing around them to confine the charcoal) would have to be brought back every day; and the Superintendents all refuse (except Robertson, to whom I did not mention this point) to bring them back free, as is done in other states in similar cases. This arangement, too, is where the coal is *made* off the railroad and has to be hauled to the road for shipment; which renders it convenient, instead of handling the coal, just to lift up wagon-body and all with the derrick and put it on the flat. I think we could easily devise a movable railing, or sort of lattice-work, which could be affixed around a flat-car; somewhat larger at the top than at the bottom, like a coal-wagon: about five feet high; so as to hold about nine hundred or a thousand bushels, on each flat car. As soon, therefore, as you can send me the items of expense I have mentioned, embracing cost of manufacturing &c, I think we can be in condition to close a binding contract.

It is probable that we may find it much more profitable to buy a timber-privilege on some small tract of land a short distance below Macon, – say, near Eastman – and establish a colliery there. This would save a great deal of freight. It is also likely that we could sell a considerable quantity of charcoal in Macon, and in Atlanta, at a price which would be much higher than that of our larger contract. If this last should prove true, it would go far towards paying expenses of transporting charcoal all the way from Brunswick to Altoona; and thus enable us to utilize the sap-pines on your land: – a thing my heart has been set upon for a long time.

Altogether I think there is reason to believe that such a contract might give an easy, pleasant, and profitable business to
you. If I can make the contract at ten cents a bushel, I feel very
sure the business will be *exceedingly* profitable. Probably, by
keeping quiet, we could engage all the *refuse-slabs* of the mills
along the M. & B. R. R., and concentrate them at some convenient point for a colliery; saving thus even the expense of
cutting down the trees.

———— This is a very disjointed and incoherent letter written
amid a huge storm of wind and rain, which has confined in my
room three very noisy little visitors of Charley's, who, together with that young gentleman and Sidney *Jr.* are acting in a
manner highly unfavorable to a clear statement of a business-
proposition. I wish very much that I could have a conference
with you: for a letter is unsatisfactory, at best, where so much is
to be said and discussed. As *I* cannot leave, until my dear
Comrade has passed all her trial, – cannot you arm yourself
with all manner of data about prices of wood-cutting, reliability
of labor-supply, &c &c, and run up here for a while? I suppose
they will soon be selling the usual return-tickets for summer
travellers, on the M. & W. R. R: and I will feel greatly pleased
and honored if you will be my guest at the hotel for a week.

About the coal lot;– so many circumstances (which I have
not time nor space to detail now) led me to believe that the
lot must be desirable on some other account than that mentioned
by Gov. Brown, that I had determined to go up there as soon
as it was possible for me to leave Mary, and investigate.
Yesterday, however, a friend brought Mr. Eaton (one of the
partners owning the " Vulcan Mines," situated two miles from
the " Castle Rock ") to see me, and he kindly promised to do
what he could to ascertain the facts I want to know, immediately on his return to the mines. He is to write to me. His
opinion coincided with mine, when I explained the facts to
him, and he thought it best to hold off until we could see
exactly what we are about. Of course, 'tis possible it may be
all a mistake: but it will be at least much more satisfactory
not to act in the dark.

— But I fear this long letter will weary you, dear Father, and
must close. Mary is across the street visiting Mrs. Wallen. She
suffers much pain from occasional cramps, and is otherwise a

little out of sorts. The boys are both half-sick with fresh colds. We have had an unprecedented wet season, and it seems as if the entire universe was saturated with moisture. I am very well.

Please make my acknowledgements to Hal for his kind letter; and kiss dear Janie for me: and believe me, dear Father, always

Your Son

Sidney Lanier

P. S.

I ought to have mentioned that we had a charming visit last night from Mr. & Mrs. Duncan, Miss Barnes, and Mrs. Screven, during which many inquiries were made after you, and wishes expressed for you.

S. L.

To Charles Day

Marietta, Ga. June 28th 1873

My dear Father:

I sent you a telegram announcing the happy termination of my dear Wife's sufferings, in the birth of a noble boy.[63] I now add a line, later, to say that the Doctor has just been in to see May ('tis now 7 ½ P. M., more than twelve hours since the baby's birth) and reports all progressing as favorably as possible. Though Mary's sufferings were of course very great, yet her pain has been less than ever before; and matters were as smooth and prosperous as well could be on such an occasion.

The young boy is a charming fellow, and causes a tender wonderment in the breasts of his two older brethren such as is a sight to see. They are both frantic about him and want to handle him and pet him to such a degree that he is in great danger of being pulled to pieces by his friends.

Pardon this *Ms.* wh. has been written quite in the dark. We all send love to all.

Your Son

Sidney Lanier

[63] Henry Wysham Lanier, born June 28, 1873, at first named William (see note 104, below).

To Charles Day

Marietta, July 1st 1873

My dear Father:

I write a short bulletin, merely by way of giving you a sort of daily record of Mary's condition. All seems to go well: and, except some severe pains caused by the appearance of the milk; she has not had aught to complain of beyond the weakness necessarily incident to the time. Today she furnishes a plentiful supply of milk for the boy: – more, indeed, than he seems able to consume: but I presume the supply will accommodate itself to the demand.
Our Dr. Dunwoody assures me that all is progressing prosperously.

I fear, (from your letter, received today, of 28th) that Mary had drawn quite *too lively* a picture of my disappointment in the matter of the charcoal business.[64] Of course I *was* disappointed: but not to any great extent, for although I was enthusiastic in the project, yet I had not allowed myself to build any hopes upon it. I would be glad if Harry would ascertain, (whenever he can do so without trouble) what quantity of slabs is turned out by such mills as are between Macon & Brunswick, per day: and what is the average size of the same. I have sent to the Charcoal-man of McNeil's furnace, to inquire if these slabs will make charcoal.

The boys are in tolerable condition, though neither of them seems to be as hearty as usual. I am somewhat under the weather.

Mary joins me in a great deal of love to you: and to Hal and Janie.

Your Son,

Sidney Lanier

---

[64] On June 24, 1873, Mary Day Lanier had written her father that she and her husband had both collapsed when Mr. Day's letter arrived expressing his lack of approval of Lanier's charcoal project: " to you it was only a new suggestion; to him it was the deep thought, day and night, of three weeks. . . . I begged him to write again, immediately, and more strongly– He said, sadly,– ' What would be the use? I've told them the facts and they can't see it as I do– and, as usual, I am powerless.' "

To Robert S. Lanier

Marietta, Ga. July 4th 1873

Dear Father:

Yrs. anent the baby was read with pleasure and thanks by the mother thereof. Both of those persons are progressing admirably. Mary has had far less suffering than ever before, and I have great hope of her health, hereafter. The boy has a nose marvellous like unto a bull-terrier's, and limbs like a blacksmith's: insomuch that, in virtue of his general bigness and sturdiness (for when he fairly sets himself to crying, 'tis like a simoon and general cataclysm,— portending the Wreck of matter and the crush of worlds) I am minded to call him William, — after that large-thewed and large-souled one, who has, at present, I believe, no namesake in the family.

I had hoped to be in Chattanooga by this time, arranging to make a thorough and reliable estimate of our coal lot: but the cholera-news from there this morning is alarming (I learn by private advices that there were 28 deaths yesterday), and I don't know now when I can get there. This unexpected obstacle quite throws me out: for many of my movements depended, in one way or another, on this.

Harry has written me the estimates of charcoal-burning at Brunswick: after seeing which, I have entirely given up all idea of the charcoal project. It could be successfully carried out, I think, by buying timber privileges, of sap-pines, on the line of the Brunswick Railroad near Macon: but I could not give it personal supervision there,— and so must let it alone. I shall get about Seventy (70) dollars for my San Antonio paper.[65] I will write Bacon to be on the look-out for any opportunity which may present, enabling me to get support while I might write the history of Georgia.[66] When does the Legislature

---

[65] Lanier was paid $63.00 for his essay, " San Antonio de Bexar," published in the *Southern Magazine*, July and Aug., 1873 (see letter from Turnbull Brothers, Aug. 9, 1873).

[66] R. S. Lanier had written, July 1: " I want you to write the history of Georgia. Bacon has spoken to me about it several times. Says he would see the Gov[r] & further your wishes— perhaps arrange the position you wish— if you like. I told him to do what he could." (Lanier's friend A. O. Bacon was at this time a member of the Georgia legislature.)

meet? It would suit me very well to live at Atlanta next winter. I have some other projects for the summer. Please send me Twenty (20) dollars by return mail, if you can.

Mary begs me to send a great deal of love to Mama, and to yourself. We learn, by the way, that your friend Mrs. Rowland, is married,— to Mr. Harris, of Rome. We will be rejoiced if you can get away, as you anticipate, and call on us.

Your Son

Sidney Lanier.

To Virginia Hankins

Marietta, Ga, July 17th 1873

My dear Child: Are you by " the glassy cool translucent wave " (as Milton hath it) of Burwell's Bay? [67]

How I crave a walk with you along those enchanted sands, in this golden weather!

It may be I will have one, if you do not leave Shoal Bay too soon. In a couple of weeks, (D. V.) I shall start for New York, bent on the very maddest of art-projects that a crazy brain ever conceived: yet I am going to play at my play, I will have my humor unbalked for once. On the way, if you will speedily write me that you are at Shoal Bay still, I will come by to see you, if nothing happen. God prosper it!

Know, meantime, that here is a wonder and a miracle again, the same being another man-child that is born unto my house. The Mother thereof prospers marvellously: at this moment she sits by me, in full view of the green mountains, (through our window,) and sends you a fervent kiss and as much heartsome arm-clasping as a letter may convey. Meantime I send you the picture of my Charles as desired by Madame Rebecca.[68] You should see this same boy, *now*! He is beautiful as any dream, and is full as loving as he is lovely.

[67] The quotation is from Milton's *Comus*.

Virginia Hankins had written Lanier on June 2 that she was going to Virginia at the end of the month to spend the rest of the summer at " Shoal Bay," Surry Co., probably with the Wrens, to whom Lanier refers below.

[68] Rebecca Alexander Smith, with whom Virginia was making a temporary home, at Scotland Neck, N. C.

I pray you write me, fully. Convey my warm and friendly remembrance to Mr. Wren and his family: ah! how some beautiful moments come to me when I think of that lovely place.

The July no. — of the Southern Magazine contains the first half of a history of " San Antonio de Bexar " by me. Shall I send it you: – or have you it? 'Tis but a poor piece.

Address me here. I am always, dear Friend,

Your Faithful Friend

S. L.

To Charles Day

Marietta, Ga, July 20th 1873

My dear Father:

I fear you were surprised. (I hope not annoyed) by my telegram yesterday.

Indeed, I only sent it after much deliberation, and with much regret: but I was under an alternative to be indebted for a favor either to you, – or to another person: and I chose you. Some of my projects, (which I had not expected to mature for a month or two, yet, but which culminated sooner, and before I was prepared, as I would have been otherwise) required me to make a loan: [69] and Mr. Van Wyck, the banker, here, very obligingly offered to let me have the money in any way I wanted it: but in course of our conversation, I gathered that it was a regulation of his company (as indeed with all banks) to have *two* names on all paper: and, although he kindly enough offered to forgo this regulation, yet I did not care to be obliged to him in that way: and so, (inasmuch as my brother was I knew not where, – somewhere about Blount Springs or Montgomery, – and as I did not know where my father was) I telegraphed you, simply in order to carry out Mr. Van Wyck's rule of having two names on his paper. I shall have means to meet the draft at maturity, and I beg that you will give yourself no

---

[69] A possible explanation of one of Lanier's " projects " is suggested by the surviving receipt (Charles D. Lanier Collection, Johns Hopkins University) for a sterling silver Boehm flute, which Lanier had apparently bought from H. C. Wysham of Baltimore, sent by the Adams Express Co. It is marked: " Recd payment . . . 7/25/73." The flute cost $240.00. (See also the following letter and the conclusion to Lanier's letter to his brother, May 24, 1873, above.)

concern whatever about it; at the same time, thanking you very heartily for your prompt answer.

Mary continues to improve: and, *malgré* the colic, so does the baby. He is a truly noble boy, and I take great delight in him. Mary begs one to say to you that in consequence of the weakness of her eyes, she has not written you, but sends her kisses in my letter.

We see the Duncans often, and Mrs. Screven: who always inquire about you. Tell Janie I went to Miss Roberts' this afternon to play the flute for Miss Green (the invalid) who is visiting there on the litter that I had built for Mrs. Wallen last year; & the ladies inquired very particularly and affectionately about her. (Janie). We rejoice,– after the manner of the wicked – that that slim thorn, Mr. Ritter, has been drawn out of the flesh of Brunswick, and congratulate Hal and Janie upon this signal revenge that Time hath brought.

May and the boys join me in all manner of love to you, and to Hal & Janie and Charlie [Taliaferro]. You must be a happy quartette, and we long to embrace all four of you.

I am always, dear Father,

Your Son

Sidney Lanier

P. S. My extra copies of The Southern Magazine are just arrived, and I send you one by the morning mail.

S. L.

To Clifford A. Lanier [70]

Marietta, Ga. July 21st 1873

My dear Clifford:

Your letter is here, and gives me the pleasure of knowing that you are (or, by this time, have been) far from the haunts of Montgomery men, and that the great hills and trees set you to thinking of deep matters.

[70] Excerpt previously published, *Gulf States Historical Magazine*, II, 14 (July, 1903). The last three sentences and the signature have been cut out of the MS; they are reproduced here from a contemporary copy made by Clifford Lanier.

In much reading and reflection upon the relations of mind and body (to which you refer), I have found occasion to establish for myself – among some others not now pertinent – one general principle which is constantly being confirmed and which will save from much error any one who loves to meditate upon this fascinating subject. The principle to which I refer is about (for I won't now take time to put it into very precise scientific form) this: that whilst there is a remarkable parallelism between the phenomena of Mind and the phenomena of the nervous system (a parallelism which Herbert Spencer has detailed with a wonderful insight and supported by a prodigious number of illustrations), yet it is always unsafe to assert, on this account, anything like a *dependence* of mind upon matter; much more to erect a theory that mind is made of matter, in any way.[71]

For mark that, in the first place, it is only with a *certain portion* of the human frame that mind seems to be particularly connected. It is true that a musician's musical faculty might be paralyzed by a blow on a particular portion of his head: indeed Dr. Mettauer asserts that when I was ill with erisypelas, the various portions of the brain which were successively distended with blood in consequence of the progressive inflammation set up by the disease around my head, betrayed their functional distinctness very clearly. But on the other hand I might have had my leg cut off, (in which event a large number of nerves as well as other tissues would have been sundered) without producing any effect whatever on my mind. Now it is certainly as fair to infer from this latter fact that mind is *not* made of matter, as to infer from the former that it is; and these contradictory phenomena imperatively drive us away from *that* direction in searching for an explanation.

Which brings me to say, in the second place, that a suggestion you make is directly in the path of the theory which has always seemed to me to offer the best solution of the two conflicting classes of phenomena above referred to. Suppose I take a violin

[71] A copy of Herbert Spencer's *The Principles of Psychology* (New York, 1871) survives in Lanier's library, Johns Hopkins University. Much of Lanier's letter is clearly based on his reading of this book.

The reference in the following paragraph is probably to Lanier's illness in the spring of 1865; Dr. Mettauer has not been identified.

which is out of tune: I may play it with perfect accuracy, that is, I may make exactly the motions required to play perfectly on a tuned violin: yet the result will be unmusical and discordant. So, again, suppose that one of the strings is tied down to the finger-board so as to lose its vibratory capacity: that tone, and all tones represented by that string, will be dumb.

Now in both these cases the hand that plays, the bow that is drawn, the mind that directs; are all in perfect order, *they* are not crazed, nor paralyzed: it is *only* the string that is affected.

Applying this illustration; the body is a violin, the mind is the player thereupon. If a string be out of tune (and it is well established that the body *has* strings, each of which makes its note when drawn on, and each of which *may* be out of tune) the result is, the disjointed talk of a crazy man. If a string be tied down so as to stop its vibrations (as for instance when the head is struck, and a piece of its bone presses upon and paralyzes some particular functional portion of the brain), then the playing hand and bow may play just as usual yet no sound comes: and so the mind may act as usual, yet no functional phenomenon appears to the senses.

Now, confining the attention to the latter instance, it would be just as legitimate to argue, that because no note came from the tied string, *therefore* the hand of the player was made out of strings and was tied down, – as to argue that a musician's mind, whose musical phase did not manifest itself in consequence of a pressure upon some part of his brain, was therefore made out of brain, *i. e.* of matter.

In fine, I cannot but believe that the failure of any portion of the body to respond when the finger of the soul is pressed upon it, is an utterly insufficient circumstance to prove that the soul is made of the body or is in any manner dependent upon the body for anything else than mere *manifestation to the senses of others.*

As for the immortality of the soul; – why, surely the soul *is* immortal: but just as surely (it seems to me) matter is immortal, also. Curiously enough, there is more argument (outside of Revelation, and *just as much in* Revelation) for the immortality of matter, than for that of the mind. For the experience of man is multitudinously full of the utter disappearances and *apparent* destruction of *minds*: but no man has ever known an atom of matter to be destroyed. When a man dies, his mind, so far as any one can see, hear, feel, taste or smell, dies and is utterly blotted out: but no particle of his body perishes, that remains, palpable, and through every change of its form can be accurately determined by weight and measurement to amount to precisely as much as before, i. e. to have lost no particle of its matter. Thus human experience, while it reveals uncountable instances of the cessation of soul, reveals no single instance of the cessation of matter; and, to that extent, gives greater ground for the belief in the immortality of the latter, than in that of the former.

But when we come to Revelation, the assertions of the everlasting life of the body are equally as positive as of that of the soul. True, the earth (i. e. as it now is,) passes away, and the body passes away: but the new earth and the new body, – the corruptible which has put on incorruption – survive throughout eternity, and these are, beyond question, the old earth and the old body, regenerated by some such infusion of a new spirit as that which renders the sinful soul a fit inhabitant of Heaven. In fact, the little thought I have been able to give this part of the subject in my life (alas, one has to be brave enough to be ignorant of *so* many things!) leaves me in great doubt whether God has made *anything* to perish forever, in the literal meaning of that term. For, giving the matter its most general turn, it seems derogatory to the idea of God's power to believe that He could not accomplish His purposes without making something which must utterly pass away when it has accomplished its purpose. It is only *earthly* Carpenters that have to leave worthless chips!   ″

―――――――
                   ″

Mary progresses rapidly, and is at this moment sitting in her chair by the window, in the sweet morning air, looking very lovely. She sends you her fervent love. The small man is a gem. He impresses us already with a sense of something large and noble and generous. He gives my heart a kind of twinge, – just such as a glove-stretcher gives a glove! – when I take him in my arms.

I enclose a letter from our kinsman in S. C., who is, I am told a very good man and an honest withal.[72] You must send

[72] Probably one of the Eason family of Charleston, S. C.

him a copy of " Thorn-Fruit." I'll send one of " T. L." My motions have been greatly delayed by the re-appearance of the Cholera at Chattanooga: but I hope to get through with that business, and to be in New York in a couple of weeks from now. An impulse, simply irresistible, drives me into the world of poetry and music. When Life, Health, Passion, Bent-of-Nature, and Necessity, all grasp me with simultaneous hands and turn my face in one direction, – why should I hesitate?

It is nothing but weakness which has kept me so long in doubt.

My hope and plan is to get a foothold in N. Y. during what remains of the summer, and, either to spend the winter there, or to return to Atlanta where I have some inducements to write the history of Georgia and pass the winter months in *that*, returning to New York in the late Spring – as health and interest shall seem to indicate. I am keen to finish my Jacquerie, and to present some of my Woods-translations on the flute, and these are the (temporarily) ultimate ends of my present work.

Do present a prodigious amount of love, the sister-variety, the cousin-variety, the aunt-variety, the grandma-variety to the appropriate persons.

What a garrulous pen this is!

Forgive it, – being the pen of

Yr faithful

S. L.

To Mary Day Lanier [73]

Atlanta, Ga., August 6th 1873

I scratch a note to thee, My dear and most sweet Loving-Heart, which shall tell thee that I played, all yesterday afternoon, duetts of Walckiers with Mr. Sham, in my room at the hotel, whereat Mr. Sham was completely transported: that in the evening I was conveyed by Mr. Guilford to the Hall of the

[73] This letter is written on the stationery of the H. I. Kimball House. In a letter of Aug. 2 (4?) to Charles Day, Lanier had written: " I expect to start to Macon tomorrow, (spending the night in Atlanta, to fill an engagement there) and reaching Macon on Wednesday. I will probably remain there a day only, being anxious to get back to my darlings here: but may have to stay over longer."

Mozart Club, where I found a goodly number of ladies and gentlemen, to whom I did play with "immense" success, both my pieces being vigorously encored, and many congratulations and fair sayings, as well as some flowers, being poured in upon me: that, I did meet at the same place Madame Muller, with whom, betwixt the acts, I held high converse of deep matters, and who, (as I foolishly tell thee for thy good loving partiality's sake) did openly declare to thine that he was a star: that I played with more satisfaction to myself than ever before, and feel quietly hopeful of an artist's mastery over my instrument in greater assuredness than I have yet dared: that I leave for Macon at half-past one, that is, in about an hour: that I am a little tired, (tho' not too much), wherefore I write little, the same being irksome to my sword-arm: that I am all one thee-longing, being, when I am not by thee, always that mere hollow Thee-Expectancy that thou art good enough to call thy

Husband.

To Robert S. Lanier

Marietta, Ga, Aug 13th 1873

Dear Father:

I arrived here safely on Sunday morning,[74] and found all my little family sick with terrible colds. They are all now getting better, but I myself am in the midst of a combination of malarious chill (brought from Macon) and the epidemic cold now prevalent here.

Will you please attach a card with my name on it to my baby-carriage, and get a drayman to carry it out to the dépôt and ship it as freight to me at this place? If, too, you can find the black-walnut towel-rack belonging to our set of furniture, I will be glad to have it shipped at same time.

The boys have had an infinity of fun with the chocolate: tho' they don't know it is chocolate, yet: a piece of information we have kept in reserve. Charlie desires thanks returned to Pringle for his book.

All send love,

Your Son
Sidney Lanier

[74] Aug. 10. (Lanier had apparently spent three or four days in Macon.)

To Virginia Hankins

Marietta, Ga. Aug. 19th 1873

No, My dear Friend, the power of my friendship needs no extraneous Chivalry to keep it clinging to the old vows. Indeed I never think to examine it, to analyze it, to ask it why and how. My desire to meet you is a quite simple, original, indivisible, imperishable Want, (like what the philosophers call an Ultimate Element,) within me, and I no more think of enquiring whether it may not be compounded of separate ingredients than I think of scientifically investigating my thirst, when I have it.

Why should I? There are so many things in life that a man of any maturity must bring himself to love by *reasoning*, and to which he gives his affection as an act of free grace! I do not know if this is particularly true with me,– but I'm sure I find the love-*compelling* sort of people growing fewer and fewer, and my tastes growing more and more keen, more and more merciless in rejecting the thick-skinned and the mercantile, more and more sensitive to slightest infractions of that fragile and vigilantly-guarded material out of which a tender heart builds its aspirations. Why, then, I say: when I find myself loving and honoring you, and prizing you as a Wonderful Friend, – find myself, further, drawn and bound so to do by a Power which seems infinitely tender and sweet and whose behests I obey with indescribable gladness and with unquestioning faith; why should I call myself to account?

— On the whole, I think I rather enjoy a fling at my friendship for you: for it gives my heart an occasion to assert itself, and an opportunity to speak forth how highly it holds you!

My visit to New York is somewhat delayed. It is probable I will not go until you are back in Halifax — is not that the name of the Station? I hope this may be so: for you will be far easier for me to reach, at Scotland Neck, and I shall be greatly driven; – not to speak of my fear of those old-time chills-and-fevers of Surrey: – and not to speak, moreover, of my strong preference to see you somewhere *else* than in Surrey, *now*. Let me know your precise movements.

My wife sends you a fervent kiss. I wish my boys knew you.

     God keep your eyes, your feet, and your heart, — wishes
Your Friend
Sidney Lanier

To Charles Day

Marietta, Ga. Aug. 21st 1873

My dear Father:
                    Mary has been sorely lamenting the recent
infrequency of our letters to you, and has been bitterly abusing
both herself and me for being so busy and so no-account. I have
managed to make her go over to Mrs. Wallen's tonight, for
an hour, and am writing you in her absence. She has not been
so well, of late, and has been at times somewhat discouraged
by the provoking return of some old troubles. The Dr., however, assures us that it is but temporary, and easily remediable:
and the troubles themselves are not nearly in such degree as
formerly.

     Really we both wonder how our days pass. It does seem as if
we were scarcely up and dressed, and through the routine of
the thousand little duties inseparable from a household that
boasts three sturdy boys, before night comes, and bed-time.
I have some work which occupies as much of my time as I dare
devote to it: [75] and when that is over, the time I can give to
my sweetheart and my boys seems wretchedly short.

     The money is now deposited in bank, here, to meet the draft
which I drew on you. Please allow me to thank you again for
your prompt kindness and confidence in response to what must
have been a very unsatisfactory telegram.

I have been exceedingly desirous to go to Dade [County, Ga.]
and see what can be done with the coal lot: but each time when
I have gotten ready, the Cholera has broken out afresh, and
prevented me.

     The boys are getting over their colds. Such a summer as we

---

[75] Several of Lanier's letters during this summer that have been omitted from
this edition refer to his being engaged in writing magazine articles. One of these
was probably the expanded form of "The Texas Trail of the 70's," the surviving
MS of which is dated: Marietta, Sept. 1, 1873 (see note 56, 1872); another,
his critique of Hayne's poetry (see note 89, below); a third, "San Antonio de
Bexar," the article alluded to in the postscript to this letter.

have had! I think two days out of every three, since we came, have been rainy: and this August has been a really cold month, most of the time.

We long to hear news of Janie. Mrs. Johnson (Eugenia) came round yesterday afternoon, and drove May and the boys out in Mr. Duncan's pony phaeton. I was absent in Atlanta; where I played last night at a Concert, – very acceptably, I believe, to the audience.[76]

I hope Hal improves his resting-time. To him, and to all who are with you, we send fervent love.

Your Son

Sidney Lanier

The Magazines have been sent. I waited, in order to forward both numbers at once.

S. L.

To Harry C. Day

Marietta, Ga., August 26th, 1873.

My dear Hal,

Your dispatch announcing the birth of your daughter [77] and the prosperity of herself and her mother was read by us a little while ago, amid many fervent wishes and aspirations for all three of you. Three of you, my dear Boy! *Your* daughter: how odd, and how sweet, it sounds! And how much this little Lady is going to love you!

'Tis what I could have wished for you, exactly.

God grant she may be a pure little star, with indefinite abilities in the matter of burning through clouds, and shining above storms, and otherwise glorifying the dreadful tempests, and still more dreadful calms, of life.

Meantime, however, Farewell the downy bed of ease. Farewell the long night's sleep unbroken by a single sound (save perhaps that heavenly snore of Janie's), Farewell the sovereign

---

[76] This was a concert at James's Hall on Wednesday, Aug. 20, 1873, for the benefit of the parsonage of a new Catholic Church; Lanier played two flute solos: *Macbeth* and *La Sirene* (see Atlanta *Daily Herald*, Aug. 20, 1873).

[77] Mary Louise Day.

glory of being the only thing your wife has to think about and to look after, Farewell all these sweet things: — you are dethroned and another is in power, *Le Roie est mort, Vive La Reine.*

The worst of it is that *La Reine* doesn't come into power, exactly, yet, by reason of youth: but the true Power is that of the Regent,— the abominable, diabolical Nurse. May the Devil confound all nurses, say I. A dozen times a day, young man, you will have to bow your head in abject submission and let The Nurse walk over your prostrate form, walk, nay, stand on you, and see-saw, as it were, with one foot on your favorite corn and the other grinding your once-proud nose into fragments. I recoil in sadness from the picture of the meek, humble and battered Ruin you'll be when I next see you, and, — only begging my dear Janie to try and temper the wind (of the nurse's tyrannies) for you, now that you are a shorn lamb, I remain your and her sympathizing brother,

S. L.

To Virginia Hankins

Marietta, Aug. 30th 1873

Au revoir, then, it shall be, dear Friend: for I straightway write a hasty line to say that you must not put off your school, for my departure is delayed probably a couple of weeks. I hope to see you sometime about the middle of September, but my movements depend much upon " circumstances beyond my control," and therefore I do not pretend to write more definitely.

Whatever happen, — if God Almighty do not say no — I will see you this time, and we will have a quiet ride or walk there by the Roanoke, and draw a little breath of the divine air of true Friendship.

How I long for it!

Do not look for me until I come.

I will come, D. V.

Yr. Friend

S. L.

To Charles Day

Marietta, Ga. Sep. 3rd 1873

My dear Father:

We rejoice to hear of the general improvement, spite of drawbacks, of the two ladies that Harry owns, and only wish there were some way in which we could minister to the comfort of both of them.

We are all in tolerable condition. Mary has a great deal of work to do since our old nurse was compelled to leave: but Rena is a perfect trump, and has come out stronger than ever in our moment of need, so that May gets along far better than I had expected. We find great difficulty in getting a nurse to replace our old Mauma. Servants are dreadfully scarce, here, and are far, far above any necessity to labor.

Mary looks brighter and stronger than I have seen her in a long time, and if she had *you*, I think she would be as happy as is consistent with the doleful fact of *me*.   I hope to be able to rent a cottage of four rooms in Atlanta, for the winter, and have meals furnished from a restaurant. I am convinced that people spend far too much of their time in worrying over bad cooks and stoves and fearful kitchens. It is possible I may go to Atlanta tomorrow, in order to see what can be done towards perfecting these arrangements; and in order to meet Uncle Clifford who will probably be there in attendance on the Supreme Court.

I took up the paper you accepted promptly at maturity. Today, a matter which I had not expected quite so soon, obliged me to make a loan of $250. for 30 days, and I took the liberty of drawing a similar draft on you. Please accept it: but give yourself no concern about it, as I shall have the funds in bank to meet it.

The boys are in pretty good condition, though Charley has to be driven to his meals every day, and I am fearful that his lack of appetite shows something wrong. I have been very unwell, but am quite out of the woods now, and becoming bright and strong again. I am greatly grieved by the sudden death of my friend [William] Hopson,—of which you will have doubtless heard before this reaches you.

We all send a lot of kisses which you are to distribute impartially betwixt dear Janie and the fair little ladye; How I should like to smoke a pipe over it all with my dear old Hal! Mary unites with me in kind regards to Mrs. Lamar. What a comfort she must have been to Janie !

Your Son

Sidney L.

To Mary Day Lanier [78]

Wilmington, N. C. Sep. 14th 1873

Fancy, dear Sweetheart, a man playing a long run or Cadenza, which began with most sweet tearful notes and proceeded with a rapid rush of tones surcharged with fresh pathetic recollections,—and suddenly, in the very height and sweet acme of the flowing music, coming upon a

This adjuration, being interpreted, meaneth that I was horrified to learn yesterday afternoon just after leaving Augusta that the regular train did not run from Wilmington on Sundays! Had I known it ten minutes sooner, I could have had my baggage taken off at Augusta, and spent the time there, with Salem: but I only learned it as we were crossing the bridge, and so had to resign myself.

We are delayed here nine hours: having arrived this morning at 8.15, and staying over until 5.30 this afternoon.

Salem boarded the train on arriving at Augusta, and rode through town with me. I found him looking thin, but hardy and healthy from his field-sports, which have now taken on the form of dog-and-gun, since the fishing season is over. He had a kind of peaceful, philosophic and (at the same time) somewhat doggéd look, as of a man who had done some teeth-

[78] More than a hundred letters by Lanier have survived covering the ensuing eight months' absence in New York and Baltimore. Approximately one third of these have been omitted from the present edition, since they duplicate other letters here included or are concerned with his wife's domestic problems in Georgia.

gritting and vain swearing in private, and had resolved to stick out yet longer and fight a brave fight. I fear the *waiting* which is necessarily incident to the progress of the young lawyer, will be a dreadful trial to him, when the first flush of the novel exemption from the old daily grind of his newspaper life is over, and the actual fact settles coldly about him ('tis as if a man stood in a tide remorselessly rising, slowly chilling) that success means immersion in writs and demurrers and squabbles and all the varied sort of knowledge of personal feuds and consanguinities and peculiarities which is necessary to enable a Georgia lawyer to select his jurymen.[79]

I have stood the trip very well so far, though the dust and heat have been excessive. The excitement of travel usually has a good effect on me, and I should feel very comfortably this morning if I were not so enraged by the stoppage, which sends me off into fresh paroxysms of rage whenever I think of it.

Cicero—heathen though he was! puts a case as follows: suppose a great scarcity of corn in a city, insomuch that there was a famine, and the price of corn was at a fabulous height: and suppose that a hundred vessels were sailing towards that city, laden with corn, whereof one vessel was one day's distance ahead of the others: now when the master of this forward vessel has arrived in the city, and the people thereof crowd about him offering him a hundred-fold profit upon his corn, (said people being ignorant of what is to come) what is his duty?

It is his duty (saith Cicero, that heathen man) to say, Gentlemen Merchants, I will sell you my corn, but I cannot do so without informing you that there are behind me ninety nine vessels, within one day's sail of this place, all laden with ample corn, whereby the price thereof will fall far below what you offer me![80]

Now if this heathen conscience could not be satisfied to take people's money without acquainting them with *all* the facts of the case,—how is it that this Christian railway corporation,

[79] No letters from Salem Dutcher between Nov. 7, 1871, and Apr. 23, 1873, have survived. At some time during this period he had moved to Augusta, Ga., and begun the practice of law, which he had been studying for several years before terminating his connection with the New York *World*.

[80] The allusion is to Cicero's, *De Officiis*, III, xii.

whose conscience is too tender to permit sending along its passengers on the Sabbath which was made for man (and not man for the Sabbath), did not take much pains to inform me that the promises which they have diligently circulated,—of conveying people though with great dispatch &c— were only meant in a certain sense, *i. e.* provided said people did *not* travel on Sunday, and how do they pocket my money which was given them for the consideration of quick dispatch, not only without *giving* me that dispatch, but entailing on me a clear and sure loss of some four dollars in money and nine hours in time, not to speak of an indefinite and possible loss in other cases of greatly larger degree?

But what is all this I am gabbling to thee,—to *thee*, My dear loving Soul, whose last tear, now that thou art gone out of sight, still hangs trembling before my soul even as a star just after the sun is sunk: to thee, who always makest me wish that my heart might be a harp, even as the Angel Israfel's, so that the passion thereof might fall on thine ear in direct and uinter-preted beats of music? [81]

I pray thee,—for I cannot write more now—commend me to my dear father, and my three young men; and hold me in thine heart with whatever comfort a temple holds a worshipper, for I am thy devout

husband.

To Mary Day Lanier

Baltimore, Sep. 19th 1873

So ! At last I have a little moment to draw breath in, and to speak a word to my dear Heart.

In the dead waste and middle of the night, I arrived at Enfield [N. C.] (where I had concluded was my best chance to find a conveyance to reach Ginna) got off the train – which was behind time – in a monstrous hurry, at a lonesome depot, saw the baggage-man throw off my valise, caught hold of one end of my trunk while the train was at smart speed starting off, ran

---

[81] The allusion is presumably to Edgar Allan Poe's poem, " Israfel."

with it till I got a good grip, then fearlessly bade the baggage-man to cast loose, – which he did, and my poor trunk bumped on the earth with fearsome thud; – but Providence watched over me, and it fell in the sand. I got quarters, stuck my feet in my blanket, pulled up a great quantity of cover over me, and dug myself a deep place in my feather-bed—so bitter-cold was the night—and fell off into a good sleep. Next morning, I fared forth toward Scotland Neck, in a spring-wagon drawn by a good horse, and driven by an old gentleman – a Native – with whom I held much high converse upon agricultural matters until we reached our destination. I dined, sent a note to Ginna, who replied in a most sweetly-startled fashion, and at half-past four jumped in a buggy and drove to her home. The day was so beautiful that we could not stay in doors, so into the buggy again, and away through the lovely woods and past the charming residences. Here live seven Smiths, all brothers, all rich, all in the houses of their ancestors, all well-educated, tasty people, in just such a cluster of elegant country homes as I don't think is elsewhere to be found in the South. They have their own Episcopal Church, – a lovely brick edifice, beautiful with vines outside, and with a fine organ inside. Returning from our drive, they press me to stay, so my traps are brought out from the hotel, and I take up my quarters at Ginna's, – one of the Smith's where she is a guest. Everybody seems as kindly and genial as can be: next day Miss Adelaide Smith volunteers to teach Ginna's School, so that the latter may be with me : which is done, and Ginna and I, soon after breakfast, take to our buggy again and fare forth into the woods, where, arriving at a pretty spot, I stop the horse and stretch myself back in the buggy-seat, with my feet comfortably on the dash-board, what time Ginna reads me passages here and there from her book. After much quarrelling and disputing, she finishes and we drive home: then the flute comes out, Ginna sings, and I play seconds, (with a good piano, too): then dinner, rest, and in the late afternoon, we walk to the Church, climb the fence, Ginna vaulting there-over like a young fawn, wander about, then sit on an iron garden-seat in the enclosure and watch the sun go down. Home to supper: then the flute, voice and piano, Blackbirds,[82] much

---

[82] A musical composition by Lanier, probably the one written in Texas and first called *Field-larks and Black-birds* (see note 36, above).

talk &c, and the night closes. Next morning, they have out the old family carriage, and Ginna, with young Smith, drives down with me to the village, where I embark in the hack to return to Enfield. As we shake hands, Ginna says, – with all manner of wondrous lights shinging through her brown eyes – "Write and tell May that your coming has been like the Skies to me, and I shall never know how to thank her for sending you," together with other like messages.

Meantime I have had the most monstrous sore-throat that was ever concocted, the pain almost driving me mad, and now as we go back towards Enfield it becomes ravenous and gnaws me like a vulture. I go bravely to work, however, get some Iodine & Glycerine mixed, make a probang out of my toothbrush, and, what with this and Brown's Trochees, when I awoke on the Steamer yesterday morning, I found myself much better, and am quite free from soreness this morning.

Altogether the visit to Ginna was simply delicious, and I think she enjoyed it keenly. Her lot is in a sweet place and I am rejoiced to think of her lonesome life being brightened by so many friends, who all seem to be exceedingly fond of her.

Arriving here yesterday about nine, I bathed, & dressed leisurely, and finally despatched a note to Mr. Wysham,[83] about one. He came in three minutes after he received my note, but I was at dinner. As I came out from dinner, and sauntered to the desk for a tooth pick, he came up, grasped my hand, we had a word or two, made an appointment for four O'clock, and off he dashed on business. At four he came, took me to his house, where I found a charming residence, but dismantled, (his family not yet having returned), carried me straightway into his library,– both talking all the time – bustled about, and finally got us both fairly down to a duett of Kuhlau's. We had but begun it, however, when arrived Mr. Winterbotham, a fine young pianist, whom he had invited to play our accompaniments, and so we adjourned to the piano in the drawing-room. – a fine Weber. Then we had Bach's sonatas (Fl. & P.), a duo

---

[83] See note 7, above. Henry C. Wysham was at this time playing the flute in the Peabody Institute Concerts. In a letter of Sept. 25, Mary Day Lanier reported to R. S. Lanier: "This gentleman is– according to Sidney– ' a keen and faithful man of business '– a lawyer in active practice."

For the other musicians mentioned in this and the following letter, see note 88, below.

(2 Flutes) from Rigoletto, with Piano accompaniment, (magnificent, and unlike any duo I have ever heard before) then I played the Swamp-Robin [84] with much applause (though fearfully done, my mouth being dry as powder with excitement, and I couldn't get any tone at all), then Kuhlau's grand duo, (2 Fl. & P.). Then he took me to tea, and we started afterwards to Dr. [J. J.] Chisholm's, whose daughter plays much with Wysham. On the way we pass a house where some one is playing the piano. " Stop " says W: peers in through the windows, clutches me, and we go in just for a lark. Mr. [B. F.] Horrwitz, Mrs. Horrwitz, (she is playing) Mr. [James?] Gibson, the latter an accomplished old N. Y. beau: to these we enter, fall a-talking, crack a thousand jokes on the flutes, (which we secretly left in the hall) (and some of the same jokes would not at all do to repeat, though the lady got off the worst one): but presently Mr. Horrwitz goes smelling round, finds the flutes, brings them in in great triumph and noise, and we fall to playing all manner of improvised duetts. Presently they insist on *me*, and I play " Blackbirds," with stunning effect. Then we play Scotch airs for old Mr. Gibson, some other people drop in, play, play, play: then we seize our flutes, and dash off to Dr. Chisholm's; where, on entering, I am presented to four ladies, one of whom seizes my hand at hearing my name, and declares that I must pardon her for that Mrs. Eason of Charleston is one of her dearest friends and she has heard her speak of me so often &c &c. This is pleasant. Then we fall to: Wysham plays some wonderful things of De Jong's; I play our Fürstenau, & Briccialdi's Nocturne, Miss Chisholm rendering a lovely accompaniment at sight. Then Wysham plays The Kaleidoscöp, and more De Jong: then we take some two-part songs, (Virginia Gabriel's songs, unique and lovely) which bring down the house: then some sacred music, – two Fl. & P. – : then with a grand flourish from Lucia, 2 Fl. & P. we leave; W. takes me to the Allston Club (an Art Club) [85] registers me, we sit a moment, I take

[84] A musical composition by Lanier, no copy of which has survived. It was apparently first composed as early as 1867 (see note 49, 1867) but was quite possibly revised during the recent summer in Marietta (see Lanier's letter to his brother, July 21, 1873, above, referring to his " Woods-translations on the flute ").

[85] The Allston Association was a club founded in 1858-1859 to sponsor American artists, named in honor of the painter Washington Allston. From

some whiskey; and then we part, for Wysham is an early bird, and a regular withal, always retiring at half-past ten.

Thus we have had a six hours' stretch of it.

Wysham declares himself utterly astonished at my playing, in view of my facilities, and declares that my powers are simply without limit, needing only the restraint of a good musical associate, and a little practice.

He plays very beautifully, and is my superior in technique, I judge: tho' of course, I have been playing pieces I never heard, and that too under dreadfully frightening circumstances, so that I cannot say how our sight-reading would compare. He recognizes the peculiar quality of my nature-pieces: " there is, (says he) a ' natural magic,' as you call it, in your music such as I have never heard from any one else." [86] He has true ideas of expression, and is greatly pleased with mine. All his expressions go to show that he is greatly impressed with my playing.

Dr. Browne [87] has just called, and has taken up my balance of available time (in a vastly pleasant way, indeed): and so I must now close. I am well. Tonight I am to take tea at Dr. Chisholm's and we are to give a grand musical entertainment (Wysham and I, Miss Chisholm, Mrs. [Fred M.] Colston, Mr. Winterbotham) afterwards. W. calls for me at five: which will be, now, very soon after I get my dinner. W. had a lovely bouquet for me yesterday, arranged by himself. We are like two young lovers.

Embrace thy father – and my sons, for thy

Husband.

1870 to 1875 it was amalgamated with the Wednesday Club, an organization of musical and dramatic amateurs, also dating from 1858. At the time of Lanier's letter, 1873, the club rooms were on St. Paul Street above Monument. Two guest invitations extending the privileges of the Allston Association to Lanier for thirty-day periods have survived, dated Sept. 18 and Dec. 24, 1873 (Charles D. Lanier Collection, Johns Hopkins University). Lanier was later to become a member of the Wednesday Club, see note 68, 1878, below. (See Ottilie Sutro, " The Wednesday Club," *Maryland Historical Magazine*, XXXVIII, 60-68, Mar., 1943; see also Introduction to vol. VII, present edition.)

[86] In a letter to his brother Clifford, Sept. 27, 1873 (here omitted), Lanier declared: " [The] ' natural magic' of my compositions . . . is all that I now pretend to as distinguishing them from others."

[87] W. H. Browne (described in some detail in the following letter) was the editor of the *Southern Magazine*. He and Lanier had been in frequent correspondence since Dec., 1870.

To Mary Day Lanier

Balto. Sept. 20th 1873

I had not time to tell thee yesterday anything of my good
Wysham, nor how I like him: nor indeed am I in case to tell
thee anything, for my heart is so hungry for thee that had I all
the time in the world I cd. not do more than scribble dis-
jointedly to thee the glories and delight with which my good
friend has filled my heart.

Promptly at five yesterday afternoon, he came, took me to his
house for a moment to change his coat, and we then straightway
repaired to Dr. Chisholm's, where we found Miss Julia awaiting
us. Without ado we plunged into the music: Kuhlau's Grand
Trio (2 Fl. & P. F.) (how I long for thee to listen to that
sublime composition!), then the Trio from Rigoletto (2 Fl. &
P. F.), then songs with flute *obligato*: then we took tea, amidst
all manner of merry and unaffected talk the Chisholms are fine,
simple, elegant people, whom thou wdst. like – then straight
back to our Music, until Mr. Winterbotham came in, when we
repeated the Kuhlau Trio (of which the P. F. part is quite
difficult) with stunning effect: then Winterbotham played some
grand *Maenadic* strains from Tannhauser, a wonderful Taran-
telle of sombody's, a brilliant *fantasie* of Thalberg; then
Miss Julia Chisholm, being called out, gave the prayer of
Mendellsohn's

with wonderful delicacy and depth for a young girl but not as
thou canst give it: and then we had a little wine, and so
separated. Wysham walked part of the way with me. 'Tis the
most genuine case of true love thou hast ever known. W. is
noble, and sweet: a keen, faithful man of business, an ardent
music-lover, a fervent friend, with that peculiar spice of boyish-
ness which one always finds in the most loveable men when in
their sportive moods.

Little notes, like this card enclosed, flit about between us
when the cruel business separates us in the day. This morning

he appeared before I was dressed, but would not come up, on finding he was too early for me.

I enclose a caricature, wh. W. says is perfect, of the players at the Peabody Institute Concerts: and a slip containing the first of a series of articles by W. in the Home Journal.[88]

Dr. Brown, as I wrote thee, called yesterday. He brought a San Antonio paper containing a charming notice of my Article on that City, which my atrocious chambermaid has managed to put where I can not now find it, to send thee, but I will try again.

Brown is utterly unlike any idea I had formed of him. A small man, with large, prominent light-blue eyes, hump-shouldered, nervous: getting off on a subject and talking at lightning-speed until he is completely lost and forgets he has an auditor, in pursuing his train of thought: a man evidently of ardent soul, fervently devoted to the right, to such a degree as to make him forget sometimes the slow process which is necessary to reform old Wrongs which have, by standing a long time, become so covered over with little clambering vines of rights that we cannot precipitately overturn the one without uprooting the others. To call on him, and on the [Thomas] Baxters: then to have a toot with Wysham about two: then to dine: then to be carried off by Wysham to some new friends on a musical excursion wh. he has not yet fully explained to me: that is the programme to day.

Thy dear letter with enclosures, is come.[89]

''

''

O my Heart, how completely thou *Art* my Heart! Thou art in every thing I do, say and hear: thy loveliness is in all the notes

---

[88] The *Home Journal* was a Baltimore magazine, the only known file of which is in the Peabody Institute Library, Baltimore.

The caricature inclosed was an etching by Frederick Dielman entitled " A Musical Soirée " and dated " June 1872 " (see illustration). An undated newspaper clipping in the John S. Short Collection, Johns Hopkins University, identifies the players from left to right as follows: Otto Sutro, Asger Hamerik, Prof. Henry Allen, Kate Dieter (later Mrs. J. W. Breedlove) standing, Prof. Bernard Courlaender, Henry Jungnickel, and Henry Wysham. All became acquaintances of Lanier's.

[89] One of the enclosures was a letter of Sept. 12, 1873, from *Lippincott's Magazine* rejecting Lanier's review of Hayne's *Legends and Lyrics*.

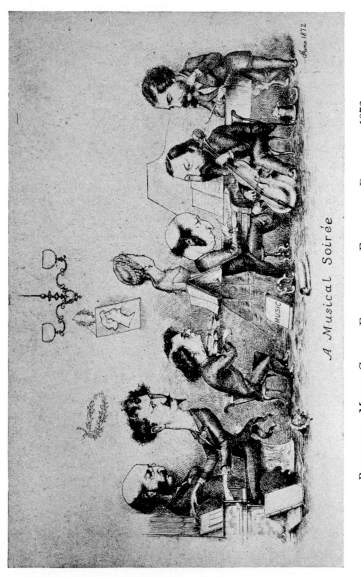

A Musical Soirée

BALTIMORE MUSIC GROUP, ETCHING BY FREDERICK DIELMAN, 1872

Courtesy of Maryland Historical Society

that come from the silver queen, it is thou, verily, that
enchantest the people: May God sphere thee, dear Wife, in
His love, as thou art sphered in the centre of the inner life of
thine
　　　husband.

To Mary Day Lanier

Baltimore, 22nd Sep. /73.

I have but time to tell thee, dear Heart, that I was taken in
tow yesterday at half-past Eight in the morning by my dear
friend Wysham, and carried to a lovely stone Church in the
Country, (first going to the house of a Mr. Perrine, a rich
Baltimorean, through the loveliest park imaginable) where we
played, during the service, three pieces, (Flute duetts, Manoah,
Hatham, and "Hark, My Soul"; all with Organ Accompaniment) to the great edification of Pastor & congregation.

Then we were taken into the carriage of Mr. Perot, and
carried to his house, a lovely villa, in the midst of a fair
paradise of beautiful grounds, lakes and trees, where we dined
and spent the balance of the day until ten at night, when Mr. P.
sent us back to town. We played a thousand things (these are
good people, but they understand that good music is always
good, Sundays as well as other days): Wysham was fairly
intoxicated with pleasure, and I too, both of us having been
all day making love in the most absurd manner: I played
"Blackbirds" twice: and we wound up with a fair batch of
hymns, 2 Fl. & P. F. and a half-dozen voices.

Today I have been calling on Dr. Browne, & Mr. Turnbull,
and have found them both very pleasant.[90] This afternoon
I am to meet the great Mr. Hamerik, and to-night we are to
have a farewell session over the duos. Tomorrow morning at
nine, I leave for New York, armed with several letters of
introduction to musical people there.

I have just met Lamar Cobb, who informs me that Uncle

---

[90] Lawrence Turnbull, Lanier's first Baltimore friend (see note 16, 1870),
had been the editor of the *New Eclectic Magazine* before it was reorganized as
the *Southern Magazine* under the editorship of W. H. Browne.

For the identity of Hamerik (mentioned in the following sentence and more
fully in the following letter) see note 91, below.

Clifford passed through Washington on Saturday, on his way to New York. I fear he will wonder where I am, and would telegraph him, if I had any idea where he was stopping.

"

If I had but one little moment of the large love that comes out of thy gray eyes into my heart! Dear God, my Child, how I long, simply, to look upon thee, a little while! Midst of all my friendly glories, I am lonesome. One near one is too far. Thou, thou, alone, art my Too-sweet, My One, and I am ever growing more completely thy

Lover.

To Robert S. Lanier

New York, Sep. 24th 1873

My dear Father:
         I arrived here last night from Baltimore. I had stopped there – expecting to stay only a couple of days – to see my friend Wysham. Having once seen him, however, I found him a soul so congenial that it was quite impossible to leave him so soon, and I stayed five days, during which he devoted himself to my pleasure, and to my profit, with a whole-souled friendliness I can never forget. Wysham is a lawyer, in full practice, but is also renowned as being one of the finest Amateur Böhm-Flute players in the world. He was pleased, beyond my utmost hopes, with my playing.

On the last day of my stay, he had Mr. Hamerick,[91] – who is director of the Peabody Academy of Music in Baltimore, and one of the most accomplished composers and *Maestros* in the world – at his house, to meet me and hear me play. Immediately after the first piece I played alone, Mr. Hamerick informed me that he was endeavoring to induce the Trustees of the Peabody Academy to supply him with funds for the formation of a large Orchestra; and he forthwith offered me the position of first flute, therein, in the event of his success,

---

[91] Asger Hamerik (1843-1923), Danish composer. From 1871 to 1898 he was director of the Peabody Institute in Baltimore, and conductor of its orchestra.

at the same time expressing himself in the most marked manner, both upon the style of my composition, and my playing, (it was one of my own pieces that I had performed.) This position would give, *per se,* $120 a month: and five scholars (Wysham declared he would guarantee *twenty,* but five would be all I wd. care for) would increase this amount to $200 a month. Thus I cd. live, and at the same time have a good part of every day to write my books and work for the position I desire in the world of letters: adding to these advantages, the further one of having daily access to large libraries, the deprivation of which I have so keenly felt heretofore.

Altogether, this plan offers so many advantages that I think it would be my duty to accept the place, and I eagerly await the result of Mr. Hamerick's negotiations now pending with the Trustees. Mr. Hamerick also gave me a strong letter to Theodore Thomas: but I am here too late to use it, as Thomas starts today (I am told) on his usual winter tour.[92] Indeed, I would not care to go with him: for I do not desire — it wd. be folly for me to attempt — to travel in this cold North during the winter.
Thus, you have my plan, so far as it is matured, and I sincerely hope it will meet your approval.

As to the Florida project you mention: – much reflection convinces me beyond doubt that this kind of writing is not my forte, 2nd that it does not pay, 3rd that there is no *career* in it at all, for one spends one's time writing that which people throw away as soon as read, – and it is my desire to write something that my boys may hear of, in the future.[93]

As for the Lecture project, it is quite impossible, for the same reason that it was impossible for me to continue practicing law, *viz.* that I cannot *speak* in a crowded room. I find that playing the flute is highly beneficial; while loud speaking is injurious. Finally, as for the loping horse and the out-door work; – while I am deeply grateful to you for the offer and

[92] Theodore Thomas (1835-1905), a German musician, who had come to America at the age of ten. In 1862 he had organized in New York his own symphony orchestra, whose concerts Lanier had attended. Later he became the conductor of the New York Philharmonic Society.
[93] The "Florida project" and the "Lecture project" (mentioned in this and the following paragraph) were apparently discussed in a letter from R. S. Lanier that has not survived; neither of them materialized.

for the spirit which prompts it – yet there are many reasons against it. For instance, (to adduce only one, of many) I am now thirty-one years old: I am determined to win myself some sort of place in men's regard: how *could* I do that, in attending to the " out-door work " of the Office? Again, my attending to the out-door work &c would not at all increase your income: and that is not large enough for us both. In short, I believe that you will readily agree with me, upon reflection, that my views are well-considered, and that the Baltimore plan is, in view of all the elements of my situation, the best. If that *fails,* I do not know what I shall do; but propose to stay in New York about a month in order to see if any other more feasible projects may not result. I have some valuable letters which I shall take occasion to present at an early day, and these will put me in the way of many things, I hope.

I have written you thus fully, because I observe from the tone of your letter that you are a little inclined to think I ought to have unfolded myself more fully to you before. But pray do not believe me in fault; my silence has only been due to my reluctance to announce plans which were before so apparently chimerical, – for I never could have reasonably dreamed of making so fine a figure, with my poor untaught music and playing, before those who have been accustomed to hear the finest music in the world, and it did really seem, even to me, highly chimerical for me to attempt to shine in music, under such circumstances: yet my dependent condition made it my duty to try that, for it seemed my last resort in order to be a self-sustaining man while I write my books.

I fear that Uncle Clifford will think me a desperate fly-about: and I wish you wd. ask him to take the trouble to read this letter, so that he may understand at least my hopes. I value his good opinion so highly, that I am willing even to bore him with my long explanations, – rather than lose it.

I succeeded in finding him today, after a long search. I arrived here yesterday afternoon about dark: and came to the St. Nicholas, thinking it likely he might be there. (I had heard of his coming to New York through Lamar Cobb whom I met in Baltimore). Not finding him at this hotel, I went up to sundry other places, after him, and only learned this morning, after I got my letters from Winslow Lanier & Co's of his being at Fifth Av. Hotel. I straightway went up there: and, after some search, found him just as he was starting for Philadelphia. As he only had one day to spare, and was already packed &c, he concluded it best not to stay. I regretted immensely my inability to be of service in piloting him about the town.

But I must close. I telegraphed you this afternoon that I had found Uncle C., fearful that the telegram he sent you yesterday might alarm you. (I wrote you from Wilmington.) I also asked in my telegram that you send Mary fifty dollars. She is in great need of it. I left her but little money, thinking that the seventy five for which I wrote you some time before leaving would probably reach her on the day of my departure. I find however a letter from her, here, in which she advises me that it had not come. If you have sent the fifty telegraphed for, and could send twenty five more to her, it would be a great help to me.

With a great deal of love, for yourself, Mama and Pringle, I am

Your Son

Sidney Lanier

To Mary Day Lanier [94]

New York, Sep. 24th 1873

O my Heart,   I found thy letter this morning.   Betwixt thy happiness in My dear Clifford & Willie,[95] – and thine unhappiness in the moneyless distress thou mentionest – my heart is quite torn. I have just telegraphed father to send thee funds, which apply as thou likest.

— I have so many, many things to tell thee ! I cannot do it, now, having just written fourteen pages to my father, wh. have tired my preposterous old right side: So will keep all details till another day.

But I *must* tell thee how fair a triumph I had on Monday.

[94] Previously published, *Scribner's*, XXV, 625-626 (May, 1899); reprinted, *Letters* (New York, 1899), pp. 74-75.

[95] Clifford Lanier and his family had stopped in Marietta on their way home from Montvale Springs (see Lanier's letter to his brother, Sept. 27, 1873, here omitted).

My good Wysham (" Harry " I call him, and he me " Sidney ")
on that day had the great Mr. Hamerick, (—Director of the
Peabody Academy of Music in Baltimore, one of the first
Composers in the world (Theodore Thomas has just brought
out his (Hamerick's) " Nordische Suite " with great effect)
and one of the most accomplished Maestros, also —) at his
(Wysham's) (*du Himmel,* what a sentence !) house, to meet
me. As soon as he came, Harry made me play " Blackbirds."
When I finished, Mr. Hamerick expressed himself in such
approval as would have delighted thy loving heart beyond
measure. He declared the composition to be that of an Artist,
and the playing to be almost perfect, with a grave and mani-
festly hearty manner which could not be mistaken: and concluded his applause by telling me that he was engaged in
endeavoring to persuade the Trustees of the Peabody Music
fund (they have an income of $40,000 a year !) to authorize
him to organize a full orchestra, in which he begged I would
accept the position of First Flutist. Kind Heaven, how my
heart throbbed with delight, – for my first thought was, of
thine enjoyment when I should at last be able to tell thee that
I had received, finally, and without any more peradventure, the
hearty recognition and approval, both for my composition and
for my playing, of one who is regarded (he is so spoken of in
one of the musical papers of this City) as a composer just below
the Classic Beethoven & Mozart, whose compositions are played
along with those of the great masters, and who has been
accustomed to hear, and to conduct, the finest music in the
world – – – –   After thus praising my work, Mr. Hamerick
went into Harry's library, and wrote me a beautiful letter to
Theodore Thomas: not a letter of extravagance, but a few
grave, sweet, courteous words, such as thou wdst. like: then,
coming down stairs, he made me play again the three main
movements of " Blackbirds," and testified anew, both while
I was playing and when I had finished, his pleasure in the piece.
    Is not this fine ? I declare that the greatest height and depth
of my glory, is the sparkle that will come into thy gray eyes
when thou readest these words.
    It is therefore a *possibility* (I *will* tell thee ! tho' thou must
not set thy heart on it much, for 'tis *only* a possibility, yet being
a sweet one, let us dream of it *together* !) that I may be First

Flute in the Peabody Orchestra, on a salary of $120 a month: which with five flute-scholars (Harry W. declares he'd guarantee twenty, but I want no more than five) wd. grow to $200 a month: wherewith we can live very nicely in Baltimore: and so, God be praised, thou and I might dwell in the beautiful city, among the great libraries, and I cd. write my books and be the man I wish to be, whilst thou, my poor Heart, thou, my long-suffering Sweet Heart, couldst be by me, also in midst of the music, the religion, and the art, that thou lovest.

I do thank God, even for this *dream.*

How *can* I close ! Yet I *must,* without delay. God keep thee, and my dear Sons, and thy father, and our good White Flower, in His best Angels' Charge, prayest thine

Husband.

I ought not to end this letter, without saying that thou couldst never dream how intense and unremitting has been the activity of Harry Wysham's friendliness. Some time I will transcribe for thee, one of his letters of introduction, in which he speaks of me quite as *thou* wdst, if thou shdst, let thy heart have the rule of thy tongue!

To Mary Day Lanier

New York. Sep. 25th 1873

Dear Heart, Sweet Heart, My Heart'[s] Heart, how I long for thee! No one is so beautiful as thou art, the counterparts of thy gray eyes have not hitherto appeared upon the earth, thy brows are unique, and thy soul is more love-worthy and more loving than all the souls that have been breathed into human bodies since the world was.

Here, in the very beginning of absence, I am desperate and full of woe for lack of thee: how will I live without my dear Mate until the winter, nay, until the next hour be past?

Sometimes I have to drown out my thoughts of thee with some overmastering excitement, so that I may keep my soul and body together.

"
––––––––––––––––––––––
"

Today I have been quietly endeavoring to advance my interest in one way and another, as well as commencing to see some friends. Thy letter of 22nd I got at Winslow Lanier, & Co's this morning. I did not stay to talk to Charles (Mr. J. F. D. is yet in Europe) knowing the load of care that must be on his mind in this great crisis.[96] The bank so far is perfectly solvent and safe – – – I then called on Foster [Higgins], and found him the same good old Fors. He received me with great cordiality. The family are all at Perth Amboy, and I am to go there and spend the night soon.

I called also on Mr. Eben, who did not recognize me at first on account of my beard, but, upon hearing my name, seized my hand and arm, and showed great sign of warmth. We had a good talk, and he then made me play a Kuhlau duo with him (I reading at sight), to his approbation. I am to see him again soon.[97] There is so much to write thee! Now I cannot do it.

Embrace thy father, and my sons for me. Tell Warren to take care of all my people: say to him that I wanted to shake hands with him when I left, but did not find him until too late; and that the board-money will be sent him.— I wrote thee and father yesterday. God send me a kiss of thine soon, prayeth thine

Husband.

To Virginia Hankins

New York, Sept. 26th 1873

How your brown eyes were shot through and through with lovely lights! during those, to me, enchanted days! Have you not seen the woods, so, when the sun was rising, and the level rays pierced between the trees deep into the hearts of the leaves?

---

[96] The financial panic of 1873.

[97] In a letter of Sept. 27, 1873, to his wife (here omitted), Lanier wrote: " I called on my Mr. Eben again this morning. . . . [He told me] that I had more ' execution ' than himself on the flute, . . . insisting upon giving me a few lessons, – for which he vows he will not receive a cent of payment! in order to polish off one or two little faults of my amateur style! " No further identification has been possible of Mr. Eben, who seems to have been an acquaintance of long standing and who is mentioned occasionally in Lanier's later letters.

Warren, mentioned in the following paragraph, was a negro servant at Lanier's boarding house in Marietta.

How sweet and how strong you are, My dear Little Friend!

The glamor of the happiness of your friendly companionship is not yet departed from me, my heart is still aglow with your friendly sympathy, and my hand feels still warm with your friendly clasp: insomuch that I can not yet speak to you save in exclamations and quick questions.

Moreover, how good you were, to give me, at parting, your book,[98] where on many pages I saw the signs of your meditations, pencilled in the margins! I did not read a line of the book: but I read "between the lines," as they say: for it was if *your heart* exclaimed, here and there, – those brief sentences, and questions, and scraps of poems. One of them I must ask you further about, when I get time.

You will be glad to know that I have had some great triumphs in the way of music, since I saw you. There is a bare possibility that I may come to live in Baltimore.

I only write a brief word, now, being in midst of many engagements. Do write me, dear Friend: addressing "care of Messrs. Winslow, Lanier & Co, 27 & 29 Pine St, New York." I beg you present my warm regards to your friend Miss Smith, who was a rare revelation of sweet womanliness and heartiness and goodness, to me, and in whose shining eyes and gracious face I saw a thousand charms wh. I cannot describe. Let me be also remembered kindly by the Messrs. Smiths, whose kind hospitality I hope some day to repay with great pleasure. Tell Mary I do not forget her.

Let me know your thoughts; and as soon as I get time, you shall have mine. Meantime I am always

Your faithful friend

S. L.

To Mary Day Lanier

New York. Sep. 26th 1873

I still have but a moment in which to write thee. It takes so much work, and so much time, to do anything in this wonderful Babylon! I will but send thee Harry Wysham's last

---

[98] Presumably a "novel" Virginia Hankins had begun writing several years

letter, rec^d this morning, and will copy off his letter of introduction to Mr. Weber, (this is, by the way, a dastardly thing
to do, – but he read it me, himself, after he had written it, and
therefore I hesitate not, for thou wilt take pleasure in seeing
what he thinks of thy lover, – and I wd. *almost* steal, to give
thee pleasure) for thy perusal, then for thy burning up.[99]

I am to go to my old friends the Dutchers to board, on
Monday. Miss Louise has just taken a house in Brooklyn, near
Fulton Ferry; – and they take such famous care of me, and I am
altogether so attached to them, that I regard the arrangement
with great pleasure. I have just called on Miss Julie (Mrs.
[Horace] Ripley) and been informed that when she ran over
to her Sister's yesterday and informed them I was here, (I had
seen Miss Julie before) Annie May seized her and nearly shook
the breath out of her for joy.

Thou wilt see from Harry W.'s letter that prospects brighten
a little for my Baltimore plan: whereat my heart is all over-
burning with thankfulness and hope and joy.

No more now, save this last floating kiss, sighed over to thee
out of the deepest deep of the heart of thy

                                        Lover.

To Mary Day Lanier

New York, Sep. 29th 1873

Thou, whom God made whilst He dreamed of Tuberoses and
red-roses and heliotropes and violets — thou, that bewilderest
my heart with thy loving-sweetness as it were a breath of air

before (see note 25, 1870, and her letter of Sept. 19, 1873, to which this is an
answer).

[99] In his letter introducing Lanier to Weber, Wysham had written: " A lawyer
by profession,– a musician by nature,– a poet for love, a writer by culture,– a
man by instinct and birth, he blends the delicacy of woman with the firm fibre
of manhood."

On Sept. 23, 1873, Wysham had written Mary Day Lanier his impressions of
her husband. His letter has not been found, but she copied extracts from it in
her letter of Sept. 25 to R. S. Lanier: " *Thus,* for sample, he writes– (referring
to some very ardent expressions of friendship [for Lanier] just uttered)–
Pardon all this,– it is very boyish, and yet he is the FRIEND I have been looking
for all my life long.' And farther on: ' Mr. Hamerik the conductor of our
Institute (Peabody) heard him play and gave him a cordial and valuable letter

drawn many-ways by those four divine flowers — thou, that art delicate-white like the Tuberose, that art glowing-warm with all artist's-passions like the red-rose, that art mystic-dreamy like the heliotrope, that art tender and faithful and true like the violet, – if my worship cd. match thy desert, thou shdst. sit higher than any daughter of men or gods.

"
———
"

Yesterday afternoon at three, I met by appointment my Aunt Helen [100] and her husband, Ronald McDonald, (one of the editors of the New York Times,) and we went forth for a long half-day in the park. We strolled and strolled, and talked and talked: Aunt H. petted me to my heart's great ease: she is a woman of wonderful intelligence and great culture, and her husband a rare modest gentleman such as thou wdst. like to know: and so we had a noble inter-souling, until long after dark, when the Park became enchanted land, and we wandered, amid much high discourse, through the fairy alleys, by the moonlighted lake and the great flashing fountains, until we all fell desperately in love with each other. With thee, too; for I told them so much of thee, and drew thee with such tender minuteness that they knew thee and loved thee and cheerfully consented that thou shdst. be of the party.

Today I have been all day moving, – 'tis so hard to do aught in Babylon! and will be henceforth at " 195 Dean St, Brooklyn." I hope now to settle down for a week or two, and get time to accomplish somewhat, and to write thee many things. I am now just leaving the St. Nicholas, to go across the river.

— So, – O well-beloved, how well-beloved Wife! fare-thee-well, God keep thy sleep and light thy dreams this night, and

---

to Theodore Thomas. He, however, tried to persuade him to stay or rather return to Balto.

" ' I think Sid would like us here, if he knew us better: at any rate he would have one Friend whose heart and soul, whose powers physical and mental (tho' feeble) would ever be exerted on his best behalf.' "

[100] Lanier's maternal uncle, William Henry Anderson, had died on Jan. 28, 1850, leaving a widow (Lydia Helen Haworth Anderson), one of Lanier's first teachers, who had later married Ronald McDonald. (Some years after Lanier's death the McDonalds were living in Grinnell, Iowa, where Mrs. McDonald died in Apr. or May, 1888.)

wake thee after the morrow is come with some sweet memory of thy

Lover.

To Mary Day Lanier

N. Y. Oct. 4. '73

I am just come from Foster's at Perth Amboy, and after a desperate run over town to attend to some necessary matters, have but three minutes to spare before going back. For they insisted I must come back for a Sunday with them, and there are reasons why I shd. go.

I played for them last night, and " Blackbirds " fell like a bombshell in the camp, exciting them to more enthusiasm than I have ever seen them display.

Thine, of Janie's death,[101] is here. I will write our dear Hal Monday.

I enclose Wysham's last.

O how my heart longs for thee! God envelope thee in some fervent sphere of Love, and keep thee and my little thee-'lings so, singeth the heart of thy

Lover.

To Mary Day Lanier [102]

N. Y. Oct. 6th 1873

O my Heart, O my Heart, how will I live longer if I cannot kiss thy hand ? Meseemeth that all life hangeth upon thine instant presence. Large Eyes, large Brows, look down on my soul from some divine height of dream-land this night, and comfort my thirsty-love.

″

″

Hither came I from Perth Amboy this morning, having spent a lovely Sunday there yesterday, dividing myself betwixt

[101] Janie Taliaferro, wife of Harry Day, died on Oct. 1, 1873, leaving a three-months-old daughter (see Mary Day Lanier's letter of Oct. 3, 1873).

[102] Previously published, *Scribner's*, XXV, 626 (May, 1899); reprinted, *Letters* (New York, 1899), pp. 75-76.

Foster's and Parkman's people.   Park lives there , in a charming
house, with his wife and his four pretty daughters.   They were
all sweet and cordial; we had a great exposition of good music:
the bay was beautiful, filled with white-sailed boats gliding past
lovely green hills and noble trees and smooth lawns: and the
sun gave the trembling waters a warm kiss that was a whole
afternoon long : – and in the midst of all my soul was so full,
so full of thee that I had nearly died of longing, being unable
to endure so much beauty without that Enlargement of my
soul which *thou art*.

Arriving in town this morning I rushed over here, to Brooklyn,
changed my dress, and went to Mr. Mcdonald's (Aunt Helen's
husband), who took me, by previous arrangement, to play for
Mr. [Frederic] Schwaab, the Musical Critic of the N. Y. Times.
We arrvied at Mr. S.'s in a fierce storm of wind and rain, got in,
and met Mr. S. – a dapper little young man, supposed to possess
supernatural knowledge in the matter of Italian Operas, being
hand-in-glove with Mantgek, and rejoicing in all manner of
souvenirs from the great artists – wh. he exhibited to us.   I
played him Blackbirds, and the Swamp-Robin; whereat he was
greatly stricken, expressing himself in fair terms and allowing
himself to be drawn into as much enthusiasm as was consistent
with his Exalted Position.   I am to go again, when he will have
an entire afternoon; and meantime have left some music for
his sister to practice on the piano.   Before I commenced to play
we had a triangular talk in which my Critic did me the honor
to expound some very orthodox theories in regard to the flute: –
which I straightway proceeded to upset with all the pleasure
in the world, by practical arguments.   He was exceedingly kind
and polite, and I have to thank Mr. McDonald very much for
the meeting, which was arranged by McD. entirely without
my knowledge.
    Thou couldst never believe how my good Aunt Helen has
completely fallen in love with me, and with thee, – whom she
knoweth, by my representation, full well.   She is all agog with
pretty plans for my welfare: and believeth that I am a great
genius and artist.   All this maketh me to be happy as a Child,
and I indulge my delight in it quite without *arrières pensées* of
any sort.

Tomorrow I am going to call on Mr. Weber, and present my letter: [103] next day on Mr. Levett, (to whom I have a letter from Mr. Hamerik) and Mr. Eben: and on Thursday night I am to meet a lot of musical people by arrangement of Aunt Helen.

So. ————————————————————————

My poor dear Hal ! How full is my heart, of him, and how I long to place my arms around his neck ! Comfort thou him, – as I know thou wilt, indeed.   I cannot write more, now. Heaven be about thee, as a light-blush lieth about a star,– saith thy

Lover.

To Mary Day Lanier

Brooklyn, Oct. 8th 1873

My poor Heart, how overwrought thou art! Thy letter showeth too much excitement. O if I cd. rest thee a moment, – thine head, thine heart, thine hand, – thy most sweet head, thy most loving tender heart, thy faithful musicfull hand!

I pray thee, Sweetheart, get thee into some quiet place, and say to thyself that God is King and Master, ordering all things, and ordering them *well*. CONCERN NOT THYSELF TOO DEEPLY: thy heart is of too delicate tissue to bear the greatness and the honesty of thy wonderful loves, if these be strained too long. What a lover thou art! And, O my dear Lady, how dearly, how dearly do I love thy loving love-worthiness!

I telegraphed thee yesterday that I was in favor of the Brunswick move for a few months. There are many reasons, outside of the main one of being a comfort to our poor Hal and a solace to thy good father, why this arrangement shd. be made. It will remove the necessity of my coming back to find thee a place in Atlanta: it will give thee and my darlings a chance to pass a month or two of winter without those distressing colds: and finally it will diminish my outgo. This last consideration is of a serious nature in the present crisis.

---

[103] The letter from Wysham, partly quoted in note 99, above.

I have such a fair presentiment of leading thee into some freer and happier life, – if I can but tide over the desperate shoals of this necessarily inactive preliminary period. How my heart burns to do this, – how my soul aches to bring thee among the people who cd. minister to thy long-unsatisfied needs, among the beautiful things of art, among the great inspiring works of man, among the noble and far-stretching glories of nature: how desperately I have struggled and am struggling to accomplish this: how many obstacles (whereof thou wot'st not) try to break my heart; how many agonies and writhings and humiliations my soul endures silently, and must yet endure ere the end be reached: – these things I will not detail to thee. They all come for want of a little money: – and I mention them simply in order that thou mayst have the additional consolation, – in the loving sacrifice which carrieth thee to B'k – of knowing that thou art also helping one who loveth thee with so overmastering passion that thy name is to him a divine talisman, thy kiss a divine glory, and thy love a divine Church wherein he hideth his heart from all evil and sorrow.

"

"

No, thou canst not take the baby: 'tis Janie's request that Gussie [Lamar Ogden] rear it, and that is sacred: moreover Dr. Hall declareth that thy health wd. be utterly ruined in attempting to nourish two: therefore hide this sorrow in thy heart, like the great-heart Lady, the open-armed Sister, the worshipful much-enduring wife, that thou art.

"

"

Let us name the boy Wysham Lanier! [104] and have Harry Wysham for his godfather! 'Tis a lovely name: and this man hath been a friend of friends: and I think, from some expressions he hath let fall, he wd. keenly like such a thing as to have this namesake (of course I have not mentioned it to him).

[104] Lanier's third son, born June 28, 1873, had at first been named for his great-uncle, William Lanier (see Lanier's letter to his father, July 4, 1873, above). In a letter of Sept. 22, 1873, Mary Day Lanier had written her husband suggesting that Henry C. Wysham, his new musical friend in Baltimore, should be the boy's godfather, "for this boy beginneth the Art-epoch in thy life." Lanier's counter-suggestion in the present letter was accepted, and the son was christened Henry Wysham Lanier.

Write me hereanent: and agree with me that this is a happy inspiration.

″

———

″

Enclosed I pray thee find a lovely fern, wh. was brought from San Domingo by a gentleman on the Samona Bay expedition, and given to Aunt Helen by him. She sendeth it to thee, with all manner of love. When thou shalt get time, write a brief little note, of thy sweet sort, to her. How thou wdst. like her! She thinketh and loveth all that I do. ″⁄″ Mr. McDonald reporteth the Times Critic as declaring that he hath never heard such flute-playing as mine.

I have nothing special to report to thee today, as to musical advancement. I pray thee kiss my dear Brother Harry many times for me. 'Tis a great, noble soul: and my heart yearneth *so* after him! God grant some happy issue to my labor, that so I may have opportunity to minister to this sore heart; as I wd. fain do.

″⁄″ I hope to get some money to thee in a few days: $150.

″⁄″ Thou wert better burn this letter of thy fine pastor.[105] When I think of him, I wonder at the poor narrow cold life I lived in Macon, – looking at it from the standpoint of the friendship which has given me so much pleasure since then, and of the beginning art-life wh. hath seemed to liberate my soul from a thousand cold bands. O Wife, Wife, how happy cd. I be, with thee by me, as *thine* artist, *thy* poet, *thy*

Lover!

TO MARY DAY LANIER [106]

Brooklyn, Oct. 10th 1873

How can there be any moment in the day when thou sittest not visibly on thy queen's-throne in my heart's foreground and smilest down to me the inspiration and the reward of work ?

---

[105] A letter from the Rev. Mr. Rees, giving an account of the death of Janie Taliaferro Day; it had been inclosed in Mary Day Lanier's letter to her husband, Oct. 3, 1873.

[106] Excerpt previously published, *Scribner's*, XXV, 626 (May, 1899); reprinted, *Letters* (New York, 1899), p. 76.

Thou art so lovely to me: and there is nothing sweet nor good in me that hath not burgeoned on some stem of *thy* planting in my soul.

"

———————

"

So thou hast been ill, and hast needed thy lover ? – I can not think about this.

"

———————

"

No, I will not write thee another Jeremiad, my last was full-enough of it. I have not a solitary trouble which does not come from the need of money, – twelve hundred dollars would make me the happiest king on earth ! – why then shd. I weary thee with details ? Most of my time and strength go towards the task of tiding over until there shall be some regular income. It *was* my hope to get an engagement as concert-soloist with Theodore Thomas : but he left town before I could find him. This I hoped wd. bridge over the time between now and the middle of November when the Peabody Orchestra-Arrangement will Commence – if it Commences at all. This was the only Concert-party I cared much to go with. I observe, however, that Camilla Urso (the violiniste) has made up a party, to go on a concert tour. She has already started: but I am told she is to be here next Sunday, and I will make a desperate effort to see if I cd. make a short engagement with her. I hope for nothing from this, however, as in all probability her arrangements are entirely completed, programmes printed, &c. Failing that, I may go into an Orchestra for a little time: but that is not likely, for no leader cares to engage a player who can not stay more than a month.

Meantime I devote myself to making friends among all sorts of people. Last night a party of some twenty people assembled at the house of one of Aunt Helen's friends in 23rd Street, to hear me play: They were all astonished and delighted, and testified the same by the most unequivocal tokens. They were pleasant people, and I enjoyed myself much among them.

My triumphs continue. Today a letter from good Harry Wysham (which I will send thee tomorrow) tells me that he had just rec'd. one from Badger.[107] (I went to Badger's day before yesterday on business and found there a magnificent great silver Bass-Flute, running down to F below the staff: and on putting it to my lips drew forth the most ravishing notes I ever heard from any instrument: whereupon I dilated upon a wind of inspiration and did breathe out strains thereupon in such fashion that the workmen gazed and grew sympathetic, so that now when I go there they immediately bring me the bass-flute: – this is THY HUSBAND , – not *me* – that I am telling thee of, – dear.)

Wysham quotes from Badger's letter: " Lanier is remarkable, Lanier is astonishing, Lanier will knock spots out of our great flautists. But you ought to hear him play the bass-flute. You would then say, let me pass from earth with those tones sounding in my ears ! If he could travel with a concert-troupe and play solos on the bass-flute, I would get orders for 50 in a month ! " &c. But thou shalt have his letter.

I enclose a slip from the Baltimore American anent the Orchestra business.

I grieve over thy many trials: but my heart is not strong enough to think of them. I dare not think of them. I pray God give thee patience for a little while, and help me towards mine end, wh. will also be end to many of thy irksome ills.

Embrace my darlings. God can only know how I yearn to take them in my arms. Write me quickly whether we shall name the boy Wysham, so that I may surprise Harry with that.

Dear Love, dear Wife, may this night be about thee like the love of thy

Lover.

To Mary Day Lanier

Brooklyn. Oct. 13th 1873

My dear, magnificent boys, how hungry and thirsty my heart is for them ! Doth my Charles fly from the terrors of solitude as of yore, and chafe for " somebody to play with? " Doth my

---

[107] A. G. Badger, a flute manufacturer. He appears frequently in the letters, as Lanier had theories of flute construction which he tried to persuade Badger to adopt.

Sidney-elf squeal anon after the fashion of the sick pig, and
retireth he to the corner as often as he did aforetime? Doth
my great magnanimous Wysham-William breathe out love and
large-heartedness from all his splendid body and comfort thee
with prophecies – which are to him but recollections – of
heaven?

And dost thou, O my lovely *Mutterchen,* sit in midst of these
three, with all thy large eyes a-beam and thy tender ministries
a-shine, my central Sweet, my dearer Self, My One that art a
finer I than I ?

— It is thus I have pictured thee to them all at Perth Amboy.
Yesterday I went down, arriving at dark. I found Daisy at the
porch, who when she saw me coming up the street, ran to
meet me: a mark of favor which Cousin Lou declares is simply
wonderful from this most retiring of Daisies.[108] After a
charming tea, we all adjourned to Parkman's house, to have
some music, as his piano accorded better with the flute. I had
carried down my own flute and Badger's Bass-flute. So, through
the springy night, to Parkman's: where, opening the door without warning, we saw, through the hall, Park with all his family
at their tea. We incontinently rushed in upon them: and I
kissed all the way round, commencing with Cousin Sarah, and
presently encountering, to my great pleasure, Cousin Tibbie,
(Mrs. Seleninoff) who was down spending a day or two at
Park's. Thus we commenced a sweet, merry, homelike evening.
Presently, music was called for, whereupon Daisy, with the
piano, and I, with the flute, took the floor and kept it a long,
long time. We played Soussman's second " Soupir " in F; then
a couple of noble airs from Mendellsohn's Elijah which were
simply ravishing on my dear Silver-souled Silvertongue; then
I played " Blackbirds ": then Daisy and I a lovely Sonata of
Kücken: and so on; then we talked, Cousin Tibbie and I, and
Lou and I, of thee and thy boys, whereof I did paint some
pictures which must have been marvellous sweet since True
Love handled the brush and mixed the colors. Then, after
another shower of kisses, and enough love sent to thee to start
an ordinary life with,– back to Fosters, I mad with longing to

[108] The people mentioned in this paragraph were all relatives of Mary Day
Lanier. Parkman Higgins was the brother of Foster Higgins—both her first
cousins.

show thy loveliness to these people and to see them pour their love into thy receptive heart. Nellie, (a splendid girl of Parkman's) begs that thou wilt send me, for her, one of the pictures of thyself taken after thine illness,– the *spirituelle* head, thou knowest,– wherewith she hath fallen greatly in love. Lily also desireth a picture of Charles. Send me also one of the naked ones. — — I have done nothing particular today. – On looking at Wysham's letter I observe that on account of some things therein, it were better not to trust the same much to the mail: So, thou shalt see it some other day when I can put it into thy hands.

Ah, happy day, most brilliant of days,– when I *can* put aught into thy very, very hand, that I do worship each finger of ! Speed it, speed it, thou God that hast charge of Time ! crieth thy

Lover.

To Mary Day Lanier

Brooklyn, Oct, 14th 1873

Thou art suffering, thou art feeble, thou art overworked and worn, – and I cannot, cannot help thee.

— I cannot even tell thee what a tumult of love and anxiety and anguish possesseth my heart, as I think of thy long-suffering and thy trials.

Pity *me,* therefore, dear Twin, – for thou hast the pitous herte of that worshipful Nonne [109] whereof thou and I know – pity me, with all thy gentle greatness, that I am far from the only place in earth that my heart findeth rest in, being the place where thou art, – and that my hand cannot even be lifted to take from thy most dear shoulders a single moiety of thy burden. This is sorrow, indeed.

— But God is great; and wise, withal. God's will be done on earth, as it is in Heaven.

''

''

Thy father's letter, with postscript from Hal, came this morning, as also thy Card. I pray thee send me not cards: I

------

[109] The allusion is to Chaucer's description of the Nun in the Prologue to *The Canterbury Tales.*

can not bear that alien eyes should see thy dear messages: – tis a fancy, foolish an thou likest, – yet, send me no more cards: but if thou art pressed, as thou must be, for time, a single line of " I love thee, Sweetheart " on a scrap of unfolded paper, – in an envelope. I will not have thy dainty words eyed by Mrs. Prettyman and daughters!

———— I am well. Weight, today, 140 lbs. M͏r Lanier has returned from Europe. I have been playing some lovely duetts today with M͏r Latham, the flutist who travelled with the Pomeroy-Suedair Concert Troupe last winter. Further I have not advanced. It is now quite too late for me to make any engagements, here, if I go to Baltimore; which latter seemeth very likely, now. Embrace the little men for

thy
Lover.

To Mary Day Lanier [110]

Brooklyn, Oct, 15th 1873

Today, I have been playing a few duos with Mr. Eben: then to Aunt Helen's for a little chat, where she exhibited to me tickets to the Opera for tomorrow night, – *Die Zauberflöte* ! – in which Di Murska, Lucca, and Tamberlik,[111] all, appear; the arrangement being for me to take her (Aunt H. – *not* Di Murska nor Lucca): all of which is kind in the extreme; then down town, where I lunched; then to attend to some financial matters, in the course of which I was waylaid, on Wall Street, by Park Higgins, who made me walk up the Street with him what time he informed me that " Louise " (as he calls Miss Kellogg) [112] was to be here on Sunday next, and that he was proposing to arrange for me to play before her, his wife having

[110] Previously published, *Scribner's,* XXV, 626 (May, 1899); reprinted, *Letters* (New York, 1899), pp. 76-77.

[111] In the following letter Lanier gives an account of the performance of Mozart's opera and estimates of the singers: Ilma di Murska (1836-1889), coloratura soprano; Pauline Lucca (1841-1908), dramatic soprano; and Henrico Tamberlik (1820-1889), tenor.

[112] Clara Louise Kellogg (1842-1916), American soprano, who had made her debut in New York in 1861, and later in London. In 1874 she organized her own troupe to sing operas in English and conducted it successfully for a number of years.

already written her anent my style of playing: tho' I don't
anticipate much pleasure from the interview, for from all I can
hear of Miss Kellogg she is fearfully puffed up with conceit,
wonderfully wrong-notioned about music (She "don't like
Wagner" – for instance – "there is nothing in his operas for
the Prima Donna to do beyond the other singers:" and She
"don't like Theo. Thomas' Orchestra, they can't accompany
a singer at all!" and other the like deliverances) and, more
than all, despises the flute, having once given Mr. Eben a
fearful rebuff, telling him, after his most brilliant piece, that
"She didn't care to hear a man pumping wind into a tube!!"
Yet, – simply for the adventure of the thing – if they *do* arrange
the meeting, I'll go.

O, My Child, how I can play, with a couple of months'
practice! Thou wdst. not know my playing now for that wh.
thou heardst at Marietta. The instrument begins to feel me,
to grow lithe under my fingers, to get warmed to life by my
kiss like Pygmalion's stone, and to respond with perfect enthusiasm to my calls, even as thou dost always to all my demands
upon thee.
It is like thy Soul, dear Soul, made into Silver! How can the
people but respond, if I have thine exquisite inner Self speaking
by my lips!

Some nights ago, on entering a restaurant to get my tea, a
gentleman hastily arose and grasped my hand, – whom I soon
discovered to be our old acquaintance Maas, the tenor. He
seemed greatly pleased at seeing me: told me he was singing
in Trinity Chapel and belonged to a fine quartette Club, went
into raptures over my flute (wh. I had with me) and finally
begged that I wd. meet them at some time. Today the invitation
comes for Saturday night, and I'm going to accept, as I desire
to make as many musical acquaintances as possible.
A telegram from Hal this morning about the Coal lot, – from
Brunswick.
————"———— Thus, my life.
But O my God, how thirsty are my eyes for a sight of *thine*
eyes! God clear them of all clouds of trouble, and brighten
them with visions of His love and His glory, – humbly prayeth

Thine   Husband

To Mary Day Lanier [113]

Brooklyn, Oct. 17th 1873.

Tis but a little time I have to write thee, today, dear Heart: and to supplement my brief I send these fine sweet words of Ginna's. She talks as very few women talk to a *friend*: that is what it is, verily, and naught more than that: – friendship. There is a cool and sweet deliberation about these friendly words from a Woman that is enchanting to me. It is as different from the impetuosities of love, as a violet, with its limpid dew-drop, away down deep under cool fern-shades and rock-shadows and glen-silences, is different from a great red rose burning in the sun.[114]

I went last night with Aunt Helen to hear Die *Zauberflöte.* *That* was a mere farce: as indeed was all of it, save the singing of the two *prime donne,* and the chorus. Di Murska executed the most wonderful staccatos in the higher register (taking high F, (they say) at a leap, without an effort): and Lucca made all that *could* be made out of that poor bald music of Mozart's. Why do we cling so to humbugs? Mozart's music is not to be compared with Schumann's, or Wagner's, or Chopin's or Mendellsohn's, or Beethoven's. The "*magic flute*" in this opera made us laugh, and the sight of the animals (who are supposed to be charmed from their lairs by the tones of the "Magic flute") capering about the stage to the poor thin notes of the poor thin music was too absurd.

I am going up presently to see Mr Lanier and family.

God wrap thee and the boys in His Heart, crieth thine

Husband.

---

[113] Previously published, *Scribner's,* XXV, 626 (May, 1899); reprinted, *Letters* (New York, 1899), pp. 77-78.

[114] In reply Mary Day Lanier wrote on Oct. 25: "And *so*: thou art so careful as to reassure me about Ginna's fine letter! Why, Sidney! Or, was it thyself for whom the reassurance was worded? For I am *sure* that it would never have occurred to me to require it. I am almost tempted to tease thee – – – – but . . . [that] would be a shabby requital for the privilege of reading her noble letters."

To Mary Day Lanier

Brooklyn, Oct. 19th 1873

Last night I met the Symphonia Quartette Club, (of which
Mr. Maas is a member) at the house of Mr. McDonald (not
ours) in Madison Avenue. — I do protest, dear Love, that I can
never bring myself to cease feeling a certain sentiment of
hatred for myself, – when I hear all these delightful things,
and taste all these luxurious glories of wealth, – as last night
in that elegant house — without *thee.* I do not feel the soft
carpet beneath my foot, without an agony of yearning that
Life wd. allow me to smooth it, and soften it, thus, for *thy*
dear feet. If I sit in a Springy fauteuil, if I glance in the
brilliant mirrors, if I gaze on exquisite marbles and pictures,–
it is always with that *arrière pensée* of *thee.*
And so, it was with thee filling all my heart and brain, thee
throbbing in my pulses and tingling in my hands, that I moved,
talked and played last night.   How else cd. I but please the
folk? Thou knowest what a stony and *nil admirari* flock these
hard-eyed rich New Yorkers are: and therefore thou wilt be
pleased when I tell thee that thine inspirations did evoke even
enthusiasm from these passionless ones, and turned the stones
to life. — This quartette is to give a concert, in Brooklyn, on
the 12th November; and, they asked me to play a couple of solos,
thereat, with such evident sincerity that I cd. not but consent.
—   I desire some day soon, to run up the Hudson and see
thy Mrs. James. I heard of her through Cousin Sarah (Parkman's wife) who had met her some days ago. Cousin Sarah
told me that Mrs. James, on learning that Cousin Sarah was
connected with *thee,* became greatly warmed up and made a
thousand inquiries about thee, declaring that she had never
loved any one as she had loved thee. This makes me desirous
to see her. Thou hast not writ of Wysham-William ! Wh. shall
it be? All things considered I vote for Wysham.
Some time next week I hope to send thee ample supplies
financial. I fear some other arrangements I had made for thee
have not been carried out. 'Tis a dreadful time, as to such
matters. Ordinary methods of money-raising are entirely
abandoned. The banks here will not loan money on any

security whatever, to any body at all, since all feel themselves in the dark and sacrifice all friendship in order to protect themselves. But I think I will succeed in some plans, next week. If it shd. be delayed until week after next, be not dismayed. I will be sure to arrange everything. Write me of all that is needed: I do not mean details: but simply cast up in thine own mind, when thou hast leisure, everything needed to clear off all scores in Marietta, and let me know the gross amount.

I have not heard finally from Harry Wysham abt. the Balto. arrangement, but I think now there is every probability I will be engaged there for the winter.

"

"

  O Wife, dear loveliest One, cd. I put my love and longing into any sensible form, I think thou wdst. needs be bodily drawn hither to me over the waters and the mountains, by the might and huge in-grasping *vis* thereof.

— Meantime, 'till God shall smile, – that is, 'till I shall see thee – I lie forever at thy feet in the spirit, and look upward into thine eyes as into Heaven.

For the morning heavens, before the sun is up, have no gray so lustrous, so immaculate, so silver-starred, so full of half-seen, vanishing angels, so pure with charitable dews and so luminous-warm with the coming passion of the Sun, – as have thine eyes, to thy

    Lover — .

To Mary Day Lanier

       Brooklyn, Oct. 21st, 1873.

  Well, either " Wy," or " Sham," or " Wyshe " is better than " Bill ": and " Bill " he would infallibly be, as was that same " brave, sweet uncle " before him. Moreover, the project of naming him William — as I wrote it to Grandmother — was purely hypothetical, and was subject to alteration, and I do not think there is enough feeling about it to produce any pang: surely no pang that will at all equal Wysham's pleasure. Know that the loss of his three boys hath gone very deeply into his heart, and I think this fact will add much to his gratification in this partial preservation of his name. I meant it should be simply Wysham Lanier. Write me thy final approval — if thou dost approve — and I will write Wysham about it.

Eh bien, eh bien, what a revelation of sweet womanliness, of music-full spirituality, and of youthful beauty have I had in thy pretty cousin Lucy, — Park's oldest daughter! She hath been staying with her cousin Louise Kellogg in Philadelphia, while the latter hath been singing there with her opera troupe. I ran down to Perth Amboy on Sunday and met Lucy for the first time. We played together, and although her execution is limited, I have never found any accompanist like her, save thee. She hath much of thy delicacy of sentiment, and keen piercing into the glory of a musical work: and like thee she needeth but a hint, to her quick intelligence. Add to this a lovely hand, a soft pathetic voice, a figure somewhat *petite,* perfect manners, a singularly dignified bearing, and elevation of thought, — and thou hast this little woman. Thou art the only lady in the world that could keep me from falling quite in love with her.

Sleepeth the long lady on my cot? [115] And groaneth the same, squeaking withal, under this precious weight, as of old under my carcase? I fancy that canvas saying with Trinculo in the play, Well, Misery makes us acquainted with strange bed-fellows. Seriously, I do love this good female Longitude for helping thee in thy need.

Tonight, for the first time since I came hither, I indulged myself; stealing off all alone, I went to a concert in Steinway Hall in which Wieniawski [116] was to play. His execution was wonderfully neat, clean and beautiful, and his sentiment mostly very good. He did not get out the liquid, amber tone, like that monkey Vieuxtemps; he played with too much vibration, and in very *agitato* passages the somewhat elephantine shakings of

---

[115] On Oct. 13, 1873, Mary Day Lanier had written that Miss Rebecca Fraser had been assisting her with the care of the children ("sleeping on thy cot"), since she had been forced to fire her negro nurse Ellen.

Trinculo, who is inaccurately quoted below, was the jester in *The Tempest.*

[116] Henri Wieniawski (1835-1880), Polish violinist and composer, was making his first American tour at this time, 1872-1873, with the celebrated Russian pianist, Anton Rubinstein. Henri Vieuxtemps, to whom he is compared, had been heard by Lanier in New York in 1870.

his head, contrasted with the small tones of the violin, made the latter seem still smaller and somewhat disappointing. His staccato passages were too exquisite, and whenever he allowed himself to play a pure and unvibrating *cantabile* he gave me keen delight. The balance of the concert was simply absurd.

And now, O my heart's dear Heart, fare thee sweetly and serenely through the night, and may some tranquil Angel, of most rare fancy, stand at the helm of thy dreams, — crieth to thee thy

Lover.

To Mary Day Lanier [117]

Brooklyn, Oct. 26th 1873

O, wert thou but by me this wonderfully lighted morning, and couldst thou but sail with me over the flashing waters out yonder, then were time only delight, and space only a pleasure-ground, and life only glory. To look into thine eyes, and thence into heaven: to feel thy hand-clasp steadily amid the fitfuller caresses of the wind and the sunlight: to be still and at rest in the reverend sweetness of an inner perception of thy presence, and to have at the same time the fair actual confirmations of thy bird-wing brows, thy long hair, thy very, very lips: to —— but, My God ! – I will break mine own heart with this movement. ————

—   Yesterday I played duos – some lovely Kuhlau's – with Manuel Pascual, Wysham's Cuban friend. He received me very cordially: and we played very well together : but we will never harmonize *very* intimately, for while he has taste enough to like the best music, yet there is a certain something, – a flame, a sentiment, a spark kindled by the stroke of the soul against sorrow as of steel against flint – which he hath *not,* and the want of which will forever keep him from penetrating into *the deepest* of music. He is warmly enthusiastic, and wd. have played the whole afternoon with me, but I was obliged to leave, to meet an engagement.

[117] Excerpt previously published, *Scribner's*, XXV, 627 (May, 1899); reprinted, *Letters* (New York, 1899), p. 78.

Thou wilt be glad to know (to whom cd. I say such a thing but thee ? – and then, only because I know thou wdst. be glad to have assurances, from a *disinterested observer,* concerning *thy husband*) that, having now seen and played with the very best players in New York, I am of the honest opinion, after a critical and severe comparison, that thy husband can do more than they can.

———— Harry Wysham hath thy letter, and declareth, amid much glowing commendation thereof, that it hath made him love thee nigh as much as he loveth thy

Lover .

To Virginia Hankins

Brooklyn, Oct. 26th 1873

How can I describe to you, dear Friend, the lofty solace wh. your friendship brings me! Indeed, when it places in my hand a gift so rare as your last letter, – a gift wh. no other woman but you *could* have presented, a gift compounded of sunlights, of woods, of tuberoses, of maiden-reveries, of keen intellectual brilliancies, of dainty and most pure womanliness, of affectionate inquiries, and of friendly prayers for me, — what can I do but vainly long to shower a thousand testimonials of grateful delight upon the white hands and the whiter Soul that between them have wrought so sweet a thing?

Vainly long: – for alas, I am in Babylon, hot, strenuous, forcing, passionate Babylon, where True-Love must fight for itself every moment of every day and of every night or else go down in a pitiful surrender to False-Love, where Artifice compels even the modest and simple-minded people to go pranked in her guise by visiting upon them the punishment of conspicousness if they do not, and where a thousand necessities which are *not* necessities but which God for some unfathomable reason allows to seem so, imperatively demand of man many moments which he could otherwise devote to those whom he loves better than himself. Ah, how many things I desire to say to you! You are so keen, so incisive, so true-sighted; and I wd. *so* like to ask you of some matters that a man does not see through,

as a woman. But Time scarcely touches the hot world with his
feet, here. I arise in the morning, I sigh: – hey, presto, whirr! –
it is night, and I go to bed, tired as if I had held the world up
all day like Atlas.

Sometimes, nevertheless, I say, when midnight bedtime
comes, – well, tired or not, I will write Little Dainty One,
tonight: – but then, no, says my heart, write no tired letters to
her, give her a fresh moment, or none.

Thus, dear Friend, you hear from me seldom. Pray believe
that my heart sends you frequent messages, that naught fails
you save the tired hand, and that the time will presently come,
I hope, when some of my projects (of wh. I must not tell you
now, for they might fail, and then your friendship wd. have
another burden) will blossom into many fair things, – into
none fairer than the leisure to talk freely with one who gives
me infinite courage and infinite patience and infinite pleasure,
in allowing me to call myself her

Friend.

To Mary Day Lanier

Brooklyn, Nov. 3rd 1873

I came up from Perth Amboy, today, where I spent Saturday
night and Sunday.[118] I do get on famously with them all, there:
particularly with pretty Cousin Lucy, – where-anent they do cry
that thou wert better look after thine own ! Foster's family
have moved up to town.
I have some cold, — the weather hath been marvellous raw –
and feel not quite so brilliant as aforetime.
Thy cousin Mel (short for Pamela – I had mistaken the name
for *Nell,* or *Nellie,* and wrote thee wrongly –: Mel is Parkman's
oldest daughter, and a rare fine Creature) hath conceived a
violent passion for thee, moved thereunto by my description of
thee, by sundry bits of thy letters wh. I have showed her, and
by thy *sick* picture. She continually asketh, hast thou never
another of these same ?
—   O my dear Young Men ! My heart is so full of their

[118] Lanier had also spent part of the previous week there, Oct. 26-28 (see his
letter of Oct. 29, 1873, to his wife, here omitted).

loveliness. I do not see any like them, here. My arms ache to fold them all three. Fold thou them, for me, dear *Mutterchen*.

――――― God light thee a special heaven of love and faith and peace in thy heart, dear Wife, dear Wife, – prayeth thine

Husband.

To Mary Day Lanier

Brooklyn, Nov. 5th 1873

Distress not thy dear heart, that thy money goeth; money is made to spend: and, No ! thou art not a *costly luxury* [119] at a thousand times the price: —— and thou shalt have the needful amount by Nov. 15th.

――――― Last night I dined with the Winslows,[120] who have moved to their beautiful town-house for the winter. I had carried my flute by previous arrangement: and after dinner, Mrs. Edward Winslow, (– a lithe fragile little blonde, not long out of Vassar, young wife of Mr. James Winslow's oldest son, built altogether in face and form after the fashion of thy Mrs. Chandler, of old) and I moved upon the enemy with Piano and Flute. Our first piece,– the *Ave Maria* that thou knowest – made the house (in professional parlance) rise at us, and one gentleman, moved by much Champagne as well as music, drave across to us at the piano and swore that he had never heard the flute played before. Then we played and played: Songs, Gounod's Meditation on Sebastian Bach, (didst thou not hear me in the night begging for thee and calling thee with this most passionate music?) Waltzes, Macbeth, (in wh. thou hast spoiled me for all other accompanists) German Songs, Claribel's Songs, Last Rose of Summer, Sweet Home, and I know not what, finally closing with Ernst's Elegie.

— I have much to do, today. So, fare-thee-well, dear Sweetheart, yea, God fare along with thee, as it were a strong tenderhearted One leading a dainty pilgrim by the hand, – prayeth thy

Lover.

[119] Mary Day Lanier had signed her "Business" letter of Oct. 31, 1873: "Thy *Costly Luxury*."
[120] James Winslow had married J. F. D. Lanier's daughter.

To Mary Day Lanier

Brooklyn, Nov. 6th 1873

In the morning I awake, and look about for thee, and find thee not, and sigh: then I plunge into a rush and whirl, – and behold it is night, again. Thus drift the days with a headlong and passionate velocity past me.

Aye, *past* me: – for they do not carry me along, I am not part of these days, my heart is not in them, – – – *thou* art not by! Spite of their fierce rushing, – how long, long it is since I have seen thee ! O dear eyes, my twin dawns, mixt of the night's mystery, the day's revelation, the dew's charity, the stars' subtlety, the sun's passion,–O ye saintly Two, so soft and large and loving-piteous, when, when will your sacrosanct radiances shed themselves again upon me, and dissolve me into a pure spirit, and rest me and renew me ?

"

"

I have called on Judge Herring. I saw him, and Miss Mary (Harriet?). The Judge seemed about as when I last saw him: I could detect little change save a more palpable failure of memory, evinced by his propensity to ask the same question (and his utter obliviousness of receiving the same answer) a great many times in conversation. They all sent a-many loves to thee, and I did my best to impress upon them thy constant love, spite of the many occupations which prevented thee from writing them. Some time next week I will do my best to see thine other people.

Tonight, they have some friends visiting at Perth Amboy, and by previous arrangement I am to go down for a musical evening. Tomorrow-night I am engaged to the Winslows for a family festivity in honor of the sixteenth birthday of Miss Katie Lanier. Next night (Saturday), a grand musicale at Pasquale's, (the Cuban who "worried" Harry Wysham so, once, as H. W. wrote me), when we are to play trios, duetts, and solos: Sunday morning to church with Charles Lanier, and dinner with the same thereafter: Sunday afternoon (I think) Mr. Cortada, (Organist) is going to perform a grand Mass of Beethoven in his Church for my especial benefit: – and thus I could keep up the tale for ten days more. All this is besides much extra running hither and thither.

―――″――― God arrange thy days and nights about thee like alternate petals of some heavenly flower curved around the sweet perfume-spirit in the core thereof, prayeth thy

Lover.――――――

To Mary Day Lanier

Brooklyn, Nov. 7th 1873

I have just come from the Clarendon, where I have been for two hours playing Schubert's Songs with Miss Kirtland and Miss Lucy Higgins. I left *them* with flaming cheeks, Lucy's being cooled however with a rain of tears she wept while I played the *Ave Maria* of Schubert: and as for me I cannot tell when my heart has throbbed so big and fast before: for my Silver-Soul, my Other-*Thee*, spoke surely as never flute spake before, and would have melted the meanest heart in the land.
― O, can I not, some time, play these things to thy very ears, as now I play them to thy Spirit's ears?
―― I go in a little while to Pasquale's musicale: and cannot now send thee more than this brief word.
―― These be but slim letters, Sweet-heart: *Thou* wilt allow for great weariness. From *thee*, I take a little rest, knowing thou wilt give it gladly. My cold is better.
―― God dissolve thee, thou Pearl, in the wine of His love,– prayeth

Thy   Lover.――

To Mary Day Lanier [121]

[Brooklyn] Nov. 16th 1873

O my unforgetting Sweet, O my Trusty-Soul, O my Thrice-Beloved, O my Wonderful-hearted One, O my beautiful Spirit: thou dear inward Energy of all my work, thou clear spring of

[121] Previously published, *Scribner's*, XXV, 627 (May, 1899), combined with letter of Oct. 26, above; reprinted, *Letters* (New York, 1899), pp. 78-80.

my best plans, thou sweetest End of my sweetest hopes and highest Love of my highest loves, thou that art at once my blesséd Life and blesséd Death for I live utterly to thee and so die utterly to all others, thou that being my wife and my Worship art thus at once my Earth and my Heaven, thou that in making thyself Nothing for love of me hast made thyself All in my love. Thou that art in very truth my Dainty consummate Sum and Whole of everything, — hear thou the prayers and adorations that go from me to thee this day, vouchsafe some little sweet answer and responsive smile thereto that shall come into my heart subtly like a little sudden wind that ariseth and breatheth upon a flower and dieth, project thy great and strong love in fashion of a marvellous wall about my heart, utterly be about me and keep me and let me be throughout all this day nothing save only Thine.

—— For this day I have by main force cut out from all the Cruel days that have been betwixt me and thee with fullness of labor and weariness of body, and I have dedicated this sweet twelve hours to one delicious dream and meditation upon thee. *Ay de mi*; Heart, Heart, Heart, if I could spend them all gazing into thy frank and faithful eyes !

"
_____
"

As for money, there hath been nothing but disappointment after disappointment, it hath seemed to me as if God had turned over my plans for the nonce to the Devil and this latter had amused himself with me in an inexhaustible round of frolicsome malignities and thwartings. The hopes, the fears, the angers, the humiliations, the agonies, the intangible insults which I could not resent, the quite tangible failures which I could not prevent,— how can I bear to tell thee of these ? I cannot. I simply hint that they have been, — because thou art my dear, dear Wife. and thou hast the right to my whole life. Moreover I wd. not nave thee believe that the small disjointed scrawls that have latterly come from me to thee, were due to any ordinary fatigue — I had not written Harry Wysham a scratch in two weeks. I did not even know that half so much time had passed. I enclose his letter wh. awoke me to that melancholy fact. Thou wilt see that the Orchestra is to be formed: but to last only four months, – and each player to get only $60 a month. Yet I am going, without hesitation: for (1st) this will occupy but a little time, and 2nd, I can largely supplement the poor pay with a pupil or two and in other ways, and 3rd it will give me a foothold which I can likely step from to something better, – for the Peabody Academy is a literary as well as musical institution, – and they don't know all my accomplishments yet ! There's a brag: – but thou hast a lover's soul, and I will not scratch it out.

—   Until, therefore, I can get there (to Baltimore) and go to work, and see my probable income, I can not write more definitely in this regard. Thou great trusting Heart, with how many cruel *indefinitudes* hast thou been compelled to tantalize the cravings of thine eagerness !

—   Wysham demands (this is *my* term, – he *begs*) that the boy be called " Henry Wysham Lanier ": and I do not object: for that will bring [that] [122] large Soul, our [dear] *other* Harry, into our midst more often, by the calling of his name. What thinkest thou ?

——   I telegraphed thee on Thursday that I wd. send funds for all obligations in Marietta to Dr. D[unwoody] on or before the 20th *inst*. Of course I am not going to tell thee the agonies I underwent, in coming to this pass: I desired that, if thou shdst. be all packed for moving, as I supposed, thou [shdst.] go on to thy friends with free heart. I so hope thou *didst* go. I await news of thee with such anxiety as I cannot describe. Indeed I cannot think hereupon.

"

"————I have had some pleasant musical successes. I played on Wednesday night at a concert in Brooklyn, before some 800 people, and made some stir, particularly in the papers, – notices whereof I send thee herein.[123] Of course, the

---

[122] A corner of the MS has been torn off; three missing words have been restored by conjecture.

[123] Five clippings from New York newspapers of Nov. 13, 1873, noticing this concert survive in the Charles D. Lanier Collection, Johns Hopkins University. They are labelled by Lanier: the New York *Commercial Advertiser, Sun, Evening Mail,* and *Times,* and the *Brooklyn Eagle.* They speak of him as " a flutist of remarkable skill and purity of style," " an admirable artist . . . thoroughly conversant with his instrument," " a performer of fine taste and culture," and " a Southern gentleman, whose name is known to some of our readers as the author of a pleasant, wild story of love and war in the South." According to

talk in the notices about a *debut*, the *debutant*, &c. is simply absurd: 'twas no *debut* at all, I only played for the fun of it and by way of feeling the pulse of these audiences in a quiet way (for these little concerts are not ordinarily heard of at all in the newspapers) before venturing to prescribe for the big music-sick patient of New York. When I am ready to come out, which will be after I practice four months in Baltimore – I shall make my debut under the auspices of the Philharmonic, or of Theo. Thomas, – or not at all. Meantime, these notices will amuse thee. They are considered wonderfully flattering. There are so many aspiring musicians here, who work for years and years, and are never heard of at all.

Perhaps the most complete triumph I have had was on last Sunday evening, being over one Miss Alice Fletcher, – who is, by the way, a person much in the Arististic world, and is secretary of *Sorosis*, though certainly as unmasculine and as sweetly feminine and Truely womanly as one could desire.[124] She is, I am told, the intimate friend of Janauschek, – and has travelled much abroad. I wish I could spread before thee all the scene, which was very fine. But I cannot, for very weariness of my miserable right arm. Suffice it, that when I had played Blackbirds, and the Swamp-Robin, before her and an audience of some half-dozen more of cultivated people, the house rose at me: Miss Fletcher declared that nothing like it existed out of Wagner: that I was not only the founder of a School of music, but the founder of American music: that hitherto all American compositions had been only German music done over, but that these were at once American, un-German, classic,

the New York *Times*: "The most interesting incident was the début of . . . Mr. Sidney Lanier. . . . In the second part of the program the débutant was down for a composition of his own, which he names 'Blackbirds.' It is a poetic fantasie upon the strain of the Southern blackbird, which it transforms into wild, sweet music, and, as a composition it is of classic purity, and decided originality."

There also survive in the Charles D. Lanier Collection an unidentified clipping indicating that the notice in the New York *Times* was reprinted in a Baltimore newspaper, announcing that Lanier had been engaged by Hamerik for the Peabody Orchestra, and a program of the concert.

[124] Alice Cunningham Fletcher (1838-1923), ethnologist and pioneer writer on Indian music. "Sorosis" was a woman's club founded in New York in 1868, the first of any significance in America.

The allusion in the following sentence to Janauschek, the actress, was probably prompted by the fact that Mary Day Lanier had seen her in a performance of *Deborah* in Macon the previous winter (see her letter to Lanier, Feb. 3, 1873).

passionate, poetic, and beautiful: that I belonged to the Advance-Guard, which must expect to struggle but which could not fail to succeed, – with a hundred other things, finally closing with a fervent expression of good wishes in which all the company joined with such unanimity and fervor that I was in a state of embarrassment wh. thou mayst imagine !   I wrote her a note next day, desiring to make some more articulate response than blushes, to her recognition: and I have a lovely note from her in reply which *thou* shalt have in a day or two.[125]

—   On Wednesday I played flute trios with Mr Pasquale and Mr. Yzquierdo. We sat down to a bound volume of Kuhlau's trios at three O'clock, and played without leaving our seats until five. They gave me first flute. Dear Wife, dear Wife, how I craved thee, how I agonized for thee, as we breathed these miraculous harmonies and unearthly-dainty melodies ! I had taken Mr. McDonald there, with me. He could scarcely contain himself, – newspaper hack as he is ! – and his great eyes got as deep as the sea,– and nigh as moist.   Think, – Mr. Yzquierdo, who has been playing in N. Y. for years among the very best professional flutists, and who is certainly the best reader I ever saw, – says *I* am the best *he* ever saw, – I, who surely as thou knowest have scarcely read a half-dozen new pieces in any year of my musical life, – before this last month or so ! How splendid it is: I could never tell thee how I enjoy such things: for it is not I, but always *thy* husband,– in whom I have much interest.

——   And now, enough, this time. I shall dream of thee, shall kneel to thee, shall retrace thy features on my heart, shall fancy the waving of thy garments, shall light my soul's darkness with the gray glory of thine eyes from afar and feed my Sense's hunger with the red sweetness of thy distant lips, shall love thee, shall bless thee, shall pray for thee and to thee, shall utterly adore thee, – all this day, being for this holy length of time nothing more, nor less, nor other, than

Thy

Lover.

[125] Alice Fletcher's reply (Nov. 14, 1873) to Lanier's letter is reproduced in *Letters* (New York, 1899), pp. 79-80, note. She wrote in part: "Your flute gave me that for which I had ceased to hope, true American Music, and awakened within my heart a feeling of patriotism that I never knew before."

To Mary Day Lanier [126]

Brooklyn, Nov. 17th [18th] 1873

Where art thou, this pallid, snow-covered morn, O Heart, O Heart? The earth is like a widow in white: – and my heart is like the earth, I am in a pale mourning for My dear Mate, O if I might but behold for one little moment the glory and the satisfaction of thine eyes !
How wholly I am thy lover ! I say to myself, – My Sweetheart would desire that I should be thus, that I should do thus, that I should say thus: — and thus am I, and do I, and say I. I am not a man, I am a *Love-of-thee* done into flesh.

"

———

"

Last night I played at another Church concert in New York City, far up town,[127] to a very pleasant audience, with very pleasant testimonials of success. My first piece – a Concertino, of Briccialdi's, (wh. thou hast never heard) – brought down the house, in an enthusiastic *encore,* to which I responded with the inevitable Blue Bells of Scotland. My last piece was the Swamp-Robin, wh. I only ventured as an experiment. 'Twas a curious psychologic study,– to note how it puzzled most of the audience, and how the few who *did* get into it, began, as it were, to look about them and to say, – like a man who has suddenly ridden into a strange and unexpected road – Heigh, heigh, what's this ? Somebody saith, Every original writer has to educate his readers, gradually, to himself. How true this is in New York ! Here, the people are at once the boldest and the timidest in the world. When The New presents itself, here, each one waits for the other one to pronounce decisively: of course, at first, no one speaks: finally some generous and open heart says, This is a good thing: and then straightway all the people join and push the good thing to heaven. Once give them

[126] Previously published, *Scribner's,* XXV, 627-628 (May, 1899) ; reprinted, *Letters* (New York, 1899), p. 81. (The date has been corrected from the evidence supplied in the following note.)
[127] The Free Church of the Holy Sepulchre, 74th St., between Lexington and 4th Avenues. A program of the concert, dated Nov. 17, 1873, has survived (Charles D. Lanier Collection, Johns Hopkins University).

a start, – these singular New Yorkers – and they will go any length.

—— I am very well. I pray thee distribute love and kisses to my father and Mama and Pringle.[128] Tell father I will write him in a day or two.

——" And now God make thee a special soft Spring, dear Heartsease, and wrap thee in it away from these biting airs, prayeth thy

Lover.

To Mary Day Lanier [129]

Brooklyn, Nov. 21st 1873

O Heartsease, I can but breathe thee a brief fervent aspiration, this morning, – telling thee, betwixt two worship-ful sighs, that my Dane, Mr. Hamerik, was in New York, two days ago: that after a long search we found each other; that he behaved most beautifully and nobly to me, and offered to do everything in the world to make my stay in Baltimore pleasant; and that finally I concluded an engagement with him, as *Flauto Primo* in the Peabody Symphony Orchestra, for four months, commencing on the 1st Dec. prox°. We are to have four rehearsals a week, of two hours each, from twelve to two P. M: and one concert each week. This, you observe, only takes up some eleven hours (4 Rehearsals @ 2 hours each, and one concert @ (say) 3 hours) out of the week's time, and gives me a great deal of opportunity to write. I do not get as much pay as I hoped: my salary as Flauto Primo, and a solo or two (solos are paid *extra*) will barely bring out a hundred dollars a month. But I hope to make fifty more a month with a pupil or two: and then I can finish my darling Jacquerie midst of the great libraries. I am overjoyed at this prospect : and my dear Wysham already has his arms open, waiting for me x x x x

[128] Lanier assumed that his wife had already reached Macon on her way to Brunswick. Actually she did not leave Marietta until Nov. 21; and even then she stopped in Griffin to visit her friends the Munroes and the Kells, not reaching Macon until the end of the month (see Lanier's letter of Dec. 2, 1873, below, and Mary Day Lanier's letters of Nov. 8 and Nov. 30, 1873).
[129] Previously published, *Scribner's*, XXV, 628 (May, 1899); reprinted, *Letters* (New York, 1899), pp. 81-82. The last part of the MS is missing.

To Milton H. Northrup [130]

Brooklyn, Nov. 23rd 1873

My dear friend:

The cordial friendliness of your letter is so small consolation to me for the mournful impossibility of availing myself of your very kind invitation. I shd. take a world of pleasure in shaking your hand, in renewing my delightful acquaintance with your wife, and particularly in getting your baby to sleep, (– which latter operation I consider to be not far from the very acme and culmination of human delights: – more by token, I've three of my own, and I often get every one of them to sleep, on the same evening) :– but I'm just leaving town, and can't make time.

I shall be in Baltimore all the winter, and if any happy fate should blow you that way, I would be very glad to foregather with you. You should, in that event, send me your card through " H. C. Wysham, 41 Lexington St. Baltimore: " – an address that will always reach me.

Commend me, I beg you, to Mrs Northrop, and, in especial, to the baby; and believe me always

Yr friend

Sidney Lanier

To Mary Day Lanier

Baltimore, Nov. 29th 1873

O Wife !

Here, finally, is thy lover. He hath had his little fling at the people of Babylon: he hath measured his strength with the strong men thereof, the flute-players thereof, the artists thereof: he hath travelled a fearsome road there, hath suffered a thousand deaths there, hath seized many hearts there, hath had many triumphs there, hath toughened and seasoned his soul with all manner of strains and tests there: and, at last,

[130] Previously published, *Lippincott's Magazine*, LXXV, 313-314 (Mar., 1905).

having after a thousand disappointments, accomplished everything he expected (and in some particulars far more than he
could have hoped), he is here, worn somewhat, and tired, yet
with a heart full of energy and a brain full of a thousand plans
for a great and brilliant winter's work, with pen and flute.
Send him thy blessing, quickly, O brave Heart, O sweetest Soul
that God hath yet made, O thrice-lovable and thrice-beloved
Lady.

— The hardest strain of all was to sell the Policy.[181] But
I will not tear thee, *now,* with my agonies during that business.
That is gone: and I can not yet quite bear to think of it. Some
other time I will talk to thee of it. Now, I will but tell thee
that the proceeds (my share, *i. e., thy* share, *wh.* I have appro-
priated as it were mine) have just paid off all the obligations
I have incurred during the last eight months, including My
Silver Tongue, and my two fine professional suits of clothes.
These, then, are thine, and thy father's presents, — as I wrote
Harry to tell thy father.

—— Thou shdst. see thine in his rig *a la Concert.* The
Dutcher girls have quite flattered him into believing that he
is rather a passable monkey in his Swallow-tail and white tie.
Please send me here, (address care " H. C. Wysham, 41
Lexington St. &c.") gross amount due at Marietta. I have sent
funds to Dr. Dunwoody: but do not know whether I have sent
enough. I write my father today to hand thee $25, for thy
pocket money: and I also send thee herein a check for $50 wh.
thou canst have cashed at any of the Macon Banks.

— My dear Wysham had everything prepared for me here, –
even to securing nice room for me – and rushed into my arms
this morning, early. He forgets nothing, and arranges everything, with a precision as marvellous as it is friendly. I go to
my first rehearsal on Monday. Until then I occupy myself in
fighting a cold wh. I have not had time hitherto to look after.
The two days of rest from now to Monday will be simply delicious to me. Thou wdst. marvel if I shd. tell thee the work I
have done in the last seven weeks.

—— O how I stretch out my arms to thee, Wife, dear dainty
Lady, Sweetheart, Heartsease, Tuberose !

[181] A life-insurance policy belonging to Charles Day; it was sold as much to
assist Harry Day as the Laniers (see H. C. Day to Lanier, Nov. 23 and Dec. 7-10,
1873).

God take my solicitous tenderness for thee, and make it into an Angel, to sit by thee and tend thee and defend thee and comfort thee, is today's prayer of thy

Lover

Kiss Mama, and father & Pringle for me. I write father today.

ROBERT S. LANIER [132]

Baltimore, Md. Nov. 29th 1873.

My dear Father:
I have given your last letter the fullest and most careful consideration. After doing so: I feel sure that Macon is not the place for me. If you could taste the delicious crystalline air and the champagne breeze that I've just been rushing about in, — I am equally sure that, in point of climate, you would agree with me that my chance for life is ten times as great here, as in Macon.

Then, as to business. Why should I, — nay, how *can* I —, settle myself down to be a third-rate struggling lawyer for the balance of my little life,— as long as there is a certainty, almost absolute, that I can do some other things so much better? Several persons, from whose judgment in such matters there can be no appeal, have told me, for instance, that I am the greatest flute-player in the world: and several others, of equally authoritative judgment, have given me almost equal encouragement to work with my pen. (Of course, I protest against the necessity which makes me write such things, about myself: – I only do so, because I so appreciate the love and tenderness which prompt you to desire me with you, that I will make the fullest explanation possible of my course, out of reciprocal honor and respect for the motives which lead you to think differently from me.) My dear father, think how, for twenty years, through poverty, through pain, through weariness, through sickness, through the uncongenial atmospheres of a farcical college and of a bare army and then of an exacting business-life, through all the discouragements of being born

[132] Previously published, W. H. Ward, "Memorial," *Poems* (New York, 1884), pp. xx-xxi. The MS is not signed and the end of the letter is probably missing. R. S. Lanier's letter to which this is an answer has not survived.

on the wrong side of Mason-and-Dickson's line and of being wholly unacquainted with literary people and literary ways, – I say, think how, in spite of all these depressing circumstances and of a thousand more wh. I could enumerate, these two figures of music and of poetry have steadily kept in my heart, so that I could not banish them! Does it not seem to you, as to me, that I begin to have the right to enroll myself among the devotees of these two sublime arts, after having followed them so long and so humbly and through so much bitterness? If I could only make you see all this, as clearly as I *now* feel it, now when I have actually engaged in this service!

The object of my visit to New York was to see at once, by using the severest tests, – that is, by measuring strength with the best artists there – whether there was any hope for me to excel greatly, either as musician or writer; and secondly, to arrange matters so that in case the Baltimore project failed, I could get some engagement in New York, immediately.

The Baltimore Orchestra is now *un fait accompli,* and having been offered, entirely without solicitation either by myself or my friends, the place of First Flute in it, I have accepted it. Mary will tell you the details of the engagement, wh. I have written her. It is the very best place I cd. have found, just at present, occupying but little time, and thus giving me a splendid opportunity to write and study. As for the climate, I have no fears whatever. It is better than that of New York: and I have continued to prosper, physically, even in the New York climate. In spite of a wretched cold, such as would have laid me up for months at Macon, my appetite has continued good, my strength has constantly increased, and the old dyspepsias that used to drag me down are wholly unknown. I am full of energy, full of unwritten music, full of unrhymed poetry, and I look forward to a winter crowded with vigorous work and profitable study.

To Mary Day Lanier [133]

Baltimore, Dec. 2nd, 1873

Well, Flauto Primo hath been to his first rehearsal.

Fancy thy poor lover, weary, worn, and stuffed with a cold, arriving after a brisk walk, — he was *so* afraid he might be

[133] Previously published, *Scribner's,* XXV, 628-629 (May, 1899); reprinted,

behind time — at the hall of Peabody Institute. He passeth down betwixt the empty benches, turneth through the green-room, emergeth on the stage, greeteth the Maestro, is introduced by the same to Flauto Secondo; and then, with as much carelessness as he can assume, he sauntereth in among the rows of music-stands, to see if peradventure he can find the place where he is to sit, — for he knoweth not, and liketh not to ask. He remembereth where the flutes sit in Thomas' Orchestra: but on going to the corresponding spot he findeth the part of Contra Basso on the music-stand, — and fleeth therefrom in terror. In despair he is about to endeavor to get some information on the sly, — when he seeth the good Flauto Secondo sitting down far in front, — and straightway marcheth to his place on the left of the same, with the air of one that had played there since babyhood. This Hamerik of ours hath French ideas about his orchestral arrangements and placeth his pieces very differently from Thomas. — Well, I sit down: some late comers arrive, stamping and blowing, — for it is snowing outside — and pull the green baize covers off their big horns and bass-fiddles. Presently the Maestro, who is rushing about hither and thither, in a Frenchy excitement — falleth to striking a great tuning-fork with a mallet, and straightway we all begin to toot A, to puff it, to groan it, to squeak it, to scrape it, until I sympathize with the poor letter and glide off in some delicate little runs: and presently the others begin to flourish also, and here we have it, up chromatics, down diatonics, unearthly buzz-ings from the big fiddles, diabolical four-string chords from the cellos, passionate shrieks from the clarionets and oboes, manly remonstrances from the horns, querulous complaints from the bassoons, and so on. Now the Maestro mounteth to his perch. I am seated immediately next the audience, facing the first violins, who are separated from me by the conductor's stand. I place my part, (of the 5th Symphony of Beethoven, which I had procured two days before, in order to look over it, — being told that on the first rehearsal we would try nothing else except the 5th Symphony) on my stand, and try to stop my heart from beating so fast, — with unavailing arguments. Maestro rappeth with his *baton,* and magically stilleth all the

Letters (New York, 1899), pp. 82-84. (The second flute player, mentioned at the beginning of this letter, was Louis J. Doetsch).

shrieks and agonies of the instruments. " Fierst," (he saith, with the Frenchiest of French accents, — tho' a Dane, he was educated in Paris) " I wish to present to ze gentlemen of ze orchestra, our fierst flutist, Mr. Sidney Lanier, — also our first oboe, Mr. (I didn't catch his name)." Whereupon, not knowing what else to do, — and the pause being somewhat awkward — I rise and make a profound bow to the Reeds, who sit behind me, another to the Celli, the Bassi, and Tympani, in the middle, and a third to the Violins opposite. This appeareth to be the right thing, for Oboe jumpeth up also, and boweth, and the gentlemen of the orchestra all rise and bow, some of them with great *empressement.* Then there is a little idiotic hum and simper, such as newly introduced people usually affect. Then cometh a man, — whom I should always hate, if I *cd.* hate anybody always — and, to my horror putteth on my music-stand the flauto primo part of Niels Gade's Ossian Overture: and thereupon the Maestro saith we will try *that* fierst: horrors! They told me they wouldn't play anything but the 5th Symphony: and this Ossian Overture I have never seen or heard! — This did not help my heart-beats, nor steady my lips, — thou canst believe! However, there is no time to tarry, the baton rappeth, the horns blow, my 5 bars rest is out. — I plunge.

—O my Heart, O my Twin, if thou cdst. but be by me in this sublime glory of music! All through it I yearned for thee, with heart-breaking eagerness. The beauty of it maketh me catch my breath, — to write it. I will not attempt to describe it. It is the spirit of the Poems of Ossian, done in music, by the wonderful Niels Gade.

I got through it without causing any disturbance. Maestro had to stop several times on account of some other players. I failed to come in in time twice in the Symphony. I am too tired, now, to give thee any further account. I go again to rehearsal tomorrow.

— I sent thee a letter containing check for $50 on Sunday. Also sent $175 to Dr. Dunwoody, desiring to know how much more was needed. I am so eager to have some word from thee: all I know is that thou wert in Atlanta on the 21st. That is eleven days ago!

— Thou Heartsease, thou Tuberose, thou Heliotrope, God have a care upon thy blossoming, — prayeth

Thy Lover.

To Mary Day Lanier

Baltimore, Md. Dec. 9th 1873—

O My poor Heart, My poor weary, sleepy, overworked, over-worn, strained, tired, and infinitely-dear Heart, I have just read thy letter out of the nursery, where thou hast been laid up of thy lame foot, my heart hath travelled back through all the wearisome croupy nights, through all thy sufferings, I am all alive and throbbing with thy pain, O my God, how tender is my heart to thee, dear, patient *Mutterchen,* thou faithful Wife, thou lovely Soul, thou Heart'sease!

Every day last week we had a rehearsal,—two hours each—, and I had such a cold and catarrh as would have made Angels weep, methinks: yet I managed to crawl up, each day but one, to the Academy. On Saturday night we had our first grand Symphony Concert, and made the most brilliant opening, they say, of any series of concerts ever given in Baltimore.

— I will give thee details of this, send thee programmes, tell thee a thousand pleasant things wh. are daily said and done to thy lover,— when I get time, only saying now that Mr. Hamerik is greatly pleased with my Orchestral playing, and that we have a beautiful Orchestra of thirty-five fine players. I long to talk to thee of all these things; but I am just moved to my permanent quarters, must go to rehearsal presently, have several matters to arrange first, will write thee again tomorrow, fully. Meantime, I enclose a charming note from Miss Alice Fletcher, of New York, (Secretary of Sorosis!);—and beg God to wrap thee in violet petals of His Love, as tenderly as would thy

Lover.

(I should have written thee weeks ago that Harry Wysham desires Gussie Ogden to be Godmother. *I* will write *her* tomorrow, and ask her. That will antidote my fault a little, I hope, in not sooner telling thee: there was no intention of having Mrs. Wysham as godmother: hereanent is a long tale I must tell thee some time. Kind Heaven, will my heart last, till I see thee?

To Mary Day Lanier [184]

[Baltimore, Md.,] Dec. 11th 1873

Let no pang crop thy heart about the money : the amount is not larger than I expected: I will manage it.

Thou Heliotrope, thou Sweetest Sweet was ever kissed, thou poor lame One, thou crazed One with Bedlam about thee, O God, how my heart seemeth to beat all about thee as the blue heaven doth sometime throb anxiously about the earth, apprehensive, love-timid, agonized with devotion. Yesterday, Harry Wysham wrote thee, a most rare sweet letter. This morning came thine saying that, now he had *me*, he must write *thee*. Harry's devotion is untiring, boundless, infinitely-varied. I take all my meals at his house, save breakfast, which is served in my room. I secured a pleasant place, only a few yards from Harry's, only ten steps from Mrs. Saidee Bird's,[135] (who hath seized me, and hath begged me to visit her house as it were home, and hath said sweetest things of thee, and of thy lover's playing which she heard Saturday night at the *Concert*) and just across the square from the Academy of Music.

I have been called on by a host of delightful friends, and have all manner of invitations. I must immediately commence to respond to these, some of which have lain over too long. How many, many pleasant things I could tell thee ! But I've been writing all the morning, – *necessary* letters — and my arm is fearsomely tired.

I read Harry one of thy letters yesterday. If thou cdst. have heard him ! He was amazed, and delighted beyond descrip-

---

[134] Excerpt previously published, *Scribner's*, XXV, 629 (May, 1899); reprinted, *Letters* (New York, 1899), pp. 84-85. Mary Day Lanier and the children had gone to Brunswick to spend the winter (see her letter to Lanier, Dec. 10-11, 1873).

[135] Mrs. Edgeworth Bird had known Lanier in Macon, and during the ensuing years she was to befriend him in many ways. In Baltimore she lived on Mt. Vernon Place, opposite the Peabody Institute.

tion: amazed at thy powers, delighted at thy lovingness, sweetness, womanliness, artisticalness. Here let me whisper a secret,
to which I must not again refer save when I see thee. I penetrated it in a few minutes after I first went into the house.
Mrs. W. is a weak woman, without any womanliness, and a
strong devotee, without a spark of religion. Verb. Sap. My
poor Harry!

I send thee a programme of our Concert last Saturday night.
It was brilliant, and thy lover failed not, – though half-dead
with cold, and though called on unexpectedly.[136] I am better
today. — The Music lifts me to a Heaven of pain, – without
thee ! — We are now rehearsing the *Symphonie Fantastique*,
of Berlioz: wh. representeth an opium-dream of a love-sick
young man. Tis wonderfully hectic, and parts of it wonderfully
beautiful.

God put thee in His heart, as thou wert a drop of rare Essence
in a Vase, — prayeth thy

Lover.

Write me at " 161 St. Paul St."

---

[136] A program with the pencilled annotation: " Blackbirds. S. Lanier. See
newspaper clipp Dec. 8th? 1873," and a clipping from the Baltimore *Gazette*
have both survived (Charles D. Lanier Collection, Johns Hopkins University).
According to the latter.

" Not on the programme, but between the parts, Mr. Hamerik, desiring to
introduce to the Baltimore public his new acquisitions, the first oboe, flute, and
bassoon, called upon Mr. Stovasser, who plays the former instrument, for a
solo. . . .

" Mr. Sidney Lanier, first flute, was next called upon. Although evidently
appearing under protest—for Mr. L. was suffering from a severe cold—Mr.
Hamerik's witty introduction brought him from his seat in spite of himself, and,
like a faithful artiste, he quietly proceeded to do his best. He played, without
accompaniment, a composition of his own called ' Blackbirds.' Of classic purity,
this work is filled with the most bewildering harmonies, all founded on a theme
which translates, without imitating, a flock of those glossy birds in the midst
of quiet fields, and trees, and streams. . . . His performance was warmly
received."

The Peabody Orchestra season lasted from Dec. 6, 1873 to Mar. 28, 1874,
and consisted of eight " Symphony Concerts " and seven " Students' Concerts,"
given on alternate Saturday evenings. Circulars announced this as the " Eighth
Season of Concerts," but it was only the third under Asger Hamerik's direction
(see Introduction, vol. VII) and the beginning of Lanier's professional career.
Since a complete file of programs survives at the Peabody Institute, no effort
has been made to supply in footnotes the full and correct titles of the compositions referred to in Lanier's letters.

To Mary Day Lanier

Baltimore, Md, Dec, 12th 1873

I have just come from thy Mrs. Saidee Bird's. How I wish I might tell thee but the half of the pleasant things she had to impart to thy lover! She seemeth to know how rare-sweet *thou* art: and this maketh me her friend immediately, and wholly.

Our Norah Freeman [137] hath " come out," greatly. Knowest thou that she is now teaching music, and supporting herself quite independently thereby? This giveth me great regard for her. She is a near neighbor of mine.

So, indeed is everybody. Mrs. Machen,–(Minnie Gresham) [138] abideth just across the street, and, I hear, hath expected me to call ere now. I had been waiting for her husband to call on me (for, now that I am *quasi* a professional musician, I am a little sensitive) but I learn he hath been out of town ever since I came. So, I will e'en gie her a call, anyhow.

I am just off to dine with Mr. Wilmer, an old comrade of Clifford's and mine, who hath married and settled in Baltimore, and promptly called on me.[139] Met Dr. Browne this morning, and we are arranging an evening with Col. R. M. Johnston.[140] Tonight I am to go with Harry to visit his friend, Mrs. Wyman. Last night we called on, and played duos for, the Perrine's: night before, ditto the Perot's.—Of course I must make friends of all these people,—in the interests of music.

— But, O God, O God, Heartsease, how full is my heart

---

[137] Daughter of Lanier's Macon friend, Harriet Freeman (later Mrs. Fulton).

[138] Minnie Gresham of Macon was a close friend of Gertrude Lanier; she had married Arthur Machen of Baltimore the preceding winter (see Mary Day Lanier's letter to her husband, Feb. 12, 1873).

[139] Skipwith Wilmer had been with the Lanier brothers in the Marine Signal Office at Wilmington, N. C., in the fall of 1864.

[140] Richard Malcolm Johnston (1822-1898), a Georgia author and educator, best known for his local color fiction, beginning with the *Dukesborough Tales* (1871). He had moved to Baltimore in 1867 and established his school, Pen Lucy, at suburban Waverly. An intimate friendship between Johnston and Lanier ensued, beginning late in 1873 or early in 1874– though the earliest surviving letter is dated Nov. 6, 1877. (See Lanier's letter to his wife, Feb. 3, 1874, and note 22; also Francis Taylor Long, " The Life of Richard Malcolm Johnston in Maryland, 1867-1898," *Maryland Historical Magazine*, XXXIV, 305-324, Dec., 1939.)

ever of thee; of thee only! God convert every star into a tender-apprehensive spirit about thee this night, prayeth

thy Lover.

To Clifford A. Lanier

Baltimore Md, Dec. 16th 1873

Your letter has just reached me, having been forwarded from New York.

– I have not written you, in answer to your last, – because sometimes one has to shut up one's heart a little while, tightly, in order to keep one's control of it. Scarcely a day, indeed, when I do not see, in going about the streets of these great cities, the forlorn faces of the starving, of the rag-people, of the criminals, of the all-wanting, anything-grasping folk who are rogues by birth and by necessity and who suffer, suffer, throughout life. What can one do *quoad* these people, whom one cannot possibly relieve? One can only shut one's heart with a great gulping sigh, and say to oneself, it is God's world, He understands; I do not, let me be still. This one *must* do; otherwise one is paralyzed by one's sympathy, and hindered from work.

–And if so with the rag-pickers, – how much more, O my darling, my sweetest Man's-heart in the World, My One Love among men, my noble and patient Soul, my dear, steadfast Friend-and-Brother-and-Playmate-and Comrade-and-Exemplar-of-Knighthood, all in One, – how much more must I hold my heart firmly, to keep it from utterly breaking – when I think of you, after all the patient and toilsome years, struggling with debt and poverty and a dismal future!

If I think of it, I cannot work. – I only allow myself to know it. It is down in my soul's background. I *must* keep it there. If it should stay in the front, – I should do like those desperate regiments in battle, who have nothing left save to die, – I should charge it, and fall.

– In answer to your question as to my occupation; – I'm (Heaven save the Mark!) *Flauto Primo* in the Symphony Orchestra of the Peabody Institute; work, – to go through four rehearsals each week, of two hours each, with one Concert, each week, of three hours duration, – making in all eleven hours a week, of labor: pay, – sixty dollars a month! But that is not all my work. I have the Jacquerie to finish; I am getting up a cheaper Method for the Boehm Flute than the one now in existence (which costs $7.^{50}, while mine will not cost more than $2. to $2.$^{50.}$) : I am also getting a lot of music ready to publish: and expect to have a pupil or two on the Flute, ere long.

I have invitations to the best houses in Baltimore, and many friends have called on me. I could never tell you the kindnesses and sweet things which are done and said to me daily.

But, kind Heaven! Yonder is my Heartsease, whom I adore more and more every day of my life, in Georgia: and my three splendid ones, my beautiful little men: – when am I to see them? God only knows. Sixty dollars a month is not much: – but it is exactly sixty dollars a month *more* than I can make in Georgia, and *is* so far on the road to independence that I will not abandon it for anything in the world, – except for something that will *pay seventy* dollars a month.

Embrace all for me. Write me at " 161 St. Paul Street, Baltimore, Md." I must be off to rehearsal in a little while – If I could only kiss you, dear Clifford! – Anyhow, I am always your faithful loving

S. L.

To Mary Day Lanier

[Baltimore, Md.,] Dec. 17th 1873

Will I never get time to talk with thee, my Heliotrope, My Sweetest Sweet, My One Love, My Clear Star, My brave and patient Heart, My dear End-of-all-longing?

Here is my fair neighbor, Mrs. Byrd, just come over in person to my door to bid me to dinner with her; Harry Wysham to join us in the evening, when we are to play flute duos for her. I am just from rehearsal: The Fantastic Symphony, The Overture to Masaniello, and a most exquisite Hunting Overture of Méhul. I must rush away to Mrs. Byrd's. I am full of naught but thee, I desire naught but thee, I work for naught but thee, my Hope is to be with thee, my joy, my Heaven, is to look into thy gray eyes.

I must tell thee that I won thy lover some hearts last night. Harry W. and I went to Mrs. Wyman's, a magnificent house, full of all manner of beautiful things. It was her reception night. After a simple duo, I played my Swamp Robin, amid profound silence; and thereafter came many sweet and earnest testimonials;—too earnest to be mistaken—that I had gone through the shells of the folk, into the Souls thereof. What is thy Letty Yonge's name? I must find her out.

— O my Loveliest One, O my dear Wife, for whom I long unspeakably every hour, art thou indeed " all one heart-ache for thy husband " ?

— God cure this ache of thine, soon, crieth thy

Lover!

To Mary Day Lanier

Baltimore, Md, Dec. 18th 1873

Thou givest me daily proof that thou art the sweetest lady in the world: thy letters are incomparable, they breathe a violet-fragrance of womanliness, of love, of trust, of religion, into my heart, so that I am like one that hath within him a warm and fervent and perpetual spring, full of flowers that no winter hath any power upon. Occasionally I read a sweet strain to Wysham, and he seemeth as he were lifted into a glimpse of some Heaven whereof he had dreamed. Would God I had no work in life save to sing thee to the world, dear worshipful Lady! – And I get no consolation save in believing that all I do, of good, of noble, of sweet, of charitable, of unselfish sort, is but a *eulogium* of thee put into act, which, if men do not recognize it as such, is at least seen so to be by all them that be Above.

Here are enclosed thy shoe laces: wh. I found only after a long search. The man said one of them was a pair (!): but I bought two for safety. As for thy shoes: they will be made here. Must I tell thee the truth? I was too ill in New York to attend to them, after thine instructions came. Several times started I with thy plans and specifications: but had to give it up, for very weakness.

Yesterday, for instance, (–thou askest for my daily life–)
I rose at Eight: dressed, not with enthusiasm, the same being
to me an ever increasing bore. At nine, Henry, serving-man,
brought in my breakfast, the same being a chop, a couple of
very soft-boiled eggs, and coffee: at ten, I walked down town,
called at Harry's Office for my letters, read same, attended to
some little matters here and there too minute to mention, such
as having my watch regulated, &c, got back to my room at
half-past eleven, out with my flute, took a turn at a difficult
run in the Masaniello overture for ten minutes, then over to
the Academy Hall, to rehearsal. From twelve to two, with my
Orchestral brethren, I worked at the Fantastic Symphony, the
" Hunt of Henry IV " Overture, and the Masaniello: all of us
making mistakes occasionally, but altogether doing pretty well,
and getting new ideas of the *ppp* and fff (in one place in the
Fantastic Symphony the 1st flute has p.p.p.p. (4 of 'em) and
the words *presque rien*, over the same passages!). Home from
rehearsal, and just pulling off my hat in my room, a lady is
announced: who proveth to be Mrs. Byrd. She insisteth I shall
come to spend the balance of the day at her house. I go: at
half-past three we have a jovial dinner, *we* being Mr. & Mrs.
Hull, (brother of Geo. G. Hull – – – Athens people formerly,
now living in Baltimore), Mrs. Byrd, her daughter (lately
married, Mrs. Smith,) and daughter's husband, her son, Edgeworth Byrd, Mrs. Tom Baxter & myself. We leave table at
five, we four gentlemen go to the billiard-room, and play a
couple of games, I then steal away to mail a letter to thee, and
one to Harry with Mortgage, note &c, therein. Meantime it
hath been arranged that Harry W. shall come, who hath not
yet met Mrs. Byrd: so I run over to his house at half-past six,
rouse him up, take tea with him & Mrs. W. (Isobel is in N. Y.).
We then shoulder our flutes and our music, and march upon
Mrs. Byrd, arriving, they have coffee: during wh. in come Mrs.
Johnston (Col. R. M. J.'s wife), Miss Baxter, Mr. Poullain,
and Mr. Baxter. We adjourn to the parlor, a boisterous party
enough. Presently out with the flutes: play, play, play, I cut
into all their hearts with the Swamp Robin (wh. they all declare
to have the soul of the Georgia woods in it), Harry makes at
'em with the great Flute passage of Wm Tell Overture, then
we play an Andante of Kuhlau, for two flutes, then all sorts

of skirmishing, flutes and Piano &c &c. Then we take our leave amid all manner of pleasant sayings and invitations: come to my room, dash into a duo of Kuhlau's; then Harry leaves, (he is a man of regular habits, nothing ever keeps him beyond his regular hour, of ten and a half, for retiring) and I breathe a prayer to thee on the Bass-Flute wh. Badger has sent me to keep and sell for him, – and fearful I may forget it, sit me down and write off a memorandum of it, (of the prayer, I mean): then to bed, sending a sigh of fervent love and blessing to thee and my three beautiful men.

I have no pupils, yet: having been quite too unwell, and too busy in the intervals of sickness, to make any move that way. Next week I may do so: but I am ruminating other projects which may change my determination in that regard. Whereof anon.

Tomorrow I draw some pay, as *Flauto Primo.* I lay it at thy feet, first fruits of my musical labor. Thou must take some ten dollars thereof, (or, of course, as much as thou wilt) and expend the same in Xmas presents for the little ones. I had meditated sending them a box of toys and candies from here: but I cannot possibly get time to select the same. If I can, I will do so yet.

I am always begging God, dear Friend, dear Love, dear Sweetheart, dear Wife, thou exquisite All-Sweet,—to make me worthy to be thy

Husband.

To Mary Day Lanier [141]

Baltimore, Md. Dec. 20th 1873

For this enclosed $25 (and $5 more, wh. I have kept) I have played the first flute parts in Beethoven's Fifth Symphony; The Ossian Overture: The Staccato air of The Magic Flute: The Nordische Suite: The Overture to La Dame Blanche: The *Symphonie Fantastique,* of Berlioz: the Mendellsohn Concerto in G. minor for Piano & Orchestra: The " Hunt of Henry IV

---

[141] Previously published, *Scribner's,* XXV, 631 (May, 1899); reprinted, *Letters* (New York, 1899), p. 89, where it is misdated Dec. 26.

Overture " of Méhul: the Rondo Concerto, of Chopin, for
Piano and Orchestra: and the Overture to Masoniello.

If they wd. only pay me by heart-beats, by agitations, by
mental strains, by delights, by agonies, – then I wd. I wd. be
already grown rich on these aforementioned pieces. They say,
however, that I play them very nicely: and that is some reward.
— I sent, a week ago, to Dr. Dunwoody, funds to discharge
the entire balance due at Marietta, and I devoutly hope that
by this time everybody is paid off.[142] As thou askest so earnestly,
I will tell thee that I am still in debt, after ruthlessly expending
every dollar of thy policy-money, some three hundred dollars.
I must try hard to work out of this: and have but little time.
But I keep my heart up. Thou must not trouble thine herewith.
Thou hast enough.

Tomorrow night we have our Second Grand Concert: The
Symphonie Fantastique, The Méhul Overture, the Masoniello
Overture, the Concerto (Rondo) of Chopin (J. N. Pattison,
of New York, plays the Piano Forte part): these are all the
Orchestral pieces. There are besides a song from *L'Africaine*,
with flute obligato which Wysham is to play, and some baritone
songs.

– How stretched my heart is! I love thee more and more every
hour.

– I am better, in health. Write me of thy foot. Kiss thy father
for me.

God warm the air about thee, dear Heliotrope, with His Heart,
saith

Thy Lover.

I made the P. O. order payable to Harry in order to save you
the trouble of identifying your signature to the Postmaster.

S. L.

---

[142] On Dec. 10, 1873, Mary Day Lanier had written that the Marietta indebted-
ness came to $400.00: "Pray tell me . . . if we can meet it without new debt."

To Mary Day Lanier [143]

Baltimore, Dec. 21st 1873

Last night, we gave a magnificent concert. The house was crowded. Read the enclosed *Carte,* showing the fare we spread before the people. O my God, how I did sigh and long for thee, dear Heartsease: had I thee, the music wd. have been complete, life wd. have been utterly full, my heart wd. have bathed itself in a sublime sea of passionate content.

The Orchestra was inspired. The *Symphonie Fantastique* — as difficult and trying a piece of Orchestration as was ever written — was played to a marvel. Dost thou not remember that I once put *thee* into music? So, in this *Symphonie,* every movement centreth about a lovely melody, repeated in all manner of times and guises, wh. representeth the Beloved of the opium-eating musician.

—— I will make a *Symphonie* with thee for its melodic cynosure some day, wh. shall be more lovely than Berlioz', because thou art more lovely than any one that Berlioz cd. have known.

— Then the "Hunt of Henry IV," O my Sweet-Heart! It openeth with a grave and courteous invitation, as of a cavalier riding by some dainty lady, through the green aisles of the deep woods, to the hunt: a lovely, romantic melody, the first violins discoursing the man's words, the first flute replying for the lady. Presently, a Fanfare: a sweet horn replies out of the far woods: then the meeting of the gay cavaliers: then the start, the dogs are unleashed, one hound gives tongue, another joins, the stag is seen, hey, gentlemen! away they all fly through the sweet leaves, by the great oaks and beeches, all a-dash among the brambles, till presently Bang! goeth a pistol, (it was my

---

[143] Previously published, *Scribner's,* XXV, 629-630 (May, 1899); reprinted *Letters* (New York, 1899), pp. 85-87.

A month later, after a repetition of the Méhul overture described in this letter, Lanier wrote to his brother Clifford, Jan. 31, 1874 (omitted from the present edition): "'The Hunt of Henry IV,' . . . ever since the first morning we rehearsed it, has filled me with the most vivid visions of you, and of the green ravines and generous bosomed mountains where you and I hunted, before care was, and before we were men. . . . Positively, all this is as clear, in the music, as if you and I were again in the mountains, with Uncle Will and the hounds! — and I must add, that I don't, in general, like 'Programme music.'"

veritable old revolver, loaded with blank cartridge for the occasion, — the revolver that hath lain so many nights under my head and (God hold my heart together!) *thine,* – fired by *Tympani,* (as we call him,) the same being a nervous little Frenchman who playeth our drums), and then the stag dieth, in a celestial concord of flutes, oboes and violins. O how far off my soul was, in this thrilling moment! It was in a rare sweet glen, in Tennessee, the Sun was rising over a wilderness of mountains, I was standing (how well I remember the spot!) alone, in the dewy grass, wild with rapture and with expectation, yonder came gracefully walking a lovely fawn, I looked into its liquid eyes, hesitated, prayed, gulped a sigh, then, – overcome with the savage hunter's instinct, – fired, the fawn leaped convulsively a few yards, I ran to it, found it lying on its side, and received into my agonized and remorseful heart the melting reproaches of its most tender, dying gaze. — But luckily I had not the right to linger over this sad scene: the conductor's *baton* shook away the dying pause, on all sides shouts and fanfares and gallopings "to the death," to which the first flute had to reply in time, recalled me to my work, and I came through brilliantly.

— The Chopin Rondo, Concerto for Piano and Orchestra, I cannot begin to describe to thee. It nearly killed me, with longing for thee: – for thou wdst. have understood it, as I did, thou wdst. have recognized the wondrous delicate, yet intense, thoughts which pervade it, the " Zäl " as Liszt calleth it. Herein the flute hath some lovely replies and dialogues with the piano, in solo; and the horns are exquisitely brought forth. – The songs were not particularly fine, tho' very enjoyable, The Masoniello overture thou hast of course heard before. It was played very brilliantly.

—— Today Wysham and I played a beautiful *Adagio Patetico* during the *Offertorium* at St. Paul's: – the largest church in the city. We had an Organ accompaniment, played by a glorious organist: and as the two spirituelle silver-tones went stealing and swelling through the great groined arches of the enormous church, I thought I had never heard flute-notes so worthily employed before. The people were greatly pleased: and Wysham was delighted.

Alas, so it is cat and dog twixt Wysham and his wife. She,

poor creature is in my judgment not quite right in her mind. She subjects him to such painful scenes: he has to steal his flute away to avoid them, whenever he plays in public! She is a fearsome soul.

I dined with Mrs. Bird today, and left there bearing some fervent messages of love for thee. She hath been my constant and true friend, and I shall love her, – I know thou wilt also – all my life.

Some day, when thou art in the humor, send her one of thy dainty notes, in a few words. I take such delight in expressing to her my worship of thee!

– Now God fill thy heart with the exquisite satisfactions thou hast poured into mine, prayeth thy

Lover——

To Charles D. and Sidney Lanier, Jr.

Baltimore, Md. Dec. 22nd 1873

My darling little Sons:

Papa sends you a hundred kisses apiece, and wishes you the merriest Xmas that ever two boys had in this world. Have you both told Santa Claus, up the Chimney, what you wanted him to bring you? How I wonder what Charlie asked for? And what did my nimblewits Sidney want? You must both write me and tell me what you told old Santa Claus. I hope he will bring you both some fire-crackers: but you must mind your eyes, now, if you don't want them black as a crow's.

And do tell me when you write, what little Harry Wysham thinks of fire-crackers, and Xmas generally. I really suspect he wouldn't give one good swig of milk for all the crackers in Brunswick: – but then he's young yet, you know, and he'll learn better as he grows older. And as for little Sister, I am perfectly sure she wonders what can possess those horrid boys to be wasting time on toys and poppers and things when they *might* be sucking milk out of a bottle: and I wouldn't be surprised if she didn't get up a Missionary Society before long to send out missionaries among those misguided boys and teach them to be quiet and to drink their milk very mild.

Anyhow you must try, – especially you wild Nimblewits ! – not to run Mama entirely crazy, – and Uncle Hal, and dear Grandpapa. O My, what a time Uncle Hal and Grandpapa will have, if you don't keep quiet! Papa can see them, now, dancing a wild dance of despair:

over your noise and your capers and your screeches.
And now Papa wants you do to to do him a favor: that is, first, to kiss Uncle Hal and Grandpapa for him: next, to put your arms around Mama's neck, and tell her she is the loveliest, the dearest, the daintest, the most worshipful-sweet Mama in this wide world, and kiss her six times apiece for your loving

Papa.

To Robert S. Lanier

Baltimore, Md. Dec. 23rd 1873

My dear Father:

I had hoped to hear some account of home matters from you, before now, in reply to my request therefor: but suppose Uncle Clifford's illness, of which I heard through Mamie, has thrown a great deal of hard work upon you, and so I have contented myself with such brief snatches of home news as Mamie has been able to write betwixt her four children, her Dentist and her lame foot.

I have not been well for four weeks past, though I have managed to keep at my immediate work without interruption save for one day. I believe my performance in the Orchestra has given satisfaction to the *Maestro* and the people in spite of my bad cold, & the two Symphony Concerts we have given have been very brilliant and successful.

I am much better now, and hope to do a great deal of hard work for the balance of the winter. I have a number of good friends, whose attentions have been very marked, and I have the strongest hope of gaining such a foothold here as may lead to something permanent.

Mary's account of Uncle Clifford's last illness gives me great concern. I heard through Mrs. Gresham, (whom I met at a friend's house some days ago) that Uncle C. was about to leave for New York, to consult physicians upon his disease. If this be so, I hope he can find a day to spend with me here, on his way back. Please tell him so.

Clifford sends me a melancholy account of matters in Montgomery. I fear he is wasting his time in that place: and I greatly wish he could get an opening somewhere in the North, where life does not seem to be at such a dead standstill.

I send you all a merry Christmas, with my love and hearty wishes. Tell Mr. Pringle I should heartily like to set off a pack of fire-crackers with him, and my two rascals.

Your Son

S. L.

To Virginia Hankins [144]

Baltimore, Md.
Dec. 23rd 1873

My dear, dear Friend: If I cd. only tell you with what satisfaction my heart turns to you,—to you who are so beautiful and who shine so steadily in all weathers!—from the waves and tempests and shifting phases of my life. Never howls the wind so loudly but I can hear your calm voice, singing songs of Land,

[144] Previously published, *Southern Literary Messenger*, II, 10-11 (Jan., 1940).

of Harborages, of faithful Anchoring-places: never is the night black enough nor the intervening wave high enough, to shut out from me the constant vision of your friendly-lighted eyes.

Of how much value this is to me, you cd. not know without knowing the fluctuations of my life,—of health, of fortune, of work. These I have not the heart to sadden you with. I will only tell you, I am God's shuttle. He whisks me back and forth, from Heaven to earth, from earth to Heaven. What He is weaving, I know not.

— I only try to make as good a shuttle as I can.

— At this present, (this much of my personal affairs I *ought* to tell you, because your friends here do not know *all* I am doing) I am in Baltimore writing my " Jacquerie," wh. I hope to have ready towards Spring. I wanted to write it here because there are some books in the library of the Peabody Academy here wh. I desire to consult.[145]— You must know the doctors told me some months ago that my solitary chance for life was to quit my profession,—the law. I resisted this conclusion until I found it was simply irresistible. Then, what to do? My father who makes enough for both of us, begged me to live with him, at home: but this I *cd.* not do, — dependence, even upon him, wd. be utterly intolerable to me,—so l left Macon, resolved to strike out something of independent livelihood, in whatever humble way, in the world of art,—that being the only thing I know how to work at, save the law. So, on my way to New York, the Director of the Peabody Academy, here, astonished me by offering me the place of *Flauto Primo* in the Symphony Orchestra supported by that institution. This opportunity to help interpret the great works of the Mighty Musicians was too delicious, I *cd.* not resist it; and so, after attending to some business in New York, I came back here Dec. 1st, and am now fulfilling my engagement. We have a magnificent Orchestra:

---

[145] Sometime before (Mar. 15, 1871) W. H. Browne had examined the Peabody Library in answer to Lanier's request for authorities bearing on the Jacquerie and reported: " There is a treatise entitled ' Recherches historiques sur les Routiers et la Jacquerie,' in the 20 vol. of J. M. C. Leber's *Collect*ⁿ *des Dissertations relations à l'histoire de France.* Paris 1838.

" There may be something in the ' Précis des guerres entre la France et l'Angleterre ' (coming down to 1490) in 4 vol. C. B. Petitot's *Memoires.* Also in Buchon's collection of Chronicles– but I fear these voluminous and rare works are not accessible to you."

the delights, the ecstasies, the manifold Heavens, through which
I pass in playing with them,—are not to be described. But so
far I have been too ill to do any work of moment, save to attend
the rehearsals and concerts of the Orchestra. I am now better,
however, and hope to fill my winter with work.

I have been led to give you these details, by having met,
here, your friend Dr. [Reverdy] Johnson, who has very kindly
invited me to his house:—I feared, (you understand) that he
wd. write of my being seen periodically playing with the Symphony Orchestra and that, if you knew that, and nothing more,
you might be led to think me an eccentric and unreliable sort
of creature. That *you* shd. think anything small, or less than
high,—of *me* – – – I cannot bear at all, and so, *voila,* I have
" explained." [146]

Your *critique* of Middlemarch was exquisite. I knew that
you wd. see the perfect art with which Dorothea Brooke is
made to find rest for her great heart in the adoration of
Ladislaw. Is it not wonderful that so many women do not
know their own needs, and fancy,—as must those who disagreed
with you on this point,—that an ardent, high, pure, independent, fearless, manly soul, like that of Will Ladislaw, could
not satisfy with its adorations, the heart of Dorothea Brooke,
simply because there was lacking a certain smug air of sub-
stantial-ness, of success-in-life, of dull routine-ish respectability
in him? My God, dear friend, do I not know the unutterably
sad faces of the women who have made this mistake, do I not
see them and mourn over them daily? —But if you will ask my
wife, she will tell you that through all phases of suffering, of
bereavement, of poverty, of trial, or solicitude,—she has never
for one moment been *unhappy,* because she has known that she
was loved, has been visibly worshipped and actually adored,
each day more than the last, by a soul wh.,—whatever else
might be said of it—was at least certainly fervent and sincere
and faithful.

This is the End of life, the height and sweet Acme of it:—to

[146] In her reply, Dec. 31, 1873, Virginia Hankins said that she had heard of
Lanier's being in Baltimore through her friend Dr. Johnson, whom she urged
Lanier to cultivate.

Her criticism of *Middlemarch*, referred to in the next paragraph, was contained
in her letter of Nov. 1, to which Lanier's letter is an answer.

be worshipped, in faith and love. Is not that the Desire of God? And are we not made in His image?

I knew that your poetical keen instinct for truth and right wd. never mislead you in such a matter.

Convey my warm remembrance to all your friends. I often long to see the brilliancies that gleam in Miss Ad's [147] eyes: and I hope sincerely that some turn of life may throw me again at Scotland Neck.

Write me at " 64 Centre St, Baltimore, Md." Your letters are so rare, and fine, and noble:—if your feet and hands were not so small, I should call you Dorothea Brooke!

Whatever I may call *you,* I always thank God that you are good enough to allow me to call *myself,*

Your Friend

S. Lanier

To Mary Day Lanier [148]

Baltimore,   Dec. 25th 1873

Heartsease, Heartsease, why am I not learning my heavenly lesson out of thy gray eyes today? What doth God desire, that He keepeth me apart from thee, in whose presence only am I complete ?   — Well, there be tempests that blow one petal of a flower away from its mate-petal, and keep it whirling: – let any man say *why* !

———————— I am just come from St. Paul's Church, where ten musicians of our Orchestra (among them myself) were engaged to help make the music for the Grand services of the day. We were a 1st Violin, Viola, 'Cello, double bass, Clarinet, French horn, bassoon, two flutes (Wysham & I), and great organ: with a choir of about forty boys and men, and some female voices. The service was nearly three hours long: and Music, music, all the time. We opened with the Overture to Mozart's " Magic Flute ": (wh. was, I am free to say, a most abominably *outré* affair for a church service): and then played

---

[147] Adelaide Smith, in whose family Virginia Hankins was living.
[148] Previously published, *Scribner's,* XXV, 630-631 (May, 1899); reprinted, *Letters* (New York, 1899), pp. 87-89.

with the choir throughout the service. This is a fearfully and wonderfully ritualistic church: A Shrine is in the front-centre, flanked by two enormous lighted candles, and arched over by a number of smaller ones. Three clergymen, and a number of acolytes, boys, &c, assisted in the service. The close was very impressive. The rector marched in stately fashion down from his dais: the other clergymen, the acolytes, and the choir, filed, two and two, behind him: all marched down into the body of the church singing a fine chant, then filed to the left and so went in procession across to a side door giving into a room in the rear of the church, through which all passed, still singing. The chant was kept up long after they had disappeared, and the door was shut: and as the voices receded, and receded, until finally nothing but the clear treble of the boys cd. be heard, 'twas dramatically very beautiful.

Some of the pieces were magnificent : and the crash of the organ and voices and instruments rolled gloriously among the great arches. *All* of them wd– have been fine: but some of the music was composed by the father of the rector, and was not properly phrased, though containing a few good ideas.

Next me sat Mr. Ghiberti, 1st Clarionet. Presently, the communion-service came on. This, Ghiberti watched with great curiosity. It was the first one he had ever seen ! When he saw the Priest blessing the bread, he leaned over to Wysham (who is a devout member of this Church) and asked, with great interest, " Does he eat *all* that ? " Afterwards, when the bread was distributed to the kneeling people, I observed him make gestures of much disgust at the smallness of the portion given to each, and finally he informed Wysham that *that* wd. not begin to be enough for *him* !

And O these heathenish Germans ! Double-bass was a big fellow with black moustache, to whom life is all a joke wh. he expresseth by a comical scowl: and viola was a young Hercules, so full of beer that he dreamed himself in heaven; and Oboe was a young sprig, just out from Munich, with a complexion of milk-and-roses like a girl's, and miraculously bright spectacles on his pale-blue eyes; and there they sat, Oboe, and Viola and double bass, and ogled each other, and raised their brows, and snickered behind the columns, without a suspicion of interest either in the music or the service. Dash

these fellows, they are utterly given over to heathenism, pre-
judice and beer, they ought to be annihiliated, if they *do* get
control of the Age, life will be a mere barbaric grab of the
senses at whatever there is of sensual good in the world.

——   I am going in a few moments to Mr. Perot's, where I am
invited to take my Xmas dinner. I have done nothing all day
but dream of thee. I placed thee beside me in the church, and
sometimes my heart quite broke when in looking around, out
of my dreams for a moment, I found not thee, but only the
small choir-boy who, – in default of a music-stand, held my
music for me.

——   If worship can make thy day sweet, – be Today thy
sweetest of days ! crieth thy

lover.